WEST AFRICAN CHRISTIANITY:
THE RELIGIOUS IMPACT

To Kelefa
and Sia Manta

'I see things as they are
And ask, "Why?"
You dream of things which were not
And ask, "Why not?"'

WEST AFRICAN CHRISTIANITY
The Religious Impact

LAMIN SANNEH

ORBIS BOOKS

Maryknoll, New York 10545

Second Printing, March 1990

The Catholic Foreign Mission Society of America (Maryknoll) recruits and trains people for overseas missionary service. Through Orbis Books Maryknoll aims to foster the international dialogue that is essential to mission. The books published, however, reflect the opinions of their authors and are not meant to represent the official position of the society.

Originally published by C. Hurst and Co. (Publishers) Ltd.,
38 King Street, London WC2E 8JT.

U.S. edition 1983 by Orbis Books, Maryknoll, NY 10545

Typeset in Great Britain and printed and bound
in the United States of America

ISBN 0-88344-703-7

ACKNOWLEDGEMENTS

The material in this book formed the substance of post-graduate lectures I gave first at the University of Aberdeen, Scotland, and at Harvard University. I am grateful to my students at these two Universities for their critical interest and challenge. I talked extensively with Professor Andrew Walls of Aberdeen, and am grateful to him for his stimulus and encouragement. Professor Richard Gray at London read an earlier draft of the book and has helpfully called my attention to many details of fact, interpretation and style. I am very grateful to him. I am similarly indebted to Christopher Fyfe of Edinburgh who offered his authoritative encouragement when I was still undecided about the project. I have learnt much from the work and collegial friendship of Dr Adrian Hastings and of Professor John Hargreaves, both of Aberdeen. Some of the intellectual stimulation for the book came from my association with the Ecumenical Association of African Theologians. I am grateful to my esteemed colleagues there. The many other sources on which I have drawn for intellectual sustenance are too numerous to mention by name, but some of the obvious ones are indicated in the bibliographical notes.

With this venture into the publishing world I can again repeat the words of those who stand in grateful tribute to their publishers. Christopher Hurst has laboured tirelessly in the cause of this book, and his unfailing courtesies and patience, matched only by an unyielding professionalism, cannot be repaid or forgotten.

It remains as usual to record my appreciation to my family: Sandra for doing the index and for her invaluable support and forbearance, Kelefa for letting his father have undivided share of what might have been a hotly contested interest in the typewriter, and Sia Manta for not developing much more appetite for the swivelchair. All accepted my promise of compensatory devotion to the family, all the more indulgent in view of habitual shortcomings on that front. Formed in such habits, I am encouraged to crave the indulgence of the reader for other faults and shortcomings in this book, the more attributable to my personal responsibility for having been the recipient of much generous help and rich stimulus. It is a sufficient reward if the book transmits something of that help and stimulus.

L.S.

Harvard University,
Cambridge, Massachusetts,
January 1983

CONTENTS

MAPS

INTRODUCTION

The subject of Christianity in Africa does not lack sponsors and advocates. A glance at the bibliographical material supplied in this book is enough to show that even in our part of the field the available resources are truly impressive. Why, then, a new book on the subject?

The most obvious thing to say is that we still lack a general regional survey of the field. There are a number of detailed studies that have explored parts of it in varying degrees of thoroughness, including a good number of edited works. However, their focus remains much narrower than what is attempted here, both in geographic range and in historical scope. It is possible to group these detailed monographs and others together and get a sense of the wider range involved. Yet, in another sense, they do not easily add up. To treat West Africa, for example, as a coherent unit requires the establishment of standards of analysis and interpretation that go beyond the aims of either a monograph or a collaborative work.

The second reason for a fresh initiative lies with the nature of the subject. Christianity in Africa has had more than its share of the attention of Western writers, including throngs of social scientists and their disciples, most of whom are interested in everything except the Christian religion. It is as if in our concern to describe the sunlight we concentrated on the shadows, using that derivative relationship as the justification for a reductionist approach. This book, by contrast, is concerned with the straight religious aspect of Christianity, and tries to demonstrate the continuity of the theme through the range of historical experience. To do this clearly and consistently would seem to be a new departure in the field. But the fact that it can be attempted by just looking carefully through the available material suggests indeed that it lies very much on the surface, and no great skills of insight and interpretation are required to unearth it. If anything, the greater challenge would seem to be in restricting the abundance of sources within manageable proportions and to providing a swift enough undercarriage to cope with the weight of evidence. Now that it has arrived at the stage of being launched upon the world, others must decide whether they too have been struck by the light it has not sought to elude.

The third reason is more utilitarian, and it concerns the great demand for something of this kind. Every year some 3000 students take the Advanced level paper of the West African Examinations Council in the subject. They and their teachers have had to forage about for the necessary academic sustenance. I hope that this book may shorten their days of hunting and gathering. The special requirements of such academic examinations have deeply influenced the structure of the book. But a syllabus, although it may prove a faithful bill of fare, can be totally inadequate when used as a recipe. I have in fact departed significantly from it when analysing and interpreting the material, partly in the hope that in any future work of revision the syllabus itself may be adjusted to take account of new developments and possibilities. It has stimulated this particular enterprise, and it is a rich enough reward if some of that stimulus is reciprocated.

The nature of the task

Although I have taken the general reader for granted, I hope not to have departed too radically from the concerns of the specialist. In this regard I have put forward an interpretation that is my own, but one that nevertheless attempts to do justice to the evidence. It is based on the view that the African, as the agent of religious adaptation, has played a far more critical role than his missionary counterpart whose role as historical transmitter has too often been exaggerated. Those responsible for this unbalanced presentation include not only Western writers but a surprising number of African ones who often promote it by making it the basis of the nationalist cause. But to detach the African factor in this way is to misunderstand the history of Christianity in its African transformation. It is also to underestimate the religious aspect of Christianity's interaction with African religions, an aspect which received its most pronounced expression at the hands of Africans. Western missionaries for their part squeezed Christianity into a conformist pattern that was largely in accord with the imperialist tradition, paying more attention to creating an acquiescent African population than to issues of religious assimilation. Of course certain individuals were exceptions to this rule, but the inhibiting effect of missionary 'hardware' can scarcely be doubted.

The historical roots of the preponderance of African agents over the Western missionary are firm and clear. It is by that factor, more than any other, that we have to explain and assess the apparent failure of missions between about 1480 and 1785, the period covered by Chapters 2 and 3, and the corresponding success in the period between about 1785 and 1885, described in Chapter 4 and subsequently. In that century Christianity had thrived from its Sierra

Leonean taproot and brought to bloom a new generation of Africans who would be responsible for the future direction of the continent. And when the wind of an aggressive imperialist drive flattened much of the continent before it and scattered forces of disruption in its initial impact, African Christianity had by then become sturdy enough to contemplate separation from mission as an appropriate form of resistance. This was the period between 1885 and about 1915. Even in that volatile political atmosphere, it is a striking fact that African Christian spokesmen were concerned with the religious implications of the threats that confronted them. Alongside them were others who decided on a political response and campaigned actively to follow that path.

To fuse the theme of the African religious response with the political theme and annex it as a sub-plot of the great nationalist cause is to overlook the explicit religious concerns of those involved. An indigenous Church, for which many strove, was to precede the nationalist state with which it was not identical. The unmistakable import is that the empirically distinct national Churches of today had their equally distinct empirical roots in the past, and an investigation of those roots is a necessary stage in our appreciation of their important and separate contribution. Thus a recognition of the African factor is by now long overdue and is of inestimable value in the rediscovery of the real origins of African Christianity.

Once accorded the pride of place that is his due, the African Christian agent begins to extend his claim over a much wider area, including the statistical advance of the cause where the Western missionary has traditionally asserted pre-emptive rights. The extension of mission to Abeokuta and Badagry, for example, or the ill-rewarded toils of a stint in the Gambia, have been by African instrumentality. The same could be said of the Niger Mission, not to mention the spectacular instances of the movements founded by the Prophets William Wadé Harris and Garrick Braide. This in itself is not surprising. What is remarkable is the stubborn slowness of Western missions to recognise this and to act accordingly. Sometimes an individual may rise, such as Henry Venn, who sees this point and then boldly makes it the shibboleth of policy. Because it is a rare occurrence when it happens, such individuals rise to heights of pre-eminence in appropriate contrast to the general flatness of the scene they survey. What needs to be recognised is that the African factor, far from being the administrative construct of enlightened missionary policy, had existed independently as the logical outgrowth of the theological nature of mission. The concluding material in Chapter 9 investigates this in some depth. The corollary to mission is 're-mission', the internal adaptation of external mission. Other alternatives deny mission if they reject that corollary or postpone its fulfilment. In that case 're-mission' goes underground and becomes the leavening work of the Spirit within which the Western missionary is confined to the extreme margins, given to occasional awakening to events after they have been irreversibly solidified by exposure.

In the period between 1915 and 1930 an astonishing phenomenon was to hold the centre of the religious stage, and this was the growth of prophet movements and charismatic Churches. Chapter 7 deals mainly with this. Many academic careers and ecumenical reputations have been made from giving attention to this phenomenon. Yet it is a curious irony that the African student who desires a general sympathetic introduction to the subject will feel thwarted by the multiplicity of detailed studies and a plethora of articles in learned journals. To cut a swathe through the mass of material that at present exists and is rapidly increasing was not an easy task. In the end, with the contemporary situation still in some flux, I decided, I hope for more than reasons of mere indolence, to impose a historical limit and treat mainly the roots and extent of Christianity Independency in West Africa. In addition, I have placed more stress on the African religious foundations of Independency than the social or political, this being in keeping with the general interest of the book.

Approach and interpretation

This may be the natural point to say a little about the approach I have decided to adopt in this work. The African religious response to Christianity seems clear and consistent enough to deserve serious attention. This means interpreting the history of Christianity by reference to African religious models, with local African agency as an indispensable link in the historical chain of tranmission. The process of interpretation through which Christianity has been successively submitted, proceed from its Judaic and then Hellenistic transformations to its contemorary Western incarnation, is not a fixed and exclusive series of episodes long concluded but a dynamic process that has now attained the high-water mark of its African career. That we should continue to use Western charts to navigate this new confluence of the Gospel and Africa is one of the paradoxical legacies of an ethnocentric Western world-view. As to why, in addition, we continue to flounder there should be even less mystery. This should then make our task of recovery that much easier. If ever there was a time for doing this, it is now.

We need a shift in our categories of data compilation and analysis to take adequate account of the new African Christian material. In faithfulness to that material there must be a genuinely plural tradition of academic scholarship to reflect on the data and to reconstruct it as a faithful component of the African world to which it belongs and from which it speaks to us. To try to erect on the back of this material a newfangled notion of an exclusive academic orthodoxy of one approach or another is to continue to press claims of superiority by which the continent had once been dispossessed. The spirit of religious tolerance, fuelled by the tradition of open enquiry and access in matters religious, so characteristic of African traditions, should find a counterpart in an academic community of a plurality of approaches. Because the feast before us is extraordinarily rich, the risk of excessive infusion from one approach only out of the range available is correspondingly great.

That risk has not been entirely avoided, particularly by social scientists, with thick clouds of controversy now swirling round the heads of combatants as to who can lay the greater claim to the African lamb of sacrifice. For the ordinary reader in Africa the academic debate remains largely inaccessible, so that a new form of the Berlin Congress which ushered in the era of the 'Scramble' is being staged over Africa's intellectual and spiritual terrain. Yet however alienated the modern African may be from his new intellectual masters, he still retains *de jure* and *de facto* possession of his intellectual and religious hinterland, whatever the skirmishes that may be fought on the hazy strip of theory. That hinterland is to be seen in local universities enveloped in massive folds of rite, music, myth and symbol. Genuine challenge, whether of the alternative call of other religions or of scholarly interrogations must be welcome as a necessary irritant to the process of religious assimilation. But we would be in manifest error if we thought that challenge could come only from outside, that traditional religions were some sort of neat package that insulated their devotees from the pressures of the world by propelling them outside the gravitational pull of history. The entire phenomenon of spirit possession or ecstasy, for example, was proof of the radical stock-taking that went on within traditional religions and cultures. To formulate this phenomenon in articulate intellectual categories may be new, but it is preceded by an older spiritual enterprise. It is that enterprise which illuminates the new African Christian material by investing it with an access route to the deeper mysteries of the religious outlook.

In the material on Christian Missions and Modern Education (Chapters 5 and 6) I have tried to re-assess the evidence in the light of the African factor. The use of African languages and local agents in the work of Western missions was indispensable, though we are often left in the dark about the real identity of such agents. It is still necessary to stress this African agency even when missionaries appear to accept (or reject) only those who had been to a degree 'westernised', as if such assimilated Africans (such as the Creoles of Sierra Leone) had also renounced their eternal soul. In any case 'assimilation' usually amounted to no more than a stammering acquaintance with Western civilisation, not to be compared to the infinite accumulation of millennia of cultural influence that psychologists say constitutes the collective archetype of the race. But, since history must judge such things, Africans presided over the momentous changes of the time with competence and foresight. A glance at some of the names of these historic agents described in Chapter 6 below is enough to show the scale of their achievement.

It is now time to say a little about the important subject of religious pluralism in West Africa. Once over lunch with a distinguished scholar of religion at the Faculty Club of Harvard University, the question of the resilience of African religions came up in the context of new forces that have entered the continent. It soon emerged that in spite of the public appeal of the new factors clamouring for allegiance, African religions have continued to fill a fail-safe role when the other options had been tried and had failed to cope with personal problems. In the strictly historical way in which I have approached the problem (Chapter 8 below), very little could be said about the up-to-date situation. But it would be surprising if the main outlines of the matter have altered significantly.

The field of inter-religious encounter in Africa has suffered excessive neglect in the past. Apart from a few popular remarks made in front of the camera or the microphone, or faintly distrustful proposals offered in academic sources, the matter has largely been left to plunder by rival partisans from both sides of the Christian-Muslim scene. Often what happens is that a guilt-stricken Western conscience seeks relief through an over-indulgent recital of the failings of Christianity in face of Islam and traditional religions, with a gullible African audience completely mesmerised by the lucid force of a medium they aspire to emulate. In the face of this negative legacy it would seem that a dispassionate demonstration of the source material is called for. In an area where caricatures and stereotypes circulate freely it is necessary to seek to erect such a massive wall of evidence as may obstruct the proliferation of the more resistant strain of prejudice that thrives from popular demand. Once again, by retaining the African factor as the most reasonable focus, the enterprise is more than truly joined. Its merit is that it allows us to assess the respective impact of Christianity and Islam through the eyes of African religions, and in so doing release these two missionary faiths from the fixed, motionless time-frame in which they have been frozen and submit them to the animated surge of history where nothing stands still. At a stroke we are freed from the elusive search for the 'pure' faith, either in Africa or elsewhere, and with it a certain relief from having to defend a utopian past that never existed. With mis-spent energies once again gathered and re-channelled for fresh use, we may now devote our time to the real business of investigating the process whereby Africa captured the two religions for herself. Both the method of that interaction and what emerged at the end of it should help to extend and enrich the wider field of religious enquiry. In the past we have mainly repudiated both these factors, thus draining the two missionary religions of all historical significance. By restoring the African factor, therefore, we have come a long way toward a genuinely historical view of religion.

Implied in this methodology, of course, is the idea that both Christianity and Islam are themselves just two options in a field where other options exist. Since all such options are kept alive by communities of personal adherents, it seems a reasonable course to describe them in dynamic terms, of acceptance and rejection, of assimilation and resistance, of 'propensity towards' and 'disinclination from'. Such comparative standards are the engine that powers religious movements and hitches them to the juggernaut of history.

There is a need also to treat African Christianity as a legitimate tributary of the general stream of Christian history. The North African Church of the early centuries, the Coptic Church of Egypt as well as the Ethiopian Orthodox Church should all be seen as manifestations of the on-going history of Christianity on the continent. As long as Western Christianity continues to consider itself as the true and sole guardian of the heritage of the Apostles, so long will it continue to appropriate the North African Church as a European phenomenon, with a corresponding repudiation of other manifestations of Christianity, such as the great Orthodox Churches of the East, as false or inadequate. But since Western political hegemony over much of the world has largely receded, the power basis that had sustained such an ethnocentric view of Christianity has also largely crumbled, although the accompanying mental habits have lingered in the unexamined lumber-rooms of history. It is therefore a more propitious time to challenge Western ethnocentrism and to press for a comprehensive view of Christian history in which the West's own contribution is retained by submitting it to a comparative critique. The fact that the old habits still lurk behind exaggerated claims for Western pre-eminence in the missionary enterprise, for example, suggests that the time for a radical reappraisal cannot come too soon. African and other Third World scholars ought to address themselves to the whole matter of the missionary heritage and history rather than allow it to be taken over as an exclusive Western preserve. Without this Third World dimension, mission would languish as the flawed instrument of alien subjugation, and an important part of Christian history would thereby be lost. In view of the Third World's own significant contribution in the field, such a loss would constitute a near-catastrophic diminution of accumulated labour, and should not be allowed to happen.

The African Christian stream in the present stage of its accelerated development has entered upon a vast and majestic course, a swift and vigorous career that remains at bottom consistent with the lively pace set for it by the host environment, whatever the outward checks and surface disturbances. For reasons of academic study we are often compelled to arrest that flow and divert the course into analytic channels. The reason is that the science we practise constrains us to deal only with fragments and across some rather obscurely academic barriers. When we have finished with such leisurely spectacles we must be free and encouraged to imagine a luminous synthesis through which the commitment of communities moves and shines, one that does not stand still but stirs constantly with the variegated richness that animates those communities. Any impartial observer genuinely interested in how human communities assemble and project themselves would have to admit that an event of colossal importance was taking place in African Christianity. He would be equally impressed if he pondered for a moment the route by which Africans arrived at this great sea. From a tiny drop, which on the fringes of the desert had almost evaporated, has been condensed the rain-clouds which in the fullness of time were to burst over the rest of the continent, producing the broad stream which now meets our view in the following pages.

1

AFRICAN CHRISTIAN ANTECEDENTS IN ANTIQUITY

It is our duty to proceed from what is near to what is distant, from what is known to that which is less known, to gather the traditions from those who have reported them, to correct them as much as possible and to leave the rest as it is, in order to make our work help anyone who seeks truth and loves wisdom.
                                                          Al-Biruni (937–1050)

The spread of Christianity to Africa is better known from the richly documented and more recent period of the nineteenth century, but the roots of that contact can be traced back to the very beginning of Christianity itself, when Africans played a prominent role in the life and expansion of the early Church. Using Scriptural materials, historical sources and oral traditions, we can piece together a coherent account of these early African pioneers and the contribution they made to the Church.

Scriptural materials

The great Church Father Origen, to whom we shall refer again, writing in 220 AD, said that Christ could not have been born at a better time and place. The rule of Rome had encompassed the then civilised world. The political fragmentation of earlier times had been overcome as Rome united distant provinces under central control, created a unified administration and linked them by an efficient communication and transport system. The birth of Jesus therefore became an event of more than local significance. His teachings could spread to all corners of the empire bursting out from the relatively inconsequential district of Galilee along the oft-plied sea-lanes and the constructed highways which embraced the far-flung empire. It was indeed as part of the centralisation policy and efficient system of the Roman administration that Jesus came to be born in Bethlehem where his parents had had to go for the census that was being taken. The Gospel of Matthew says that after Christ was born his parents — for the safety of the child now being hunted down by Herod, the district governor of the Romans — had to flee to Egypt. That in effect is the first tradition connecting the African continent with the Christian story.

Nothing more is told of this episode in the life of the Holy Child, nor indeed of life in Egypt. Egypt of course was part of the Roman imperial system. The Nile had been developed as an important communication line and a trading artery.

An account written about A.D. 60, probably by a Roman citizen of Greek origin, describes how the author sailed from Alexandria in Egypt up the Nile for some 800 kilometres, crossing the Red Sea and later reaching the vicinity of present-day Aden. It is clear, as other Scriptural references will show, that people and news travelled vast distances. One of the results of this was to produce a growing community of informed people who were able to keep in touch thanks to the remarkable postal system of the time. Although as refugees in Egypt the child Jesus and his parents would presumably have sought obscurity, it is surprising that no other source describes their presence there.

The African theme emerges again only towards the end of the life of Jesus, by which time he had created a strong fellowship among his disciples and his active preaching career had come to an end. The oldest known document of the New Testament, the Gospel of Mark, being largely the eye-witness account of the Apostle Peter, says that after the trial of Jesus he was led to the place of Crucifixion. On the way they met a man called Simon from Cyrenia, whom they compelled to carry the cross behind Jesus. Cyrenia was a Roman province in Libya. The Gospel of Mark adds that Simon was the father of Alexander and Rufus. We are not told who these men were, although it can be taken for granted that the Gospel mentioned them because they would have been familiar to a section of its audience. There is only one other quick reference in the New Testament to one of these men, and that, like Mark's Gospel, comes from a source strongly connected with Rome. In his letter to the Christians at Rome the Apostle Paul mentions Rufus along with others, such as Priscilla and Aquila, whom we shall again encounter in the company of a prominent Christian figure from Alexandria. Rufus is merely singled out as being 'chosen in the Lord', a phrase we may interpret as given to Christian service, apparently living at that time with his mother. It would appear that Rufus belonged to the growing Gentile Church which the Apostle Paul was actively fostering, a point of some significance for Africa which was about to become one of the most important outposts of the wider mission to the Gentile world. There is mention of Alexander in other Apostolic writings where he appears to have split with the Church. But it is hard to connect this Alexander with the Simon of Cyrenia.

In the next milestone of the Church's life, mention is made of people from both Egypt and Cyrenia at Pentecost where the disciples received their collective commissioning to undertake Christian mission which the book, called the Acts of the Apostles, chronicles in fair detail. Shortly after Pentecost the disciples encountered strong persecution which led to the martyrdom of one of their number,

Stephen. This compelled them to leave Jerusalem and they were scattered in numerous towns and districts where the numbers of Christians grew. According to the Acts, among the people who spread Christian teachings were people from Cyrenia who helped found the church in Antioch where the disciples were first given the name Christians. We are given the name of a man from Cyrenia, Lucius, who was active with the church at Antioch. There was also Simeon, identified simply as a Black man, possibly from the Ethiopic countries.

Elsewhere in the Acts we are given details of the baptism of an important government official designated as an Ethiopian palace chancellor, but more probably from the renowned kingdom of Meroë. He is described as being in the service of Queen Candace. He was on his way to Jerusalem to perform duties connected with worship to Yahweh, being himself an adept. According to a tradition preserved by the Church historian Eusebius, writing in the early fourth century, the name of this 'Ethiopian' official was Judich. As the story is recounted in the Acts, the Apostle Philip was urged to go and meet Judich in the Gaza where he found him reading from the Book of Isaiah a passage which expounded the theme of the recent Crucifixion of Christ. Philip is said to have explained this to Judich on enquiry and also at his request to have baptised him in a roadside pool. We shall never know for certain what role Judich played in introducing Christianity to Meroë; but history tells us that Meroë grew to be a prosperous and flourishing Christian kingdom in the Upper Nile valley, lasting several centuries.

In the young church at Ephesus the Alexandrian convert Apollos was very active. Priscilla and Aquila met him there. A gifted man, he had only heard of the teaching of John the Baptist, who preached the baptism of repentance. Priscilla and Aquila took him aside and confirmed him in the Christian way. Apollos was obviously endowed with exceptional powers of oratory. The Apostle Paul, for example, found that there was a strong personal following for Apollos at Corinth where his supporters constituted themselves into a separate community. We do not know if Apollos himself encouraged this separatist development, but it is significant that when specifically invited to go to Corinth he declined, content merely to say that he would when it proved convenient. It may well be that, like Paul, Apollos was only concerned to spread the teachings of Christianity rather than sponsor a separatist cult. In this he seems to have succeeded. Nevertheless he has left his stamp on the Church both in Asia and in Europe.

Scriptural materials begin to thin out at this point, but the story begun there continues to take on a brisk pace in other sources. Both from the fact of the centralised administration of the empire under Rome and from the personal contribution of individual Africans, the early Church struck firm roots on African soil. Although the flowering of that ancient tradition has largely passed, there is still a strong fragrance of that achievement left in the Ethiopian Orthodox Church and the Coptic Church in Egypt.

Historical sources and local traditions

Historical writers and oral traditions preserve the continuity between the early Church of the Apostles and that of the great Church Fathers; through that continuity the African aspect has survived. For example, Eusebius carries a tradition that John Mark, the author of the Gospel of the same name, came to Egypt in the service of the Church. He travelled to Alexandria where he helped establish Churches. Even today Mark is accorded special reverence by the Coptic Church in Egypt who regard him as their founder. Whether or not Mark actually founded the Coptic Church, the tradition which claims that he did appears firm, and historians who venture behind that tradition will find themselves in unfamiliar territory. Of the same order is another tradition according to which the Apostle Thomas came to Egypt and did some Christian work there before going on to India. This was about 52 AD. An obscure reference also claims an Ethiopian association for him. The Egyptian connection with the Apostolic Church is extended by a claim that in the year 180 the Alexandrian Church commissioned one Pentaenus for service to India, and if the Thomas tradition is authentic it would lock neatly into this later claim. What is clear is that the route to India via Egypt and down the Nile was an established one, and Christian agents as well as travellers going about other business followed it regularly. There is no reason, therefore, to discount it either for reasons of logistics or because of lack of interest in the project on the part of Christians. To complete the picture this begins to create, there are strong traditions in India itself that the Apostle Thomas founded Churches in South India, including the Orthodox Syrian Church of the East, with a membership today of about a million and a half, and the Mar Thoma Syrian Church with about 350,000 members. These traditions maintain that Thomas went to Madras where he met martyrdom. The site of his reputed death is preserved as St Thomas Mount, about 8 miles south-west of Madras city.

At this point the Apostolic initiative passes into local enterprise, with local Christians determined to establish and spread the faith in the manner in which the Apostles had passed it to them. The subsequent history of the young Church in Africa suggests that the labours of the first disciples yielded much fruit. Still utilising historical sources and local traditions, let us turn our attention to the manifestation of Christianity through local churches as well as in individual contributions.

The Kingdom of Axum

The rise of Axum in the northern part of the Ethiopian highlands is held by historians to be connected to the decline of Meroë which it replaced in power and influence. At the beginning of the Christian era, Axum had become the most important ivory market of north-east Africa. It had a splendid and impressive capital full of stone monuments. Its rulers became Christians in the middle of the fourth century, a time which coincided with the apogee of the kingdom, which had by then successfully challenged and defeated Meroë.

Numerous details are given in the traditions of how Christianity first came to Axum. The historian Rufinus, writing in the fourth century, says that two brothers from Tyre accompanied a friend on his way to India. The brothers, who were Christians, were Frumentius and Aedesius. They took the familiar route through Egypt and up the Nile. They stopped in the port of Adulis within the kingdom of Axum for victualling, but the crew and passengers ran into trouble there when they were set upon by the local people, who cut them down, with the exception of the two brothers. Brought before the king, who took pity on them because of their youth, they were kindly treated and given royal appointments at court. Frumentius became secretary-treasurer and Aedesius cup-bearer. But their royal duties did not take up all their time, and they spent the rest of it collecting the scattered Christians in Axum, most of whom were merchants and other foreign residents, and organising services. Additional church buildings were constructed and congregations multiplied.

Although Christianity was an important influence in Axum the king himself remained unconverted. After his death succession passed to his son Ezana, who was too young to take the reins of power, and a period of regency followed in which, if we may believe the account, power devolved on Aedesius and Frumentius who together shouldered the responsibility of government in which they schooled the young Ezana. They also appear to have taught him Christianity, for the young prince converted to the faith on becoming king. Yet from inscriptions he himself made it is clear that his adoption of the faith was not wholehearted, so that, with the rising tide of the Roman Christian power lapping on his shores, diplomatic and political considerations may not have been entirely absent from his motives. Whatever the degree of sincerity in the king's adoption of Christianity, the new faith was destined to make a major breakthrough in the kingdom.

Aedesius and Frumentius left Axum soon after the installation of King Ezana. Both returned to Syria, but Frumentius passed through Alexandria where Patriarch Athanasius received from him reports of the progress of the cause in Axum. Seeing the enthusiasm of the young Syrian the Patriarch had him ordained and consecrated bishop for service in the Axumite kingdom. The date for this is not fixed with any precision, but Frumentius is said to have visited Athanasius during the latter's reign from 346 to 357. Frumentius is rightly regarded by the Ethiopian Orthodox Church as *'Abba Salama'*, 'father of peace'.

Egypt and North Africa

The Alexandrian Church. The Church which first existed in Egypt, like that in North Africa (chiefly Carthage and Cyrenaica), was Roman-influenced. Only later, in the second half of the third century, did it spread beyond Roman and Jewish circles to reach rural populations. Historical records of the period suggest that a long-enduring contest took place between Christian teachings and indigenous religious traditions, and even though Christian altars appear to have displaced the traditional altars on which sacrifices were made, many of the old religious habits survived under Christianity. This point will emerge more sharply in later chapters.

One of the strongest centres of Christianity in Egypt was Alexandria. The fact that it was firmly within the orbit of the Roman Empire, with all the facilities for communication and travel, meant that news of Christianity could travel there quickly. But, equally important, it was the home of some 200,000 Jews who provided a recognisable bridge to Christian teaching. Alexandria was to develop into an important centre for the church, boasting a famous Catechetical School presided over by people like Clement of Alexandria (*c.* 150–215 AD). Learning flourished there, with Jewish and Greek scholars carrying on a vigorous tradition of study and philosophical reflection. It was in Alexandria that a serious attempt was made to interpret Christian teachings in the light of Greek philosophical thought, a process begun under Jewish scholars. Clement made his mark there, though he was not a native of that city; belonging to an élite, he stressed the element of reason in religion and established it as an important foundation of faith. The seeds he sowed in his teachings were to attract the attention of splinter groups.

One of his pupils was Origen (*c.* 185–253), who was to eclipse him in learning and fame. In 203, after Clement left Alexandria, Origen, then only eighteen, was appointed to succeed his teacher at the Catechetical School which he successfully guided through a time of fierce persecution and gave it an enviable pre-eminence in the Christian world. He laid the foundations of a scholarly analysis of Scripture, working with both the original Hebrew texts and the Greek of the New Testament documents. But he also developed a coherent theology of the nature of God, revelation and salvation. Open-minded and deeply learned, Origen carried on his shoulders the immense task of bearing witness to the church throughout the world of learning, which he also enriched with rare gifts of the spirit. A tangible form of that was the great St Gregory of Cappádocia, in Asia Minor, who was converted by Origen while the latter was working and living in Caesarea. By such endeavours Origen was forging links to extend the chain of Apostolic teaching and example which first brought the church to Africa. When we come to look at St Augustine, the fifth-century North African theologian, we shall find there the same links with Apostolic teaching and the same motivation to interpret Christian doctrines in the contemporary context, in Augustine's case in the context of the collapse of the Roman empire.

Before turning to the Coptic Church in Egypt we should perhaps mention another major development in the Alexandrian Church, namely monasticism. The teachings of Jesus on poverty, purity and prayer within a fellowship of disciples stimulated the Alexandrian church to embark on the monastic life. Egypt, with its desert and caves and the palm-fringed oases sprinkled in the sand, provided an appropriate setting. With the help of keen spiritual tools men carved for themselves temples of retreat and self-denial which would catch a reflection of the immaculate Christ. Antony (251–356), who had his own roots in agricultural life, having been born at Koma near Memphis on the Nile, was a Coptic Christian who turned to the monastic life with all the severity of that calling. He sold all his possessions, endowed the poor and abandoned society for a life of solitary retreat in an old fort. But later the monastic life evolved into a community affair, with Pachomius (290–345) leading the way. The monastic life blossomed under Pachomius who introduced into it rules of communal life, later organising the monks into orders, each under an abbot. Thus constituted and organised, monasteries acquired a prestige and influence which far exceeded anything that their meagre resources had originally suggested.

The Coptic Church. Before the coming of Christianity the Copts were an ancient Egyptian people who practised the old religions of the Pharaohs. They lived mostly in rural centres, attached to the land and the flocks they tended. As the existence of the Catechetical School at Alexandria showed, the church in Egypt originally comprised Greek-speaking Christians, with an important Jewish influence. Christianity continued to be the religion of a cultured, educated urban élite and had not yet seriously penetrated village communities. But, for whatever reason, there was a significant change, beginning about the middle of the third century, when Coptic villages and towns along the Nile embraced Christianity. This precipitated a crisis within the ranks of the adherents of local religions. Often Coptic Christians, accused of disloyalty and seen as a subversive force, were persecuted by their opponents. But we need to use caution in assessing the worth of these reports of persecution. A certain literary flourish sharpened the outlines of such stories to give them a dramatic effect which was not always in keeping with standards of accuracy. Nevertheless, in whatever way the style of the persecutions was exaggerated, there is sufficient evidence that Christians suffered, willingly or unwillingly, at the hands of officials of Rome. Eusebius, who seems to have made the subject a special concern of his, says that he was himself present in Thebes on the Nile when a wave of persecutions engulfed the Coptic Church. Many apparently refused to abjure their faith and accepted death willingly. These persecutions succeeded in driving the Coptic Church into itself so that it became little involved in projects to spread Christianity beyond Egypt, apart from a period of relationship with the Ethiopian Orthodox Church. Instead, the Coptic Church came to be sustained by a strong liturgical and sacramental life. This received a strong boost from the translation of the Scriptures into Coptic, beginning in the fourth century. Today, the Church has some 5 million members, but still suffers from many of the disadvantages of a minority religion in the now Islamic Egypt.

North Africa. Following the Third Punic War (146 BC) the Romans dismantled the Carthaginian empire and took Tunisia, once its heartland. Carthage under Rome became the purveyor of grain to Rome and other Italian cities, with the produce entering Italy through the port of Ostia Attica. The Punic population was virtually decimated in Carthage, but the Berbers remained as the base of the Roman plantation system. Christianity had made some inroads into Tunisia and the Algerian hinterland but until the early third century it was confined mainly to unofficial and native circles. And then the Church burst into new life under the brilliant and highly individual figure of Tertullian, a lawyer by training, by disposition a rigorist and by natural endowment a writer. He is regarded as the father of Latin Christianity in the sense of having created a Latin vocabulary for Christian theology. He was the first to formulate and coin the term 'Trinity', marshalling reasons as to its central place in the Church's teachings.

Persecution and schism

Born in North Africa in 160 AD, Tertullian witnessed the persecution of many Christians which he recorded in the dramatic words, 'The blood of the martyrs is the seed of the Church', meaning by this that those who lapsed from the faith during periods of persecution could not be re-admitted except through the baptism of blood as martyrs, an extreme position many reached only through schism. He brought a lawyer's sense of advocacy to issues of religious tolerance, believing that persecution was not only harmful to society but in deep conflict with the highest principles of Roman law. In 195 Tertullian converted to Christianity under obscure circumstances, but later stepped over into the Montanist movement, an ecstatic religious sect which prophesied the imminent return of Christ. Tertullian imposed a rigid, rationalist pattern on Christian theology and appeared at his best when engaged in controversy: against Rome because of what he regarded as the corrupt and unjust world over which it presided, against the pre-Christian heritage of his people because he believed it to be contaminating; against the leaders of Eastern Christianity because of their woolliness, and against the bishops because he believed them to be presiding over an imperfect church. Like Clement of Alexandria with whom he disagreed, Tertullian was deeply affected by the Church's experience of persecution. He died about the year 220.

Power shifted in time from Alexandria to Carthage, and although a time of severe testing awaited it, the North African Church became a citadel of Christianity second only to Rome. Between 220 and 256 three important councils met there. At that time the Church was labouring under great difficulties as Roman authorities tried to check its growth and curb its power. An edict was promulgated by the Emperor in 250 requiring Christians to appear before local commissions, renounce their faith and sacrifice to the Emperor on pain of torture and even death. Cyprian, the much revered bishop of Carthage at that time, went into hiding and only re-emerged in 251 when the persecution abated. But by that time the authorities had succeeding in squeezing many Christians into submission, creating by that threat controversy in the Church about what to do with repentant renegades. Cyprian tried to steer a middle course. He convened a church council which adopted a moderate position of admitting the lapsed after some rigorous penance. This held the two wings of the Church together and Cyprian's authority was consolidated, held in esteem alike by those who later seceded from the Church and those who remained behind. Cyprian was arrested and tried for his episcopal role and executed in September 258. His martyrdom elevated his stature in the eyes of the Donatists who sought death as a prize of faith.

The periods of intense persecution under the Emperors Decian in 250 and Diocletian from 303 till 312 had far-reaching effects on the Church in North Africa. In the first place it stiffened the anti-imperial resolve of African Christians. This resentment against Rome coalesced around the movement called Donatism which made resistance to Roman political orders its *raison d'être*. Matters came to a head in 312 when Caecilian became the victorious episcopal candidate of the citizenry of Carthage. A rebel council was hastily convened to denounce the election of Caecilian and to install a rival bishop who died the following year in 313, to be succeeded by Donatus whose name became attached to the movement. The radical

political views of the Donatists came into the open. By the Edict of
Milan of 312 the Emperor Constantine decreed religious toleration.
Informed of the troubles in Africa, Constantine decided to back
Caecilian and to exempt the clergy in communion with him from
levies. He had a meeting called — the Lateran Council — to rule
against Donatus. The Council was dominated by Italian bishops.
These actions established the foundations of a close alliance between
the Catholic church and the Roman power in Africa. They also
resulted in the permanent alienation of the Donatist Church, which
began to spread widely. In the year 336 it could call on the support of
270 bishops, a number which had increased to 400 by the end of the
fourth century. The authorities, alarmed by the progress of Donatism
and unable any longer to ignore it, decided on a collision course. In
316 Donatist basilicas and other Church property were expropriated.
This opened Pandora's box, and a period of violence and outrage
followed in the Donatist reaction. A shaky peace was contrived in the
late fourth century when the Berber chief Gildo, also a recognised
official of Rome, formed an alliance with the Donatist bishop
Optatus. But this did not inhibit the Donatists, who launched a
movement to dispossess rich landowners and suppress remnants of
Catholicism in areas under their control in the western parts of
Numidia. This alliance of Gildo with the Donatists was not without
significance for his own later attitude towards Rome. In 397 he
rebelled against Rome by witholding the shipment of grain, thus
threatening it with starvation. The Roman senate acted promptly and
despatched an expedition against him. He was captured in 398 and
died soon afterwards.

Thus the persecutions achieved the permanent disaffection of
African Christians, placing them outside the Catholic Church and its
Roman sponsors. Secondly, it fomented internal disputes, with many
unwillng to forget what they regarded as betrayal on the part of those
who lapsed during the Diocletianic persecution, leaving an
accumulating legacy of schismatic sentiment. And thirdly, it drove a
wedge between the native population, who now flocked to the
Donatist sectarian standard, and the Catholic Church now firmly in
the Roman imperial camp. Thus the religious issue of re-admission of
the lapsed into the Church became overlaid with opposition to
Roman domination, with a trace of economic resentment at excessive
taxation and the burdensome effects of the plantation system. Even
the conversion of Constantine and his avowed policy of religious
freedom offered little prospect of reconciliation. On the contrary, his
intervention against the Donatists merely succeeded in hardening
their position that the Catholic Church was now an instrument by
which the Emperor intended to secure their repression. What began
as a movement to resist corruption in the Church developed into a
vengeful, if fitful, nationalist struggle. Under the Emperor Julian

(361–4) and his policy of retracting support for the Church, the Donatist reaction flared up in bursts of violence in North African cities until it threatened to consume the Catholic Church.

It is tempting to treat this episode in the history of the ancient Church in Africa as a regrettable side-issue of the much grander theme of the remarkable progress of the Church elsewhere and to miss its implications. However, it is important to resist that temptation. We should take note of the following points. First the church became mixed up with the issue of foreign domination. When the Berbers embraced Christianity under Donatism, the result was a situation of inevitable conflict with the Catholic Church and therefore of potential schism. Secondly, the decentralised nature of the Berbers' political life made them unamenable to the central authority of the Church and prone to extremist solutions; political or religious compromise, often the result of a consensus on procedures for settling differences, was replaced with sectarian claims. Thirdly persecution upset the delicate balance between the native and the Romanised elements in the Church, and the Donatists took advantage of the declining fortunes of imperial Rome by rolling back the frontiers of the Catholic Church. Fourthly, there was no native Scripture and consequently no permanent tool for the creation of a durable Christian community reared on its own cultural roots. Last but by no means least, there was the ever-present problem of internecine struggle and competition for dominance among the Berbers, which infused a spirit of turbulence into their religious life; in this the Church was caught up. It will be seen that many of these factors are highly relevant to the much later history of Christianity in West Africa and elsewhere.

Augustine

The small flame which the early disciples tended on African soil appeared to be flickering in North Africa as the divided flocks of rival bishops contended with each other, buffeted by the harsh winds of schism. Then arose a man who revived the Apostolic impulse and adorned the Church with some of its finest gifts of mind and spirit. This man was St Augustine, born in 354 in North Africa and dying there in 430. Although he failed in his patient wooing of the Donatists he succeeded at a strategic conference of Catholic and Donatist bishops in June 411 to stem the tide of Donatist revival, which finally had to be checked by imperial force. Yet Augustine did manage to help the Church recover some of its lost prestige among local people and gave the African Church an authority which profoundly influenced Papal and conciliar pronouncements on faith and doctrine. In his celebrated book, the *Confessions*, Augustine provides more than a straightforward autobiography, giving rare insights into the background of the Church's teaching and ideas current in this time. The torch he lit in that and other books like *Retractions* and the *City of God* has continued to illuminate the far corners of the world of Christianity, establishing their author as a supreme master not only of his age but even of ours. Let us look briefly at the African side of his life, paying attention to elements of continuity with the contemporary African church.

When Augustine became a Christian he was in Milan. The power of Rome was then rapidly declining and Christianity was still a minority religion, with many of the wealthiest citizens and officials still attached to the old religions or to a degenerate Neoplatonic philosophy with its hedonistic culture. One of the influences which led to the young Augustine's conversion was the example of monastic life which the monks of Egypt had founded. After his baptism he went to Hippo near Carthage to live as a monk. Later he was ordained priest and in 395 became bishop of the city where he continued to live for the next thirty-five years. One of his activities was to conduct meditations on the Gospel of St John. Although his house and the basilica were situated near the fashionable suburbs of Hippo, with large houses and gardens, the diocese over which he presided embraced village churches and private chapels in the hinterland and adjoining the hill-town settlements of the Donatists. As his reputation grew, he was called upon to make numerous visits to Carthage where he was consulted on many questions. En route he would visit his disciples and fellow-bishops, few of whom could have known at that time what a towering pillar the man was destined to become.

After he returned from Milan where he had been baptised by St Ambrose Augustine never again left Africa. He became absorbed in the routine and details of a provincial society of which he was the main focus. Accounts speak of his unusual capacity for friendship and affection, always ready to welcome visitors to his house for meals and discussion though he led a semi-monastic life. He made many friends and was treated with respect by leading citizens, both Christian and non-Christian. He carried on a copious correspondence and was tremendously active as a teacher of his people. At this time Rome remained largely pagan, and after the collapse of the empire many of its leaders, deeply anti-Christian in feeling, fled to Africa. It was partly the challenge of meeting their criticisms that caused Augustine to set forth his views in the *City of God*. In the *Confessions* Augustine was able to enlarge the provincial details of his life and fix on them a crisp but timeless quality. Similarly in the the *City of God* Augustine marshals arguments based on factual details and contemporary sources (he was poorly furnished with the latter) to create a monumental structure held together by a heavenly vision. In this too the soil of Africa clings to his achievement. In Book XXII (24) of the *City of God* he writes evocatively of the Africa he knew:

The manifold diversity of beauty in sky and earth and sea; the abundance of light, and its miraculous loveliness, in sun and moon and stars; the dark shades of the woods, the colour and fragrance of flowers; the multitudinous varieties of birds, with their songs and their bright plumage; the countless different species of living creatures of all shapes and sizes. . .

Then there is the mighty spectacle of the sea itself, putting on its changing colours like different garments, now green, with all the many varied shades, now purple, now blue.

Conclusions and prospects

Let us, in these concluding paragraphs, attempt to summarise the main outlines of the story of Christianity and its contacts with Africa. The infant Church, like the Holy Child before it, felt the full impact of contemporary political and social events, and in the struggle to interpret the message of Christianity numerous obstacles were encountered and not always overcome. But whatever success there was in those early beginnings some of it could be credited to African Christians, some of whom had met Jesus personally and were present in Jerusalem, Antioch and other places when the Christian movement began. Similarly some of the Apostles appear to have landed on African soil, encouraging the setting up of churches. There is little doubt that Africa as well as other lands came firmly within the horizon of the first disciples and that Christian teaching was intended to apply to all peoples without respect to status, colour, political belief or geography. It is a matter of historical record that Africans participated fully in the mission of the Church, and this is a matter of some significance for us today. In another way Africa was representative of the Church in other lands. Orthodoxy flourished in the Church, but so too did heresy and unconventional doctrine. The Churches in Africa in our own day reflect this diversity of tradition, with a similar challenge of translating the Church's teaching into the local religious and cultural idiom.

In the time of the early Church, the Sahara and the difficult terrain of the mountain Berbers sealed off the church from active contact with sub-Saharan peoples, whom Christianity was to reach mainly by way of the sea. But a similar geographical barrier was to interpose itself between the coastal and forest belts of Africa, where Christianity had made a deep impact, and the savannah regions in some of which Christianity was only being introduced in the twentieth century. So, in spite of the enormous strides the Church has made in Africa, with something like 170 million Christians, some obstacles have remained. But in the fluctuating fortunes of the African Churches, the tradition of the Apostles, especially in its Scriptural form, has struck deep roots, binding those Churches as a recognisable extension of their historic witness, no more protected from the pressures of the world than they were.

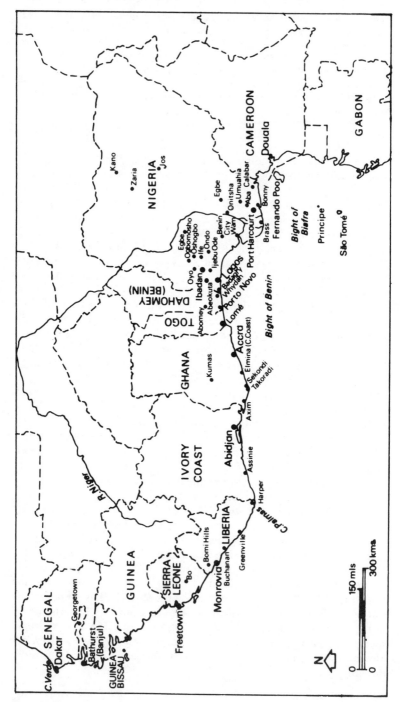

West Africa

2

THE EARLY PIONEERS:
THE CHURCH COMES TO WEST
AFRICA, 1471-1703

The Church must bear in mind that among these very enemies are hidden her future citizens; and when confronted with them she must not think it a fruitless task to bear with their hostility until she finds them confessing the faith. In the same way, while the City of God is on pilgrimage in this world, she has in her midst some who are united with her in participation in the sacraments, but who will not join her in the eternal destiny of the saints. . . In truth those two cities are interwoven and intermixed in this era, and await separation at the last judgement. St Augustine

Christianity in Islamic North Africa and Egypt

The attempt to establish the Church in North Africa suffered major setbacks, and it was in a much weakened form that it was swept away by the rising tide of Islam in the seventh century. The Muslim armies quickly spread over Egypt and North Africa to which they gave the name *'Maghrib'*, an Arabic word meaning 'the West'. Christian remnants were easily mopped up or squeezed into acquiescence, while Islam obtained a bridgehead for attacks into the Iberian peninsula. A few Christian communities existed in Mauritania and in ports scattered between Tangier and Tripoli; these were valuable to the Muslim rulers for the lucrative trade they attracted from Europe. Consequently they were granted permission to worship in their own churches and have priests, but they were forbidden to do any missionary work. Even the puritanical rulers of the Almohad dynasty maintained this policy of toleration for Christian minorities because of the value of the trade they carried. There were also many Christian elements in the armies of the sultans as bodyguards; chaplains were assigned to them. A third group of Christians were refugees from Islamic Spain who came to settle in Morocco. They were called Mozarabic Christians and spoke Arabic as their first language. The word 'Mozarabic' is an adaptation of the Arabic *must ^carib*, and it means people of foreign or mixed descent who became naturalised as Arabs. From the thirteenth century these people formed a separate and important community and were recognised by Pope Innocent IV as constituting the Moroccan Church. The Berbers on the whole had

15

their links with Christianity dissolved and when they emerged from their mountain villages to face the power of Islam, they did so as sectarians affiliated to the extremist Kharijite movement. The double barrier of Islam and the Sahara sealed any hopes of the Church spreading from North Africa towards the south, where Islam was meanwhile making progress.

In Egypt the Coptic Church was incorporated as a protected minority of the Islamic state which exacted a heavy price for its continued existence. Christians were required by state policy to pay tribute, offer hospitality to Muslims, and distinguish themselves from the rest of the population by means of their dress; they were forbidden to erect new churches or monasteries or to display any aspect of Christian practice, and they were to ensure generally that no Christian symbolism obtruded in any way on Muslims. During persecutions in the eighth and ninth centuries, churches were destroyed and orders issued which led many Christians to embrace Islam. For example, in 744 some 24,000 Christians turned to it on the promise of the governor that they would be spared taxes imposed on all other Christians. Egypt also blocked attempts by Christian Ethiopia to establish contacts and links with the outside world. Egypt's fear was that Ethiopia might form military alliances with Christian Europe, then in the grip of a fever for Crusades, and thus prove a costly neighbour on its exposed southern flank. A group of Ethiopian pilgrims in Jerusalem in 1345–7 complained that the Sultan of Egypt had imposed a ban on Ethiopian travellers through his country to prevent them slipping through to Europe. Because of the unhappy, persecuted Copts in Egypt, who traditionally looked across the country's southern border for help, Ethiopia had been involved in a number of military operations against Egypt. For example, in the reign of Sultan al-Salih (1351–4) a wave of persecution broke out against the Copts, and Patriarch Marqos (1348–63) sent word from prison to the Ethiopian King, who immediately mobilised a huge army against Egypt. News of the troop movements reached Egypt and it was enough to secure the Sultan's capitulation and the Patriarch's release.

Although Islam and Christianity were struggling to win advantages in a game of power politics, there were many others who tried to establish a basis for continuous contact on religious matters. It is this theme which we must now follow, for it leads into the subject of how the Church eventually came to West Africa.

The Franciscan and Dominican religious Orders made several attempts to begin missionary work in Egypt and North Africa. St Francis of Assisi himself visited Egypt in 1219, accompanied by a group of Brothers Minor. He met the Sultan and is said to have preached to him. A Franciscan mission visited Tunis in the same year, but met with hostility and failure. Another determined group of five Franciscans went to Morocco in 1219, deliberately courting and receiving the martyr's crown. Members of the Dominican Order also travelled to Egypt where by 1234 they were relatively well established, working mainly among Christian soldiers and Christian slaves of whom there was a considerable number. The Dominicans worked patiently by preaching and teaching and giving instruction to Muslim inquirers on Christian worship. They also emphasised the need for special training for work among non-Christians, associating themselves with centres for the study of languages, especially Arabic, in North Africa. Perhaps the most outstanding Christian figure involved with Muslims was Raymond Lull who visited Tunis in 1292 at the age of sixty, anxious to wage a spiritual crusade with the 'art of loving the good' (which was also the title of a work he had written two years previously). That proved a disappointment, for he cut short his trip. In later life, in a mood of remorse, he made two boisterous trips in which he incurred first imprisonment and then martyrdom.

These setbacks did not exhaust the desire to spread Christianity or the energy needed to carry it out. On the contrary, they merely drove Christians to find fresh outlets for opportunities of service. It is important to see these developments both in the context of the transformation of the mediaeval European Church into a popular and secular institution (both St Francis of Assisi and Raymond Lull epitomise this) and in terms of the prevailing urge to penetrate distant lands to advance the interests of commerce, increase scientific knowledge and, in the process, abandon the hitherto futile attempt to do missionary work in Muslim lands. In this way Islam proved a catalyst both in stimulating profound changes within the Church and in diverting surplus energy into new, untried fields.

Medieval Christianity and the missionary movement

When changes were in progress within the medieval Church, the involvement of Christians with Islam provided scope for lay leadership and popular support. Wealthy dukes and princes gave money and land and well-to-do merchants and aristrocratic families rallied round the Church, so giving it a new lease of life. The church building became a landmark in nearly all areas, and although sharp differences remained among social classes and in regional variation, everywhere the uniform if not unifying weight of Christianity was being felt in increasing measure. For one thing, peace and order began to return after the upheavals which reached a peak with Muslim attacks in the eighth century. The symbol of the new political order was the Frankish king Charlemagne (*d.* 814), who was crowned as Holy Roman Emperor on Christmas Day, 800, in Rome. Although this sowed the seeds of future conflict between Church and state when Pope Innocent IV disinvested the Emperor Frederick II in

July 1245, it provided a basis for relative stability. Furthermore, while the authority of the Pope was certainly not everywhere uniformly acknowledged, the institution of hierarchical authority was nonetheless secure. Its effectiveness or power to take initiatives in local religious life, however, was severely restricted.

What contributed more than anything else to fostering a sense of Christian identity and vocation were the great Orders which mushroomed over the face of Europe. In many places this was in direct response to what was felt to be the threat of Islam. But very soon it became tied to forms of pre-Christian religious life. These Orders were founded on monasteries where the process of synthesising the new faith in the milieu of primitive folk religion, Roman and Gallic polytheism, and the spirits and deities of local shrines took a new and lasting turn. Churches and chapels were usually constructed on the sites of old religious sanctuaries and shrines, and the Church calendar was replete with feasts and festivals devoted to local deities and spirits. The traditional religious burial customs survived in the practice of using the grounds of the church building as a cemetery, thus bringing the old notions of duel and ordeal within the consecrated bounds of both the churchyard and the evil-chasing power of the church bell. Indeed, rituals connected with the dead came to assume an enormous importance. These ceremonies preserved the traditional belief that the spirits of the dead maintained links with the living whose *familia* (i.e. spiritual double) was now to be brought within the greater brotherhood of the dead. The monks, aided by the nobility and the clergy, presided over this popular religious revival. Even the great reforming Order of Cluny, endowed by a powerful duke in the tenth century, actively fostered the commemoration of the dead, a service for which they became renowned, and suitably rewarded throughout Europe. They consequently won over the aristocracies of France, Spain, Hungary and the Empire.

If the monastery as an institution was the symbol of this new religious age, then one individual epitomised its spirit: Bernard of Clairvaux. The monastic institution was to symbolise the new synthesis involving the dogma of the Church and the pre-existing religious customs so that the Church had cast over it a layer of popular religious culture which brought it much closer to the older traditions. However, this rich climate of religious interaction produced abuse and excesses, and the call went out to reform the religious life by reorganising the monasteries. It was here that Bernard of Clairvaux was to leave his mark, his house at Clairvaux founding some sixty-five daughter-houses under the energetic Cistercians. Many of the Orders which eventually reached West Africa in the fifteenth century and later sprang directly from this monastic legacy, both in their acquired sensitivities to popular religious customs and in their unitary view of faith wherein Church and state co-operated for man's salvation and welfare. Thus, although the period of incubation under review remains largely out of sight from the West African point of view, it nevertheless developed features which were highly relevant to the issues of religious interaction and synthesis which the Church faced in West Africa. At first, fired by the ascetic ideals of the great monastic movement, the early Christian pioneers in West Africa saw their mission in terms of consolidating the gains they had made in the successful assimilation of European folk religion, assuming that in the West African context the traditional religions would play a similar responsive, secondary role. This attitude survived, so that even when, later, missionaries were furnished with better documentation on African religions, the notion of an indigenised Church remained largely a remote possibility. Of course we can now clearly see that local religions were the only meaningful point of contact for most Africans, as indeed they were for medieval Europe. This is now comprehensible not only because of renewed interest in African religions but also because we now have the comparative tradition of early monasticism. We are thus in a position to appreciate that the meaningful adaptation that was going on in African Christianity was mainly as a result of the underlying vitality of African religions.

The Cape Verde Islands, 1402-1652

The role of lay and secular people in the expansion of Christianity in Europe, especially in the Catholic Counter-Reformation, was also prominent in the extension of the Church to the Cape Verde Islands. As early as 1402 the Canary Islands, further north off the Mauritanian coast, were colonised by a Norman baron, and Spanish Franciscans did missionary work among the native Guanches. The Franciscans then went to work in Madeira, discovered in 1420, and to the Cape Verde islands, discovered by the Portuguese between 1456 and 1460. The islands became an important base for slaves in transit, and it was from these islands that European factories, such as that at Gorée in the mouth of the Senegal river, were supplied with provisions. Slaves were also used to develop several of the islands, including Santiago.

As in the Congo, so in the Cape Verde islands Africans educated in Lisbon were encouraged to become priests and to take an active part in the work of the Church. Fr António Vieira, a Jesuit priest, spent a week in the islands during the Christmas season of 1652, and has left a description of the role of African priests there. He writes admiringly of the African clergy: "There are here clergy and canons as black as jet, but so well-bred, so accomplished that they may well be envied by those in our own cathedrals at home.'[1] After the War of Succession between Spain and Portugal in 1475, most of the north Atlantic islands were ceded to Spain except Madeira and the Cape Verde islands. These continued to serve as an entrepot for ships in the export of food to places along the Upper Guinea coast. The slave trade also increased and with it the islands' importance. It was hoped that the islands would nurture a mulatto population who would take Christianity to the African mainland, but this hope failed. It became obvious that African Christians in the Cape Verde islands were going to be sucked into the orbit of Portuguese and Spanish expansion rather than act as a transmission point for the outreach into West Africa. Indeed, Africans enslaved and transported to the Western hemisphere were later to return to West Africa as carriers of Christianity, but that era had not yet arrived.

West Africa and the first Church: Ghana, 1482-1632

In the extension of Christian missionary activity to West Africa in the fifteenth century lay and secular leadership played an equally decisive role. The men who provided the necessary support and on whose enterprise the fifteenth century missionary depended were independent kings, princes and industrious merchants and bankers, most of them with a devout, if not always altruistic, interest in helping the spread of the Church. Where West Africa is concerned, we may conveniently divide the Christian age broadly into three. The first period, from the disappearance of the Church in North Africa to about the fifteenth century, we may call the incubation period. The Church disappeared from sight but important changes had come over it, including a fresh vitality with which it was to burst upon lands outside Europe. The second period we may date from about 1450 to 1750, when Christianity was transported to West Africa, mostly as a sterilised European institution, safely quarantined in hygienic enclaves along the coast whence it occasionally timidly emerged to make local contact. Often it returned from such wary ventures still effectively insulated against cross-cultural influences and with more pronounced symptoms of its European condition. Trading forts and castles built along the coast sheltered the early missionaries, but at a price. The Church became an adjunct of the commercial enterprise, unable — except perhaps for Warri, the Congo and Angola — to generate an independent confidence in its own message, and suffering the side-effects of sudden changes in the trading fortunes of the forts. True, it made inroads into ruling circles, but its impact was marginal. The first converts, including a few scheming rulers and trading clients, became infected with African suspicions of European intentions. Isolated from the castles and forts, these converts

1. Boxer (1969, 1977), p. 259.

eventually lapsed from the faith. The third and much more successful period of the Church in Africa began in the second half of the eighteenth century, and continued through much of the nineteenth and twentieth centuries.

There is a solitary, elusive reference to Christianity in West Africa before the arrival of the Portuguese in the 1470s. There is a report — believed to be a forgery — that in 1364 the French founded a church on the Elmina coast to which they gave the name Chapel of the Mother of God.[2] Most authorities dismiss that report as contradictory and worthless. The first incontrovertible evidence of European presence in Ghana dates from January 1471. In that year two captains working for the Lisbon merchant Fernão Gomes landed at Shama on the coast where they found a fine natural harbour and a watering place. These two men were João de Santarém and Pedro de Escobar. They were surprised to find that gold was easily available for barter trade, and before long they had staked a monopoly claim to Shama and the adjoining coastal area. Faithful to the will of Prince Henry the Navigator (*d.* 1460), recognised since 1419 as the spirit and architect of Portugal's seaborne expansion, they also planted huge wooden crosses at every place where they stopped: Prince Henry's fame rested not only on his great interest in and encouragement of naval expeditions and the geographical knowledge acquired in the process, but also on his Christian zeal. He saw action against the Moors at Ceuta in 1415, and in 1455 was specially commended in a Papal Bull for his devotion and apostolic zeal in spreading the name of Christ. More important, the Bull gave the Prince authorisation to conquer and possess distant lands and their wealth. It is of course true that many men employed in the work of expanding Portugal's fortunes overseas were stirred by less elevated motives than those of their great patron, Prince Henry, and that traders conscious of huge profits to be made dashed their feet against the stumbling block of the Church and plunged after trading concessions. In the ten years between 1471 and 1481 much gold was reaching Portugal, and reports of this success encouraged unlicensed Portuguese traders as well as Spaniards to sail down to the Elmina coast. The competition became so fierce that the Portuguese decided to protect their monopoly control by building a fortified castle on the coast from which they could exclude others.

It is not our business here to investigate the history of Portugal's rise as an imperial power. But among the many factors the religious and the economic were oustanding. A contemporary adventurer expressed it as follows. He and his companions crossed the seas, he said, 'to serve God and His Majesty, to give light to those who were in darkness, and to grow rich, as all men desire to do'.[3] This

2. See, for example, Tracy (1845).
3. Parry (1964), p. 33.

combination of religion and wealth, linked to loyalty to the King, was to impose a siege mentality on the first missionaries. The secluded life in the forts and castles undercut the principle of open access to the Church. The fact that missionaries came in the company of foreign traders, many of whom sold guns and sowed discord between rival chiefs, served to weaken the Christian cause. And with the best will missionaries were themselves hampered by sickness and deaths, and by their ignorance of local conditions. Nonetheless much valuable work was done and much useful knowledge and experience obtained in that period.

The first concrete reference to the presence of Christian missionaries in what is today Ghana occurs in a context which suggests extreme lack of confidence. On 19 January, 1482, Diogo da Azambuja landed at Elmina, known locally as Edina, at the head of an expedition of 100 artisans and 500 soldiers. The size of this force indicates that many perils were expected by the expedition. A clue is given as to where most trouble was expected. We are told that on the day after the landing, Diogo da Azambuja and his men appeared before the local inhabitants 'smartly dressed but with hidden arms in case of need.' After those preliminaries, the party proceeded to celebrate Mass (the first ever recorded in Ghana). The altar was set up at the foot of a tree on a hillock over which the royal Portuguese flag was hoisted. The expedition was conscious of the historic significance of what they were doing, and were thus obviously moved to scenes of great emotion. The Mass, they later wrote, 'was heard by our men with many tears of devotion,' and with the fervent hope 'that the Church which they would found there might endure until the end of the world'.[4] Their devotion was real enough but their hope proved vain, as we shall see.

Following the Mass Azambuja had a meeting with the ruler of Elmina, Nana Caramansa. *'Mansa'* is a Mandinka term meaning 'king' and occuring in Portuguese sources for other places in West Africa, such as 'Niumimansa' in the Gambia estuary and 'Casamansa' for an area now lying within the republic of Senegal, the southern province of Casamance. Some writers think Caramansa is a form of *'Kwamina Ansa'*, although that still does not explain how the Portuguese came to adapt it in the way they did). A Portuguese trader operating in the area and on good terms with Nana Caramansa had arranged the meeting.

The building of Elmina castle

Several details are given of this meeting. Azambuja is said to have made a proposal at the conclusion of this hasty meeting to establish a fortress on the very spot where he met the chief. But Caramansa

4. Debrunner (1967), p. 17.

showed no enthusiasm for the project: it would be better, he suggested, to maintain some distance between them to avoid possible friction in the future. To force Caramansa's hand, Azambuja invoked the latent rivalry between Elmina and Shama where the first party of Portuguese had landed and where, Azambuja said, the ruler would be happy to have a fort constructed; surely, the Portuguese told his host, Elmina would not want to be dominated by Shama. The chief understood the ominous hint and perhaps saw the point that the Portuguese intended to play an active role in local political relations. He gave his consent to the proposal, although it is unlikely that his fundamental qualms had been removed.

Soon after this audience with the chief the Portuguese began work. But no sooner had they started than they ran into trouble. They started breaking up rocks along the shore, a place where the inhabitants had normally conducted religious ceremonies, and this action disturbed sensibilities. The local people rose in anger against the workmen and were only prevented from harming them by the timely intervention of Azambuja who negotiated a temporary truce. Work then proceeded at a furious pace to avoid costly delays. However, the local people were unappeased, and they denied the foreigners access to nearby water supplies.

The Portuguese were in no doubt that the Church they came to represent could survive only if it was given shelter within a fortified castle presided over by themselves, a Church which marched in step with the profit-seeking machine of Portuguese commerce. One of their oft-repeated ambitions was to extend by their action the influence and authority of the King of Portugal, a message they drummed into the ears of Caramansa and other African rulers who could not have failed to perceive in all this a number of far-reaching political implications.

As soon as the palisade and citadel were completed, a church building was constructed which came to bear the name of São Jorge — St George — the patron saint of Portugal. The fort itself was named the 'Castle of São Jorge'. A chaplain was appointed to serve the church within the fort, and in time provision was made for four priests to serve at the castle, although it was difficult to find men to fill the posts. Similarly, in spite of the clear aim to convert Africans, this could hardly be done from within the security of the castle. The chapel became preoccupied with its own internal life, seeking to fulfil the conditions imposed on it by charter of offering a daily Mass for the repose of the soul of Prince Henry the Navigator and a weekly votive Mass to the Virgin Mary. There was also a requirement for liturgies concerned with the commemoration of the dead. These requirements emphasised the juridical and spiritual links of the chapel with the secular and lay leadership of the medieval European Church. The Order of the Knights of Christ, founded in 1319 in

Portugal, had been given complete spiritual jurisdiction over all churches founded in West Africa and 'southwards to the Indies'. By a Bull promulgated in March 1456, Pope Calixtus III had empowered Prince Henry, as Grand Prior of this Order, to name incumbents to all benefices, both of secular and of regular clergy, to impose censures and other ecclesiastical penalties, and to exercise the powers of an Ordinary within the limits of his jurisdiction. It was in this way that the church of São Jorge at Elmina came to be devoted to Prince Henry and was brought under the obligation of saying Mass for the souls of all deceased members of the Order of the Knights of Christ.

While the immense contribution of Prince Henry to the discovery and exploration of Africa and much of Asia and the Americas is not to be doubted, the church of São Jorge unintentionally placed a psychological barrier between itself and the African people. The great Prince deserves better than to be the handy whipping-boy of the patriot, but the church he helped to bring to West Africa and on which such a heavy responsibility rested had more pressing business to hand and became an unwitting prisoner of its own history, unable to match the imagination and enterprise of its patron.

The King of Portugal took seriously the obligation imposed on the church of São Jorge to say Mass as prescribed, and in September 1501, he threatened that unless such Masses were said the stipend of the priests concerned would be reduced. The King also wrote to Pope Alexander VI for authorisation to demand this of all churches in West Africa, and this was given in May 1503. However, the changes envisaged in these and similar efforts never materialised. Local conditions in West Africa militated against the institutional transplantation of the church.

Diogo da Azambuja and the chaplain made strenuous efforts to try to convert Nana Caramansa, but all to little avail. As long as Nana Caramansa remained unconverted so long did the people of his chiefdom. But we can see why Caramansa refused Christianity. His office as chief required him to preside as the ceremonial guardian of the religious customs of his people. Secondly, the abrupt nature of the coming of Christianity and the fact that it was made to represent an external sovereignty alienated traditional rulers. After a period of good relations with the Portuguese, African rulers might become ready to accept Christianity, or a form of it, but in the initial stages suspicion predominated.

The King of Efutu converts

Then in 1503 the Church achieved a breakthrough. The King of Efutu and six of his ministers embraced Christianity, and their example was followed by other palace officials and principal title-bearers, together with their families. The number was estimated at

300 by one Portuguese eye-witness, who may have been inclined to exaggerate the size of the conversion. This eye-witness, Diogo de Alvarenga, said that he and the vicar subsequently helped to put up a chapel for the King at his request.

We should now try to assess the significance of this conversion. In the first place it was not 'mass conversion' as one modern writer claims, unless by this he means that there was a large number of converts. It was clearly a matter of the palace élite converting rather than the ordinary masses. As such, political and economic considerations must have played an important role, with the King of Efutu perhaps attempting to use the Portuguese as a lever against other rulers. Similarly, he may have thought of diverting as much as possible of the trade with the Portuguese into his area, and presumably felt the rich presents he had been given by them to be a sign that European traders would look to him. Thus the political and economic relations existing on the coast would have exerted a powerful influence on the decisions of rulers to accept or reject Christianity during the period we are considering.

In any case ten years from this event reports indicate that most of those who had converted had lapsed, including the King of Efutu himself. In 1513 a Portuguese trader, Affonso Caldeira, sent a letter to King Manoel saying that the current King of Efutu was still desiring baptism. Nothing had been heard about the faith of his predecessor.

Life in the castle

The castle at Elmina continued to dominate Portuguese relations with chiefs just as it had enabled the Portuguese to pre-empt rival European traders along the coast. The castle in fact became a model that was copied by the Chartered Companies in later times. Its advantages were obvious. Above all it enabled a European population to establish permanent residence in West Africa from which trade was conducted, ships could be refitted and local markets supervised and directed. One modern authority describes how the castle constituted a self-sufficient community, with a clerical and mercantile staff and workmen skilled in all the essential crafts. It also preserved the feudal aspects of Portuguese social life. There was a governor who was paid a salary, and under him were ten men, also salaried. A surgeon and two commercial secretaries were the highest paid officials apart from the governor. The chief trader was also paid a salary together with four men working under him. There were thirteen officials who were normally assigned military and general duties. The King's chaplain was paid a salary and said daily Mass for the soul of Prince Henry. The priest-in-charge and two other chaplains, all of them paid a salary, taught the mulatto children in the castle, although in theory their chief task was to carry Christianity to Africans outside the castle. That missionary work was to be done under the Patron Saint, Francis of Assisi. These people, plus the works superintendent, all received officers' salaries. In the junior ranks were the apothecary, a barber trained to bleed patients, the infirmary supervisor, the overseer of the oven, a blacksmith, a cooper, two carpenters, two masons, a tailor-darner and two bombardiers or armourers. Then came four women who kneaded dough and served in the infirmary as nurses. Every person was entitled to a daily ration of four loaves, some wine, and once a month to three pints of olive-oil and honey, and six pints of vinegar. This arrangement continued from its establishment in 1529 till 1607 or perhaps even to 1637 when the Portuguese lost the castle to the Dutch.

In 1529 Estevão de Gama was appointed Captain and Governor of Elmina and with him came a royal order to establish a school at the castle for the purpose of instructing local children in the Christian faith. This reference to Christianity and education opens a theme of revolutionary significance for Africa, although clearly in those early days the results were poor. Estevão da Gama was charged by King João III to 'take special care, to command that the sons of the Blacks living in the village learn how to read and write, how to sing and pray while ministering in church. . .'[5] Generous financial incentives were provided to carry through this educational project, all the money coming from the King's share of the gold trade at Elmina. A school was to be established with fifteen pupils as the upper limit. Although numerous details are given of the method of establishing the school and its financial welfare, surprisingly little is told on how it actually operated and what it achieved. This may indicate that the success of the school was limited, especially since the unfamiliar language of Portuguese was to be the medium of instruction.

The Order of Hermits of St Augustine

With the involvement and interest of the King of Portugal in the Christian enterprise at Elmina, there began to be pressure from Lisbon for better results. Reports had reached the capital that the work in Elmina was slackening and that priests put in charge there had been attracted to trade or were careless in carrying out their priestly duties. Unable to control the Elmina clergy from the distance of Portugal, the King in 1554 turned for help to the Order of the Society of Jesus, otherwise known as the Jesuits. A letter was sent to the Secretary to St Ignatius Loyola in Rome, but the Jesuits did not respond to the King's earnest entreaty. Efforts were then directed at another religious Order, the Hermits of St Augustine, which despite their name did not owe their foundation to that Saint. His illustrious

5. Wiltgen (1956), p. 16.

patronage was merely adopted for it, and it remained a Portuguese Order.

The Augustinians arrived at Elmina in 1572. They were Fathers Pedro da Graça, José de Moraes, Jerónimo da Encarnação and Gaspar dos Anjos, the Superior of the group. Elmina was divided for pastoral purposes into four wards, each under one of the missionaries who taught catechism and reading. A village church was built consisting of a cross and an altar in an open space and regular services were held there. It was intended to turn this makeshift place of worship into a permanent, brick-walled church building where Christians would be taught their prayers and new inquirers instructed. There was also a plan to introduce residential segregation for Christians by restricting them to a part of Elmina near enough to the castle for them to be protected from non-Christian influences. As it was, Christians lived in a mixed population with their non-Christian relatives and neighbours whose ways, it was believed, contaminated the Christian life. In 1573 two more missionaries arrived, Domingo de Santa Maria and Atanásio da Cruz. In 1574 the Governor of Elmina, Mendo de Mota, arranged for a monastery to be built for them and their companions.

Provided now with a permanent base, the missionaries started penetrating the surrounding communities. Two of them remained at the monastery, while the other four divided into two groups, one visiting Komenda and the other going to Efutu, both within safe distance of Elmina castle. Some encouraging signs were beginning to appear. In 1576 the reigning King of Efutu asked for and received baptism, and was joined by six of his sons and three nephews. His counterpart in Komenda similarly received Christian baptism with his eldest son. The Chief of Abura followed. Efutu lies some 8 miles inland from Elmina, Abura about 10 miles to the north, and Komenda 9 miles along the coast to the west. It is clear from this list that the missionaries were going over familiar territory; as we have seen, Efutu had already been introduced to the faith in 1503 and this was repeated in 1513 — but on both occasions political and economic factors seem to have predominated over any religious motive. It could not have been very different in 1576, nor could Abura and Komenda have acted any less from expediency. All of them shared the same fate.

Faced with the increasing presence of Europeans, also with an increasing number of African religious and commercial clients, the local populations in Efutu and Komenda reacted with violence. They attacked the missionaries and clubbed them to death. Then they destroyed the chapels, and desecrated the articles of holy office: priestly vestments, images, altar cloths, the missal and the Eucharistic elements. Only Father Pedro da Graça, who had been absent visiting stations along the coast, escaped.

Reasons for failure of mission

Why did the Augustinians suffer this extreme fate? History is silent on this question, but we should try to answer it. The fact that Portugal was consolidating its control over local trade must have had something to do with it: the missionaries symbolised the extension of hateful Portuguese domination in local affairs. Secondly, the intrusion of Christianity into royal courts and palace circles threatened the position of traditional religions whose keepers would be anxious to try to prevent their further erosion by Christianity. To understand this better we have to think of the King representing central authority and the devotees of the traditional religions representing power at the periphery. When the King embraced Christianity he challenged the latter and thus upset the normal balance between his prerogative and the authority of the elders. For this reason, the attack on the Augustinian mission needs to be related to internal political tensions in Efutu and Komenda. It probably came when it did because the psychological moment was right; the Superior of the mission was away on pastoral visitation; and Efutu and Komenda, receding beyond the immediate shadow of Elmina castle, felt sufficiently free from intimidation to rise in revolt. We can thus see that for Africans too Church and state — i.e. the sphere of the divinities and the abode of politics — are interwoven and inseparable. Nevertheless the experience of the Augustinians was not typical. It was the only instance of violence towards European missionaries in the whole history of Christianity in Ghana.

The Sacred Congregation of the Propaganda Fide

After the sacking of the missions at Efutu and Komenda the work of the Augustinians ceased. An interlude of over fifty years followed during which trade flourished, especially that in slaves for which Elmina remained the principal outlet. Then in about 1631 there was a request to Rome from clergy at Elmina for special priestly powers, and this re-awakened interest in West Africa. The letter was eventually discussed at the session in September 1631 of the Sacred Congregation of the Propaganda Fide in Rome. The letter was accompanied by detailed descriptions of St George Castle at Elmina supplied by one of the former governors. What emerged from the session was a formula designed to remove abuses among the clergy at Elmina, reform the priestly office and clarify questions of jurisdiction between Elmina, Shama and São Tomé. The vicar at Elmina was granted certain episcopal rights, although the full office of episcopacy which was sought was refused. Elmina's subordinate position under São Tomé was reaffirmed. Another vicar, stationed at Axim, also on the coast, was subject to Elmina.

Such a tidying up of church affairs in Ghana might have carried a strong church to greater heights, but as it was the church was weak, deficient in leadership, impeded by complex political considerations, misused by men with worldly ambitions and in the end compromised by association with the Castle and its traders. This picture of cardinals solemnly discussing the faith at Elmina with the Pope must strike the onlooker as over-optimistic. Discussion of the matter became the specialised concern of European bodies overseas and the pressure of Portuguese incumbents in West Africa. The goal of a permanent African church still lay some way in the future, but the coming of French, Spanish and Belgian Capuchins brought its attainment much closer.

The era of Capuchin missions, 1637–1703

The French Capuchins. In 1633 two priests belonging to the Capuchin monastery in Saint-Malo, Brittany, landed on the Guinea coast. One of them, Fr Colombin, had apparently been invited by a French trading concern to accompany its expedition to West Africa. The French had begun to show interest in the trade at Elmina in 1582 when they tried in vain to set up a French post within the Castle itself. Fr Colombin recorded many details of the popular religion at Komenda, where he stopped briefly, later presenting a report of his findings to the Capuchins. His account vividly portrays the strength of traditional religions. Fr Colombin had been led to two clear conclusions. First, religion was an inseparable part of life for Africans, affecting every sphere of life, and was highly developed. Secondly, the traces of Catholic Christianity he found intermingled with African religious elements suggested that there was a need and a basis for missionary activity to revive African interest in the Church. However, Fr Colombin appears to have been over-optimistic in his portrayal of Christian prospects in West Africa, understandable if he wanted to arouse confidence but unrealistic in the light of previous attempts.

Following Fr Colombin's report, the responsibility for undertaking a mission to West Africa was assigned to the Capuchin Order in Brittany in July 1634, and three years later six French Capuchins landed at Abiany, later called Assinie (today in Ivory Coast), some distance from the other major forts along the coast. It was a turbulent time, with the rival trading nations of Europe competing for control of the shore line and with the Dutch forcing the Portuguese out of Elmina. Yet the orders under which the Capuchins sailed assumed unrealistically that they could control local affairs and impose on events a rigid apostolic pattern of obedience to the Church's teaching. Events were to disprove this assumption.

Even the party's landing was inauspicious. Fr Colombin's canoe was overturned by powerful breakers just short of the shore, and he had to be rescued by his African helpers. At first the missionaries were welcomed by the King of Assinie and services were held amid the usual emotional scenes. But it was not long before local reaction to their presence came to the surface. At a public tribunal called to decide their future, there was a hostile display of arms although it was agreed by the decision of a majority to allow the missionaries to stay. However, the local spirits, clearly angered by this, came to the aid of their protégés in the shape of a deadly fever. In less than a year four of the six priests had died, and the two survivors, Fr Colombin and Fr Samuel, were left with the faint hope that French ships would land at Assinie and come to their help. But the rough seas, as well as the fact that Assinie had never been an important centre of the coastal trade, prevented ships from landing there. After a year of vain promises the missionaries ran out of bargaining chips. The King of Assinie stopped the language lessons they were being given and local people stopped food supplies and withdrew protection for their personal belongings which were confiscated without recourse. Clearly Fr Colombin and Fr Samuel were hopelessly exposed, and they decided to escape by stealth on the night of 12 August 1638, making their way to the Portuguese fort at Axim. Although they were hopeful of resuming their work at Axim, this could not be done. Local opposition remained strong and they had to struggle to survive, the Axim people demanding that they trade items of merchandise to earn a living. They stayed in Axim for a while and then left for the Portuguese island of São Tomé, with the hope of reaching Benin City. This plan too failed. São Tomé fell to the Dutch who promptly arranged for the priests, including Fr Colombin, to be deported to Brazil in October 1641. That effectively ended the work of the French Capuchins in that part of West Africa.

Spanish Capuchins at Takoradi and Arda. During the time of the founding of missions in Ghana vigorous attempts were made to penetrate Benin City. It was while trying to reach Benin that one such mission landed in Takoradi. In April 1651 a group of seven Spanish priests and two brothers, under Fr Angel de Valencia, dropped anchor there; they went ashore and met the local people. In a stay of three weeks, they met some eager inquirers but were reluctant to do any work there lest it deflect them from the work they planned to do in Benin. Anxious however, to receive the seeds of the Christian life, the local people had twenty of their children baptised before the priests left.

The expedition, however, ran into trouble. They were led to Shama where the Dutch Governor at Elmina, angry at the presence of the Spaniards in his territory, arranged to have them held prisoners at Elmina Castle. Some escaped, but eventually the two priests who remained were granted release and sent to Benin. However, they never reached it and instead ended up in São Tomé, haggard and demoralised.

In 1658 Toxonu, the King of Arda, sent two emissaries to the court of Philip IV of Spain, requesting missionaries. The request was passed to the Capuchins at Castile where the two Africans were baptised and given the names Felipe and António. The idea, to be developed by later missionary organisations, was that Africans would be trained to carry forward the work of the Church among their own people. Related to that was a scheme, again of enormous significance subsequently, to communicate the faith in the local language. A Spanish catechism was translated with the help of Felipe and António into the language of Arda. Spurred by the prospects of gathering a rich harvest of souls in the then Dahomean kingdom, eleven Capuchin missionaries set sail for Arda, arriving there in January 1660, clutching copies of the catechism they had prepared.

The King of Arda's interest in Christianity was typically bound up with diplomatic and economic considerations, and the missionaries were subjected, again typically, to delay and indecision. Finally the King confined them to the coast and forbade them to preach Christianity, a remarkable turn-around. Felipe, the senior emissary of the King who had been converted in Spain, recanted his new faith and abandoned the missionaries. In the unsettled atmosphere of European coastal trade and its equally unsettling impact on African political relations, it was perhaps understandable that missionaries should find their work impeded by what must have appeared to them as the necessarily hostile influence of Pagan religions. In terms of the strong tradition of missionary activity which arose from the general ferment of the Reformation and the Counter-Reformation, it is equally understandable that people in Europe should have wanted to share the faith with Africans. What is surprising, however, is that after so many false starts and bitter setbacks the Church should have wanted to persevere with the missionary enterprise. Without necessarily probing the religious motive, the historian must attempt to show that this persistent missionary tradition is integral to the character of the post-medieval church, and ultimately to Apostolic teaching. Similarly, African resistance to the Church needs to be studied in the context of European activity on the West African coast and the climate of mutual mistrust it created.

Following the orders restricting them to the coast, the Capuchin missionaries went through a period of terrible disappointment. Cut off by a thickening fog of official neglect, they lost five of their number through death within a year, and the remaining six, shaken and deprived, wearily returned to Spain. West Africa must have appeared to them like a vast sponge, at one moment ready to soak up missionaries and Christian religious ideas and at another squeezing them out in sudden contractions without much visible change. Despite the superficial impression of receptiveness, missionaries appear to have encountered in West Africa a subtle but stubborn resistance to the Church. Yet there were some gains on both sides, although for Ghana the full achievement of securing African collaboration alongside missionary initiative still lay some way in the future. At least it was clear that missionaries were willing to pay with their lives for the realisation of the dream of a West African Church, and this was just as well, for that future was to be filled with the unmarked graves of a far greater number than had died in the centuries between 1450 and 1750.

Capuchin work at Whydah. Still reeling from the disappointment of the Assinie mission, the French Capuchins were approached about the possibility of restarting work on the Guinea coast. Unconvinced by assurances that the Dutch had relinquished their territories to the Portuguese following the 1661 peace treaty between the two countries, the Provincial (leader) of the Capuchins in Brittany set up investigations to determine the true situation. It was found that, contrary to what had been maintained in Rome, the Dutch still retained power in West Africa and consequently it would be impossible to send Catholic missionaries to a Protestant-dominated area.

When the next opportunity came it fell largely to a Capuchin priest from Flanders, Fr Célestin, to answer the call. Accompanied by Fr Bénédict, he sailed from La Rochelle in October 1681, arriving a month later at Whydah (today in the republic of Benin). This time most of the trouble they had was with the resident French traders. For whatever reason, the latter resented the priests in their midst, and it was only the kindness of the Protestant Dutch and English which enabled missionary work to begin. Then Bangaza, the King of Whydah, took an interest in the personal welfare of Fr Célestin and provided him with food and lodging in his palace. Fr Bénédict had by this time left Whydah. Recognising the central and inalienable position of the King within the religious tradition of his people, Fr Célestin felt rightly that the progress of the Church in Whydah would have to be along different lines from those pursued previously. Assuming that children could be nurtured in the faith and gradually introduced to the discipline of the Church, he thought that schools should be established to begin this educational process. He held classes for the King's sons, teaching reading and writing and lessons in worship. He then wrote enthusiastically to his superiors in Flanders about his vision of Christian schools and the urgent task of founding enough in West Africa to meet the emerging challenge of an African pastorate, which he saw reaching beyond the limits of royal residences. A bold vision, but resources were limited. And then in

1683–4 the Royal African Company which was operating in Whydah, and under whose auspices Fr Célestin and Fr Bénédict had come there, collapsed, and with it any prospects of developing Christian work. Fr Célestin died on his way back to Europe in December 1684.

The Capuchin chapter of missionary enterprise in West Africa thus came to a sombre close. The balance-sheet of some two hundred years of dogged heroism showed dismal results. It was left to the French Dominicans, and later to the Holy Ghost Fathers and Protestant churches, to carry the flame of faith from their failing hands. The race was not abandoned.

The French Dominicans, 1687-1703

French Dominicans in Whydah. After the collapse of the Royal African Company, the Guinea Company was founded, with the sponsorship of Louis XIV of France. Under its auspices a further attempt was made to establish mission stations along the coast, from Whydah to Assinie. On a voyage bound initially for the West Indies, Fr François travelled via West Africa and landed at Assinie in 1686. But complex political and economic rivalries put paid to any idea of settling down there. Komenda at first looked promising, but the fact that the King there was trying to play off rival European interests against each other to secure his own political survival meant that missionaries would be allowed very limited initiative. Also Komenda was firmly within the sphere of interest of the Dutch who promptly apprehended the ruler for allowing supplies to reach the French party. He was humiliated and held to ransom for 8,000 francs in gold.

When the ship next called at Whydah, a receptive atmosphere was found to be prevailing there and Fr François, encouraged, went back to France in order to organise a mission. He came back in December 1687, accompanied by a group of Dominican priests. After a leisurely cruise down the coast he arried at Whydah in February 1688 with two companions. King Bangaza who was still reigning, approved the idea of a school proposed by Fr François, and promised to send his own children there. Ambitious plans were drawn up and submitted for approval to religious and commercial authorities in France. Once again the dead hand of fate fell on the plans. In 1688 the Palatinate war broke out and Louis XIV, who had championed the West African project, was too preoccupied to heed the plans of Fr François, who died the following year. When the war ended in 1697 nothing remained of the plans except sad memories. Nevertheless, it seems fairly certain that even if the mission had ever got started, its close association with Louis XIV and aggressive French mercantile interests would have stifled it at birth.

Assinie: another false start. The death of Fr François inspired some of his associates to renew the mission he had begun. Fr Loyer, a Dominican priest serving in the French West Indies, was urged by a fellow-priest to go to West Africa for this purpose. In April, 1701, he sailed for West Africa, having as companion a colourful local adventurer called Aniaba who claimed the throne of Assinie as Crown Prince, with the reigning ruler acknowledged by the French as regent. Aniaba was baptised in Paris with pomp and ceremony, in the presence of Louis XIV. His departure was turned into something of a state occasion, arousing great hopes. Aniaba had lived in Paris for nearly fourteen years and was obviously well educated, but the high hopes he had raised were dashed when the French discovered that he was a war captive and not of royal blood. More important, they found that once in Assinie he was going to prove a troublesome ally and that the reigning King, Akasini, would be more compliant with their wishes even though his value to the Christian mission was less obvious. Provided that trade and commerce could be assured, the French were prepared to postpone the final judgment which the missionaries were impatient to bring. Deeply embarrassed by Aniaba's elaborate deception, the French suppressed the truth about him. Later missionaries, such as a Catholic priest writing in 1956, felt haunted by his spirit and wrote in high moral tones to assuage a sense of guilt.

The mission of Fr Loyer, built on the sand of Aniaba's grand hoax, collapsed under the weight of his own tempestuous personality. He hated the religious practices of the people, despised their manners and poured scorn on their hospitality. He depicted the people in the most antagonistic way possible, writing at one point: 'I can say without exaggeration that of all the peoples of the earth, the most malignant, the most thievish and the most ungrateful are the Negroes'.[6] Even a charitable, sympathetic account of the cause he came to serve described him as having 'erred' in his treatment of local people. He cut himself off from those he desired to convert, hardly justifying his presence. He remained at the trade fort called Saint Louis, built in 1701, waiting for relief supplies and a boat to take him away and in March 1703 he boarded a Portuguese slave ship and made his way home via São Tomé, Brazil and Lisbon. He symbolised the frustrated hopes of the whole era of missionary activity in West Africa. No less than African rulers, European traders were unwilling to allow religious factors to stand in the way of commerce and profit, and often expected priests to serve as purveyors of ritual to the trading companies. The city of God in the Church may be fairer by far, but men were happy to prosper in the broad area of overlap with its worldly rival and leave the necessary separation to an indefinite future.

6. Wiltgen (1956), p.91.

3

MISSIONARY ACTIVITY IN BENIN, WARRI AND SÃO TOMÉ, 1480–1807

You say that your law is not a false law. I believe you. If I thought it was false, what would prevent me from destroying your churches and driving you away from them? What would you say if I sent a troop of [our tribes] to your country to preach their doctrines? You want all [Africans] to become Christians. Your law demands it, I know. But in that case what will become of us? Shall we become the subjects of your King? The converts you make will recognise only you in time of trouble. They will listen to no other voice but yours. I know that at the present time there is nothing to fear, but when your ships come by thousands, then there will probably be great disorder. . .

Chinese Emperor, 1723 (adapted by C. R. Boxer)

We have remarked in the previous chapter on attempts to bring the Church to Benin City and on how Elmina was placed under the jurisdiction of São Tomé, whence missions to Benin City were to be directed. In this chapter we shall look closely at early Christian missions to Nigeria from the fifteenth century to the mid-eighteenth century. First we must give a brief account of São Tomé and Príncipe, islands lying in the Gulf of Guinea.

São Tomé and Príncipe, 1470–1707

These islands were first discovered by the Portuguese about 1470, and at that time they were uninhabited. They were colonised by white settlers from Portugal, including levies of Jewish children deported in the 1490s. Later a labour force of African slaves was secured from a variety of tribes on the mainland. São Tomé proved a rich source of sugar, and a plantation system worked by slaves was soon developed to meet the rapid rise in European demand for that commodity. The island experienced an economic boom for most of the sixteenth century, and the Portuguese promptly transported the system to Brazil. São Tomé itself became the capital of Portuguese commercial interests in Lower Guinea just as Santiago in the Cape Verde Islands was for Upper Guinea. In 1534 a bishopric was established there, with responsibility for Lower Guinea and even beyond. Augustinian priests, for example, used the island as a centre from which they tried to introduce Christianity into Whydah. In the sixteenth century trade mostly in slaves carried by interlopers flourished between São Tomé and Angola, and it was from there that the trans-Atlantic slave trade was started by way of the infamous 'middle passage'. This was in November 1532, when the Portuguese ship *São Antonio* carried a cargo of 201 slaves to Santo Domingo and San Juan, with a rapid increase in successive years — by 1534 the number shipped had more than trebled. Christianity in São Tomé was still a European affair. There were African Christians, but since Africans were prized chiefly for their labour, religious scruples about their souls were not allowed to interfere with economic considerations. Consequently, although a few Africans were ordained as priests, they occupied an inferior place in the Church. Instead the Portuguese seem to have encouraged the Mulatto population to take a lead, but ironically they saw the Mulatto as a barrier between themselves and the Africans. The Mulatto clergy, offered the chance to avenge their sense of racial inferiority *vis-à-vis* the whites, took the opportunity to despise the Africans, especially their African fellow-clergy. In 1707, for example, the Mulatto canons of the Cathedral Chapter petitioned the King that no more Africans should be appointed as priests in the Cathedral. Earlier, in 1595, a bishop had alleged that Africans would only accept baptism at the hands of white priests, since they despised their fellow Black Africans. There are several contradictions here and they would not concern us if they did not have a profound significance for the fate of Christian missions in West Africa. The slowness in creating an African clergy, a logical next step after the sending of missions to baptise converts, impeded the growth of the Church and undermined the whole justification for embarking on mission at all.

São Tomé, as a bastion of imported European values, continued to preside over the affairs of the mainland, particularly in the strenuous attempts to reach Benin City. It is in this context that we should now proceed to examine the history of its hinterland neighbours.

Benin City, 1472-1707

The first Portuguese voyage through the Bight of Benin is attributed to one Ruy de Sequeira in 1472, although no immediate attempt was made to follow up this discovery. Then, in January 1480, two caravels made a voyage to the Rio dos Escravos, 'the Slave River', in the Niger Delta, to obtain some slaves then needed to exchange with African traders for gold; they obtained some 400 slaves. After João II ascended the throne in Portugal in 1481 he started to encourage trade on the Guinea coast, taking the title 'Lord of Guinea'. A declared policy of the new King was to use African rulers as agents of christianisation. In 1486 there was an expedition to the Delta area and its immediate hinterland, led by João Afonso d'Aveiro, and it was on this or similar expeditions that the Portuguese first came into contact with the kingdom of Benin, which made a deep impression upon them. It was a kingdom of considerable size and power, and the Oba held several chiefs and petty rulers under his authority. If the Portuguese were going to make any impression in West Africa, then obviously Benin City was the place from which to start. The kingdom thus came to constitute the centrepiece of the Christian strategy of the Portuguese, although it was soon to be superseded by the Congo.

Travellers normally went by boat to Ughoton (the port of Benin and politically subservient to it) and thence by land to Benin City. The Portuguese received some encouraging signals that Benin would be reached by Christian missions, but this was only in the early stages. The Oba, Ozolua, took an active interest in the strangers and asked the chief of Ughoton to accompany them back to Lisbon. By the end of the fifteenth century, however, Portugal's relations with Benin had reached a low point. Men sent there sickened and died, and trade failed to develop. The Oba and his people refused Christianity, so that one despondent Portuguese was driven to write: 'The manner of life of these people is full of abuses, fetishes and idolatry'. However, Benin continued to interest the Portuguese: they could obtain slaves from there and they discovered valuable beads, called by them *coris*, which fetched good prices. Cotton cloth also figured in their trade with Benin. The Portuguese Crown established a monopoly right over the much-valued Benin pepper, strictly forbidding other European merchants to engage in the trade. The Oba of Benin similarly imposed restrictions on the trade, forbidding any but his own royal agents to sell the commodity to Europeans. Ughoton became the principal outlet. Early in the sixteenth century this pepper trade was destroyed by the discovery of new fields in India, and Ughoton was abandoned as a pepper port although contacts with Benin were maintained. From 1514 Príncipe became the base for operations in Benin, a period which coincided with bad relations between Benin and Lisbon.

At about this time the Oba professed an interest in Christianity, but coupled it with a request for arms from Portugal. The Portuguese King Manoel encouraged the Christian element but held back on the arms. He would, he said, comply with the request for arms once he was satisfied that the Oba was 'a good and faithful Christian'. In a letter, King Manoel demanded that the Oba acquit himself by granting favourable treatment to Portuguese traders, hardly the recipe for amicable relations. In the meantime the Oba had some Portuguese mercenaries accompanying him on military campaigns, and it was during one of these that priests arrived from Portugal in Benin City. In 1516 the Oba sent one of his sons with the sons of some of the chiefs to be baptised by the missionaries, who also received permission to construct a church in Benin City. Although tradition claims that such a church was built, no evidence has survived to this effect, and it can therefore be no more than conjecture. The Oba died in late 1516 or early 1517. Nothing further is heard of the missionaries there. In May 1517 the vicar of São Tomé and three other priests arrived in Príncipe on their way to the court of the new Oba whom they wanted to introduce to Christianity. This particular mission failed to reach Benin City, and no further attempts were made for the next twenty years or so. Christianity lost its influence at the Benin court with the death of Ozolua. Some Christian remnants were to be found among a handful of free Edo and those slaves who had converted in Portuguese service, one of whom, Gregorio Lourenço, an interpreter, gave a female slave as alms to the church of São Tomé. Such Christians, without ministrations of a priest, weakened with time. It was a much diluted faith that the missionaries of later times found in Benin and surrounding areas.

In 1538 King João III of Portugal sent out another mission to Benin City, consisting of two Franciscans and a member of the Order of Christ. This time the Oba had not asked for the mission. When the mission arrived in Benin City, it found Gregorio Lourenço still alive and several African Christians being held captive by the Oba, who had himself been baptised as a boy in 1516. Little of that early contact with the church survived the Oba's boyhood. His reception of the missionaries was unfriendly, and it began to emerge that he had adopted a stern policy towards Christianity, forbidding the dissemination of Christian teachings or the baptism of those close to his palace, including the wives *(sic)* and children of Gregorio Lourenço. However, the Oba was not completely opposed to Christianity, and allowed the missionaries a chance to expound the religion, which they proceeded to do in a rather bellicose manner. They failed to impress the Oba, who made it clear that he was not prepared to change his religion. The priests persisted, and forced their way several times into the Oba's palace, each time finding the doors shut in their face.

In addition to attacking the religion of the people of Benin, the missionaries warned the Oba of the 'perilous condition' of his soul and condemned the practice of human sacrifice. In a letter to King João III, they denounced the Oba for anointing himself with human blood and, to cite their words, offering sacrifices to the devil, persisting in idolatries, diabolical invocations and many other superstitions, abominations and errors. Clearly they exaggerated, but the reference to human sacrifice occurs for the first time in that letter and, surprisingly, is not repeated in later sources. If it is to be relied on, the conclusion must be that the new Oba was personally responsible for introducing the practice in Benin City, perhaps for internal political reasons. If his power was threatened by the Oghene, the high priest of the imperial cult, and other subordinate chiefs, then he may have thought he would acquire supernatural status by being anointed with human blood. Furthermore, it would recognise his role in the ritual as initiator and arbiter and thus turn the tables on his rivals.

With the uncompromising attitude of the missionaries, Portugal's relations, notably in trade, with Benin began to suffer. Portuguese traders found themselves stranded in the kingdom, with the Oba refusing them any help. The missionaries were detained and forbidden to leave until an ambassador had arrived from Lisbon. Meanwhile other European traders were appearing in the region: the French, English and Dutch were soon to replace Portuguese commercial power in Benin. By then it was an open secret that religious missions to the kingdom stood little chance of success, although more than one daring attempt was made to reach it.

The Kingdom of the Itsekiri (Warri), c.1574-1807

The Itsekiri kingdom, called Warri in modern sources, was related through dynastic bonds to Benin, although it in fact followed a policy independent of it. Christianity was introduced into the kingdom by a group of Augustinian monks led by Fr Francisco a Mater Dei, who acquired great authority there. (This is thought to have been between 1571 and 1574). Fr Francisco baptised the Olu and his son, who was named Sebastian. Sebastian himself became Olu in 1597, and although a serious enough Christian, he had great difficulty getting priests to settle in Warri; the poverty of the state and the deadly malaria fever prevented a strong Christian mission from being established. The priests depended on the trickle of trade that flowed from Warri to enable them to enter and work in the kingdom. São Tomé remained the base for such priests, and even those who visited Warri were mostly reluctant. Sometimes trading in slaves was recommended to the missionaries as an ironic inducement to maintain themselves in Warri. But the vagaries of the trade, combined with the disinclination of priests from São Tomé to go to Warri, made this suggestion unattractive, and in the end circumstances prevailed to preserve moral scruple. The Augustinians were withdrawn in 1584. It was not till 1593 that a party of Franciscans visited Warri from São Tomé. But within four years most of the priests died. A more satisfactory solution to the problem would have been to train natives of Wari to serve as priests. But the manner in which the Bishop of São Tomé, Francisco de Villanova, tried to do this by sending Domingos, the son of the Olu, to Portugal for priestly training showed a lack of appreciation of African political tradition. As heir apparent, Domingos would come to serve the political interests of Warri, including upholding the institution of polygamy, a role which would conflict with the priestly office. In any case the popular basis of Christianity is not secured by cultivating it in the hot house conditions of the royal palace. Domingos in fact married before he left Portugal around 1611, having been absent from Warri for more than ten years. He returned with a large retinue, bearing with him the inflated hopes for the progress of the Christian cause in Africa. These hopes were soon abandoned, with the Bishop of São Tomé making the acid comment that the Prince was unsuitable for the priestly office envisaged for him.

Although Domingos continued to encourage Christianity in Warri after he succeeded his father as Olu shortly after 1620, the old obstacles to mission were not overcome. Priests were only persuaded with the greatest difficulty to visit the kingdom, and those who went grew faint-hearted or found other avenues for their talents; some turned their hands to trade. The Olu and his entourage did everything to encourage Christianity in Warri, but their enthusiasm was not matched by the devotion of the people. After 1640 efforts were made by the Propaganda Fide to sustain missionary interest in Warri by using Spanish priests. (Spain and Portugal, which had been united under the Spanish Crown from 1580, had now separated again). This aroused the strong Portuguese suspicions that the Propaganda Fide was being used as a screen by Spain in order to infiltrate pockets of Portuguese influence in West Africa. It is well to remember that Rome did not recognise the new Portuguese Crown until 1668, lending credence to Portuguese fears of partiality. Reports continued to tell of the imminent decline of Christianity in Warri where the lack of priests appears to have posed an insuperable barrier.

In the 1650s, with the accession of a new Olu, Dom Antonio Domingos, son of Domingos by a Portuguese wife, interest revived in a mission to Warri, which came to be increasingly confused with the kingdom of Benin. The Governor of São Tomé put his weight behind a project to send a mission to Warri, on one occasion offering considerable financial payment and five slaves, but no one took up the challenge. The Spanish Capuchins who tried to reach Warri were detained by a nervous Portuguese authority in São Tomé and refused access. Probably at their instigation, the Olu of Warri wrote a letter to the Pope in 1652 asking for priests to be sent to his kingdom[1]. This and another letter to be referred to later cannot be unreservedly accepted as genuine, the pious fervour of the document probably serving as eager recompense for the failure of the Spanish Capuchins to achieve their object of reaching Warri. Nevertheless Rome responded promptly and a group of Italian Capuchins, led by Fr Angelo Maria d'Aiaccio, went to Warri in 1656. Fr Angelo Maria and a companion, Fr Bonaventura da Firenze, reached Warri from São Tomé and spent four years travelling through the kingdom, their

1. Ryder (1960), pp. 11-12.

efforts apparently being amply rewarded with conversions among the Itsekiri. But the confident progress of the Christian chariot soon collided with the defensive reflex of Portugal experiencing a commercial decline on the West coast, and the activity of the Italian priests was halted. Expelled from Warri as commercial spies, they arrived in São Tomé where immediate arrest and suspension from their mission awaited them under orders of the Vicar General. They were later cleared of all charges and reinstated. However when Fr Angelo Maria and a fresh party of eight Capuchins tried to return to Warri in 1663, the Portuguese still refused them permission. In this and similar disputes with Rome, Portugal was trying to defend one of its most jealously guarded prerogatives, the *Padroado,* which vested in the Portuguese Crown rights and privileges over Catholic missions and ecclesiastical establishments in Africa, Asia and Brazil, as well as genuine concern over safeguarding what little remained of the spheres of Portuguese commercial interest.

In the end Portuguese obstructionism coincided with a decline of the Warri trade, thus effectively damping the earlier interest in undertaking a mission to the kingdom. By 1673 the Olu was complaining that more than ten years had passed since a priest visited his kingdom, adding that many Warri Christians had reverted to traditional religious practices as a consequence. At about the same time a Franciscan priest had arrived in Warri, and through him the Olu appealed to the Portuguese Crown for help with priests and also for more regular trade with Portuguese carriers. Portugal replied that it was beyond its power to compel reluctant traders to go to Warri, suggesting instead that the Olu should make his kingdom more attractive for trade. Since a mission to Warri depended on a revival of trade, nothing came of the Olu's request, which Portugal in fact referred to São Tomé. But Warri continued to place unbounded confidence in Portugal's power to secure the interests of the kingdom, and in 1685 another petition was despatched to Lisbon asking for missionaries. In 1689 the Prefect of São Tomé spent a year in Warri, during which time he is reported to have made important gains for the Church. This was Fr Francesco da Monteleone. He returned to São Tomé after Warri to resume his prefectorial duties. The mission despatched to Warri in 1691 by Fr Monteleone to continue the work proved a disappointment. Its leader, Fr Giuseppe Maria de Busseto, was not committed to his charge. Furthermore, he died only one year later. The others abandoned the mission and either faintheartedly returned or fell to trading. The Olu, still confident, sent a letter with the returning priest, Fr Protasio, appealing for priests and a demonstration of Christian perseverance.[2] This letter, like that mentioned above, cannot be regarded as undoubtedly an authentic transcript of the Olu's message, and even if it was, then something

2. Ryder (1960), pp. 15-16.

more than a straightforward devotion to the Christian cause must have prompted it, such as the hope that a Christian alliance with Portugal might help to defend his weak and exposed kingdom from some external menace. Since we do not know that for a fact, it is simplest to see the letter as another attempt at dressing up the less than candid behaviour of the mission. But perhaps the hint in the letter that some pressure might profitably be put on Fr Protasio to return to Warri and worship in the church building being constructed according to a plan he himself left behind may be a genuine reflection of the Olu's veiled criticism of the priest.

The Olu's request to Fr Monteleone failed yet again in its objective. São Tomé was itself experiencing a severe shortage of priests, and in any case attention was now being directed to Benin. Fr Monteleone undertook an abortive and costly mission there dying at Ughoton on the way. In 1696 two Italians, Frs Bonaventura da Brescia and Felice da Piagine, visited Warri but fell gravely ill almost immediately, so that this mission too proved abortive. Then in 1709 the Italian Capuchin Prefect, Fr Cipriano a Napoli, journeyed to Warri and his subsequent report painted a sombre and pessimistic picture of Christian prospects in the kingdom. Two Capuchins who had preceded him to Warri the year before were engaged in hand-to-mouth trade to survive and had undertaken little in the way of priestly or missionary duties. Fr Cipriano was also struck by the pervasiveness of traditional religious rites, which had succeeded in diluting the faith of those few Christians still clinging to vestiges of Catholicism. However another party of Capuchin missionaries resided in Warri for the two years 1715-7, striking a more optimistic note in their estimation of Christianity in the kingdom. Nevertheless it is clear that such as did exist of Christianity in Warri was largely a court religion, restricted to the Olu and a few of his officials and their families.

Under these circumstances political changes in the palace had repercussions on Christianity in Warri. For example, the Olu — who styled himself Don Agostinho — continued the policy of his predecessors in looking to Portugal for support for the Christian cause in his kingdom. He died around 1732 and his brother who succeeded him dropped the Christian policy of previous Olus and retracted support for local Christians. Church services ceased, a statue of Christ which had been a pious gift from Príncipe was destroyed after it failed to bring relief when the country was stricken by drought, and the church building came to be used as a byre for animals. When an attempt was made around 1733 to revive Christianity in Warri, the Olu refused to co-operate with the priests. Not until the 1760s was new hope aroused with the accession of a new Olu. In 1770 a native of Warri, Canon João Alvarez, and another priest, Fr Felix, were sent on a mission there, but they proved an incompatible pair, with Fr

Felix quoting and encouraging reports in Warri against Alvarez to the effect that 'the Almighty had never intended negroes to be priests'.[3] Fr Felix returned to São Tomé early in 1771, convinced that this was the reason for their failure. He had entered the familiar dead-end of racism.

As if to prove him wrong, attempts were made by Portugal to direct a new mission to Warri from Brazil. The Englishman Captain John Adams, who visited the kingdom around 1795, remarks that several emblems of the Catholic religion were present in the royal palace — 'crucifixes, mutilated saints and other trumpery. Some of these articles were manufactured of brass, and others of wood. On enquiring how they came into their present situation, we were informed that several Black Portuguese missionaries had been at Warri. . . endeavouring to convert the natives into Christians; and the building in which they performed their mysteries we found still standing.'[4] Adams concludes that the Olu was a stalwart upholder of indigenous custom, crediting him with over sixty wives and his subjects with even less fidelity to Christianity. This Olu was called Manuel Otobia and was still reigning in 1799. He was succeeded around 1807 by an Olu whom the Governor of São Tomé addressed as King João. The Governor was writing because reports of the decline of Christianity in his kingdom had reached alarming proportions. He asked the Olu to help the Christian cause, defend Christians against the Ijaw, and mitigate the hardship which has fallen on them because of heavy or unjust taxes. The Governor then invoked the name of the Portuguese authority to try to secure the Olu's compliance. Little resulted from this.

The material circumstances of Warri militated against the successful establishment of Christian missions in the kingdom. Portugal's chief commercial rivals in West Africa, such as the Dutch and the English, neglected it because of its lack of opportunities for lucrative commerce. Christianity in the kingdom suffered from this enclave position. Whatever determined efforts might be made to reach it from the outside, Warri remained isolated and irrelevant to the calculations of the main trading powers. The litany of endless requests for help shows the Olu occupying an isolated diplomatic position from which he had to sue for recognition. The rest followed from this: the unwillingness of priests to remain in Warri and the sorry plight of those who did; the reluctant patronage of Portugal; the grudging response from São Tomé; the trickle of trade that broke hardly any new ground; the willingness to compromise in order to attract even the most adventurous; the embellishment of requests from Warri with such exaggerated deference as to be hardly compatible with kingly office, and so on. The eclipse of Catholic

3. Ryder (1960), p. 21.
4. ibid., p. 22.

missions in Warri took place in spite of explicit royal support, suggesting a qualified role for rulers in the process of religious change.

Capuchin missions to Benin, 1640–1748

We have discussed in the second part of Chapter 2 the work of Capuchin missionaries from France, Spain and Flanders in Assinie, Arda and Whydah as well as Axim. We saw the initiative of Fr Colombin in bringing missionaries to West Africa. It was a similar initiative of his which encouraged Capuchin missionaries to try to reach Benin City in the seventeenth century. We should also remember that the work of the Capuchins was supported and directed by the Sacred Congregation of the Propaganda Fide.

A fact which we passed over in Chapter 2, but which influenced the success or otherwise of missions to Benin City, is that from 1640 Portugal was engaged in a war against Spain and the Netherlands. After that year the Pope refused to recognise the new government in Portugal in its capacity of directing overseas missionary activity. Spain then sought to profit from Portugal's disqualification, although the decline of the latter in West Africa allowed the Dutch and the English to enter the scene and gave Spain little prospect of gaining a stronghold there. Portugal also retained São Tomé and Príncipe.

In 1648 the Propaganda Fide assigned the Benin mission to the Spanish Capuchins of Valencia and Aragon. The Protestant powers that controlled the trade of Benin made no attempt to spread their religion there. Fr Colombin had visited both Benin and Warri in 1640, and described the people favourably, saying they and others in the region 'are truly gentle, civilised, friendly to priests, exemplary in their behaviour, and receptive to all good teaching[5].As at Komenda in Ghana, here also Fr Colombin became over-enthusiastic. He wrote of Benin:

In this kingdom the people may very easily be led to embrace the Faith, and priests can live here with greater ease than in other parts of Guinea because of the healthy climate, and the fertility of the soil, and because the people are more generous. Their language is simple. . . 'These people have their pontiffs, priests and other ministers for the performance of their rites. Their king is so greatly feared by his subjects that when they but hear his name spoken, they all fall prostrate and adore him with fear and unbelievable reverence. Thus from this it may be imagined that if the king were converted to the Faith, the rest of his subjects would easily be won over.'[6]

The Propaganda Fide were further encouraged by a report from Fr Francisco de Pamplona in 1646, when he returned from the Congo

5. Ryder (1969), p. 100.
6. ibid.

where he had been serving, that a Benin mission would by-pass the Portuguese and make it unnecessary to use São Tomé. An added reason, he said, was that the Oba had converted to Christianity — which was not true.

The Propaganda Fide proceeded to appoint a mission to Benin City, consisting of twelve priests with Fr Angel de Valencia as prefect. Three of the priests died before leaving Spain, but the remainder left Cadiz on 12 February 1651. The Spanish captain of their ship, more anxious to lay up treasures on earth, spent over two months trading along the coast between Cape Palmas and Takoradi. This group of Spanish Capuchins, whom we described in Chapter 2, had a brush with the Dutch at Shama and were eventually arrested and confined to Elmina Castle. Seven priests were able to continue the journey to Benin City, taken there by the vice-prefect, Fr José de Jijona. By the time they arrived at Ughoton they all were ill, some too much so to travel. The vice-prefect and one of the priests then pressed on and arrived in Benin City, but after much negotiation they failed to get an audience with the Oba. The vice-prefect then returned to Ughoton to consult his companions about his stalemated mission. There Fr Angel de Valencia and the other Capuchin priest detained at Elmina rejoined them, but within the space of six days three priests died, including Fr José. Another was too ill to make the proposed return visit to Benin City, and was left in the care of two other priests. The remaining two members of the mission reached Benin City on 10 August 1651, led this time by the prefect, Fr Angel de Valencia. He too faced stubborn resistance in his efforts to obtain the Oba's ear. However, more determined than most, he at last succeeded in insinuating himself into the audience hall of the Oba who appears to have listened politely and with interest to what the man of God had to say.

The missionaries were offered lodgings in the palace, with the promise that the Oba would be pleased to see them again. However the offer was not made good. Obviously palace officials, who had blocked earlier attempts to reach the Oba, must have felt deeply concerned at the political implications of a christianised Benin court, and as a result tried to prevent the priests from establishing themselves in the city. At their second and, as it proved, final audience with the Oba they presented gifts to him and to the most important chiefs. The Oba undertook to build a church, going so far as to indicate its site. The Oba's mother similarly showed interest in the religion of the priests. Taking this as a signal that Benin was ready to receive the faith, Fr Angel summoned his three companions from Ughoton; the work of evangelisation was about to begin in earnest.

He had reckoned without the determined opposition to his mission that was gathering pace around the Oba. The Oba's chief minister, probably the *Uwangue* who held great power in the affairs of the pálace, erected a curtain of secrecy between the missionaries and the Oba. When the missionaries tried over several months to see the Oba, the chief minister refused to arrange it. Twice he ordered the missionaries to go back to Ughoton and twice they refused, believing that the chief minister had acted without the Oba's authority. The prefect tried to get round this barrier by presenting the Oba with a chiming clock through a messenger. The Oba was suitably impressed but sent it back with a request for the prefect to explain why it had stopped working. The wary chief minister, seeing through the trick, handed back the clock to the priests, saying that the Oba and his people would manage without it.

Precautions were taken to ensure that the priests did no work in Benin City, and they were restricted from travelling to other parts of the kingdom. The Edo-speaking interpreters they had been promised never showed up, thus effectively cutting them off from the local people, and the few Edo who knew any Portuguese were forbidden to give the priests any assistance. When they thought of undertaking language lessons a chief announced that an oracle had warned the people not to provide any help. Their supplies were fast running out, as were their hopes of establishing a Benin mission. Only the providential arrival of some English traders saved them from disaster. With that help their spirits revived enough to make them think of making one more desperate attempt to catch the eye of the Oba.

They chose as the arena of their daring project the major ceremony of human sacrifice when huge crowds poured into the city and they could wander among the people without arousing too much suspicion. The prefect and Fr Felipe de Hijar were to carry it out. On that occasion some 2,000 leading citizens were present in the city. At one o'clock in the afternoon the priests decided to enter the huge courtyard, and took their place under one of the galleries under it. However, after the main ceremony of offering sacrifice was over and the Oba and his officials started moving around, the missionaries were found out. They described what happened to them as follows:

We. . . then stepped into the middle of the courtyard and began speaking aloud to the king and chiefs of the evil they were doing in making those sacrifices. . . But we had hardly spoken when [they] rushed furiously upon us and swept us through the courtyard with great violence; they did not stop until they had thrust us out and closed the door. When we tried a second and a third time to re-enter the courtyard with those who were still going in, they prevented us. Finally they drove us out of the palace altogether. Around the gate was gathered a huge crowd who mocked us all the way to our house[7].

In the end the two priests were expelled from the city and were led under escort to a secluded house about 14 miles away. There they

7. Ryder (1960), p. 119.

suffered great hunger and hardship until some Dutch and English traders showed them Samaritanly mercy. Finally they were able to reach Príncipe, their mission unfulfilled.

Those left behind in Benin City suffered hardship but no maltreatment. One of them, Alonso de Tolosa, gave an account of how they were able to visit the Oba's mother and his brother-in-law, both of whom had expressed sympathy with the religion of the missionaries. The people of Benin too (on the whole) showed an encouraging interest in the mission. However, those opposed to the mission proved too strong, and the priests were compelled to withdraw from the city and rejoin their companions who had taken refuge in Ughoton.

Reasons for failure of the Benin mission

We must try to explain the apparent failure of the mission to Benin. It is clear that the Oba and his close circle of royal relatives remained favourably disposed towards Christianity, but it is equally clear that the *Uwangue* and palace chiefs were opposed to the religion of the priests. It would thus appear that there were divisions in the palace. In his religious policy the Oba was opposed by an alliance of the *Uwangue* and a powerful body of palace chiefs whose strength *vis-à-vis* the Oba was growing, thanks largely to the trade with the Dutch and the English. For example, the missionaries often complained that the Dutch and the English had been working hard to get the chiefs of Benin to discourage Christian mission. Probably the missionaries, in their despondency, turned their suspicions of Dutch and English activities into firm proof when failure seemed inevitable. However, it is possible that the trade which the English and the Dutch brought to Benin benefited the chiefs on the periphery of the palace, enabling them to control the policy of the Oba, so that he could not embark on an independent religious policy without their consent. Thus the political reality of a clear shift of power away from the Oba at the centre to the *Uwangue* and the palace chiefs at the periphery determined the poor response to Christian missions in Benin. When the priests approached the Oba directly, they brought out this weakness in the Oba's constitutional authority: he was not his own man.

The other element in the situation, apart from the political one, is the religious issue. Historical sources tell of the power of traditional religion in Benin and of the considerable influence wielded by the *Uwangue* in palace affairs. The *Uwangue* was entrusted with naming the successor to a deceased Oba; he often did this in collaboration with the *Iyase*, the town chiefs, but his was the decisive voice in who became the new Oba. The position of the *Uwangue* rested on his religious function, and at the height of his effectiveness he held ruling

Obas under his authority. One account describes how the *Uwangue* 'enjoyed so much authority with the king that the latter was entirely under his influence, and nothing whatsoever was decided in the kingdom without his advice'.[8] Consequently the Oba was secluded, being allowed to leave his palace only once a year and in the meantime he was required to submit to the ritual details of the state religion over which the *Uwangue* and the chiefs presided. It may have been fear of the court religion being eroded by a foreign religion that decided Benin's religious authorities to reject Christianity. If the traditional religion were weakened, the authority of the *Uwangue* and all those with an interest in the old practices would be undermined. An astute man, the *Uwangue* organised an effective boycott of the religion of the missionaries.

But not all the labour of the missionaries went in vain. In Príncipe they discovered that the kingdom of Itsekiri was different from that of Benin with which it had hitherto been confused in Rome. Itsekiri (Warri), as we saw, had been introduced to Christianity and its ruler, long mistaken for the Oba of Benin, had shown himself ready to encourage Christianity in his kingdom. The confusion in Rome led to misdirected efforts in the mission field, but once they were aware of the true position, the priests endeavoured to go to Ode Itsekiri to encourage the existing Christian community and to use it as a stepping-stone to reach Benin. Itsekiri was in fact incapable of supporting an independent mission; nevertheless the authorities in São Tomé and Príncipe, representing the Portuguese Crown, treated the missionaries as subjects of an enemy power (Spain) and deported them to Lisbon.

Italian Capuchins: Warri and Benin, 1655–1748

When the Propaganda Fide received the reports of the deported missionaries who cleared up the confusion between Warri and Benin, it was decided to designate the new missions authorised to go to the area as 'Mission to Warri and Benin'. This was done in 1655, with the Italian Capuchins replacing the Spanish in an effort to placate the Portuguese. To make the point even more explicit the new mission went to Lisbon to seek Portuguese authorisation and to request that São Tomé to be allowed to act as a base for work in Warri and Benin. However, the Portuguese were not entirely satisfied, and they reduced the size of the mission to four, turning back the Prefect among others. That suggested the shape of things to come, for when the remaining missionaries arrived in São Tomé they encountered serious difficulties. Two priests visited Warri from São Tomé after being subjected to official delays, and when they returned they were arrested and suspended from their duties on the authority of the Vicar

8. Ryder (1969), p. 17.

General, an incident already mentioned above. They were put aboard a ship bound for Lisbon in 1662, the victims of Portugal's disproportionate determination to protect the *Padroado* and cling tenaciously to the few remnants of its former power along the West coast. The missionaries were in fact accused of coming as spies, and of trying to infiltrate pockets of commerce still controlled by Portugal.

However the Prefect of the mission succeeded in delivering a letter from the Propaganda Fide to the Oba of Benin, who appears to have responded favourably to the idea of missionary activity in his kingdom. When the Prefect and his companions, then under Portuguese deportation orders from Europe, were cleared of all charges in Lisbon, he appealed to the Propaganda Fide to revive the small flame of interest which his contact with the Oba had kindled. The Propaganda Fide responded promptly with enthusiasm, and eight missionaries were selected. But as we saw earlier, this party of Capuchin priests, led by Fr Angelo Maria, had their path blocked by an over-anxious Portuguese authority. They were refused travel documents and so could not travel. The claim that the Oba was keen to receive the mission therefore could not be proved. The new obstacle of Portuguese opposition was to make Benin City even less accessible than before.

New hopes and old failures

The Propaganda Fide made no further attempts to reach Benin for another twenty years, so discouraged had Rome become by Portuguese obstruction. A new move was launched in 1683 to get the Benin mission restarted, but this time from Angola. The prefect of the Capuchin mission there, Giovanni Romano, obtained the agreement of the Portuguese authorities to bring a mission to São Tomé bound for Benin and Warri. The Bishop of São Tomé was contacted from Lisbon and asked to permit a mission for Benin to be based there. In June 1684 Francesco da Monteleone, an Italian Capuchin, arrived in São Tomé to begin preparations for the work in Benin. But unfamiliar problems caused familiar frustrations. The Bishop of São Tomé died in 1685 and da Monteleone found himself saddled with priestly duties on the island. Giovanni Romano in Angola was unable to send the help he had earlier promised. When the governor and the officials of the cathedral in São Tomé wrote to the Propaganda Fide for urgent and substantial help, they did not get it. The Propaganda Fide could only send out three priests instead of the eight asked for. Three were sent but only one arrived, and he was dying. Eight new priests arrived in January 1691, most of them in a deplorable state of health. Three died within a few days of landing and two more were dead by 1693.

Not until 1689 was da Monteleone able to visit Warri, and from there he tried to reach Benin. He was then escorted on a river boat to the borders of Benin where his plans to continue his journey had to be abandoned because the local chief, then in dispute with Warri, refused to allow him to disembark. By the time Benin got wind of this the missionary had turned back, so that the boats that Benin sent to fetch him returned empty.

However Fr da Monteleone was able to go to Arbo and Mobor, outposts of the Benin kingdom, where he said he saw confirmation of the desire of the Bini people for Christian work. He was clearly labouring under a self-inflicted illusion. Nevertheless on his return to São Tomé he set about organising a strong mission to Benin. The vice-prefect of the island, however, refused to authorise it on the odd grounds that the Oba was not baptised. Fr da Monteleone agreed to postpone the mission to a more appropriate time, but meanwhile sent letters to the Oba, and when he received a friendly reply he drew the optimistic but unfounded conclusion that the Oba and his kingdom were eager and ready to embrace the Christian faith. Early in 1695 a fresh group of Capuchin priests arrived in São Tomé, and Fr da Monteleone was at last able to fulfil his cherished dream of leading a mission to Benin. He left São Tomé on 8 September, bound for Benin, but his wish was not to be fulfilled. He fell ill at Ughoton and died there in November. Benin was then in a state of war and the unrest would have hampered missionary work even if the priests had been able to get there. In a report to the Propaganda Fide in Rome in September 1696, the vice-prefect concluded that missions to Benin could achieve nothing. The main reason he gave was the state of civil war in Benin. But another reason may have been the unfriendly attitude of the Oba's court to Christian mission, and if this were the case the vice-prefect would omit it from his report for fear of jeopardising future missions.

In 1709 the new Capuchin prefect of São Tomé led a mission to Benin but returned disheartened. According to the report of the mission, the Oba and his chiefs refused to see the priests, including the prefect. It was impossible, they said, even to attempt any work in Benin — which must have been a true reflection of the prospects for Christian mission in Benin. However, within a year the Oba is represented as having written letters to Rome requesting the sending of Christian missions to his kingdom. The language and style of these letters, particularly one sent to the Pope, would make it unlikely that they could have been the work of the Oba or any of his officials; they were written in a deeply pious style with a devotional seriousness such as could only have come from someone deeply rooted in the Church. No such person existed in Benin City. Were the letters a forgery? Probably they were, but it is also probable that they were based on an actual historical incident. In 1712 the governor of São Tomé received an official letter from Portugal advising him that the Oba of Benin had responded favourably to a mission of two priests the previous year and had requested the establishment of a permanent mission in his kingdom. The governor was ordered to investigate this reported change of policy; clearly some contact had been made, but it is hard to imagine that the change had been on the scale suggested in the letters. A pious scribe, perhaps one of the Capuchin missionaries, must have inflated the subject with his own high hopes.

A Capuchin mission was established in Benin City in about 1711 but after three years it ceased work. One of the missionaries, Fr Celestino d'Aspra, reported that he and his companion had given up their work there because the people 'were most obstinate in their errors, and they worship the devil: but there are some who would follow the Holy Faith, were it not that the king will not give them permission and freedom to profess it[9]. What must have happened is that between 1709, the time of the abortive visit of the prefect of São Tomé, and 1711 when the Oba requested a permanent mission, civil war in Benin brought to power a new Oba, named Ozuere, who may have welcomed the Christian mission in an attempt to supplant his opponents in the traditional religious camp. But Ozuere reigned only a few months spanning the years 1710-11, and any mission which he may have requested or which depended on his continuance in office would have shared his fate. Thus historical sources which say that Benin in 1710-11 was prepared to change its long-standing opposition to Christian missions may be correct and not necessarily in conflict with other accounts of Benin's traditional unfriendliness towards Christianity in 1709 and again from 1711. The internal political unrest in the kingdom would explain the discrepancies.

After the departure of Fr Celestino d'Aspra in 1713 no more Capuchin missions were sent to Benin. Capuchin prefects in São Tomé continued to keep an eye on developments in Benin in the hope of reviving the work there, but little more was done. One last hopeful attempt was made in 1748 by the then prefect in São Tomé, Fr Illuminato di Poggitello, who set out for Benin, encouraged by reports, all too familiar, that the Oba was prepared to welcome a priest. This time the report proved true, but Fr Illuminato was told he would have to undertake the mission at his own expense. Weakened by illness and lack of provisions, he abandoned the idea and turned instead to Ode Itsekiri. That brought a formal end to missionary contact with Benin. In the three centuries of vain attempts to penetrate Benin with the Christian Gospel, little concrete had resulted. The cost had been heavy and the gains were few.

The reason for the failure is straightforward enough. Christianity was too closely identified with existing European interests to be able to follow an independent course in African states. Traders and commercial agents working for European concerns might adopt the

9. Ryder (1969), p. 119.

religion, but only so long as they remained tied to European bases. For the rest, considerations of local conditions would be decisive. Furthermore, many European traders ignored arguments of religion in pursuit of profit and were not averse to restricting missionary work if commercial reasons demanded it. The fact that missionary ventures were promoted as the schemes of European kings also hampered their progress in Africa, because of the political price which would have to be paid by African rulers who accepted Christianity. With conflicting political claims among European powers, such adoption of Christianity would have turned African rulers into minor clients. Few of them would knowingly have submitted to playing that role in either an active or a passive way.

But it would be unrealistic to blame the failure of Christian mission on European factors alone. There were real problems on the African side too.. In the past many writers have blamed the failure partly on the fact that mission was undertaken by Europeans, whom Africans never trusted because of the racial difference. The historian must not set out to prove or disprove arguments of racial prejudice, but only to show where, if proven, they have influenced events. It is much easier to measure the influence of local political considerations on attitudes to mission than the influence of intangible factors like racial prejudice, particularly since the same racial factor did not prevent African rulers from participating fully in European trade. Similarly, the influence of African religions must have exerted a powerful counter-pressure against mission. Two other relevant considerations must be taken into account. One is that during periods of political stability and relative social peace Christian missionaries found it almost impossible to establish their work. Some minor rulers, seeking to expand their power, might encourage missionaries, but their limited motives, plus the fact that they could not afford to antagonise their major political competitors, often stopped further Christian expansion. In some cases, missionaries were too few or too ill to take advantage of such limited openings. The second consideration is that during periods of severe social and political unrest, African rulers might be willing to welcome missions, and if European military intervention was promised or threatened, that often eased the path for the spread of Christianity.

In West Africa during this period, all the circumstances were unfavourable to the establishment of Christian mission. Fresh hopes were constantly being aroused, only to be shattered on the unyielding rock of African resistance. Yet new forces were working to erode that resistance, and in the subsequent upheavals brought on by European trade, mainly in slaves and guns, African societies, increasingly overshadowed by an advancing column of gunboats, were conditioned and eventually compelled to accept new influences, and consequently Christianity gained a foothold. It is now time to turn to that extremely successful period of Christian expansion.

4

THE ESTABLISHMENT OF CHRISTIAN COLONIES IN WEST AFRICA: SIERRA LEONE AND LIBERIA

[The] population, bowels and surface of Africa, abound in valuable and useful returns; the hidden treasures of centuries will be brought to light and into circulation. Industry, enterprise, and mining will have their full scope, proportionably as they civilise. . . Tortures, murder, and every other imaginable barbarity and iniquity are practised upon the poor slaves with impunity. I hope the slave trade will be abolished. I pray it may be at hand.   Olaudah Equiano (1789)

Founding of Sierra Leone: African colonists from London

In chapter 2 we divided the history of Christianity from the West African point of view into three distinct phases. We called the first phase the period of incubation when the Church disappeared in North Africa and Egypt only to burst upon the rest of the world, including West Africa, with the new life acquired in its European transformation. We saw in chapter 3 that the Church's specific European identity was to pose a serious barrier to its spread in West Africa. We might call that whole period the era of frustration. In this chapter we shall describe the remarkable conjunction of historical circumstances and social forces that created a hospitable environment for the diffusion of Christianity between 1787 and about 1893. We could call it the era of promise. The religious map of Africa was permanently changed as the new religion was carried into numerous communities by the wide-ranging activities of African agents. The basis of this expansion was the notion of a Christian settlement into which freed slaves would be concentrated under Christian nurture and from which Christianity would emerge as an attractive religion. Because it would share the distinctive character of its African setting, it would not therefore be an alienating force. Its foremost proponents would be Africans, and it would be supported by the labours and contributions of those who professed it. In this way Christianity would encourage the habits of useful industry and self-reliance, shedding along the way its repelling European identity.

It was a bold vision conceived within a partnership in which Europe would provide the material support in which it was rich, with

53

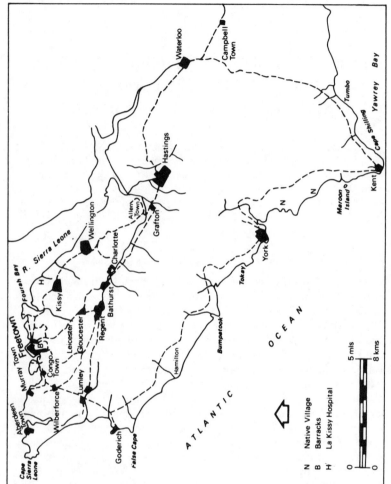

Freetown and its environs.

Africans supplying the people with the motivation to sustain the Church. The slave trade would thus be effectively undermined and the heavy burden of guilt on Europe's conscience would be lifted. The fact, of course, remains that despite such lofty ideals, missionary Christianity shared many of the interests of colonial rule, and when the time came for Africans to demand the withdrawal of missionary control, it was seen as incompatible with genuine Christianity. All the elegant phrases about African self-reliance and indigenous leadership appeared to have been forgotten, and the object of missionary prayers for a strong, indigenous Church in Africa came to be seen as a threat and a betrayal. That is a warning to us to distinguish carefully between the political interests of the missionary establishment and the genuinely religious dimension of Christianity, a dimension which Africans eagerly utilised as they came to grapple with new economic and political forces. That theme is developed further in Chapter 7. But its roots reach back to the establishment of Christian settlements in Sierra Leone, and it would therefore be appropriate to describe the origins of those settlements and their social and religious character in some detail.

In a famous legal judgment in England in 1772, Lord Mansfield declared that slavery was alien to the law of the land. Although the judgment was not directed at the institution of slavery as such, it was exploited as an authoritative ruling concerning the illegality of holding slaves. There were many African slaves living in England at the time and they accordingly considered themselves free. The specific case in which Lord Mansfield handed down his judgement concerned a slave called James Somerset. The Somerset case, whatever its technical status in law, was a momentous social event, showing that in many influential quarters public opinion was in advance of the law. It set in motion a bitter campaign to get the slave trade abolished and slavery itself made unlawful.

Two Africans living in England at the time were Ottobah Cugoano and Olaudah Equiano, the latter also known as Gustavus Vassa the African. Cugoano was a Fanti from Ghana and Equiano was an Ibo from Nigeria. Both wrote books about their life and experience as slaves, Cugoano's being published in 1787 and Equiano's in 1789. Cugoano urged the British government to take active steps, such as sending a fleet to West Africa, to suppress the slave trade. Equiano for his part appealed for the banning of the slave trade on the grounds of economic inefficiency. He argued that legitimate commerce would bring far greater profits to England than the meagre returns of a cruel, wasteful traffic in human merchandise. It is a theme which was to recur often in the writings of nineteenth century missionaries and was to prepare the way, somewhat unwittingly, for the economic investment policy of colonialism. In addition, both Cugoano and Equiano called for the extension of Christianity to Africa, seeing it as an ally in the campaign against the slave trade and as a force by which to achieve the modernisation of Africa. Cugoano himself wanted to return to Africa as a missionary to his people, a desire which fired many emancipated slaves, particularly those from the United States and the West Indies, to follow the missionary trail.

The first attempt to send a group of ex-slaves to what is now Sierra Leone ran immediately into problems. The Committee for the 'Black Poor' in London agreed to fit out a party of Africans for re-settlement in Sierra Leone, but Henry Smeatham, the brains behind the idea, was later found unsuitable for what Granville Sharp and others intended as a Christian experiment. It was Sharp who had brought the test case of James Somerset before the English courts and thus established himself as a foremost promoter of the cause. He had given the Sierra Leone project his strongest backing; thus when Smeatham was retired on moral grounds, he worked actively to resume the scheme, and one was put together. However, when the party was ready to sail in January 1787, fever broke out and departure was delayed. Another attempt was made the following month, but as the convoy of four ships sailed through the Channel, a storm blew up and disabled two of the ships. The others limped back to port and the attempt had to be abandoned. When in April yet another attempt was made, it suffered the fate of the previous ones. In the process of taking the Africans and their white women companions from London to Portsmouth, many fell ill and died, while some others, believing that the venture was ill-starred, lost heart and gave up the idea altogether. But a faithful remnant of 411 persevered, and set sail, arriving in Sierra Leone at Frenchman's Bay on 10 May 1787, led by Captain T. Boulden Thompson. However, the settlers were to go through a fiery furnace of adjusting to the climate and the environment. Some fourteen of them died before reaching Sierra Leone and within three months of arriving, a third of the entire party died. By March 1788 only 130 of the original number were alive. Granville Sharp, determined to make the scheme a success, arranged to send out another party. Volunteers were hard to find in spite of Sharp's evident enthusiasm. In the end only thirty-nine people, including two English doctors, agreed to go.

The main attraction for prospective emigrants to Sierra Leone was the promise of land and the prospects of acquiring wealth through lawful enterprise. It was widely believed that this would achieve the gradual extinction of the slave trade and the dissolution of the institution of slavery. But the promises turned out to be unrealistic. Land was extremely scarce and had to be carefully negotiated for with distrustful rulers. What land there was proved difficult to cultivate because of the underlying gravelstone. The Sierra Leone Company, which was formed from subscriptions with the idea that immediate profits would be made and shareholders amply rewarded, merely went on accumulating losses. Disease and death took a horrific toll of those who survived the journey.

As an immediate economic proposition the venture was obviously foolhardy in the extreme. But the settlement did not live by bread alone. The humanitarian pressures which had led to the sending out of the first settlers continued to build up and philanthropists, armed with specialised knowledge on the conditions of slavery and the harsh trade that kept the festering canker spreading, redoubled their efforts to try to abolish the slave trade. An essential part of their armoury was the existence of a settlement like Sierra Leone, and if that went down the cause would suffer a disastrous setback. In May 1787, Thomas Clarkson got Granville Sharp and Samuel Hoare to press ahead for abolition, and this group of philanthropists chose William Wilberforce to champion the cause in Parliament. Less than a year later, a Committee of the Privy Council was set up to hear evidence on the slave trade, and in May 1788, the matter was raised in the House of Commons. Sharp, faced with parliamentary delay, turned to private sources for support and a petition was sent to Parliament asking for the incorporation of the West African venture as the 'Sierra Leone Company': a bill incorporating it was introduced in April 1791. With the coming into being of the Company, there was a dispute over the role of Granville Sharp: he was pushed out of the Company because of his uncompromising ideals. and replaced by Henry Thornton, a banker, who was more likely than Sharp to stress the economic side of the Sierra Leone settlement. He remained, however, a close ally and friend of Wilberforce.

The first settlers went to a place they named Granville Town in honour of Sharp's pioneering work, but it collapsed after some four years. However, the vision it embodied lived on. Granville Town itself was situated on the 'Province of Freedom', which was another name for the settlement; the settlers lived in a close-knit community, practising self-government, useful labour and mutual succour. Sharp's removal from the scene, which almost coincided with the failure of the settlement at the Province of Freedom, saw the beginning of a change in the direction of the settlement. Sharp was a well-intentioned and virtuous man, but his ideas were too theoretical to be of practical value, and in the context of the distant, unknown land of Sierra Leone, seemed extremely speculative. Still, the encouragement he provided for the initial idea of a West African settlement had been tremendous, and if he erred it was towards excessive idealism, not distrust of the African, as was to characterise the history of the settlement in the period of European imperial penetration of the continent. In any case those who prided themselves on an unsentimental knowledge of hard economic reality and who had taken over the affairs of the settlement were to fare even worse, for the Sierra Leone Company as an economic proposition was to be on the rocks soon after its establishment.

Under its new charter, the Company arranged to move forty-eight of the original residents of Granville Town to a new site near Fourah Bay in 1791: that site, also called Granville Town, became a village of seventeen houses. The first Granville Town had been burnt by a local ruler, King Jimmy, as a retaliatory action against what he considered violations by the Company's servants on his territory. Since it was clear that the settlement was too small to be viable, attempts were made to replenish it by recruiting more volunteers, with the operation being directed from London, where the Company had its headquarters.

Nova Scotian settlers

At about this time, news came of exactly the sort of people who might find new hope in a settlement like Sierra Leone and who, by their willingness to emigrate, would reinforce the claims of those opposed to the slave trade. These people were former American slaves, who had enlisted in the British army during the American Revolutionary War and fought gallantly. But they were unhappy with the life they lived in Nova Scotia where they had gone after the war; instead of the freedom and land promised them, they worked as farm labourers with no hope of ever owning land. Thus they were a disgruntled group, who felt ill-rewarded for their sacrifices, and harboured an understandable distrust of officialdom. One of their number, Thomas Peters, travelled to London to bring the grievances of the Nova Scotian Blacks to the attention of influential individuals. He met Sharp and was befriended by Thornton who suggested settling Nova Scotians in Sierra Leone. Peters returned with plans to organise the first emigration. In January 1792, about 1,200 free Blacks sailed from Nova Scotia, arriving in Sierra Leone three months later. The whole enterprise had cost nearly £9,600, which was paid for by the British government. One modern writer describes their landing in Freetown thus:

Their pastors led them ashore, singing a hymn of praise[. . .] Like the Children of Israel which were come out again out of the captivity they rejoiced before the Lord, who had brought them from bondage to the land of their forefathers. When all had arrived, the whole colony assembled in worship, to proclaim to the [. . .] continent whence they or their forbears had been carried in chains —

'The day of Jubilee is come;

Return ye ransomed sinners home.'[1]

The optimism of the Nova Scotian settlers was to prove their most valuable asset in the difficult years that followed. They had received a

1. Fyfe, *History of Sierra Leone* (1962), pp. 36-7.

foretaste of what was to come on the voyage when sixty-seven of their number died. Thirty-eight died within weeks of their arrival. In the heavy rainy season a year later nearly 100 died. Then in September 1794 the French attacked the settlement and caused heavy destruction of life and property. Ever-present was the threat of attack by the Temne and the general insecurity of life that created. In the climate of rising expectations of a better life, the settlers, twice uprooted from their land, resisted official attempts to tax them, and rebelled rather than give way. The land question remained a serious source of grievance. Within a few years of the Sierra Leone Company being started, financial losses made its collapse inevitable. In 1806 it was decided to introduce a bill in Parliament making Sierra Leone a Crown Colony. The bill was enacted into law in August 1807. On 1 January 1808, the Crown took over formal responsibility from the Company. However, that did not by any means solve all Sierra Leone's problems, the most serious of which remained the continuing slave traffic, the most lucrative source of revenue for neighbouring rulers and one from which the Colony and its inhabitants were excluded by the terms of the Slave Trade Abolition Act of 1807 as well as by the nature of the settlement itself, being a refuge for the victims of the slave trade. A direct consequence of the slave traffic was the diversion of much valuable trade from the Colony, which accentuated the problem of agriculture as an alternative source of livelihood. After the first and second Temne attacks of 1801 and 1802, for example, the acreage under cultivation fell dramatically from 650 almost to nil. There was a gradual return to the land, but many enterprising Nova Scotians entered trade as middlemen selling goods of European manufacture to hinterland areas with Freetown as an important commercial base.

The story of the abolition of the slave trade belongs more properly to a separate history, although its effects on a settlement like Freetown were immediate. We should at this point turn to the background of the missionary movement in West Arica, taking particular note of the role that Africans played in it. It will be necessary to break the strict rules of chronology in order to say a little on each of the major Christian missions involved in the Sierra Leone settlement. We shall examine in turn the role of the Church Missionary Society, the Wesleyans, the Quakers and the Roman Catholics. Although the Baptists were strongly represented among the settlers, the Baptist Missionary Society, one of the first Protestant missions to be founded, did not have a presence there. On the other hand, the Quakers, who had a worker in Freetown at an early stage, did not have a formal mission attached to their work, which was supported by the Methodists. The Catholics, apart from the few individual early pioneers, arrived rather late on the scene, although their work belongs with the general theme of missionary history. Such gaps and peculiarities will have to be borne in mind in the following section.

Missionary activity in Sierra Leone

The Church Missionary Society and related bodies. In 1799 a group of Evangelical churchmen belonging to the Church of England founded the Church Missionary Society (CMS), a name which it adopted in 1813. Its founders were lay and clerical and they obtained the support of Wilberforce, Thornton, Macaulay and other members of the 'Clapham Sect' (a group of pious Church of England Evangelicals). Before 1815 the CMS tried but failed to attract Englishmen to the mission field, and it turned instead to Lutheran Germans trained in Berlin. In 1804 the first two missionaries, Melchior Renner and Peter Hartwig, went to Sierra Leone for work primarily among the Susu. That first initiative went wrong. The two missionaries stayed for two years in Freetown instead of the recommended one year in which they were supposed to acclimatise themselves before going out into Susu country. Also they quarrelled violently so that great crowds used to gather outside their house to listen. It was obvious they could not work profitably together. Peter Hartwig abandoned the missionary vocation, disappeared into Susu country, not to convert but to become a slave trader. He was not the last missionary to find slave-catching more appealing than soul-seeking.

Undeterred, the CMS sent out three more missionaries, all Germans, in 1806: Leopold Butscher, Johann Prasse and Gustavus Nylander. Nylander was to be the pioneer agent of the CMS in Sierra Leone, and he stayed in Freetown as Company chaplain, thus representing the Established Church in Sierra Leone. He became a teacher in the government-sponsored school. Nylander thus symbolised the connection between government and mission. He also created a formal connection between mission and education, so that the chapel and the school marched hand in hand. Within four years of arriving in Freetown, he had more than one hundred pupils under instruction. In 1810 the Governor built Nylander and his Nova Scotian wife each a new school-house, and towards the end of that year the enrolment had gone up to 150 regular attendants. In sharp contrast to his educational achievement, Nylander failed to attract people to his chapel. The services he conducted were poorly attended, not because the local settlers were uninterested in religion, but mainly because most of them were adequately provided for by their own pastors. The European population, on the other hand, the natural constituency of Nylander's colonial chapel, turned against church attendance. The chapel fell into disrepair and had to be abandoned and Nylander ministered to his dwindling flock from his house instead.

In 1818 Nylander left for the Bulom Shore to do missionary work and had a fruitful time there. He composed a *Bulom Grammar and Vocabulary,* and translated St Matthew's Gospel into that language, the first Scriptural translation in Sierra Leone, although in 1801 Henry Brunton, back from the mission field, published a Susu grammar and some catechisms in Scotland. Brunton's books were the first to be published in a West African language.

Of the other two missionaries, a few remarks must suffice. Johann Prasse, originally accompanied by Leopold Butscher, went with Renner to the Rio Pongas for work among the Susu. The CMS continued to uphold the theory that the concentration of missionary effort in Freetown, with its corrupting European influence, was without long-term advantage. Hence the preoccupation with a mission to the Susu with which Prasse became closely connected. Butscher, however, returned to Freetown to head the Christian Institution at Leicester in 1814, where he taught stone-masonry and other practical skills. Yet his distinction was not in the work of his hands but in the ideas he formulated on slavery. What he had to say on the subject was in advance of his time, and it was not till 1839, when Thomas Fowell Buxton published his *The Slave Trade and its Remedy,* that belated attention was drawn to what Butscher had said as long before as 1812. From his experience among the Susu, Butscher said that the slave trade had been the most important source of income for inland peoples and that abolition had threatened the very foundation of economic enterprise for those peoples. Seizing slaves on the high seas, as had been the policy of the British Government, did not strike at the root cause of continued enslavement; what was needed, Butscher said, was an export commodity that could genuinely replace slaves. It should therefore be the single most urgent objective of both missionaries and government to develop an alternative source of wealth for African societies. In this way Butscher set about trying to secure the sympathy and co-operation of government officials and thus helping to provide a firm basis for government and missionary partnership. He was instrumental in getting Governor Maxwell (1811–15) to devise an administrative scheme for the settling of recaptives. Similarly he brought Charles MacCarthy (of whom more presently) to the attention of Church and government circles in England. Butscher had been kindly treated by MacCarthy at Gorée opposite the mouth of the Senegal River when the missionary and his ship had run aground on some rocks during the return journey from England. MacCarthy, because of his French ancestry (his father was French), had been in French service as a military commander at Senegal, but he was equally willing to serve a Protestant power if it advanced his personal career. His later appearance on the Freetown scene was to represent a watershed in the Colony's history. Leopold Butscher is owed some of the credit for that.

MacCarthy evolved a bold and imaginative plan in connection with the resettlement of the recaptives, but this is probably best taken up in connection with social and educational improvements in Chapter 6 below. What may, however, be introduced here is MacCarthy's relations with the CMS. His predecessor, Maxwell, had set the precedent by placing the CMS in charge of all education in the recaptive villages. In 1815 a plan was drawn up, which will be described more fully below, committing the CMS to the education and spiritual care of the recaptives in the growing colony villages. When MacCarthy took over (1815–24) he pushed ahead with both the recaptive scheme and the educational plans. Although a Roman Catholic, MacCarthy became a devoted servant of the missionary cause through the CMS, impatient only that the mission was not making converts fast enough. He criticised the then Colonial Chaplain, William Johnson, and threatened to report him to the Archbishop of Canterbury for refusing to baptise willing inquirers in the recaptive population. Johnson insisted that such inquirers must be adequately instructed before baptism, but MacCarthy thought he was being unduly cautious. MacCarthy continued to quarrel with Johnson until 1821 when he went up to Regent, where Johnson worked, to see for himself what was happening. He and his officers were amazed by what they found, an orderly community drawn up under silken buntings and singing hymns of welcome. Johnson had also taught the children to hold their own prayer meetings. He introduced a Benefit Society to care for the destitute, and a Building Society founded on mutual aid among the village inhabitants. MacCarthy and his officers were silenced by Johnson's spectacular success and returned to Freetown suitably chastened.

The endless quarrelling among CMS missionaries sapped morale and hindered their work. The Parent Committee in London decided, after Butscher's intervention, to send out someone to try to sort out the problems. The man who came out in 1816, Edward Bickersteth, was a barrister, but he insisted on being hurriedly ordained for the mission he was about to undertake. His main brief was to assess the worth of the long-standing Susu mission which all agreed had been a failure. Urged by MacCarthy, Bickersteth recommended that the CMS take a greater interest in Freetown and the wider Colony area. But he did not, as again urged by MacCarthy and others, recommend the abandonment of the Susu mission. Rather, he remained surprisingly unimpressed either with the progress or potential of the recaptive villages he saw. His harsh criticisms of the inadequate care for recaptives goaded the CMS and the colonial administration into taking some definite action. This coincided with the plan MacCarthy was to implement under the Parish Scheme, as will be made clear subsequently.

The CMS remained tied to the theory that agriculture would be far more beneficial to the freed slaves than a literary education. Consequently it showed only a spasmodic interest in education until well into the mid-nineteenth century. By contrast, it sponsored agricultural projects at great expense and trouble when all the evidence pointed to their futility. In 1824 it dropped all pretence of trying to support book-learning when it gave up the recaptive schools in the villages, keeping only the Colonial School in Freetown itself; it turned instead to farming with great enthusiasm. In 1822 a plan was received from a London Quaker, William Allen, to reorganise villages on the lines of Mennonite communities in south Russia: each villager would be housed in a six-roomed cottage with cowshed and pigsty, growing food to feed his family, with cotton or coffee for an export crop. The first such village, Allen Town, founded with 200 recaptives near Hastings, never really established itself in spite of its beautiful mountain setting. Macfoy, who became its first superintendent, decided he would do better, like everyone else, by trading than by farming. He resigned in 1831 and then, converted by his wife, learnt to read and then began distributing the Psalms to a congregation he gathered himself. The congregation sang hymns it did not yet understand, so eager was it for Christian instruction. The CMS meanwhile pursued the illusory goal of tropical abundance, turning its back on the far greater abundance of a spiritual harvest. Needless to add that such agricultural schemes were much more familiar to many of the missionaries, with their roots in croft, cottage and stable, than to the Freetown settlers.

From 1841 onwards the CMS redoubled its efforts at founding centres for practical instruction. Henry Venn, the influential CMS Secretary and a man of remarkable foresight in other matters, succumbed easily to the myth of tropical abundance when, in 1841, he became Secretary of the CMS. The Society started an Industrial School where the pupils were taught carpentry, tailoring and the art of growing cotton. At the Grammar School, which it founded in 1845, the boys were taught the usual academic subjects, but they also had to learn to plant cotton. Yet, in spite of the enthusiasm shown for it, cotton was always an abysmal failure. Those who invested in it reaped only ruination. Even Macaulay, a moving spirit of the Sierra Leone Company, who had first dismissed the idea of a successful cotton crop when he was based in London, adopted the idea with the zeal of a convert when he became governor of the settlement between 1796 and 1799 (he acted 1794-5).

Two schemes were tried by the CMS, both aimed at stimulating indigenous leadership in the Church, although it is fair to add that the Sierra Leone settlers had shown remarkable leadership in their village chapels even before they saw any missionaries. One was the Auxiliary CMS, a local arm of the Society, intended to encourage local support for mission — a support given not only with financial contributions but in personnel and property. The other was the Native Pastorate, a scheme conceived by Venn as a fitting development of the notion of African self-reliance. In 1860 Edward Beckles arrived from the West Indies as bishop, with a plan to found a Native Church. On All Saints Day in 1861, the CMS handed over nine parishes to the Native Church Pastorate, with support for the work of the latter supposed henceforth to rest mainly on local parishioners. Only Freetown and a few outlying parishes were retained. The nine pastors became clergy of their own church, not employees of the CMS in England. The Legislative Council in Freetown voted money for the Pastorate on the grounds that its pastors were the only representatives of authority in the villages, sometimes with a policeman or two. Government support ceased in 1876 in a cloud of controversy and sectarian bickering, and extra money had to be raised from increased membership contributions. In 1875 the CMS went on transferring more churches to the Native Pastorate. In 1878 Holy Trinity Church in Freetown, a fashionable society meeting-house, popularly known as 'Vanity Fair', was handed over to it. By these and similar measures the CMS tried to divest itself of religious support for the work in the Colony. In its original form, the Native Pastorate anticipated by nearly a century the call of the Churches in Africa in the 1970s for a moratorium on mission, what Henry Venn vividly referred to as the 'euthanasia' of mission.

Wesleyan missionaries. Some of the material on Methodism will be carried over into a later section of this chapter. The missionary component is our chief concern here. Much of the initiative for encouraging missionary activity in Sierra Leone lay with local leaders. The first band of Wesleyan missionaries arrived with Macaulay in March 1796 to work among the Fulbe. Two were ordained ministers and the rest were craftsmen to teach new skills. They were accompanied by their families. However, the prospects of plunging deep into the country in search of the Fulbe in the Northern Rivers filled them with foreboding. On the morning they were due to sail they renounced the missionary vocation and asked to be taken back to England.

In 1806 Joseph Brown, a leading Methodist preacher and one of the Settlers, wrote to the English Wesleyan Conference asking for a missionary. Eventually the Rev. George Warren and three schoolmasters arrived in late 1811. Warren died in 1812. Three years later, in 1815, the Rev. William Davies, a Welsh missionary, arrived, to be followed by others. But many died soon after arriving. Of nine who came between 1819 and 1829, seven died in Freetown. Hampered by a scarcity of volunteers and afflicted in the field by disease and death, the missionary contribution became a diminishing factor, with the work being carried on mainly under the strong direction of independent Creole communities. (The term 'Creole' was used with increasing frequency in the second half of the nineteenth century and referred to a composite of the descendants of the old settlers, the Maroons and the large recaptive population). Much of the work remained in their hands. One such outstanding leader was John Ezzidio, a Nupe recaptive who was landed as a boy from a Brazilian slave ship in 1827. He rose to become an exhorter, class leader and local preacher, and a distinguished and devoted servant of the cause, using his considerable wealth to support the work. But he was ill-repaid for his exertions.   Faced with the increasing burden of running the Church, Ezzidio felt that a full-time missionary would be the solution, and consequently requested the English Methodists to send out a missionary. In response they sent Benjamin Tregaskis — with disastrous consequences, for he divided the flock, sowed seeds of sectarian antagonism and in the ensuing confusion erected a personality cult centred on himself. When Ezzidio died, pursued with vindictive venom to his grave, Tregaskis was seen to rejoice openly at the graveside. But Tregaskis' unbounded energy was to serve him in good stead as he sought to rule both the Sierra Leone and the Gambia Churches, leaving very little to anyone else. He left in 1874, prised away by London amid continuing controversy over his role in the field. He was a generation too early, for had he come out in the era of the 'Scramble for Africa' and its colonial aftermath, he would have been in better company. As it was, he came to Freetown at a time when Africans were the decision-makers in the church. Both Ezzidio at Freetown and James Ferguson at Badagry were representative figures of that earlier era, taking the lead in asking for missionaries, and seeing them 'as helpers, not as guides or instructors'.[2] Tregaskis thought differently. His story and that of the Methodists is continued in Chapter 6.

The Quakers. Officially the Society of Friends, the pacifist religious body better known as Quakers   did not have a missionary organisation. However, among them were some of great influence involved with the Sierra Leone, for they were foremost in the campaign against slavery and the slave trade and thus had a natural interest in the establishment of a free settlement in West Africa. One of the early Quakers connected with Sierra Leone was the enterprising Afro-American pioneer Captain Paul Cuffee, from Massachusetts, whose ambitious plans to encourage the Afro-American colonisation of Sierra Leone and discover new sources of legitimate trade will be described shortly. A London Quaker, William Allen, was instrumental in setting up Paul Cuffee in business. Both men were interested in creating a healthy commercial

2. Fyfe, *History of Sierra Leone* (1962), p.69.

climate which would discourage the traffic in slaves and help in the expansion of Christianity.

A remarkable Quaker with strong Freetown and Gambian connections was Hannah Kilham, a friend of William Allen's. While living in London she learned the Wolof and Mandinka languages from two sailors, and in 1824 and 1827 she visited Freetown. Hannah Kilham believed that it was essential to teach African children in their own language, using material from their own background, and in 1830 she returned to Freetown to put her ideas into practice. She opened a school for recaptive girls in Charlotte village, teaching in Mende and *'Aku'*, the latter probably a variety of Yoruba. She also developed ideas on using English as a second language, a foretaste of developments in recent times: the idea was to construct a special vocabulary adapted to suit local needs. Her ideas for this and on African languages were revolutionary for her time and are only now beginning to gain acceptance by ministries of education in independent African countries. Hannah Kilham opened a bookstall at Bathurst village selling tracts and textbooks to local people. She lived a peaceful life at Charlotte even though the village had been without a superintendent to keep order. In fact it was too peaceful for her, and in 1832 she went to Liberia to see how it compared with Sierra Leone. She was there for a few weeks and on her voyage back she fell ill and died at sea.

Hannah Kilham not only made education authorities sit up and think, but she forced the Quakers in London to rethink the whole question of the rightness of mission. Many of her friends wrote with indignation that her work remained unsupported by the Quakers, and appealed for a more positive attitude. In the brief time that she was on the scene, she contributed enormously to the reawakening of Quaker interest in the plight of the less fortunate in other lands.

The Roman Catholics. An early Roman Catholic missionary in Sierra Leone was the elderly Portuguese Jesuit Balthasar Barreira, who settled there in 1605, ministering to a largely Portuguese trading community and occasionally preaching to Africans. He baptised several kings and travelled up the Scarcies river. However, his attempt to baptise the Susu king was defeated by a travelling Muslim cleric from the north. Barreira left the country in 1610, leaving the Jesuits and later the Capuchins to carry on the work. The mission did not make much headway, and closed in the eighteenth century. A few African and Afro-Portuguese converts continued to profess the faith, which received some encouragement from the rare and sporadic visits of priests. The English, trading with the Royal African Company, were appearing increasingly in the area and supplanting Portuguese trade. With the waning of Portuguese influence the Catholic influence waned too.

Among the remnants in the late eighteenth century of the Portuguese presence in the area was 'Signor Domingo', the Temne chief at Royema, an area adjoining the Sierra Leone Company. Although this dignitary was a Roman Catholic and knew Portuguese and was able to read it, he sent his son to England to be educated, a sign that the Portuguese star had waned in his part of Africa.

In 1822 hopes were raised that a permanent Catholic mission would be founded in Sierra Leone. Anne-Marie Javouhey (beatified in 1950), founder of the Sisters of St Joseph of Cluny, a teaching and nursing order, visited the French colonies in 1816. In 1822 MacCarthy invited her to visit Bathurst, Gambia, and she reorganised the hospital there. She went on to Freetown and did the same for the Liberated African Hospital, staying on to nurse the sick during the yellow fever epidemic. She fell ill herself but recovered and returned to France in September 1823. Nothing came of that visit, and Anne-Marie Javouhey never revisited Africa; nor was a chapter of her order established there.

Then in 1842 a leading Catholic missionary, Edward Barron, Bishop of Constantia, paid a visit to Freetown where there was still a small Catholic community. Bishop Barron, an Irish-American, had been associated with the Venerable Francis Libermann who founded the Congregation of the Holy Ghost as a missionary order. Bishop Barron left Freetown without starting a Catholic mission there, work at that time being concentrated on Gabon. However in 1859 Monsignor de Marion Brésillac, the founder of the Society of African Missions, which was to be active in eastern Nigeria among other places, arrived in Freetown with a staff of priests and lay brothers. This followed the creation the previous year of a nothern Vicariate under the Monsignor's direction. However, 1859 was a hard year in Sierra Leone. At least 500 people died in seven months from various diseases: yellow fever, measles and smallpox. Forty-two Europeans, including the Catholic priests, were among the dead.

After the death of Brésillac, the Society of African Missions went to Dahomey (Benin) and left Sierra Leone to the Congregation of the Holy Ghost who were already established in Senegambia. The Holy Ghost Fathers did not appear in Sierra Leone until 1864 when Father Blanchet, joined by the Alsatian priest, Fr Koeberlé, and two lay brothers, Brother Wurm (from Alsace) and Brother Matthews (an Irishman) arrived. An epidemic in 1865 carried off a quarter of the European population, including Fr Koeberlé, but the other missionaries survived, and Fr Blanchet remained there until 1893. In 1866 they were joined by others, including three nuns of the order of St Joseph of Cluny. A church, St Edward's, was built and a school started. In 1870, when the Franco-Prussian war blocked support for the mission, the government in Freetown voted £150 for its work. Two nuns died in a yellow fever outbreak in 1872. The following year

Fr Gommenginger took over the Catholic mission and started penetrating into areas beyond Freetown. He founded a mission at Port Loko where he was well received by the local people; however, Port Loko was a centre for the other Protestant missions, and the Catholics were excluded from the town. They went instead to the Rio Pongas and adjacent areas, attracted by the presence of the French in those parts. In 1893 the missionaries founded a small mission at Bamani among the Mende. It was destroyed in the wars with Bai Bureh in 1895, although the missionaries and their agents escaped harm.

The Catholic missions, unlike their Protestant counterparts, did not move quickly to train an indigenous priesthood or work actively to produce a self reliant Church on the lines of the Native Pastorate. No doubt this is the consequence of the nature of the Church and its historical circumstances and not of any deliberate policy to suppress Africans. Nevertheless, the conspicuous concentration of power in white missionary hands tended to suggest and confirm the view that the Catholic church was indifferent to genuine African aspirations. However, its contribution to social welfare and educational advancement was significant in its own right.

The local population

Freetown, as intended, became the microcosm of the historical and social experience of Africa, an experiment compounded of the elements of historical tragedy, economic exploitation, foreign paternalism, religious idealism and the dream of an African utopia. Such a concentration of elements was matched only by the great variety of social backgrounds represented in the settlement. In less than a hundred years Freetown would become the home of people drawn from all parts of the African continent and beyond, neither the pure sunny utopia of the romantics nor the trap of the devil, as its critics made it out to be. In its own brief history, the settlement reflected something of the bitter history of the people for whom it existed as a refuge. The waves of settlers who arrived in Freetown, particularly the early ones, encountered difficulties no less daunting than the ones they were fleeing from. From that unpromising beginning emerged what by any standard must be considered a notable achievement.

The Black Poor and the Nova Scotian Settlers. We have already described the story of the landing of the Black Poor, very few of whom survived. The name 'Black Poor' is of course a misnomer. Cugoano and Equiano, for example, would be included under that term in spite of both being men of letters. Many of the others had been in regular employment on ships. Some had been living contentedly in England. Furthermore, the Black Poor was not a census category into which people were carefully introduced. It may have appealed to philanthropic circles whose support was eagerly sought for the new settlement in West Africa, but it described little of the economic circumstances of the Africans concerned. Their extreme plight in Sierra Leone showed how little prepared they were for life in Africa. Only a pitiful remnant survived to merge with the next wave.

As has already been seen, nearly 1,200 settlers arrived from Nova Scotia in 1792. They were not the first to come to Freetown; previously there had been settlers from England who succumbed to the climate. Thus the arrival of the Nova Scotians provided an element of stability. The Nova Scotians gave the name 'Freetown' to the settlement at Granville Town where they went to live. Some of their outstanding leaders, to be described in more detail shortly, were David George, Thomas Peters, Moses Wilkinson, Luke Jordan, John Ellis, Cato Perkins and William Ash, all of African ancestry. We should also add the names of prominent women among them. The Settlers, as the Nova Scotians were called, occupied a clearly defined residential area of Freetown where their women owned substantial property, some of it the best available. Sophia Small, a successful Settler trader, put her profits into property, and built a large house, valued in the 1790s at £900. Martha Burthen also owned a large plot of land which passed to her daughter's family. Lettice Demps similarly owned a large plot of land which her grandson, the Rev Scipio Wright, sold off in small building lots in the 1850s. Martha Hazeley was another successful woman, and her daughter Phillis who went to school in England, opened a school after her return which taught reading, writing, arithmetic and needlework for a fee. She later married the German missionary Nylander, and she was not the only Settler woman to marry a European missionary. Many of them became mistresses to respectable officials, including governors; however, these officials did not always marry such local women, although the liaisons brought them increased economic opportunities. A European carpenter married the daughter of Sophia Small and acquired a large family fortune from Sophia's estate, and a large house was sumptuously constructed out of the proceeds of this wealth, at a cost in about 1815 of £3,500.

Although clearly the settlers were great entrepreneurs (for that was to prove their life-line in their new home), they had deep religious roots as well. They arrived in Freetown as convinced Christians, many of them far more knowledgeable about the Bible and Christian doctrine than some of the missionaries sent to minister to them. One writer says: 'Christianity was for them dynamic and personal; no matter of doctrine could be indifferent; the personal experience of the individual and his sharing in fellowship with others — the sense of being the people of God — was a matter of profound importance.'[3]

3. Walls (1959).

Religion forged a fresh identity among them.

Many Settlers, men and women, took a leading part in Christian life. Mingo Jordan, originally employed as a teacher by the Company, was made Church Clerk. However, he had his own private chapel built by his congregation who gathered there every morning before sunrise and again in the evening to pray and witness. These fairly numerous private chapels were always full, in contrast to the missionary churches, such as Nylander's, which were often empty and fell into disuse. When missionary help did not arrive or failed, the Settlers took matters into their own hands. The Settler Methodists, for example, started their own mission work at York Village and at Hastings. Money was collected to put up permanent building, as at Wellington in 1830. Within ten years most villages had at least one or more chapels. Ironically, the authorities did not always look upon all this religious activity with favour, and consequently restrictions were brought in to regulate it, often with little effect. When we come to consider the rise of African Independent Churches in the twentieth century (Chapter 7) we shall see a similar attitude of official hostility towards local religious enterprise. Despite such hostility, Africans continued to practise Christianity in their own way. Settler women preached and gave personal testimonies in the chapels. Amilia Buxton had her own congregation in her house, and there were many others like her.

One contemporary eye-witness account of the life of the Settlers in Freetown speaks warmly of their religious devotion: 'I never met with, heard or read òf, any set of people observing the same appearance of godliness; for I do not remember, since they first landed here, my ever awaking (and I have woke at every hour of the night), without hearing preachings from some quarter or another.[4] They attended church on Sunday devotedly, dressed in their best clothes. Their language was deeply influenced by that of the Bible, with Scriptural phrases liberally sprinkled in their letters. Religion thus became the rock out of which the tenacious Settlers carved a future for themselves and their new home. Research now being done into their earlier background as slaves in the United States suggests that there too religion was the factor which enabled them to survive the ferocity of the slave regime. It is this quality which, perhaps more than any other, explains the success of the modern missionary movement in Africa, for it linked up with the deep piety of the Settlers and those who came after them.

The Maroons. The Maroons were descendants of slaves who fled to the mountains of Jamaica after the armies of Oliver Cromwell invaded the island and drove off the Spaniards in 1655. In the difficult mountain terrain the English occupation forces found it impossible to

4. Falconbridge (1794), p.193.

dislodge the Maroons, who continued to wage a guerrilla campaign. They were later joined by the Koromantees, slaves of Ashanti origin who had escaped from their masters. In 1739 the English authorities decided to conclude a protracted, expensive war by signing a peace treaty with the Maroons, whereby the Maroons would be allowed to retain their mountain strongholds and maintain their laws and customs without interference from the English. In return they would side with the government and its troops in the event of an invasion or domestic insurrection. They also agreed to hunt down and return runaway plantation slaves. In the 1760s when there was a slave revolt the Maroons fulfilled their promise by joining government forces to put it down. In 1795, however, two Maroons were arrested and flogged by government authorities. The Maroons felt the treaty had been infringed by the government, and felt justified in disowning the accord and resuming the guerrilla war.

The government at first attempted to meet them with force; however, unable to beat them with conventional forces, it decided to use dogs to hunt them down, hiring bloodhounds from Cuba for the purpose. The Maroons, with a superstitious fear of dogs, decided to adopt the path of surrender rather than face the canine curse. They were promptly rounded up and embarked on a ship bound for Nova Scotia, a measure the authorities thought would rid them once and for all of the problem of the Maroons. However, finding the Nova Scotian climate harsh and inhospitable, the Maroons agitated to be moved from there. After negotiations and reluctance on the part of the authorities to accede to the demands, it was decided to send them to Sierra Leone, Parliament agreeing to compensate the then Sierra Leone Company for the cost of transportation. Finally, in August 1800, 550 Maroons set sail for Freetown where they held steadfastly to their customs, refusing to adopt Christianity or accept schools for themselves. They were determined, even in ignominious defeat, to remain an indigestible irritant within the system. But they made two notable concessions: one was that they agreed to abandon their warlike ways and adopt instead the path of conciliation and consultation in the running of their lives, and the other was they allowed their children to attend Christian schools and even to embrace Christianity. The older Maroons kept to their marriage customs and funeral rites, repudiating the rule of monogamy as an unacceptable imposition. They settled first at Granville Town but were quickly moved to Freetown where they contributed gallantly to the defence of the embattled settlement.

The Maroon children who accepted education did well, on the whole, in their studies, and many later rose to positions of prominence in the social and economic life of Freetown. For example, in 1809, Governor Thompson commissioned the Maroon general, Montague James, to administer the Colony along with the Sheriff; in the 1820s William Brown was in charge of the Colonial Pharmacy; Thomas Patrick Thorpe, practised medicine first in Freetown and finally in the Gallinas country; Stephen Gabbidon and Herbert Williams prospered in business, using their English contacts to control a good share of the import trade; and John Thorpe, who traded and lost heavily in the Sherbro, turned to farming in Wellington Village and became a prominent member of the community. This John Thorpe was the brother of Thomas Thorpe whose son, John Thorpe (Jr.), was to make history in the Colony. He went to Freetown school and, taking up law, was admitted as an attorney in 1830; he then resigned, went to London and was admitted there as a Notary Public. In November 1832, he registered at the newly-founded University College, London, to study Natural Philosophy and Law, becoming the first person from the Colony to enter a university. On his return he resumed practice as an attorney.

The Maroons were also prominent in religion. They built a church and let it out to the Wesleyan missionaries. Samuel Thorpe, of the Thorpe family, earned his living as a trader but acted as a Methodist preacher. His amorous exploits were unfairly to earn him notoriety.

The Maroons found complete integration into life in Freetown extremely difficult, although many succeeded in acquiring local loyalties through marriage. One such was Joseph Green Spilsbury, son of a Maroon mother and an ex-Colonial Surgeon, who did well in trade and in 1839 invested his profits in a substantial piece of property. However, there were a few malcontents who would not be silenced, and made a stir with talk of repatriation to Jamaica. The authorities wanting to discourage them, refused them free passage, but a wealthy Maroon widow, Mrs Mary Brown, purchased a schooner of her own and put it at the disposal of her compatriots. On 1 January 1840, a determined group of Maroons sailed back to the West Indies. Some of them were to regret their action and eventually returned to Freetown. In fact the Maroon community, whatever its sense of ethnic separateness, continued to grow and prosper in Freetown in spite of the proven case for repatriation.

The Recaptives. The settlement of Freetown was both the consequence and the cause of abolitionist pressure which achieved a significant victory by securing the abolition of the slave trade in 1807. Hailed in numerous quarters as a milestone, the abolition nevertheless threw up immense problems, chiefly to do with re-settling those who were landed from confiscated slave cargoes on the high seas. It is easy now to see that such 'recaptured Africans', as they were called in the 1820s, provided an unprecedented opportunity for the spread of Christianity, but at the time matters did not appear in that light, although even then the signs were clear. Settled into orderly and well-regulated villages around the Freetown peninsula, the recaptives,

who came from every part of Africa and beyond, represented the
concentrated potential of Africa's population resource. By
penetrating them with the Christian Gospel, the Church would arrive
at the human crossroads of Africa. Relieved of the burden of
bondage, the recaptives were now to bear the new burden of
Christian responsibility towards the rest of the continent.

A Vice-Admiralty Court was established in Freetown under the
terms of the Slave Trade Abolition Act of 1807 to hear cases of slaves
illegally transported. Slaves condemned in the Court ('condemned'
in this sense means that the Court established that the slaves had been
illegally taken and were in the process of being transported, in which
case the judges could certify them as slaves in order to buy them back
through compensation and set them free) were forfeited to the
Crown, which paid their captors compensation. Many such
recaptives were apprenticed or enlisted in the forces, but their
numbers continued to rise, calling for a carefully thought out plan to
tackle the problem. During 1810, for example, some 80,000 slaves
were being illegally shipped according to an official Commission of
Inquiry estimate, many of them to the markets of Cuba and Brazil.
They were carried on American ships sailing under Spanish colours,
with the Spaniards and Portuguese themselves carrying an
increasingly large number for their colonies of Cuba and Brazil. By
the end of 1811, nearly 1,200 recaptives had been 'condemned' in
Freetown, and a Superintendant was appointed to look after them.
By now they outnumbered the Settlers from Nova Scotia and the
Maroons. Forty-two recaptives, originally from Cabenda at the
mouth of the Congo River, some 2,000 miles away, were settled at
Leicester Village where a Maroon captain, Charles Saw, was put in
charge. By July 1814, the number of recaptives in Freetown was
estimated at nearly 6,000.

In 1816 it was decided to establish a mission and administrative
department for the recaptives. The CMS agreed with Sir Charles
MacCarthy (who died in the Ashanti war in 1824) to re-direct its
energies from the unresponsive Temne to the Colony. As Governor,
MacCarthy decided to reorganise the village system around Freetown
under a new plan he called the Parish Scheme: the entire peninsula
would be divided into small villages or parishes, each under a
clergyman who would be paid an annual salary from public funds.
The recaptives would be allotted land on which they would grow food
for themselves. There would be a chapel — with provision for
required attendance — which would also serve as a school. Before
1815 there were only three such villages: Leicester, founded in 1809;
Wilberforce (formerly Cabenda) in 1810, and Regent (formerly
Hogbrook) in 1812. Before 1820 ten more villages were named,
among them Gloucester and Kissy in 1816, and Wellington, Hastings
and Waterloo, all in 1819; Charlotte and Leopold (the latter renamed

Bathurst) were named in 1817; in the late 1820s, when over 8,300 recaptives were landed between 1828 and 1829, two new villages — Murray Town and Aberdeen. Many of these villages were to produce outstanding Christian leaders. Hastings, which produced more than its fair share of these Christians, including the first African archdeacons, was proudly known as 'the Bethlehem of West Africa.'[5] Murray Town, for its part, was the home of Sir Samuel Lewis, the first African to be knighted and an outstanding Methodist lay leader.

We have referred to these villages as the human crossroads of Africa. Let us now take a closer look at the social make-up. We have mentioned recaptives from the Congo and we should add that there was a separate quarter for them at Congo Town. At Leicester, there was a Bambara community; the Bambara people belong to the land of Mali, and are linguistic relatives of the Manding, many coming from the town of Segou on the Niger. At Gloucester there were Wolof from Senegal, Mandinka, Susu, Temne, Mende, Fanti (Ghana), Ibo, and people from the Congo. At Bathurst there were Wolof, Bassa and others from the Rio Pongas in Guinea. After the disbanding of the Royal African Corps in 1819, some freed slaves and recaptives were pensioned off and settled in Freetown, and many of them went to a village named Gibraltar Town (a number of the servicemen had served in Gibraltar). At Regent the population included Bulom, Kono and Susu from the Colony area, Bassa and Gola from the Kru coast, and Ibo, Efik, Kalabari, Yoruba and Hausa, all from the Bights of Benin and Biafra in Nigeria. Mende recaptives were called Kosso and were settled at Kosso Town. Then there was Fula Town, a prosperous area of east Freetown where Fulbe traders went to settle and do business. The Fulbe represented Islam, which received official encouragement from most of the governors and which by a curious turn of fate was advocated by many spokesmen as the religion best suited to advance the interests of the Sierra Leonean inhabitants. A teacher of Arabic from Timbuktu earned a comfortable living working in Fula Town and later in the century an impressive mosque was constructed there, lending an oriental flavour to the local skyline. Fulbe caravans from deep in Fula country in Guinea came down to trade in the Colony and lodged in Fula Town. Recaptives also came from Cameroun, Dahomey and Nupe. To go outside West Africa, there were freed slaves in Freetown who originated in Angola, Zambia or Malawi, Burundi and even Mozambique. When you add to this lively meeting of cultures the numerous European agents in the general area of Sierra Leone, then you have a remarkable mosaic of humanity having in common the harsh experience of the slave system, the unifying exposure to the Freetown environment and at a pinch, the English language. Most of the recaptives, uprooted from their homeland and abandoned to the mercy of alien influences, were

5. Fyfe, *History of Sierra Leone* (1962), p.526.

grateful for the sense of security and personal dignity afforded them under Christian nurture. They were all within earshot, if not part of the hymn-singing, Bible-loving and spirit-filled village congregations that proliferated in that fertile climate. Christianity had become for them the tree of life that bore abundant fruit.

A notable Recaptive: Samuel Ajayi Crowther. Slave ships were often impounded by the British Naval Squadron about 800 miles and sometimes twice that distance from Freetown, and led under escort for the long and perilous journey to Sierra Leone. Many died on the voyage. Some were children when they were enslaved. One such was John Wright of Hastings, captured at the age of six at Ilaro in Yorubaland. He spent eight years in servitude passing from hand to hand before being sold into the international slave market. He began the long voyage to the New World, but was seized by a British cruiser of the Preventive Squadron. The ship was brought to Freetown where it and its cargo were condemned. John Wright was freed and, at the age of fifteen, sent to school at Waterloo in 1838.

A more famous case was that of Samuel Ajayi Crowther whose connection with the Niger Mission is examined in chapter 7. Crowther hailed from the Yoruba town of Oshogun which was attacked by Muslim forces loyal to the Fulani Caliphate of Sokoto and forced to capitulate and accept humiliating surrender terms imposed on it by the Muslim victors. Women and children were captured and enslaved, and the town was left in smouldering ruins. One of those taken captive was Ajayi Crowther, then aged fifteen, who changed hands several times before being sold to a Portuguese ship in April 1822. But before the ship could sail it was seized by the British Preventive Squadron and led into Freetown harbour. Ajayi Crowther was taken off it along with the other slaves, enfranchised and taken to Bathurst village where he was given the name Samuel Crowther after a missionary benefactor. In 1826 this missionary took him to England for a few months and on his return he was employed as a teacher at Bathurst before being taken into the Christian Institution at Leicester, which had been set up, under Butscher and others, as a training school for recaptive children. A promising few, like Crowther, went on to train as teachers and missionaries. Crowther left the Institution with his wife and in 1829 went to Regent as schoolmaster, then to Wellington. Used to good effect as an agent of the CMS, Crowther joined others in urging that Society to undertake an active mission to hinterland Africa. The dream of a Niger Mission, largely that of Thomas Fowell Buxton, was born out of this pressure. Crowther, as will be made clear later, took a leading part in that mission, largely at the insistence of Henry Venn. He was sent to the CMS training college in London, ordained a priest in October 1843 and, before returning, published a *Vocabulary of the Yoruba*

Language. Back in Freetown he preached in Yoruba to meetings in Kissy, attracting interested Muslim inquirers. Crowther's own views on Islam were uncompromising, but no more so than the missionaries of his time. He returned to Abeokuta in 1845 where he met his mother and sisters. In 1864 the Fourah Bay Institution, renamed Fourah Bay College, was re-opened amid CMS doubts about its value, (see Chapter 6) and Samuel Ajayi Crowther, who had been its first pupil, paid it a visit. Crowther was consecrated in Canterbury Cathedral in June 1864, as Bishop of West African countries beyond British jurisdiction. He ended his days in Nigeria where, in humiliating circumstances, he was compelled to relinquish responsibility for the Niger Mission, and died in December 1899, aged over 90.

Religious groups in the Freetown settlement

A brief sketch of the main religious groups among the settlers in Freetown may be provided at this stage. Four denominations are involved: the Baptists, the members of the Countess of Huntingdon's Connection, the Methodists and the Quakers. Although the Swedenborgians had a representative in Afzelius, they had no mission or church in Freetown.

The Baptists. The man who led the Baptist community was David George, born in the 1740s to slave parents on a Georgia plantation, where he was converted. He fought in the Revolutionary War as a loyalist, and paid the price of defeat, fleeing to Nova Scotia where he founded a Baptist Church at Shellburne in 1782. He was driven from there for baptising a white woman, but carried on preaching in the area and later in New Brunswick. When Thomas Peters returned from London with the idea of gathering Nova Scotian blacks for re-settlement in Sierra Leone, George made up his mind to emigrate, together with his Baptist congregation. When he arrived in Freetown he built a Baptist chapel and led his people in relations with John Clarkson, the first Governor of the Colony. When Clarkson left for London, David George accompanied him with the intention of meeting English Baptists and seeking support for the work in Sierra Leone; the English Baptists donated some money for the building of a church and promised help to train a local candidate for the Baptist pastorate. George also desired to undertake missionary work among the adjacent Temne, but unrest there prevented work from starting. A man of obvious enterprise and devotion to the cause, David George contributed immensely to the awakening of missionary opportunity in Africa, with himself setting the example. When he died in 1810 he was succeeded as leader of the Baptist flock by Thomas Peters with whom he had sailed from Nova Scotia.

The Countess of Huntingdon's Connection. Selina Countess of Huntingdon had led a dissident group within the Established Church in England in the eighteenth century, stirred by the Methodist revival. Some of her supporters went to the American colonies and spread the movement three. A member of the Connection ordained by Lady Huntingdon herself, John Marrant was an Afro-American born to free parents in Charleston, South Carolina. He served in the British Navy and, wounded in action, he left the U.S. for London and subsequently Nova Scotia, taking with him his attachment to the Connection. He died in London in 1791, and the leadership in Nova Scotia fell to Cato Perkins, who was to distinguish himself as spokesman for aggrieved Nova Scotians against officials of the Sierra Leone Company and was to lead a protest group to London with a petition in 1793. The Huntingdonians later joined the settler rebellion against the government when the petition was refused. William Ash, a Connectional leader, died by drowning in 1801. Cato Perkins died four years later and the leadership passed to John Ellis, a Maroon from Jamaica via Nova Scotia; Ellis lived to an old age, dying in 1839, when he was succeeded by Anthony Elliott who had arrived as a boy from Nova Scotia. However, in 1825 John Ellis had written to the Connectional Conference in England, asking for a formal relationship to be established between the two — without result. Then after 1839 two members of the Freetown congregation visited London, somewhat reviving interest among members of the London chapel in their African co-religionists whom they described as their 'sable' brethren. But again, apart from such pleasant sentiments, little was achieved by the visit.

Under Elliott's leadership the congregation grew, with chapels in half a dozen villages around the Freetown peninsula where schools were also maintained. The preachers and superintendents of the Connection were in secular employment and gave their services to the Church free, thus sparing their congregation what would have been a heavy burden of support. But the rapid increase in numbers following the re-settlement of the recaptives in the villages made it necessary urgently to seek outside help. Elliott besought London with letters of request for help, but all in vain. Then in 1850 a son of Elliott was in London and met some members of the Connection Committee who relented and agreed to invite an older son of the leader to visit England. This led to the visit of John Elliott, who spoke to the Annual Conference and surprised members of the Connection with what he told them of the strength of local congregations in Sierra Leone. There were at the time eleven chapels, forty-eight preachers and eighty-nine class leaders, all of them governed by Huntingdonian articles and code of discipline. In 1852 a local preacher, Scipio Wright, was brought to England and ordained into the ministry of the Connection. In 1853 the Huntingdonians sent an English minister, the Rev. George Fowler, who reorganised the Church administration and opened a part-time institution for ministerial training. He spent a year doing this before returning to England. The people returned to the normal pattern of having to get on with the work without missionary help.

The local members of the Connection were aware of what their unaided efforts had advised in the missionary extension of the Church, and they committed themselves to the missionary task of the Connection. One of them wrote, with such sentiments on his mind. 'All hearts were glad to see the Gospel carried by black men to black men, for the first time without any European being present.'[6] He was right to sense the efficacy of African agency in the spread of Christianity.

The Methodists. Methodism was prominent in the drive to recruit settlers in Nova Scotia, where John Clarkson used the chapel in Birch Town to appeal for volunteers. In 1791 he called on the Black population to come to Sierra Leone, promising them free land. The Wesleyan leader of the Nova Scotians was the patriarchal Moses Wilkinson, already blind and lame, but determined to lead his people home. His companion and foremost preacher was Luke Jordan. Wilkinson, like Jordan, had been a slave on a Virginia plantation, and had escaped during the war, coming to Nova Scotia, and the two of them had travelled together from Nova Scotia, Jordan becoming a 'captain' or headman of a company during the voyage. Once in Sierra Leone the Methodists, under their leadership, defended Settler rights against the Company and ordered their members not to pay quit rent, a form of taxation they saw as a denial of their free status and a repudiation of the promise made to them before they left Nova Scotia. It was an understandable over-reaction born of deep distrust of officialdom which had twice betrayed them — first on the slave plantations of America and later in Nova Scotia. The Nova Scotian Methodists, reared in the independent spirit of a land without an Established Church, adopted a critical attitude towards the authorities. Their congregations continued to grow, and their system of Church government, with its class leader, exhorters, catechists, local preachers, synod and the weekly collection allowed them to expand on their own resources.

In 1798 they built a chapel, and there the old and infirm Moses Wilkinson preached his fervent sermons. Another leading preacher, Joseph Brown, wrote to the Wesleyan Conference in 1806 asking them for a missionary (who arrived in 1811), a decision prompted by the increasing burden of the work. Many were to regret having made such requests in view of the dictatorial attitude that some of the missionaries adopted; for example, John Garvin, who came out as a

6. Fyfe, *History of Sierra Leone* (1960), p. 260.

teacher in 1793, stayed on as preacher after he resigned from the Company and tried to turn Wilkinson's own people against him. John Ezzidio, already described, suffered an even worse fate at the hands of a missionary he had himself requested. Although missionaries eventually arrived, a long delay always ensued between the request and the response, by which time the local congregations had learnt to get on without them. When confronted with official moves to disband their chapel in 1821, the local Methodists formed a new society and met in their own place of worship, the Rawdon Street Chapel, completely unconnected with the Wesleyan Conference in England. Even in the villages outside Freetown, where missionaries were well received, local Methodists continued to take a leading role. John Lambert, a man of African descent, discharged from the military, started the first Methodist class meeting in Sierra Leone. Many continued to work actively in education, opening schools, providing money to operate them and training as teachers to run them. Many more were well-to-do, a few of them highly influential men in public affairs. One of the most successful of them was Sir Samuel Lewis, on whom more will be said in a later chapter.

The Maroons, described above, also formed their own congregation. Charles Saw obtained a plot of land to build a church, of which the walls and roof were raised in 1822. After completion the building was let out for fourteen years to the Wesleyan missionaries, rather then being given to them outright; the Maroons, like the Nova Scotians, were unwilling to allow the missionaries unfettered control over their religious affairs.

The recaptives later split away from the Nova Scotians and, under Anthony O'Connor, an African, went on in 1844 to form the independent West African Methodist Society, one of the first African Independent Churches. In 1835, when the lease of the Maroon chapel was up for renewal, the missionaries refused the terms demanded and walked out of the Church. Thenceforth the Maroons worshipped under their own pastor, John Gray. The several congregations in the villages — over 2,000 strong — under the Nova Scotian preachers Joseph Jewett and Prince Stober joined them in the secession, leaving only a small Settler remnant at Rawdon Street.

The Quakers and other religious interests. There were many other individuals who came to Sierra Leone to better their personal circumstances, certainly, but also to repay their debt to Africa, and their idealism and commitment saved them from failure or ruin when nothing else justified the continuance of the Freetown experiment. One former slave who had made the journey from Nova Scotia went to his original village and met the man who had sold him; he gave him a present for having been unwittingly the instrument of his becoming a Christian. Henry Washington, a former slave of George

Washington, the first President of the United States, came to Freetown determined to improve his situation by embarking on scientific farming. There was Paul Cuffee, formerly of New Bedford, Massachusetts — a pious and industrious Quaker who traded with his own boats. In 1810 he crossed the Atlantic in his brig *Traveller,* with the intention of establishing a trading base in West Africa, but soon after arriving in Freetown he received letters from Wilberforce and from William Allen, a fellow-Quaker, inviting him to England. He returned to Freetown in 1811 and induced one of the Methodist groups to organise themselves into a co-operative trading society which would grow or buy produce to sell abroad directly and thus break the monopoly of European merchants. The contacts Cuffee had established in London would act as agents and brokers. The scheme appealed immediately to the sturdy Settlers, and a prominent Methodist, John Kizzell, became the first president of the Friendly Society of Sierra Leone, as the co-operative was formally known.

Cuffee returned to America with the idea of leading out a batch of Afro-Americans who by their example of dedication and skill would stimulate enterprise in Freetown and strengthen links with Africa. But the war of 1812 interrupted his plans, and he was only able to return to Freetown in 1816. When he did so, he came with a sawmill, trade goods and thirty-four settlers, some of them skilled artisans. He went back to America with African produce which he tried to sell at a profit, planning with the proceeds to buy goods to take back to Sierra Leone, but the scheme failed for he could only sell the African produce at a loss. He himself died soon afterwards in 1817, and his Friendly Society declined permanently. But the American Colonization Society, jolted into action to some extent by Cuffee's ideas, resumed the experiment of settling Afro-Americans in West Africa, a scheme from which Liberia was to be the direct result.

The story of Edward Jones, an Afro-American from Baltimore, Maryland, and an ordained priest of the Episcopal Church of America, fits into this pattern. In 1831 he came out to Freetown as a schoolmaster. He went to Kent village on the south-western tip of the Freetown peninsula, and from there to the Banana Islands further south. He married the daughter of Nylander, the pioneer missionary of the CMS. From Baltimore too came the Rev. Daniel Coker, an Afro-American and a co-founder of the African Methodist Episcopal Church who accompanied the first batch of settlers of the American Colonization Society; he went to live in Sherbro Island and later moved to Yoni. Thomas Macfoy, an Afro-West Indian, came with his family in 1818. He became Superintendent of Wellington Village and later, when the Methodists were expanding, he along with a few others received a local preacher's licence and was put in charge of the mission of the local church.

Freetown and the stimulus to mission: Badagry and Abeokuta

In 1837 two Hausa men, emancipated in Trinidad, arrived in Freetown on their way to Badagry, at that time a slave mart in the Bight of Benin. Many in the recaptive population were encouraged by the plans of the Hausa men, and three recaptives bought a ship jointly, renamed her the *Queen Victoria,* furnished her with trade goods, and with sixty-seven passengers set sail on 1 April, 1839, bound for Badagry.

The voyage was a success, and on their return Thomas Will, the Aku king ('Aku' was a term very loosely applied to liberated slaves of Yoruba origin), supported by leading members of the Nupe and Hausa Creoles, petitioned the government to allow them start a colony at Badagry under British protection. They sought permission to trade and develop legitimate commerce and also to take Christianity to the Bight of Benin. They asked for a missionary to accompany them and help them in the new settlement. As one modern writer correctly puts it, 'the initiative was theirs, the plan conceived by Africans in Africa, not round a missionary society table in London'.[7] The British government refused to be involved in such an enterprise, 1,000 miles from Freetown, for they were anxious to avoid the implications of imperial expansion suggested by the scheme; however, they would not stop the people going privately. After overcoming initial fears about their personal safety, the recaptives resumed the mission to Badagry. Before long a stream of settlers started arriving there from Freetown, carried in ships owned by themselves and supported from their own funds. Their example inspired others, and a cycle of people coming and going between Freetown and Badagry was initiated.

John Langley, a recaptive of Ibo origin and an old friend of Crowther, raised money from local contributions to support the Niger Mission to his own people. The Niger Mission, apt to be neglected in hard times, went through a revival during the years of emigration to Badagry, and was in fact constructed out of the solid achievements of those who sustained the Badagry enterprise which proved that a venture into Nigeria was both viable and necessary. One of the first emigrants to Badagry was James Ferguson, a Wesleyan Methodist convert. Impressed with what he first saw, he wrote encouragingly to the Wesleyan Missionary Society in London asking for a missionary to be sent out. In Freetown Wesleyan recaptives started a fund to pay for work in Badagry. In 1842 the Rev. Thomas Birch Freeman, technically from the same background as those of the 'Black Poor', a Wesleyan missionary based at Cape Coast, visited Badagry and reorganised the recaptives there in a congregation. He also went further inland to Abeokuta, where he

7. Fyfe, *History of Sierra Leone* (1962), p.212.

celebrated the first Eucharist in the palace of the king, who received him warmly.

At Hastings Village, prospective emigrants appealed to the CMS for a missionary to accompany them. The man chosen, Henry Townsend, had his passage paid by the three Aku men who owned the ship in which they all sailed: he was later to prove a thorn in Crowther's flesh. A leading Christian layman from Hastings, Andrew Wilhelm, sailed too, his passage paid by church members. Townsend returned to London from Badagry via Abeokuta to urge the CMS to enter the extended field permanently. Wilhelm returned to Freetown, and at Hastings gathered a large group of church members and led them to Badagry; before he left he presented his house at Hastings to the CMS as a thank-offering. The tide of emigration, begun so sluggishly, started to swell. Many Egba recaptives decided to return home to Abeokuta. Some went singly, others as families. Townsend met a woman at Abeokuta who had left her husband at Hastings only to regain the husband she had originally had before her captivity, and was now comfortably established as a dye trader. Some recaptives went to Cape Palmas as builders, some to Fernando Po as accountants and clerks, and others even further afield.

There was a significant Muslim element among the emigrants. One example may suffice. Muhammad Savage, the Muslim Aku headman at Fourah Bay in the east end of Freetown, bought ships and got at least fifty of his people to sail in a group to Badagry. Among this group was Muhammad Shitta Bey, then aged fourteen, who became a successful trader in the Niger and turned into a generous patron of Islamic religious causes. In 1885 he built a splendid mosque in Lagos for £4,000, and contributed generously to the building of the equally splendid Fourah Bay Mosque at Freetown in 1892. Appropriately he received a decoration from the Sultan of Turkey for his liberality. The Islamic religious theme is developed further in Chapter 8 below.

To return to the Christian theme, recaptives in Freetown went on to show an enthusiastic interest in their fellow-countrymen in Nigeria in spite of the lack of governmental or missionary encouragement. They set about a vigorous campaign of fund-raising in order to build a 'Freetown Church' in Abeokuta. Nigerian recaptives led exemplary lives of piety in Freetown. A Hausa recaptive, called Emmanuel Cline (after a German missionary), amassed a huge fortune from trading in the 1830s and when he died in 1858, he left the CMS the land needed to build a church. This was on his vast estate at what came to be known as Cline Town. Faced with such examples of devoted Christian service, the fainthearted CMS was stirred into life. Steps were taken to revive educational work in Freetown and to press ahead with the Church's wider mission. The corrosive effect of

European influence on Christians, fear of which had caused the mission to hold back, had clearly been exaggerated. Perhaps the missionaries had instinctively felt too that Creole success at adapting Western influence to African conditions might make them unnecessary. Both fears were unjustified. Nigeria was to prove one of the most significant fields for the missionary enterprise, and all due credit should go to the unsung heroes of the first outreach from Freetown.

The Freetown religious setting: Christianity and African religions

A natural question to which we must now turn is how the Christianity of the settlers interacted with African religious practices. This is only a small strand of the wider inter-religious mesh with which Chapter 8 below is concerned. Its Freetownian manifestation needs to be briefly unravelled.

The recaptives preserved a great deal of their religious customs and traditional practices although they were living in villages which were self-consciously Christian. The village organisation in fact acted as a stimulus for the re-assertion of African values, both religious and secular, with village companies serving a role similar to traditional political institutions. The interests that developed around these companies became a screen behind which the recaptives perpetuated ancient practices. Sometimes the authorities, alerted by instances of betrayal or vengeful 'leaks', stepped in to proscribe a company or benefit society as 'un-Christian' and dangerous. But they were dealing with the tip of the iceberg; most of the time they remained oblivious to the mass of activity going on away from the censorious eyes of officialdom. Much of that hidden phenomenon is surprisingly accessible through the comments and observations of contemporary witnesses. The details given here are intended merely to show that African religions continued to possess a vitality which Christianity did not destroy. It can be convincingly argued that the religious culture of Christianity, as opposed to the political role missionaries contrived to impose on it and one which many African writers have uncritically accepted, contained at its core a magnetic appeal for the old religions. From this perspective it is not surprising that traditional religious practices thrived in areas deeply influenced by Christian teaching.

Mende traditional worshippers, in the village of Sussex, in an attempt to secure a state of amicable co-existence with official Christianity, met for worship at an alternative time on Sunday mornings in 1851 to avoid a clash with the Methodist missionary. Two CMS missionaries encountered an impressive sacred image in Kissy in 1833, with bloodstained face, two horns, and a large bowl placed before it half full of chicken blood. In two smallpox outbreaks, one at Aberdeen in 1857 and the other at Fourah Bay in 1859, traditional religious powers were sought by the local inhabitants, including Christians; at Aberdeen a sheep was sacrificed and at Fourah Bay kola nuts were used in divination. Both Crowther and his distinguished colleague, the Rev. (later Bishop) James Johnson, also of the Niger Mission, were deeply involved in arguments about African religions: for them too, these religions were real enough to deserve serious attention. Among the recaptives of Yoruba origin, the Aku, Crowther found the cult of Shango, the Yoruba god of thunder and lightning, particularly strong. In addition the system of Ifa divination was well preserved and widely patronised. One Ifa diviner answered Crowther's persistent criticism by saying that he could not give up his trade, that he could not consent to give his medicine to any applicant without consulting his god as to whether he should give it or not; as Ifa directed, so he would act. In other words, his profession was based on the highest principles of ethical conduct. The diviner, far from being on the defensive, had acquired a new confidence in the face of the Christian challenge. Another Ifa diviner asked the missionaries to be content with a gesture of conciliation: he had decided to incorporate Jesus Christ into the Ifa system. He told them that he asked his clients, before making any sacrifice to the gods, first to call upon the name of Jesus Christ — a piece of bold syncretism which this time put the missionaries on the defensive. The reasoning of the Ifa diviners was clear. They argued that, since their gods existed for the good of mankind, to devote attention to them must necessarily be in harmony with the worship of the God of Christianity, and they told Crowther as much. Crowther may have continued to hold to the hard line on this matter, but there is evidence that Johnson, less inhibited by public responsibility, took the lesson to heart. Both he and Crowther reported the existence in Freetown itself of a prominent shrine for Shango, where Crowther was treated to an impressive display of devotion to Shango, and where occasionally a ram was sacrificed.

Evidence of continuing devotion to Shango through the nineteenth century is available from the sources. For example, James Johnson reported that every Friday there was a solemn ceremony involving a large procession of people, with a man leading the worshippers who was dressed in female clothes and carried an axe — the traditional emblem of the god of thunder — across his shoulders. He had in his hair two or three feathers coloured white, red and black. His followers danced and sang wildly in praise of Shango. When Johnson tried to confront the devotees of the cult, an elderly man dismissed him with the telling retort that Johnson's relative youth and his status as a paid servant of the missionaries disqualified him from passing any judgement on the rites. Such encounters were to leave their mark on the man.

Even Hastings, that fitting ornament of African Christianity orthodoxy, was not too proud to be adorned with the seamless robe of ancestor worship. According to one estimate, the largest number of traditional religious worshippers was at Hastings. In 1831 there were four separate sacred Yoruba shrines there, with a predominance of religious twin figures *(Ibeji)*. Most women who gave birth to twins placed them under the protection of these figures, which were intricately carved and stood about eighteen inches high. In 1844 a Christian woman had twins who subsequently died, and complained bitterly to the resident missionary that the Church must bear the blame since it had prohibited her from getting the aid of the sacred twin figures, which she was convinced would have preserved her babies. It is remarkable that she followed missionary advice in the first place, but there is little doubt about where she thought real spiritual power lay. Still at Hastings, divination by kola nuts to determine the efficacy of an offering was widely resorted to. Funeral rites were deeply influenced by traditional religious customs: the bereaved and their sympathisers gathered at night and made the requisite sacrifices, consisting among other things of sheep, fowls, rice and rum. They concluded with a feast at home. Shango, Elagba (described as some sort of *agent provocateur* or 'devil') and Oshun, goddess of water and a consort of Shango, were the most prominent divinities at Hastings. Notwithstanding the official prominence of Christianity, Hastings was inextricably immersed in a plural religious world. Rather than seeing Christianity as a suppressive force, we should recognise its spiritual stimulus on local religious enterprise.

Hastings also boasted a number of powerful secret societies, the best organised being the *Agugu,* known in Yorubaland, its place of origin, as *Engungun* or *Egun.* It was a masquerade dance society, wielding considerable influence and power. Strenuous efforts were made to break up the society at Hastings, but the Yoruba recaptives stubbornly resisted concerted government and missionary pressure. Some idea of the resilience of the society may be gathered from the following account.

The *Egun* was believed to inhabit an invisible world of spirits. It was in fact the spirit of a dead person coming back into the world at periodic intervals to punish and reward, according to their deserts, those who remained behind. The trance-like movements of the dance induced in the *Egun* masked figure the power to see and detect evil while remaining anonymous to the spectators, and in the course of it the masked figure made startling revelations of what had occurred in the town. On the basis of this power of detection, real control was exerted over the behaviour and loyalty of the people. It assumed some of the characteristics of a political organisation, thus provoking official reaction. Oral traditions in Hastings have preserved the local version of a contest between *Egun* and missionary opposition. According to these traditions a missionary of the CMS decided to confront an *Agugu* dance by physically attacking the masked figure, 'but he only flogged a mass of empty Egugu clothes. The bodies inside the clothes had mysteriously. . . vanished. The missionary marched back to the Parsonage; his whip had dropped, but a broom belonging to one of the. . . Egugu escorts followed him to the Parsonage, gyrating, in fact executing a little dance of its own behind the worthy Cleric's back'.[8] The missionary was being challenged to do spiritual combat on a ground not of his choosing; however we define his role, whether as the disguised front of Western secularism or the lofty symbol of a Scriptural religion, he was compelled to acquit himself in the language and style recognised by his hosts. He produced a Bible, much as if it might have been a cult object, and flourished it in the face of the pursuing broom, which consequently fled from the scene, leaving the missionary unharmed. Convinced that he had demonstrated the superiority of Christianity, the missionary had missed completely the obvious implication that Christianity could engage indigenous customs only by itself being transformed into familiar categories of apprehension. The Bible as a symbol of spirit power was drawn alongside the gyrating broom infused with similar power. At his place of residence, the missionary was within the proper limits of the spirit power of the Bible, with the retreating broom conceding the point. Thus *Egun* and Christianity, at least in local perception, were debating and competing within a common spiritual discourse, rather than about whether such a spiritual world existed at all.

The implications of such an encounter for the subsequent transformation of Christianity in Africa should be self-evident, and need no further elaboration at this point. Its meaning for the phenomenon of the history of religious pluralism in Africa deserves fuller treatment elsewhere. Clearly local religions continued to play a critical role in the assimilation of Christianity, and by neglecting them, or at any rate by relegating them to an inferior position, we have lost an essential component in the indigenous religious heritage, which constituted a vital factor in the religious motivation and perception of Africans. It is a grave loss that has removed from serious scholarly attention a significant part of the wider religious world. It is a state of affairs that has done nothing to clarify the process of religious conversion, which hitherto has been viewed in extremely narrow, exclusivistic terms and has been sustained by assumptions of the intrinsically triumphant character of the truth claims of Scriptural religion. The matter needs urgent investigation in its many aspects and across the academic disciplines, for there is not necessarily one superior way of representing the human enterprise.

8. Peterson (1969), p.266.

The African contribution to the new phenomenon of religious pluralism may represent a major initiative, if only because the traditional religious world-view is not constructed out of the defeat and domination of others. Unlike the missionary religions of Christianity and Islam, which entered the African continent from outside, African religions do not require the ruin and disintegration of other cultures for their claims to be valid, nor do they commit the fallacy of propounding a universal truth and mobilising behind it an ethnocentric vehicle for political, economic and cultural imperialism.

The other point relates to the preceding. The historic meeting of different religions in Africa should help to provide a positive framework for cross-religious influences. It should thus enable us to abandon an adversary view of religious pluralism. No longer is it the case that the two missionary religions, Christianity and Islam, are poised for wresting statistical advantage from each other, with traditional religions fit only to be plucked. The truth of the matter is the other way. Traditional religions have penetrated both Christianity and Islam and endowed them with a tolerant, absorptive capacity. An atmosphere of hospitality has consequently been generated in which Christianity and Islam, along with the older religious cultures, are made to share in an open, inclusive community without a repudiation of particularity. In this sense traditional religions have performed a universal mission towards Christianity and Islam. Indigenous religions have thus coped with external pressure by genuine response. By contrast, Christianity and Islam have not always been as confident in the new atmosphere of pluralism. Their controversial pronouncements indeed suggest that it is they who felt threatened. Propounding a universal creed, Christianity and Islam were in risk of being repudiated for not being able to adapt locally; the universal way of truth they preached appeared to have evoked an attitude of inflexibility towards other cultures. It was Africa's inherited religious traditions which, for all their close ethnic ties, prepared the ground for mutual tolerance. In places where Christianity or Islam was the preponderant influence, such as in North Africa or in Europe, the atmosphere for inter-religious encounter is correspondingly more difficult.

Tribal religion has obvious limitations, but none could be more disadvantageous than those which prevent Christianity or Islam from entering more creatively into the process of inter-religious encounter. Similarly, the view of traditional religions as basically simple and static has to be abandoned. It is no more than a myth to say that it was only with the arrival of Christianity and Islam upon the scene that these indigenous traditions were rudely awakened from their inherent slumber and launched on an evolutionary career towards their ultimate extinction. Why we should devise weighty academic scales to reckon with such chaff is one of the side-effects of that primary bias. By tilting in that direction we have abandoned the main ground on which African religions continued to exercise a powerful influence on Christianity and Islam. Equally significant, these so-called tribal religions have weathered the storm of alien transplantation and struck fresh roots in foreign climes. In Freetown we have some unique opportunities to observe at close hand the stimulating effects of such transplantation on traditional religions. Something of the same range and resilience may be seen in the wider context of trans-Atlantic religious materials in Brazil, the Caribbean and, to a degree, the United States.

Some indication, however brief, ought to be given of the underlying strength of African religions in spite of great diversity. These religions share a unity of outlook on the reality of the spiritual world. They also require — and foster — an essentially tolerant nature of human community, holding a balance between individual responsibility and fulfilment on the one hand, and, on the other, community solidarity. The individual is the custodian of community values, while the community for its turn is the guarantor of collective wellbeing. Now the way forward for Christianity or Islam is through such a heritage of responsibility and relationship, loopholes through which external influences might be absorbed and assimilated. If, for example, Christians can learn the valuable lesson of commitment through mutual tolerance, they would not only learn to relate meaningfully to their particular environment but they would also overturn the divisive measure of exclusiveness by which official Christianity might attempt to impose itself.

The historical reality of religions in Africa suggests that this is not mere wishful thinking. There is in fact a direct correlation between indigenous religious vitality and heightened Christian activity. This should prompt us to look for areas of mutual influence rather than harp on themes of polarity and mutual exclusion. For example, revelation as a source of social and religious innovation might assume great prominence with the availability of the vernacular Bible, with the Sacred Text acting to fix and warrant change. Yet if we look through traditional religions we should find a corresponding category, such as, for example, the oracles and the divinatory techniques whereby religious communities anticipated or justified change and new initiatives. Of the reality of this ancient religious tradition in Freetown and of its significance for Christian communities there can be no dispute. A more delicate matter, however, is to try to judge whether — and, if so, how — Christianity might be seen in turn as a stimulus, a constraint and a force for identity, alienation or fulfilment. Some attention is paid to this subject in Chapter 8. By whichever way we finally proceed, we should give a significant portion of the credit for the success of the Sierra Leone experiment to the quiet but no less tenacious influence of

African religions which helped to shape and deepen a sense of community on the basis of which Christianity could be introduced and made to take root. True, missionary critics strained every nerve to deprecate traditional religions: where these religions showed resistance they were to be put down as grave evils, and where they showed only a faint interest in Christianity they should be denounced as fakes. But none would question the alert and attentive spirit Africans brought to religious issues. Christianity arrived in the heart of local culture by this original predisposition of Africans. We should therefore not allow missionary criticisms and denunciations to mislead us about the resilience of indigenous traditions, nor should we overlook their facilitating role in the successful implantation of Christianity. Indeed, even in the case of Islam which, as will be made clearer in Chapter 8, created a revolutionary tradition of ideological opposition to African religions, local religious predispositions survived deep into the heart of orthodox practice. The political defeat of traditional institutions at the hands of Muslim militants had by no means removed every trace of the ancient religious heritage. The essential point, on which we must conclude this section, is that in the most hostile environment, whether Christian or Islamic, African religions continued to exercise a profound influence on the behaviour and perception of religious communities. So much of the originality of the settler communities in Freetown must have derived from this ancient religious culture.

The founding of Liberia

The issue of Emancipation in the United States. As early as 1781, Thomas Jefferson, a slave owner himself, wrote to urge the abolition of slavery on the grounds of political expediency and through moral suasion. He considered slavery a 'great political and moral evil' and a 'blot in this country'.[9] But his qualms on the matter, even if they were more than just private thoughts, lacked anything like popular support, and very few public men identified with the idea of general emancipation. Jefferson then proposed that those slaves who were emancipated should be found a 'faraway' place, to be chosen 'as the circumstances of the time should render most proper'.[10] That aspect of his thoughts on the matter appealed to other politicians, and a scheme was proposed whereby emancipated slaves could be repatriated to places outside the United States — Haiti and Africa being areas which most had in mind.

Pressure was mounting on the Southern States to give attention to the matter because many of the New England States had taken

9. Cassell (1970), p.13.
10. ibid.

action. It was there that Black organisations were set up to foment the sentiment for repatriation, or what was then called 'colonization'. The desire for a return to Africa was kept. alive by so-called 'outlandish' Africans, namely those slaves recently brought to the United States from the African continent. In 1773, for example, four recently arrived slaves petitioned the Massachusetts legislature concerning their desire to find enough money to finance a scheme whereby they could return to Africa and found a settlement. In 1783 Blacks in Boston and Newport, Rhode Island, were organising themselves and articulating a desire to go back to Africa. In Rhode Island the sentiment of African colonization ran deep. In 1773 Ezra Stiles, a future President of Yale College, was urging the need for a colonization scheme in Africa, and a powerful advocate of the idea was the African Union Society of Newport, a Black organisation set up in 1780. In 1787 the Society proposed a plan to settle Blacks in Africa and got in touch with the Quaker, William Thornton, already involved in the Freetown settlement plan. When eventually the Province of Freedom was established in Sierra Leone, the Newport Blacks were reluctant to embrace the scheme, fearing that it concealed British imperialist ambitions rather than being what it set out to be, namely a free, autonomous Black homeland. The strength of feeling among New England Blacks on the desirability of emigrating to Africa and the clarity with which they expressed their ultimate political aims proved to be a weakness, for White philanthropists were unwilling to sponsor something that would repudiate the whole basis of White collaboration.

Repatriation to Africa. Repatriation to Africa under some scheme of colonization was the only answer many felt to the increasing problem of what to do with free Blacks, of whom in 1790 there were estimated to be about 60,000 in the United States. By 1820 the number had increased to 250,000. However, although theoretically free, prejudices more powerful than legal theory continued to suppress the liberty of this new social class. Robert S. Finley, a Presbyterian minister from New Jersey, rallied public opinion behind a proposal to found a settlement in Africa, and made direct contact with Paul Cuffee whose experience of life in West Africa he tried to exploit for his scheme. He wrote to Cuffee: 'The great desire of those whose minds are impressed with the subject is to give opportunity to the free people of color to rise to their proper level and at the same time to provide a powerful means of putting an end to the slave trade, and sending civilization and Christianity to Africa.'[11] It was from his exertions that the American Colonization Society was formed in 1816. Finley had envisaged that colonization was merely one side of the coin of which the other side was emancipation, and that indeed

11. Miller (1975), p.45.

was how many Blacks, still in slavery, interpreted — or, better, misinterpreted — the African scheme. Cuffee's response was to encourage Finley and his associates to look to Sherbro, then under John Kizzell. Between them John Kizzell and Paul Cuffee strengthened the case for a West African settlement, although Cuffee was inclined to explore an alternative site to Sierra Leone. As soon as the proposal started to generate a momentum of its own, however, voices were raised in the Black community against the removal of free Blacks from White America and their concentration elsewhere, either in the United States or in Africa. But the momentum could not now be stopped, and only practical considerations stood in the way. In May 1818 a reconnaissance trip to Sierra Leone and the Sherbro was undertaken for the Colonization Society by the Rev Samuel Mills of the American Bible Society and Dr Ebenezer Burgess of the University of Vermont. The report they later presented recommended Sherbro for a settlement, with Paul Cuffee as governor. The report went to Congress in Washington for action, but in the end Congress refused to act. A little later, however, President James Monroe threw his considerable weight behind the scheme and brought closer the day of its fulfilment. In 1819 he announced to Congress that two government agents were proceeding to West Africa to launch the scheme for a settlement of American Blacks.

The first step towards establishment of settlement in Africa. In February 1820 an expedition set out from New York bound for West Africa, led by the Rev. Samuel Bacon, an Episcopal clergyman and the principal government agent, and John P. Bankson, his assistant. They were accompanied by a representative of the Colonization Society, Dr Samuel A. Crozer. There were eighty-eight migrants on the voyage. The party proceeded by way of Sierra Leone and landed at Sherbro, at a place called Campelar — which, however, proved to be a fiery furnace, where the colonists were subject to extreme privation. Instead of the promised land overspilling with superabundance, the migrants found marsh and mud exuding disease. All the agents and more than twenty of the migrants died. The remainder struggled to their feet and went to Freetown to await fresh instructions. New agents were meanwhile sent out to prospect for an alternative site.

The man charged with finding a new site was Dr Eli Ayres. He was to be assisted by an officer of the United States Navy, Lieutenant Robert F. Stockton. They arrived at Cape Mesurado in December 1821, and entered into protracted negotiations with King Peter, the local ruler. The Americans, with preconceptions about Africa and convinced of the loftiness of their motives, floundered badly in the diplomatic quicksands of chiefly protocol. Worn down by King Peter's delaying tactics and impatient to force a bargain, Lieutenant Stockton produced a pistol and pointed it at the head of the petrified king and demanded a prompt end to discussions. The king capitulated and accepted the terms imposed on him. By that measure the Americans acquired, as they were to boast later, $1 million worth of land for a paltry $300 worth of trinkets, food, guns and rum. Thus it was that Liberia, willed into being by strong-arm tactics, became the collecting point for Blacks from the New World.

The settlers who had taken refuge in Sierra Leone were gathered and put aboard ship bound for Liberia ('Land of the Free'). When they arrived, they chose a spot which they called Monrovia after James Monroe, the U.S. President. The usual hardship afflicted the first settlers. The island on which they landed was without fresh water and firewood, and was exposed to attack. Disease afflicted them in their small huddle, but those who survived and could gather enough strength began making a clearing of the wild vegetation around, conscious that they were now living in hostile territory. They set about cultivating their own food and setting up dwellings. Within a short time, twenty-two buildings were erected. Dr Ayres, concerned about the diminishing supplies of the settlement, left to obtain replenishment and put Elijah Johnson in charge. Like his Biblical namesake, Elijah Johnson was required, in the hostile circumstances of the settlement and the consequent drain on morale, to reassure the small remnant and carry on some delicate political organising with surrounding rulers. Johnson's companion at this time was Lott Carey, a Black Baptist preacher from Virginia, and together they helped the settlers to move over to the mainland.

In August 1822, the Colonization Society sent its White agent, Jehudi Ashmun, who organised the settlement along more military lines, aware of the overwhelming need for defence. Prejudiced by the manner of its creation, the settlement spent the early period of its history organising for war and engaging in action. As viewed by the unreconciled local rulers, it was a humiliating concession wrung from them by high-handed action and now extended over the mainland in provocative proximity to its dispossessed owners. It was twice attacked by King Peter and his allies, and each time the attack was repelled. At one time the settlers, conscious of the value of diplomatic initiative in heading off future attacks, sought the help of King Boatswain, a powerful Mandinka ruler whose authority extended down to the coast from his hinterland capital; he appeared in person and handed down word that the Dey people on whose land the settlement was established should henceforth desist from trying to recover their land. In April 1822, shortly after this decisive intervention, the settlers moved to the mainland.

The intervention of a ruler powerful enough to restrain the Dey people could not prevent others from removing what was considered a threat to internal political stability. Who could know where such territorial encroachment would end? In early November 1822, an attack was organised against the settlement and repelled. A few days later another attack was launched, but this one ended with the signing of a truce following the mediation of Major Laing and Captain Gordon on behalf of the Government of Sierra Leone.

External tranquility did not find its internal counterpart, and Ashmun became preoccupied with quarrels and dissension within the settlement. Such problems had always existed, right from Sherbro and the brief interlude in Freetown. The administrative control of the settlement and the supervisory functions exercised by White agents became a divisive factor — which does not concern us here, except for the way in which it emphasised in many people's minds that Blacks should not relinquish the initiative in a venture in which they had most to gain — and to lose. We should, of course, pursue this Black initiative without setting it in opposition to the overwhelming sense of racial injustice inflicted by Whites.

Ashmun recognised this problem right from the start although he was slow to deal effectively with it. He allocated some responsibility to the Afro-Americans. Elijah Johnson was made commissary of stores, in charge of rations and supplies; R. H. Simpson, a fifty-year-old man from Virginia who had purchased his freedom, was made commissary of ordnance; Lott Carey became health officer and government inspector. In fact Carey assumed great responsibility for the fledgling settlement, and we shall describe his contribution in greater detail presently.

Ashmun's administration did not succeed completely in checking settler disaffection, and it soon became obvious that he would not obtain their co-operation under the existing arrangement. The settlers rebelled twice, with Lott Carey at their head, and each time they seized food stores and arms. After the second revolt Ashmun left Monrovia for fear of his own safety. In July 1824, the American Colonization Society sent out an agent, the Rev. Ralph Randolph Gurley, to investigate the affairs of the settlement. The result was a face-saving device whereby Ashmun was left in control but with significantly reduced powers. An advisory council was created in which the settlers were given a share of power. One of the consequences was that Carey was made vice-agent for Liberia in 1826.

Lott Carey was born on a Virginia slave plantation about 1780, and was converted to Christianity in 1807. In 1813 he succeeded in purchasing his freedom and that of his two children for $850. Spurning prospects of settling down in America and earning a comfortable living, Carey embarked on the voyage to Africa determined to preach Christianity to his African brethren, and he subsequently took a leading part in the pioneering counsels of the settlement. The colony was badly exposed to both disease from within and attacks from without. Carey was active on both fronts, ministering to the sick and organising the defence of the settlement. The manner of his death in 1828 is characteristic of the unquenchable energy of the man. He was preparing for an impending attack by organising the arms cache when a lighted candle accidentally set the place afire. Carey died in the flames, and all the store was destroyed. His death was symptomatic also of the early destiny of the colony. Hailed as a marvellous invention, the early settlement still was unable to run smoothly; pressed to keep up with the neighbouring settlement of Sierra Leone, it had intermittent spurts of activity and, when a consignment of recruits arrived from America, where it received impressive publicity, it moved forward apprehensively. As a settlement it tried to proceed by the heroic exertions of those who viewed Christianity as an exclusive way of life. The local populations, aware that an inexorable force had entered the land, tried a collision course or else kept watch at a safe distance: they were not willing to smooth the way of Christianity's progress in the country.

Lott Carey was unique in appreciating some of the historic difficulties of the Liberian venture, and he made a gallant effort to escape the contradictions involved. A contemporary source which was inclined to attach seditious motives to any form of Black agitation was nevertheless moved to express appreciation of the value of Carey's contribution. 'To him', it wrote, 'was the colony indebted, more than to any other man, except Ashmun, for its preservation during the memorable defence of 1822.' It went on:

In order to relieve . . . the sufferings of the people, Mr Cary [*sic*] turned his attention to the diseases of the climate, made himself a good practical physician, and devoted his time almost exclusively to the relief of the destitute, the sick, and the afflicted. His services, as physician of the colony were invaluable, and for a long time, were rendered, without hope of reward, while he made liberal sacrifices of his property to the poor and distressed. But amid his multiplied cares and efforts, he never neglected to promote the objects of the African Missionary Society. He sought access to the native tribes, instructed them in the doctrines and duties of the Christian religion, and established a school for the education of their children. . . To found a Christian colony which might prove a blessed asylum. . . was with him an object with which no temporal good could be compared.[12]

Two stages of the fitful progress of the cause of Liberia should now be described. In the first we shall recount briefly the establishment of settler colonies outside Monrovia from 1825 till the end of the second decade of the settlement. This was to lead to the establishment of the Commonwealth of Liberia in 1839, a federation of the small settlements into a corporate political unit. The second stage is a recurrent motif that runs right through the history of the settlement,

12. Wilkeson (1839), pp. 37–8.

and it concerns individuals, some of independent means, who came to Liberia for ideological reasons. Such a theme emerges strongly from about 1829 and was to persist through to 1861 and beyond.

The establishment of settler colonies

One of the first settlements to be founded outside Monrovia was Caldwell. In March 1825, sixty-six emigrants arrived from Norfolk, Virginia and settled at Caldwell. Many fell ill immediately, and Lott Carey had to intervene with his invaluable medical experience. Only three died. In January and February 1826, more emigrants arrived from Boston and North Carolina and they also settled at Caldwell, where an agricultural society was formed the next year. A sister-colony was created at New Georgia at the same time as the Caldwell colony. By 1826 farming was prospering at both settlements: Caldwell had seventy-seven farms and New Georgia thirty-three. In 1827 schools were established under the direction of the Rev. G. McGill, an Afro-American teacher. Six schools were founded with an enrollment of 227 pupils, of whom forty-five were the children of indigenous Africans. Also in 1827, a school was opened among the Vai people, with thirty-five pupils, including the sons of chiefs and other rulers. Lott Carey's school was in the same vicinity, funded in part by the Baptist Missionary Society of Richmond.

In 1830 additional schools were established in Caldwell, and by 1834 the settlement was even more prosperous than Monrovia, and was paying good wages to its workers. By 1851 it grew so large that it had to be divided into Upper and Lower Caldwell. New Georgia also continued to grow. During 1832 a large number of recaptured Ibos and people from the Congo area were resettled there. Like Caldwell and the others, the settlement became a constituent member of the Commonwealth of Liberia.

Other settlements included Edina, where, in December 1832, thirty-eight colonists arrived. Situated in Bassa country, Edina enjoyed some autonomy, although Monrovia remained suzerain over its affairs. Another was the large tract of land acquired by the Maryland Colonization Society at Cape Palmas. For $1,000 the Society bought a large area from the rulers of Cape Palmas, Grand Cavalla and Garraway, and in February 1834, the first batch of settlers arrived. The official name of the settlement was Maryland in Liberia, and the new town founded by the settlers was named Harper.

Bassa Cove settlement followed in March 1835, pioneered jointly by the New York and Philadelphia Colonization Societies. There was a strong Quaker element in the Philadelphia Society, and among the first settlers there was an influential Quaker representation. The settlement received a baptism of fire. In June 1835, barely three months after its creation, it was attacked and sacked by the local people, and the survivors fled to Edina for safety. There were strong rumours at the time that the colourful French adventurer Theodore Conneau had a hand in the attack and was masterminding events behind the scenes. Peace was soon restored, although the wary settlers did not return for several months afterwards.

Marshall settlement, so named after the US Chief Justice, was begun in April 1837 by a group of colonists and recaptured Africans. Some 392 plots were neatly laid out for the settlers to occupy, and a school was quickly created. Bexley colony was founded in 1838. Situated in Bassa country and occupying a 600-acre site on the St John's River, it was founded by Lewis Sheridan, a man of private means. Also in 1838, the Mississippi Colonization Society founded a settlement at Sinoe, which later became Greenville. Most of the settlers came from the State of Mississippi and were cotton planters. One other settlement founded under Carey's brief leadership was Millsburg, established in February 1828. The land on which the settlement was established was acquired from Old King Peter and two other rulers. In contrast to the other settlements, Carey chose a company to run the settlement. A chosen number of migrants, already settled in the country, were carefully selected on the basis of their industrious habits and given land for farming. In a census collected in 1843, Millsburg's population was 221.

What is clear from this pattern of establishing colonies is the extent to which Liberia remained an American patent and continued to bear all the hallmarks of American colonization societies involved in its founding. The control and direction of the settlements remained vested in private hands in the United States. There was no centrally controlled direction of the operation, so that what could have been established along rational, orderly lines gave the appearance of happening according to chance circumstances, and there was no institutional organ responsible for the affairs of the colonies, and no permanent body in the United States that took direct charge of the affairs of the settlers. In Liberia itself there was no counterpart to Sir Charles MacCarthy, a strong individual who could lay down some broad outline of what needed to be done. The little settlements became fragmented communities, each thrown back on its own resources. The American Colonization Society acted more like a lobby and recruitment agency than a Congressional Committee with responsibility for the colonies. Individual enterprise that could have led to great social and political achievements under clear political direction proved a source of instability. Conspicuously missing from the picture was the decisive recaptive element: over a period of forty years, only 5,700 recaptives settled in Liberia, and they were treated badly. They lived in segregated communities of their own and were not allowed to mix freely with the Americo-Liberians whose numbers remained relatively static. In the same 1843 census, the population of all the Liberian colonies, excluding Maryland, was put at 30,000, of which 2,390 were Americo-Liberians, the rest being subject races and recaptives. Political power was concentrated in the hands of the migrants. It was in effect a reversal of the situation in Sierra Leone where recaptives predominated and acted as an effective engine of expansion in other parts of West Africa. The unassimilated African element in Liberian life had the effect of preventing the natural distribution of the benefits that Christianity and an industrious life were together supposed to generate. Yet we can judge too severely; considering the obstacles the settlers had to confront, including the unpromising social background of some of the migrants, Liberia was not an inconsequential achievement.

Black ideology and Liberia

As we have already seen, the issue of emigration from the United States to West Africa was closely intertwined with that of emancipation and the search for a Black political identity. Some of the leaders of this early version of Black consciousness had first considered Sierra Leone as a possible homeland but later rejected it as merely exchanging the American form of suppression for the British. Liberia provided an alternative for some of the most persistent among the Blacks, for in theory at least it was not a creature and department of the United States Congress. The reality of course was a little different.

One of the most outstanding of early Black nationalists who emigrated to Liberia was Joseph Brown Russwurm (died 1851), born in Jamaica to a Black mother and a Virginia planter. He went to school in Quebec and then removed to Maine where his father lived. In 1824 he went up to Bowdoin College where he finished his undergraduate degree in 1826, thus becoming one of the first two Black graduates in the United States. He contemplated emigration early, having in mind at that time Haiti, but decided against it. Instead he turned to journalism, and edited the first Black newspaper in the United States, *Freedom's Journal*, in New York. He used the newspaper to give vent to his strong anti-colonization views, and launched a campaign against emigration to Africa. But the scoffer was destined to become the vigilante. He dropped his opposition to colonization on the grounds that 'full citizenship in the United States is utterly impossible in the nature of things, and that those who pant for it must cast their eyes elsewhere.'[13] He followed his own advice and in the summer of 1829 emigrated to Liberia. A highly practical man, Russwurm was also attracted to Liberia by the prospects of better economic opportunities and the availability, as he believed, of

13. Cassell (1970), p.49.

unbounded natural abundance. Yet ideological motives were always lurking near the survface of his thoughts. He wrote that in Liberia 'the Man of Colour. . . may walk forth in all the majesty of his creation — a new-born creature — a Free Man!'[14] Except for a brief visit to the United States, where he died, he spent the rest of his life in his adopted country, and was honoured by being the first Black to be Governor of Maryland Colony.

After arriving in Liberia Russwurm founded the first newspaper in the country in 1830, the *Liberia Herald,* which established itself as a leading newspaper and was in demand both at home and abroad. As a tribute to his pioneering qualities he was made Governor of Maryland Colony in 1836. The population of the colony was relatively small at the time, only 191. But it was a promising settlement with forty-seven farms under cultivation. Russwurm was immediately conscious of the need for making common cause with Monrovia and was engaged in detailed discussions with the leaders there. He also sought to extend the frontiers of his settlement in order to avoid the risks of political isolation. In Russwurm's case, intellectual suppleness narrowed the ideological distance between the desire for Black selfhood and the need for white sponsorship.

Another striking figure who made an appearance on the Liberian stage was Martin Delany, whose background was in many ways similar to Russwurm's. He was active in journalism in both Philadelphia and Rochester, New York and campaigned widely for anti-slavery causes between about 1836 and 1849. The passage of the Fugitive Slave Act of 1850 proved a turning point: until then he had lampooned the Liberian colonies, saying that their existence detracted from the importance of self-help projects through which Blacks could improve themselves in the United States, and he still believed that hard work earned its own reward, irrespective of colour. However, he discovered that no matter what their status and their industry, Blacks were despised pariahs and inescapably locked in what he called 'a prejudice of caste'.[15] He decided to train as a medical doctor and then emigrate to Liberia. Accordingly, he entered Harvard Medical School in the autumn of 1850, sponsored along with two other Blacks by the Massachusetts Colonization Society. In the winter of 1851 he and his Black companions were removed from Harvard following a racially motivated petition for their dismissal, an experience which disillusioned and embittered him. One consequence was a book he completed in April 1852, called *The Condition, Elevation, Emigration and Destiny of the Colored People of the United States, Politically Considered.* As its title suggests, it reflected on emigration as a process in the ultimate liberation of Blacks. Nevertheless, he remained extremely sceptical of the value of Liberia which he considered a mere

14. Miller (1975), p.87.
15. ibid., p.124.

dependency of the Colonization Society. When he first turned to the idea of an African settlement, Delany conceived of it as an East African venture, no doubt stirred by the exploits of Dr David Livingstone. He launched a grandiose scheme in 1858 called the Niger Valley Exploring Party. At about the same time there was an active Yoruba movement among Blacks in New York City, and emigration to Yoruba country and Lagos was being urged upon free Blacks. The cause was taken up in the *Christian Intelligencer,* a publication of the Dutch Reformed Church, and at a public meeting in New York, arguments were advanced espousing the cause of emigration, the only point of debate being whether Haiti or Liberia was more suitable, both being at that time familiar places in colonization circles. Animating the debate at the time was also the question of the relative influence that religion ought to play in such emigration. One party, led by Delany, looked for a secular settlement, but another, more representative one wanted a settlement informed by Christian values. This second party had the advantage of being able to point to precedents in Sierra Leone and Liberia, a factor that was to influence subsequent deliberations.

It was against this background that Delany's Niger Valley Exploring Party was formed. Delany recruited successfully in New York, exploiting the sentiment for the Yoruba cause, and in May 1859 he set sail for West Africa, accompanied by forty-four passengers, landing at Cape Palmas in July 1859. He was to spend nine months travelling through Liberia and Yoruba country in Nigeria. Delany met Dr Edward Blyden who appears to have forgiven him for his earlier aspersions on Liberia. Blyden considered Delany, in his usual dramatic style, as the 'Moses to lead the exodus of his people from the house of bondage to land flowing with milk and honey. He seems to have many qualifications for the task. Let him be encouraged and supported.'[16] An unexpected reconciliation with a formidable critic had obviously stimulated Blyden's imagination.

Delany eventually made it to Lagos, and wrote enthusiastically of what he saw: 'This city, from location, is destined to be the great black metropolis of the world.'[17] (He would have felt vindicated by the World Festival of Black Arts (Festac) held in Lagos in 1977). He went on to Oyo from Abeokuta, but returned without fulfilling his ambition to penetrate further inland. Delany saw much to confirm him in his views about establishing a secular settlement based on cotton growing. He promoted the idea in Britain, saying an African cotton market could prove an invaluable source in the event of a war interrupting supplies from the United States. A certain romantic excess crept into his advocacy of the scheme: pressing the case for a settlement of Blacks in Yoruba country, he wrote: 'There is no other

16. Miller (1975), p.203.
17. ibid., p.205.

people who can raise cotton like the black, for both his nature and the country are adapted for it'.[18] Needless to say, nothing concrete came of Delany's ambitious scheme. But he did feed the general sentiment of Black improvement, what today we would call Black liberation, that had sustained Afro-American interest in Africa.

Delany was accompanied to the Liberian interior by the Rev. Alexander Crummell who had in fact preceded him in Liberia. Crummell was at that time principal of an Episcopal school near Cape Palmas. The son of a Temne prince who had been stolen and sold into slavery at the age of thirteen, Crummell was born in New York city in 1819, and became a lay reader at a struggling Black Episcopal Church in Providence, Rhode Island. In 1847, after being refused admission at the General Theological Seminary in New York on account of his colour, he left for England and enrolled at Queen's College, Cambridge. He graduated from there in 1857 and then accepted an Episcopal missionary appointment to Liberia. However, he resigned from that appointment later in the year to become principal of Mount Vaughan School near Cape Palmas. Crummell believed, unlike Delany, that Christianity had a providential role to play in the improvement of Africa, and that Black missionaries were to be the chosen instruments for this historic destiny. Both his ideas and those of Delany and others were waves rising from the general sea of Black consciousness that preceded emancipation in 1865 and continued beyond it. The existence of a settlement like Liberia provided a powerful focus of ideological awareness, whatever the attitudes adopted towards it.

Of those who emigrated to Liberia for ideological reasons none had more impact than Dr Edward Blyden, of whose career we have already taken note in its Sierra Leonean aspect. Blyden arrived in Liberia in 1851, when he was only nineteen, and had an immediate effect on the place. His unusual scholarly attainments brought him to the attention of the government, and he became deeply involved in the educational direction of the country. When Liberia College was founded in August 1861, he was appointed professor of Greek and Latin Languages and Literature, as well as being involved in the teaching of Logic, Rhetoric, History, Hebrew, French, Mathematics and Natural Philosophy. The College was a three-storey building, the largest structure in Monrovia. But it remained closed while Blyden and Crummell toured the United States looking for support and students. The impending Civil War did not augur well for their labours in that direction. It is instructive to reflect that at the inauguration of the College in January 1862, Blyden, before leaving for the United States, delivered an impassioned speech on the importance of studying classics as an academic subject. Perhaps his later enthusiastic adoption of technical education was by the way of

18. Miller (1975), p.227.

making amends for his earlier scholarly indiscretions.

In 1864 the New York Colonization Society endowed a chair for the Fulton Professorship at Liberia College, and Blyden was the first to fill it. Crummell was also made a professor and put in charge of Intellectual and Moral Philosophy, and of English Language and Literature. He resigned in 1866 in a controversy involving him and Blyden and the President of the College, Joseph Roberts, who had also twice been President of Liberia. Blyden similarly played an active part in local church activities.

His talents recognised, Blyden became Liberian plenipotentiary at the Court of St James in London, having previously been Secretary of State under President Warner (1864–7). He had also been Principal of the famed Alexander High School in Monrovia. In January 1881, Blyden was installed as President of Liberia College, and continued to call attention to the College's discouragingly small enrolment and lack of indigenous support. In 1882 when the country was faced with a British ultimatum regarding the delimitation of territory bordering Sierra Leone, Blyden, then Secretary of the Interior, was requested by President Gardner (1878–83) to lead the negotiations; but it was clear that Liberia was faced with a virtual *fait accompli,* and Blyden's acknowledged prestige could do little to change it. He stood for President of the Republic in 1885 but lost. In 1886 he resigned as head of Liberia College after protracted internal disputes. The year 1888 saw the appearance of his magnum opus, *Christianity, Islam and the Negro Race.* Its impact was immediate and profound, and the issues it raised, albeit in a journalistic fashion, have continued to occupy us down to this day. It was published in London, with lively debate ensuing in parts of West Africa. Although he returned later to Liberia College as Professor of Languages, the main centre of his life and activity had now moved to a wider stage.

Blyden's sharp awareness of the significance of the rapid changes coming over African societies from contact with Europe and America drove him to attempt to develop a relevant ideology for the Black race. It is true that his conclusions often erred in their uncritical espousal of ideas on the basis simply that they were non-Western. But neither his motive nor his vision could be faulted. He perceived that the impressive and powerful engine that had arrived on the scene had hitched to it an acquisitive and unsolicitous vehicle of domination. He called it the 'heavy and crushing indifference of the car of Juggernaut,'[19] and said that the conductors of that ponderous vehicle were immune to the feelings of the people they crushed and trampled on. This indifference, Blyden went on, extended to a complete disregard of the sensibilities that might be lacerated, and a lack of any attempt to cultivate what he called 'the well-spring of a nobler life

19. Cassell (1970), p.344.

within'.[20] African populations thus became the victims of an unsympathetic apparatus of political and commercial machinery. Blyden's ability to articulate issues arising from Europe's fateful contact with Africa, and in a medium that itself was the consequence of that contact, made him an oracle of significance.

Some religious and social developments in Liberia

The religious life of the settlers was closely interwoven with their public life. Both Elijah Johnson and Lott Carey, the early pioneers, were pace-setters of a way of life that was distinguished for the way in which it maintained a blend of religion in public affairs. We should take up this point a little later, and for the moment turn our attention to other aspects of Christian activity in Liberia. In the 1830s several missionary organisations took active steps to establish bases in the country. A church was established at Caldwell under the aegis of the Western Board of Foreign Missions of the Baptist Church. The Liberia Baptist Association was organised in Monrovia in October 1835. In 1832 the First Methodist Episcopal Church building was completed and dedicated in Monrovia; it also owned a mission school, the Methodist seminary which was built on the reported site of the Poro secret society, a precocious suggestion that Christianity had successfully overrun hostile religious territory. In May 1833, the Board of Domestic and Foreign Missions of the Baptist Church was founded in Monrovia, as a consequence of which Adam V. Anderson was sent to Cape Mount as a missionary among the Vai people. In 1834 the first Presbyterian Church in Liberia was built. In 1841 the Roman Catholics, taking advantage of Liberia's tradition of religious freedom, applied for permission to establish a mission: this they obtained and in December 1841 two Catholic priests arrived to begin work.

In 1838 the Rev. John Payne and his wife arrived as White missionaries from the Protestant Episcopal Church in the United States. He was stationed at Cape Palmas for work among the Grebo people, and became superintendent of the Episcopal Mission in Maryland county, with stations now established at Mount Vaughan, Fishtown, Cavalla and other places. In 1856 he was consecrated bishop of the Cape Palmas District of the Mission, and in fact became the general overseer of the work of the Mission for the rest of the country. By 1861 there were some six important mission stations under his charge. He was assisted by four White missionaries and eight Liberian ministers, most of whom were trained in Liberia. The Mission's constituency remained for the most part the Grebo people. William Wadé Harris, the charismatic Christian figure who was to convulse that whole part of West Africa with his message, was a

20. Cassell (1970), p.344.

Grebo, and in fact was employed as a school teacher by the Episcopal Mission. When Payne retired in 1874, he had made the Episcopal Church not the fashionable pivot of society people but a genuine instrument of national advancement, with the emphasis on local support and leadership. He is fondly remembered in Liberian history.

Perhaps the life-stories of two individual migrants might suffice to show what opportunities there were for those willing to emigrate and who were robust enough to survive the harsh climate. One was John Day, who became Chief Justice of Liberia and was an architect of the instruments of independence. He was born in North Carolina in 1797, converted to Christianity at an early age and joined the Baptist church. He developed an interest in theology, encouraged in this by a Baptist preacher; but just at this time he learnt of the founding of Liberia and expressed a desire to emigrate. He completed an accelerated course of theological studies and was ordained. In December 1830, he and his wife and four children left for Liberia, and then tragedy struck: his entire family died of malaria. He carried on alone, becoming a cabinet-maker to support himself while he ministered to a local church. He acted for both the Northern Baptist Board of Missions and the Southern Baptist Convention. Even after occupying the elevated heights of Chief Justice, Day remained as he started out, namely a devoted servant of the cause. He died in February 1861. Blyden, who knew him, was greatly impressed by his integrity, and was unrestrained in his praise.

The other individual was Joseph Jenkins Roberts, the first President of Liberia. Roberts was born at Petersburg, Virginia in 1809, and came to Liberia as an emigrant in 1829, and immediately became active as a commercial entrepreneur. After the establishment of the Commonwealth of Liberia in 1839 he was made Vice Colonial Governor under Thomas Buchanan, the first Governor. Buchanan died in September 1841, and Roberts stepped into his shoes. It soon became obvious that imposing a strong central authority on the constituent members of the Commonwealth was not an easy task, and that European commercial rivalry on the coast had diminished the country's rights to collect dues and tariffs. Between 1842 and 1845 Roberts had taken measures to establish a prosperous base for the Commonwealth with increased revenue earnings and a steadily expanding territorial sphere of influence in the interior. In January 1846, a decision was reached in principle to grant independence to the Commonwealth, with the American Colonization Society willing to relinquish legal control into the hands of the local emigrant population. When the legislature of the Commonwealth met in October 1846, it was fitting that Roberts should be assisted by an able group of people that included Elijah Johnson. The matter of independence was seriously discussed and accepted in principle. In

May 1847, the American Colonization Society informed Roberts that a draft constitution had been completed. Although many were apprehensive of the implications involved in accepting ultimate responsibility for their own affairs, Roberts calmed their fears by reassuring them that the American Colonization Society had given an undertaking to maintain a close interest in the affairs of the Republic. In other words, independence would fall just short of its full meaning, a theme of considerable significance today. Independence duly came, and in the elections that followed in October 1847, Roberts was elected President. The electoral franchise was restricted to the Americo-Liberians. The settlement of the Maryland Colonization Society at Cape Palmas, made a separate republic in 1853, joined the Republic of Liberia in 1857.

Roberts voluntarily retired from politics in 1855, although he returned in 1872–5 and then assumed the presidency of Liberia College. In many ways he was a representative figure, using his economic power to build a political base which he promptly appropriated as the preserve of Americo-Liberians, especially those with lighter skin. His political critics complained loudly about the concentration of political and government power in the hands of this group. The irony of emigrating to Liberia 'for the love of liberty', as the proud motto of the early colonists had it, and then denying liberty to others in just the same way as discrimination was practised in the United States has not been lost on critics of Liberia. Roberts died in February 1876.

The constitution of the new republic was drawn up by a Harvard professor who used the American consititution as his model. There was to be a President with two Houses of Congress and a Supreme Court. As an imported arrangement it had to be modified to fit the Liberian situation, a point that was often made by people within Liberia, including Dr Blyden. Political power, however, remained concentrated in a few families, all of American origin. The United States delayed recognition of the country until 1862, afraid that a Black ambassador might turn up in Washington from Monrovia demanding privileges due him by diplomatic protocol. Britain, on the other hand, granted recognition much earlier, in 1848, following the logic of Lord Palmerston's doctrine of self-determination originally pursued in the Balkans. France accorded recognition in 1852, as did Brazil and Prussia. All this helped to ease Liberia's aggrieved sense of international isolation.

A point to be made in conclusion is the significance of Church-state relations in Liberia. Political leaders acted as patrons of churches and missions, and the state became a sponsor of religious life in the country; the President and other high-ranking officials of the state were also Church officials. The organising of Christian mission became an important element of foreign policy decisions. Internally, the Church not only became the focus of political power, but assumed an ethnic identity. Such a unified view of religion and politics is not strange to traditional African societies, as we have had occasion to point out above, but what is strange and alienating is the foreign orientation of this ethnic self-image and its scrupulous disavowal of local and indigenous sources of renewal. Consequently a cultural ghetto was created in Liberia, a *cul-de-sac* into which influences from abroad were received and then promptly transformed to serve introverted ends. Christianity did make some inroads into local populations, but always as minor satellites of the Americo-Liberian star, which had been the epicentre of the initial impact of the message. When Christianity did succeed in breaking out of its inert casing, it was from a direction and at the hands of a person that were both completely unexpected. The Gentiles of heathen Africa, as many of the settlers were educated to regard traditional Africans, might be excluded from that dispensation claimed by the settlers and their descendants, but in the Prophet William Harris their comet would rise and eclipse the past.

5

THE BAPTIST, PRESBYTERIAN AND METHODIST MISSIONS: CAMEROUN AND GHANA

It is clear that we shall have much worry in Africa with a small community [of West Indian Christians] and I cannot dismiss the thought . . . that it might have been as good or even better to have taken Christians from Sierra Leone. . .

Johann Georg Widmann

The successful establishment of Christianity in Sierra Leone, against the background of centuries of failure, was to act as a powerful stimulus for the extension of Christianity to other parts of Africa. Furthermore, it became clear that there was no substitute for partnership with Africans in missionary work, for, more than outsiders, they knew what motivated their people. Missionaries from the West, aware of the significance of the local springs of religious vitality, could no longer dispense with African agents and would themselves have to clothe their thinking in the indigenous cultures if their endeavours were to bear any lasting fruit. Thus it came about that serious attention was paid both to the urgency of using African workers and to the case for developing African languages. We can summarise these points as follows: first, Christian missions took a broader view of their work and tried to think of the whole of Africa, not just a section of it; secondly, Africans began to take their place alongside Western missionaries in the work of the Church; thirdly, African languages were developed in order to translate the Scriptures and to provide an effective medium of instruction in the schools established by missions; fourthly, trade and legitimate commerce were encouraged in the struggle to suppress the slave trade and make slavery unattractive; and finally, administrative order was imposed on African societies in the hope of facilitating peaceful progress towards the ideal of an abundant life. The constant element in all this was the African factor which, more than any other consideration, sustained the Christian and humanitarian initiative in the development of the continent.

Preliminaries

After the Emancipation Act of 1833, Thomas Fowell Buxton

encouraged the idea that the liberated Africans in the West Indies, committed Christians, should be recruited for spreading the Gospel in Africa. In 1839 he wrote: 'We want black persons from all conceivable situations . . . and every one ought to be a real Christian; but a good Providence has prepared these in the West Indies and at Sierra Leone'.[1] A little earlier, in 1835, Moravian missionaries in Jamaica had come up with the same idea of training 'native missionaries and teachers for needy Africa'.[2] The Basel Evangelical Missionary Society, about which more will be said presently, were also interested in starting work in the trading forts on the West African coast controlled by Denmark. A recruiting mission was led by Riis to Jamaica in May 1842, and from there the first batch of Christian colonists, twenty-four in all from Jamaica and Antigua, sailed for the Gold Coast. It was a hopeful beginning, for if the experiment worked it could mark the start of a radical change in traditional missionary fortunes, but the experiment failed. The West Indians served loyally enough, but however obvious their African origins, they had lost all trace of linguistic kinship with Africa and were for all practical purposes aliens in a strange land. They could not act as an effective bridge to the continent from which they had been plundered and torn. Those who survived and had families were able to provide some hope that a second generation might re-establish the links that their grandparents had taken with them across the Atlantic, but for the time being, the idea proved futile and had to be quietly dropped. Yet important lessons were learnt and the Basel Mission, fired by a burning zeal for the cause, applied itself to the task of spreading Christian teaching in Africa with more determination. From the West Indies itself came renewed hope that the impulse to undertake Christian work in Africa could be maintained and developed. We should now examine this more closely in the work of the Baptists.

The Baptist Missionary Society, 1814–1849

The Baptist Missionary Society started work among the Blacks in Jamaica in 1814, and when emancipation came it was decided to extend the work to Africa. A group of Black Christians in Jamaica was also urging that the work be extended to their continent (of origin.) The Jamaican Christians pressed the Baptists to begin this work, 'a mission to the interior of Western Africa. . . The conversion of Africa to God is the theme of their conversation and their prayers, and the object of their most ardent desires.'[3] So keen was the interest that in 1839 one Thomas Keith, a Black Christian, set out to be a

1. Groves, vol. II (1954), p.23n.
2. ibid., p.24.
3. ibid., p.28.

missionary to his own people, carrying with him nothing more than a letter of introduction from his minister. He reportedly reached the place where he had been stolen as a boy and sold into slavery. Nothing more was heard of him. But he was not alone: at about the same time, one James Keats left Jamaica with the declared intention of returning to Africa with the Gospel. He apparently got as far as Sierra Leone and then left on a ship bound for the river Congo which he intended to penetrate. He too disappeared and nothing further was heard about him in spite of earnest enquiry. With such examples of individual courage and determination, the Baptists in Jamaica felt they had no choice but to press the Home Committee in London to answer the call for service to Africa.

At first and for quite some time it was a lonely enterprise, for the Baptist missionary in Jamaica, William Knibb, who appealed to London for a mission to Africa, was rebuffed. But the pressure to go ahead with such a mission was mounting in Jamaica among Black Christians. Unsolicited gifts were received from 1838 onwards, and at one public meeting some 100 poor labourers, lacking money, offered instead one week's free labour to launch an African mission. All that was needed was vision and commitment in London. When and how would that come? With his hand strengthened by this display of interest and enthusiasm, Knibb went to London on leave in 1840 and made strong personal representations. His idea was that a group of Black Christians from Jamaica should be brought to London for preliminary training before being sent to Africa under a superintendent missionary. At a meeting in Exeter Hall, he roused his audience with an urgent appeal and led the way by pledging his own church in Jamaica to provide £1,000 towards the project. The cause was won. At a meeting in June, 1840, the Baptists resolved to initiate a mission to Africa.

It was decided to send out an exploratory party to West Africa to prospect for a mission field. Although at first it was intended to join the Niger Mission led by Crowther and Schoen, preparations for that mission had been far too advanced at that stage to allow a new party to join it. The Baptist party, led by the Rev. John Clarke and a medical man, Dr G. K. Prince, went instead to Fernando Po.

Fernando Po had been discovered by a Portuguese sailor, Fernão do Pó, in 1471, whence its name; it was subsequently annexed by Portugal which ceded it to Spain in 1778. The Spanish, however, abandoned it in 1782, and it was therefore ready to be occupied by the dominant power in the area. This happened to be the British, who in the 1830s made it a base of operations for their naval squadron which patrolled off the West coast of Africa, impounding slave ships and committing them to trial. The aboriginal inhabitants of the island, the Bubi, estimated to number about 15,000, were forest people who shunned contact with the outside world. In addition there was a population of some 800 – 900 people of mixed origin.

In October 1841, Crowther and Schoen called at the island and found Clarke and Prince hard at work among the settlers, mostly artisans and labourers from Sierra Leone, with others impounded from the slave ships. There was also a man from Cape Coast who kept a day school attended by some forty children of the settlers. Such independent African Christian pioneers were apparently commonplace. Schoen himself reports that one such individual, a Baptist called Kingdon, had attached himself to the Niger Mission as an independent religious teacher; his work suggested to Schoen that a wide mission field was waiting to be cultivated if only the Baptists would enter the work. But such wistful remarks were soon to be followed by examples of concrete response by the Baptists. Clarke and Prince went round assessing the prospects for a Baptist mission. Even though they met with encouragement in Fernando Po, they were aware that the island was only a collecting point for people originating from the mainland which they wanted to reach at first opportunity. In Fernando Po itself some 200 – 300 people gathered to hear them preach in Clarence. Five people were baptised and seventy enquirers registered. Bible classes with fifty members were started and a school with seventy pupils was opened. Then they crossed over to the Cameroun mainland. By the time they left in February 1842 to report to London, the missionaries had seen ample proof of the ardent desire and bright prospects for mission.

When sailing for London, the ship carrying the missionaries was blown off course, drifting finally to British Guiana (now Guyana). From there they went to Jamaica where they were able to report first on the promise in Africa. As was to be expected, the response in Jamaica was enthusiastic, and the party was joined by two new recruits, Joseph Merrick and Alexander Fuller, both Black Christians, when it left finally for England to prepare for the African mission. Meanwhile the Home Committee, long sceptical about such a project, had yielded and adopted Fernando Po as a first base for reaching the continent. Thus resolved, the Home Committee had now merely to welcome Clarke and Prince by re-fitting them, along with others, for the African mission. One party, consisting of Prince, Merrick (with their wives) and Fuller set out for Fernando Po, arriving in September 1843. The other party, comprising Clarke and Alfred Saker and his wife, left England in July 1843 via the West Indies for a recruiting stop, arriving in Jamaica at about the same time as the first party was landing at Fernando Po. In Jamaica some thirty-nine men, women and children enrolled as volunteers: some were going as evangelists and teachers and others as settlers. But the Jamaican Church also contributed generously to the mission. The Missionary Society provided the vessel on which the party was to sail, while the Jamaican Church met the cost of the journey to the tune of

£500, equal to the amount it contributed annually towards the African Mission, — which suggests partnership in mission on a scale surprising both for its level of involvement and for its consistency. Jamaican Christians had long called for a mission to Africa, and now their prayers answered, they backed it with self-denying sacrifice. Nothing less heroic would have equipped them for the task ahead, especially the hardships that awaited them in Fernando Po.

Clarke and his party arrived in Fernando Po in February 1844 after an eleven-week voyage. In the island itself the members of the party were stunned by the severity of the climate and the strangeness of the place. Missionary reports began to bulge with expressions of anxiety. Disease and ill-health took their expected toll. Relations deteriorated. Then in 1846 Spain was allowed to re-occupy the island. Spanish priests accompanying the new power, spurred by the legacy of the Counter-Reformation, served notice on the Baptists. Although the work continued for a while, its future was now in doubt. In 1858 the Spanish commander of the island, Don Carlos Chacon, issued a proclamation forbidding Protestant missionary work and thus effectively closing down the Baptist mission. But the reader should be cautious in handling such examples of religious rivalry: in the competition for trade and political influence European powers were often ready to allow practical considerations to outweigh confessional ones. The struggles, for example, between Portugal and Italy, and between Spain and either of them, all of them Catholic countries, suggest the complexity of the power game. The Protestant Reformation, and the Catholic Counter-Reformation it provoked, did not produce in West Africa neat distinctions of religious controversy. Any view that the world was now evenly and permanently divided between Catholics and Protestants is, for historical purposes, grossly simplistic. Thus the eclipse of the Baptist work in Fernando Po has to be attributed largely to the repercussions of political and commercial manoeuvring that has characterised European presence in Africa. We have seen numerous examples of this in Chapters 2 and 3. When such European rivalry encountered an organised African response from powerful chiefs and kings, it has often impeded the progress of the Church and turned local Christians into a more or less tolerated minority.

The Jamaicans returned to the West Indies in 1847, in which year Clarke himself also went back to Jamaica to serve another twenty-eight years. He died in 1879, aged seventy-seven. Most of the others stayed on and gave several years of valuable service on the mainland.

To stress the point made in the introduction to this chapter, missionaries on the whole had little doubt that if their work was to be effective, they would have to rely to a great extent on African agents, or, failing that, look to West Indian Christians. The example most missionary societies wanted to emulate was that of Sierra Leone, and the evidence of Sierra Leonean Christians living and working in many parts of Africa enlivened the hope that a great missionary era was dawning. However, the future of the Church in Africa would be bleak indeed without the Christian Scriptures being made available in the local languages. Hence the prompt attention paid to translation work and the transcription and development of indigenous languages. One of the most enduring monuments to the missionary contribution to Africa's development is the linguistic achievement of men like Sigismund Koelle in Freetown and Johannes Christaller and Zimmermann in the Gold Coast. Much of our linguistic knowledge, as well as historical and ethnographic material, derive from their pioneer labours. In the Cameroun too the Baptists followed in similar footsteps. Clarke's writings on the speech of the Bubi were the first record of the language of those people. Joseph Merrick also worked in Bimbia on the Isubu language: between 1846 and 1848 he translated St Matthew's Gospel, Genesis and parts of St John's Gospel into that language. He died in 1849. Alfred Saker similarly went to work among the Duala people and was eventually able to undertake the translation of the Scriptures into their language. These early Christian pioneers were laying a solid foundation for Africa's future awakening, consisting of a scrupulous inventory of the linguistic, ethnographic and religious heritage of its diverse peoples.

The West Indian connection in the establishment of Christian mission in Cameroun extended also to the founding of a Presbyterian mission there. It is therefore appropriate that at this point we should turn our attention to the history of the Presbyterian work in West Africa.

The Basel Mission and Presbyterianism in Ghana

The roots of Presbyterian missionary endeavour go back to the Evangelical awakening in the Protestant Churches in the eighteenth century. In 1730 Dr. J. A. Urlsperger founded a German Society for the Advancement of Christian Truth and Godly Piety with its centre in Basel, and groups were formed in all parts of German-speaking Europe. They were united by a deep personal devotion to Christ through reverence for the Scriptures, with the explicit desire to devote themselves to the furtherance of the Kingdom of God on earth. Certain logical developments followed. At Basel a desire was expressed to found a missionary-training seminary. In Berlin a similar project, called the Mission Institute, had been founded by Pastor Jaenicke, himself a member of the German Christian Society, and had sent out between 1800 and 1807 thirty young missionaries for work with the English Societies. When its work was hampered by the blockade of the continent and Napoleon's measures against Germany, attention shifted to Basel where it was hoped that the newly-founded Seminary would meet the same needs. The Basel Evangelical Mission grew out of this.

From the very beginning, the Basel Mission combined a strong ecumenical and international character with a profound Biblical and Evangelical commitment. It avoided theological controversy and concentrated on the Church's missionary calling. In this regard it remained in the closest collaboration with the Church's, asking only that it be free to dedicate itself to its overriding aim of spreading the Kingdom of God on earth. It thus became a service agency to the Churches, supplying the motive for missionary outreach and the men to perform that task. It did this without regard for denominational or national considerations. For example, in 1818 the first seven men who were trained at the Basel Seminary joined the Netherlands Missionary Society, while between 1818 and 1861 some eighty-six people served with the CMS. Basel missionaries began to be found in the far corners of the world, scattering the seeds of the Kingdom and pushing back the frontiers of ignorance. By the time the Mission turned its attention to the Gold Coast it had already worked in Liberia, and one of its men, Andreas Gollmer, accompanied Crowther and Schoen from Freetown on the Niger Mission.

Interest in West Africa had been maintained by various societies and by individual contact. Between 1752 and 1824 the Society for the Propagation of the Gospel (SPG) had sent out at the request of the Royal African Company English clergymen to serve as chaplains at Cape Coast. One of these, Thomas Thompson, served five years and recorded his impressions in a journal, *An Account of Two Missionary Voyages,* published in 1758. A somewhat controversial man, Thompson saw no evil in slavery and wrote approvingly of the slave trade. However, characteristically this time, he urged the necessity of developing the Fanti language and encouraging education. When he left he took three Fanti boys with him to be educated in England. Two died, but the third, Philip Quaque, was ordained in the Anglican Church and returned to Cape Coast in 1765 to serve as schoolmaster, catechist and missionary. He died in 1816 in that position.

The Danes had also been involved at the fort of Christiansborg, a garrison fortress held by their country from which they regulated the trade in the adjacent area. The chaplains who arrived in the Gold Coast were not missionaries as such, but some of them took a close interest in African life and religion. For example, Wilhelm Johann Mueller, a chaplain at Fort Frederiksborg near Cape Coast in 1662-70, argued for a missionary effort among the local inhabitants and asked for the Bible to be translated into the local languages. He himself made a modest contribution by collecting some 800 practical words and phrases. He also demonstrated some knowledge of local religious practices, the first attempt by any outsider to do so. Two other chaplains based at Christiansborg found the restricted boundaries of fortress life inhibiting. One was Johann Rask who served in 1709-12, and the other was H. S. Monrad, serving in 1805-9. Both condemned slavery and the trade that sustained it and both expressed the classic doubt about the fitness of establishing the Church in Africa under the compromising shadow of European commercial enclaves. Without a missionary organisation at their disposal, they did the next best thing, which was to encourage the African pupils enrolled in the castle school. Among the bright talents nurtured in this way were William Amo of Axim who obtained a doctorate at Wittenberg, Jacob Capitein who graduated from the University of Leiden, producing for his dissertation an ironic defence of the slave trade as being not inconsistent with Christian teaching, Frederick Svane who graduated from the University of Copenhagen, and Jacob Protten. All these men were eighteenth-century figures, the first bloom of the the Evangelical interest in Africa. Svane was a Ga and returned with a Danish wife to serve briefly at Christiansborg as a catechist and teacher before returning to Denmark in 1746. Protten also returned to the Gold Coast but disappeared into Togoland to emerge again for a brief spell in Germany. He was then at Christiansborg in 1756-61 and again from 1765 until his death in 1769. Their work highlighted the familiar problem of how to present the Gospel to Africa in a way which would minimise Western cultural interference.

The Basel Mission decided to penetrate inland from the coast in order both to avoid excessive dependence on European agency and to reach populations relatively unspoilt by European contact. Andreas Riis went to Akropong in the Akwapim mountains in 1835 where it was hoped that the climate would prove less inclement. This was followed by the opening of another station at Aburi in 1847 with the help of West Indian settlers, a fact already referred to. At first, the rewards for the high hopes that accompanied such missionary penetration were extremely scanty. The first converts at Akropong were baptised twelve years after the arrival of Riis, and it took eight years to achieve a similar result at Aburi. Following political upheavals in 1854 when the Danes transferred their forts in the Gold Coast to the British and a controversial poll tax was introduced, the Basel missionaries left Christiansborg which was under siege and went to Abokobi. There they wanted to start an experimental agricultural project but it came to nothing. However in 1857 they won a notable convert in Mohenu, a leading priest of the traditional religion who, under his new name Paul, gave thirty years distinguished service to the missionaries.

From the mid-1850s various attempts were made inland to establish self-supporting Christian communities. By 1869 there were eight mission districts of twenty-four congregations with a total membership of 1,851 — the spearhead of a much bigger drive in later years. Alongside these developments the Basel Mission established schools and educational institutions, convinced that the future of the Church lay in the hands of a new generation of educated Africans. But if such a class of Africans was fully to exploit the opportunity that modern education afforded them, it would be necessary to create the kind of environment which would counteract the evil influence of the slave trade. Furthermore, legitimate trade would not only advance European civilisation but open the way for honourable enterprise and thus inculcate in the African the virtue of honest labour. It was believed that the agricultural labour which would be required to grow crops and other raw materials would instil the values of the dignity and reward of manual work. At about the same time the Mission was facing acute shortages of imported goods and materials, a need which brought into being the Basel Mission Trading Factory. It was to play a formidable role in the trading and commercial life of Ghana as well as serving as a source of much-valued profit for the hard-pressed Mission. In 1859 it was placed in the hands of a special Trading Commission because the increased volume of business made it impossible for the Mission to cope. However it remained a branch of the Mission, at least until 1909 when it was formally separated and its employees, no longer termed missionaries, were given a separate salary structure. The work ethic, so deeply lodged in the heart of Protestant doctrine, was neatly transplanted with the intensive care of the missionary station.

The 1860s were a trying time. A second Ashanti invasion of the coast hardened opinion on the part of those who wanted Britain to give up the Gold Coast. But the Basel Mission, already heavily committed to the welfare of the country, lobbied actively in favour of retention. In the ensuing conflict between Ashanti and the British forces between 1869-74 the missionaries found themselves squeezed in the middle. Eventually the British took Kumasi, the capital of Ashanti, in 1874, but not without first encountering stiff resistance. The Basel Mission found its work hampered by the ill feeling created by this defeat and had to wait till 1896 before it could start work in Ashanti. Shortly after, in 1902, the British secured the kingdom's formal annexation.

The Basel Mission tried to build on their gains in the Akwapim region, Kibi and in the Kwahu Plateau at Abetifi. But just as the early Portuguese missionaries regarded the kingdom of Benin as the centrepiece of their drive to penetrate Africa with the Gospel, so did the Basel Mission regard Ashanti as essential to the success of their enterprise. Taking advantage of the British take-over of Kumasi, the Basel missionary Frederick Augustus Ramseyer entered that city in June 1896, and by December 1899 it was established as a mission station, although Ramseyer's lyrical delight at this historic breakthrough was tinged with a certain regret: the Ashanti approached the Mission and the school it operated with considerable reluctance. Indeed the Mission was soon destroyed in a renewed outbreak of hostilities with the British, and although Ramseyer escaped harm, the small flock of Christians was dispersed and three died, including a teacher, Samuel Otu of Larteh, who suffered martyrdom. Ramseyer returned in December 1901 to gather the broken pieces of what was left of the Mission. From that painful re-kindling a small flame of hope spread through Ashanti country, and by 1914 there were twenty Christian congregations, 800 converts and seventeen schools.

By the very fact of being a missionary society founded in Switzerland, the Basel Mission maintained the closest possible links with the Reformed Churches out of which it was born and with the Lutheran Churches. Thus its affinity with the Presbyterian Church was self-evident. Both were the stern offspring of Calvin. But the sterner circumstances under which the Scottish Presbyterians inherited the Mission in 1916 were far removed from deliberate theological counsel. The First World War had broken out and Britain, along with France, proceeded to dismantle German interests abroad. Because of the historic connection between the Basel Mission and German Churches, the British government imposed a restriction on it, deporting its missionaries of German nationality. These were embarked at Accra and deported in December 1917. By a special ordinance enacted in February 1918, the Trading Company of the Mission was liquidated and eventually handed over to the Commonwealth Trust Ltd. The measure was rescinded in 1928 and the Trading Company resumed its trading activities.

Scottish missionaries arrived in January 1917, to take over the work of the Basel missionaries. They were led by the Rev. Dr. A. W. Wilkie, sent out by the Foreign Missions Committee of the United Free Church of Scotland. The Rev. John Rankin, serving at the time in Calabar, joined him in the Gold Coast. The excellent educational work of the Basel Mission, which was in some danger of suffering from the uncertainties of the time, was ably carried on by Wilkie and his missionary colleagues; this earned him the gratitude of the Governor, Sir Frederick Gordon Guggisberg. By the time Wilkie left in 1931 the Mission had made significant strides forward. To start with, in 1926 the Basel missionaries returned to what would now become a collaborative venture with their immediate successors. In that year too the name 'Presbyterian Church of the Gold Coast' was formally adopted. The two missions, Basel and the Scottish Presbyterians, had merged and become the local church, a transition that was elsewhere fraught with difficulty. In 1930, after a fundamental revision of the Church constitution, the Synod Committee, with a significant African bloc, became the legal trustees of the Church's properties. In 1950 Africans took over leadership of the schools. Missionary men with the normal human weaknesses had achieved by their much scrutinised labours the long-cherished dream of an African Church in circumstances where the certain fruits of profit and commercial gain could, with less toil and sacrifice, have filled their pockets. 138 missionaries and their wives gave their lives for that dream between 1829 and 1913.

The Bremen Mission, 1847–1939

While efforts were made to establish Christian work in the Ga, Fanti and Ashanti areas by others, the North German Missionary Society, better known as the Bremen Mission, went to work among the Ewe east of the Volta, beginning in 1847. Four of them, led by Lorenz Wolf, sailed from Hamburg in March of that year, but by November all but Wolf had died. Wolf himself was compelled by ill-health to abandon the mission field in 1851, dying on arrival in Hamburg. His companions, who had joined him amid high hopes, faintheartedly withdrew, and with them ended that first attempt at an Ewe mission.

When a second attempt was made it was decided to start at Keta on the coast rather than imitate the earlier attempt which struck at Peki inland. Dauble and his colleague Plessing set themselves up at Keta in September 1853, with the intention of progressing inland in stages. In 1855 they accordingly travelled to Waya where, at the beginning of the New Year, they began constructing a station. In 1857 an intermediate station at Anyako was chosen. After further prospecting in adjacent country, it was decided in 1859 to site another station at Ho. In the political troubles of the 1860s and the Ashanti war of 1873-4 some of these stations suffered and the work was interrupted, but when peace returned the Bremen missionaries resumed work. A steady influx of Sierra Leonean Creoles into the area had provided a firm base from which to build, since it attracted trade to the area. One such Sierra Leonean, called Williams, counted some fifty-three people in his household. The prominence of these Creole Christians was acknowledged by the Bremen missionaries, who introduced a Sunday English-language service. It is interesting to reflect that the expanding frontier of Creole commercial and Christian activity showed the way for the more sluggish advance of British colonial rule. In 1877 Anyako was rebuilt and re-opened. The African catechist Joseph Reindorf was dispatched to open the station at Ho in 1874, with the missionaries and others following in 1875. This was perhaps a prudent calculation on the part of the missionaries to let their African agent precede them. Peki, the haunt of sad memories, was re-entered in 1877, and in 1883 an African catechist, Stefano Kwami, was resident there. Amedzofe was chosen as a mission station and work was begun there in 1889.

This was also the period of the 'Scramble for Africa', with European powers carving up the continent among themselves. The Bremen Mission was caught up by those political events, with Germany wishing to use it as an instrument for colonisation. Contrary to popular theories about the subservient role of mission under colonialism, the Bremen missionaries denounced colonialism as an enemy of Christianity. They were led in this by Franz Michael Zahn, a forceful character who contrasted the narrow national interests behind colonial schemes with the wider international nature of Christian mission. But colonialism had begun a relentless march and could not be turned back. Nevertheless Zahn felt that the Bremen Mission should stop short of playing an active political role in opposing imperialism and thus abandoning its calling, but should strive to transcend partisan politics and retain the trust of the African. He realised of course that this would be difficult. After the German take-over of Togoland, the Bremen Mission was invited to transfer its headquarters from Keta to Lome. Zahn resisted this though he yielded to pressure by establishing a station at Lome. Under his successor, who was more amenable to imperial wishes, the Mission made Lome its headquarters in 1905.

As beneficiaries of European colonial advance, the missionaries also became the victims of any deterioration in inter-European relations. This was the case during the First World War when the British deported Bremen missionaries of German nationality, along with their Basel compatriots. But the unusual policy of the Bremen folk to train African church leaders in Westheim, Germany, at the so-called 'Ewe school', enabled the work to proceed under largely African direction even though a Swiss missionary was given formal charge. Among the Africans who were prominent in this sense were Andraes Aku, Robert Baeta and Robert Kwami.

The Bremen missonaries were allowed to return to Ghana in 1925, though responsibility for school work remained in the hands of the Scottish Mission. However their history henceforth became intertwined with that of the Basel Mission, and when they did emerge after their second deportation in 1939 it was in the context of a new era of relationship between mission and Church.

The Bremen and Basel Missions in Cameroun, 1885–1914

At the Bremen Conference (of the North German Missionary Society) of 1885 consideration was given to the opportunity for service in Cameroun. However the size of the task demanded greater resources than the Bremen Mission possessed or could spare, and so a decision was taken to hand over the work there to the Basel Mission. The situation in Cameroun itself was far from straightforward. The German presence there had caused resentment among some chiefs, those who collaborated with the Germans being threatened by the other chiefs. The whole atmosphere was thus inauspicious for Christian work, and when the Germans required that the English language be replaced by German it became impossible for the Baptists, heirs of Joseph Merrick and Alfred Saker, to continue and they too handed over to the Basel Mission.

The Basel Mission arrived with four men in December 1886, but malaria struck down several within a short time of landing. The task of integrating the local Baptists into the Basel missionary work proved intractable, with separatist Churches springing up as a consequence. The German response of seeking to undercut the African separatists by founding in 1890 the Baptist Mission to Cameroun was ineffectual, and attempts to reconcile the separatists failed. In 1898, perhaps as an admission of failure, the Missionary Society of the German Baptists, with headquarters in Berlin, was formed.

Meanwhile the Basel Mission continued with its own independent work. Between 1889 and 1897 it took significant strides around Douala. Nine stations were opened and the staff of European missionaries grew to twenty-two. Again between 1903 and 1914 the Mission was breaking new ground. A propitious mission station was opened at Fumban, a large African city and a royal capital, with an estimated population at that time of 18,000. Its ruler, King Ndjoia, was able to negotiate successfully with the Germans to bring benefits to his people. He helped develop a phonetic system for his language independent of Arabic or the Roman script. He maintained an open-door policy on religious matters, first encouraging Muslims and Christians to settle in the royal capital and then eventually allowing a large church capable of holding 400 worshippers to be erected and to replace the mosque. Political calculations were important in this decision, for the King declined to become a convert himself, suggesting that personal conviction had not moved him to favour Christianity. However no Pentecostal wind of conversion swept through the city in spite of embellished hopes, for in 1913 only 217 worshippers could be claimed by the church in a city with a population of more than eighty-two times that number. Rather Fumban counted more for its strategic and commercial location. Missionary work began to radiate to outlying regions between 1911 and 1913.

In Edea to the south-east of Douala, demand for schools helped to spur on missionary expansion. By 1914 there were at least ninety outstations with 6,600 pupils and a baptised membership of 1,150. In the Cameroun Highlands to the north of Douala, a similar demand for schools opened the way for missionary penetration, and in the new climate of European imperial control it became the most accessible form of signalling submission and even disguising resistance. In 1908, in the town of Bali in the Cameroun Highlands, the chief had two of his sons baptised along with thirty-two other children. The abatement of tribal conflict, the imposition of order, the revival of trade and the concentration of population that went with it all helped to provide unprecedented opportunities for the Church.

Wesleyan Methodist Missionary Society in Ghana, 1831–1961

We have already described the work of Philip Quaque, how he returned from training in England to serve as schoolmaster, catechist and missionary in Cape Coast. The school where he taught was supported by the Royal African Company, mainly for the children of those connected with the trading activities of the Company, and was later taken over by the Colonial government. The former pupils of the school had organised themselves into a Bible Band which also called itself 'the Meeting', or the Society for Promoting Christian Knowledge (SPCK), a name they adopted from the English society of the same name. This was in 1831. As their name showed, they were keen on reading the Bible, but they could not get enough for their needs. As a group of literate men they quickly attracted the unsympathetic attention of officialdom, and consequently their requests for Bibles and for missionaries from England went unheeded. George Maclean, the leader of the merchant community on the Gold Coast, wrote disapprovingly of the request when the Bishop of London referred it to him for his advice. But the leaders of the Bible Band were not short of initiative, with men like William de Graf and George Blankson. The latter was to perform the unusual service of negotiating with the Asantehene on behalf of a hard-pressed Governor in 1853 and again in 1854.

Having failed through official channels to obtain help from abroad, the Bible Band approached a sympathetic sea captain who returned to England with the news of eager young Africans wanting Bibles and Christian instruction. This coincided with renewed interest in religious and philanthropic circles in Britain in the welfare and spiritual progress of Africa. For example, Sir Thomas Fowell Buxton, that indefatigable campaigner on behalf of the weak and despised, had addressed the annual meeting of the Wesleyan Methodist Missionary Society which met in May 1834. As was his wont he appealed for missionaries to Africa. 'Remember', he said 'the wrongs of Africa; and remember that the only compensation you can offer is religious instruction.'[4] Thus when the request from the Cape Coast Bible Band reached the ears of the Methodists, they lost no time in responding. The man who came out in October 1834, Joseph Dunwell, did so after much soul-searching, and although his doubts about his fitness for the task were never completely quelled, he

4. Bartels (1965), p.10.

embarked with an encouraging show of support for the cause from the
Bristol Methodists.

Enthusiastically received by the members of the Band, Dunwell
settled down quickly into his job. By March 1835, he had issued fifty
membership tickets. He also established a meeting place for the
young Christians and accommodation for himself. Dunwell died five
months later, in June 1835, but his flock resolved 'to remain in the
profession; for', they declared, 'though the missionary was dead,
God lives.'[5] By 1836 two Methodist communities existed with a total
of 222 members. Dunwell was succeeded by two missionary couples,
the Rev and Mrs George Wrigley and the Rev and Mrs Harrop, but
within a year all four were dead. Even at this early stage of Methodist
work, two clear needs were keenly felt. One was the demand for a
spacious enough church and school to cope with the influx of new
members, — Wrigley tried but failed to put up new premises — and
the second was the use of local languages, particularly Fanti. Wrigley
in this case succeeded in acquiring enough knowledge of Fanti to
translate portions of the Scriptures. During his brief period of service,
Wrigley was able to see the work expand at Anomabu, Elmina,
Dixcove, Aburra Dunkwa and Dominasi. Methodism had reached a
turning point.

The man who became the architect of Methodist expansion in
Ghana was the Rev. Thomas Birch Freeman, an indefatigable
pioneer who was not afraid to push ahead and confront new
problems. His energy for work was matched only by his vision, and
the limits he set to both exceeded the normal.

Thomas Birch Freeman, William Wadé Harris and Methodism, 1838 – 1957

When Freeman arrived at Cape Coast in January 1838, few doubted
that the right choice had been made at the right time. The son of an
African father by an English mother, Freeman felt instinctively
drawn to Africa and was determined to make an impact for the
Church on the continent, at great personal cost as it turned out.
Fortunately, and unusually, he was to have some fifty-two years of
active service in which to accomplish his dream. He was eighty-one
when he died in 1890, something like an evergreen in a field of lilies.

Freeman's aim was to develop African resources to cope with his
vision of the increasing challenge of Christianity to Africa, feeling
that the time available in which to do this was very limited. With
irrepressible energy he set about his task, planning, preaching,
writing, administering and, above all, travelling on his meteoric
course across the limitless horizons on which he saw the rising star of
the Church.

5. Bartels (1965), p.19.

Six months after his arrival Freeman opened a chapel at Cape Coast, and a month later he was drawing up a comprehensive plan for organising education and leadership training for the.Church in the Gold Coast. He sent this to the Missionary Committee in London, urging support for his plans, and especially for a special Christian boarding school which would train the future leaders of the Church. He convened the first missionary meeting at Cape Coast to which he invited the local governor. He appealed for support and financial contribution to extend Christian work to other parts of the country. Impatient with the vagaries of the archaic means of transport then available, Freeman went to London himself to make personal representation on his plans. This was in October 1838.

In Ghana itself, Freeman was preoccupied with penetrating Kumasi, building on the strong foundations being laid in Cape Coast as a bridgehead. He formed three Society Classes under the charge of the three founding members and enrolled children in the first Methodist school in western Ghana. From Cape Coast he also appealed constantly to the chiefs of the surrounding areas whose opposition he believed had stood in the way of Christian expansion, and spoke tirelessly about the benefits Christianity would confer.

Kumasi and wider horizons

The political relations between Cape Coast and Kumasi were badly strained, and the climate deteriorated sharply with the activities of British commercial and military agents operating on the southern flanks of Ashanti. Christian overtures reaching Kumasi across the menaced frontiers of Fantiland were accordingly resisted. However Methodist work was represented there in the person of James Hayford who was sufficiently influential with the Asantehene, Osei Yaw (1824–38), to hold Christian services in the palace. This fact emboldened Freeman and the Cape Coast Church to begin work in Kumasi in April 1839, to the ornate welcome of a royal durbar. Greatly heartened by this welcome, and perhaps slightly incredulous at the apparent willingness of the Asantehene to welcome Christianity, Freeman returned to Kumasi at the head of an elaborate party of 340 people, with two Ashanti princes for extra effect, taking with him an English carriage as a present for the Asantehene. This was in July 1841, during the reign of Kwaku Dua I (1838–67), who gave permission for the opening of a mission station. The mission remained active until 1872, when fresh political troubles forced it to shut down.

The habit of keeping royal company, once formed, tended to harden, and Freeman was again penetrating distant kingdoms and hoisting the Christian ensign before royal personages. Between 1842 and 1843 he visited Badagry and Abeokuta in Nigeria, and Porto

Novo and Abomey in Dahomey. In 1843 he returned for the third time to Ashanti and to Badagry for the second time the following year. In Abeokuta Freeman met King Shodeke and conducted a Christian communion service in the royal presence, the first man, it is claimed, to perform Christian worship there. The accounts do not speak of King Shodeke partaking in the service, although it is significant enough that he allowed it. Freeman paid a further visit to Dahomey in 1854, which led to the stationing of P. W. Bernasko at Whydah between 1857 and 1866. In 1862, with Freeman temporarily out of Church service, the Rev. William West, Freeman's successor, was brought reports that the King of Dahomey wished to meet him. Without his predecessor's sense of the royal occasion, West ignored the reports. This coincided with a time of severe testing for Christians in Dahomey, with many suffering persecution under the King's provocative policy of resisting the Church's stand against warfare and the slave trade.

To return to Freeman: when he was not travelling he kept busy, encouraging the founding of village schools to which he sent teachers from Cape Coast. When the Rev. Timothy Laing, an African assistant minister at Anomabu, called for the application of Christianity to the practical needs of the people, Freeman backed him with a project to create a theological seminary. When Methodism was taken to Mankessim in the heart of Fantiland and there encountered stiff opposition from the worshippers of Naanam, the spirit of ancestor cults, Freeman joined the battle by personally baptising 207 people in the village. The sacred shrine housing the cult was dismantled, the titular spirit toppled and a Methodist chapel triumphantly raised on the ruins of the old religion. In this spiritual battle Freeman confidently enlisted the support of modern education. In April 1876, the Wesleyan High School was opened. It changed its name in 1905 to Mfantsipim. Two of its pioneer pupils, J. Mensah Sarbah and J. E. Casely Hayford, became the intellectual forebears of modern African nationalism. In 1884 the Wesley Girls' High School was opened, the **fulfilment** of the long-cherished dream of promoting the advancement of African women. Freeman himself presided over the expansion of Methodist work, and in fact his enthusiasm led him to over-spend, and as a result he was forced to resign in September 1857. However, because his worth was appreciated, he was able to return to the service of the Church in 1873. Having closely supervised the birth of Methodism in Ghana, Freeman can justly be regarded as its father. As we shall see with the establishment of the African Methodist Episcopal Zion Church in Ghana, his contribution, direct and indirect, to the Christian awakening in West Africa was enormous.

In the interval between Frecman's resignation and re-appointment, the work was carried on by five African ministers:

Timothy Laing, J. A. Solomon, Frederick France, John Plange and Edward J. Fynn. Supported by the missionary the Rev. William West, they and a few others held the Church together and deepened its local roots. Assisting them was a West Indian from St Vincent, Henry Wharton, who offered himself for service to West Africa in 1843. Wharton was in Freeman's company when the latter visited Dahomey in 1854, although the plan to station him there was unsuccessful. Wharton eventually became Chairman of the Methodist Church in Ghana, leaving in 1872. Thus in the years between 1857 and 1873, i.e. during the absence from the scene of Freeman, the Methodist church in Ghana had made important strides towards the goal of becoming a truly national church. That indeed was the reward Freeman felt was appropriate for his labours.

Others of course had been fired by the same vision. For example, the Rev James Fletcher, then Chairman of the Methodist Church, proposed a radical africanisation scheme in which Africans would gradually take over control, both administrative and financial, of the Church, to culminate in the withdrawal of all missionary personnel. In that form Fletcher's proposals anticipated by nearly a century the demand of Churches in Africa for a moratorium on mission. Fletcher returned to London in 1881 and his ideas were never implemented in the way he wanted. But perhaps it was a kindred spirit which moved Church leaders at the 1885 Jubilee service, conducted by Freeman himself, to call for a West African Methodist Conference. The Church was defended as an institution eminently suited to the people and to be within their means, a reference there to the great success of local Methodists in raising funds and undertaking self-supporting projects, to the envy of some parsimonious missionaries. The synod of 1905, for example, reported that over £9,600 was raised throughout the Church.

The popular roots of Methodism are undeniable and were reaffirmed by the rich harvest of souls that the Prophet William Wadé Harris produced among people in Liberia, the Ivory Coast and western Ghana between 1913 and 1915. Estimates of the number of Harris converts vary between 60,000 and 100,000, suggesting a profound response to the man. Most of these converts could not read or write and had little or no Christian instruction, for Harris merely told them to hold on to their Bibles until God sent them some white men to unlock the Scriptures for them. He had thus opened a vast new mission field. Harris himself had attended an American Methodist Mission school in Liberia and was baptised in due course. However he had never been ordained, and he attributed his conversion at about the age of twenty-one to an African minister of the American Methodist Mission. Yet in his preaching, embarked on after a vision in prison, Harris concentrated on worship of one God and salvation in Jesus Christ, leaving aside denominational matters.

Many different Churches and missions responded equally enthusiastically to his movement. For their part the Methodists in Ghana felt it important to recruit the new Harris converts. The Rev. Ernest Bruce, the Methodist minister based at Axim, spoke of a general religious awakening in places Harris visited, with a remarkable devotion to the Christian life. 'Everywhere', he wrote, 'bamboo chapels and churches were built' and that people's 'thirst for the word of God and for the songs of Zion is insatiable.'[6] The Methodist missionary the Rev. Charles Armstrong found 8,000 Harris converts in Apollonia in early August 1914, all waiting for Christian instruction. Harris had passed through that area a few weeks earlier. The Methodists in Cape Coast, desirous of giving help, were prevented from doing so by two serious problems. One was the familiar question of shortage of personnel, and the other was the new restrictions imposed by the French authorities, who outlawed the use of English and also banned work in local languages, in this case Fanti and Nzima. However, the Methodists continued to follow events in Nzima country with deep interest. The Rev. William Goudie visited Nzima to witness for himself the wonder Harris had wrought. Yet despite a threefold increase in membership, Methodist reports were claiming that as late as 1923 large numbers of Harris converts were still without a church. In about 1925 the Methodist church in Britain responded to the now much publicised need in the Ivory Coast, by which time the French authorities had subjected many Harris converts to severe persecution and restricted their movement. Despite all this, it is claimed that some 50,000 people joined the Church when the Methodists opened one in the Ivory Coast.

The significance of Harris was easily appreciated. J. Casely Hayford, himself of Methodist stock, wrote movingly of the Prophet Harris and his simple but powerful life-style, describing Harris's movement as not simply a revival but a pentecost. Of Harris himself he wrote that his soul moved in a higher plane, and that he was a dynamic force of a rare order and a man who would move his age in a new way. His impact on those who came within his hearing was electric, and the effect he wrought on those whose souls he touched was permanent.[7] Harris, though above denomination, gave sanction to the deep-seated Methodist tradition of encouraging lay participation, being himself a layman of course. Hence the instinctive appeal of his achievement and style.

Other Churches, as already indicated, profited greatly from the preaching of Prophet Harris, whatever their ecclesiastical scruples. The Catholic Missionary Society of Lyons had maintained a base in Nzima country from 1908. Fr George Fischer, working in the area at

6. Debrunner (1967), p.272.
7. Casely Hayford (1915), pp. 6–9, etc.

the time, gathered some 4,000 Harris converts into a Church between 1916 and 1921. In the late 1920s the Catholics had about forty mission stations in Nzima and ten more along the Tana river, thanks to the spiritual awakening wrought by Harris. The Anglicans profited similarly. The Rev. E. D. Martinson and C. H. Elliott, based in Sefwi, occupied themselves with the aftermath of the revival of Harris. They met John Swatson, a Harris follower, at a time when Swatson was calling people to form Anglican communities in obedience, or so he claimed, to the instructions of the Prophet Harris. Such communities were called 'Christ Church' villages, after the original Christ Church at Cape Coast. So great was the impact of Harris that his converts stretched the resources of existing Churches and spilled over into a cluster of Independent Churches led by self-styled Prophets in imitation of the great man. In fact most of his followers are to be found in such Prophet-led Churches, a testimony to the indelible impression he left after only a few years of preaching in what was no more than a once-and-for-all visit in most places. Casely Hayford's unrestrained admiration is thus understandable.

The rapid expansion of Methodist work continued apace in Ghana itself, the reason in part why the Church could not respond adequately to the work of Prophet Harris beyond Ghana. Leadership training received a significant boost with the opening of Wesley College, Kumasi, in March 1924, with Governor Guggisberg presiding over the ceremonies. The Church was also very well supported by local fund-raising campaigns. For example, at the Centenary celebrations, marked in January 1933 by a special Synod, £15,000 was raised towards a Centenary fund. A commemmorative service was inevitably held at Cape Coast at New Year's Eve 1934 to mark the arrival in Ghana of the first Methodist missionary, Dunwell. Other milestones included the creation of a joint Methodist-Presbyterian ministerial training college in 1943, later moved to Legon with the name Trinity College. In 1944, after much trouble and unavoidable delay, the Fanti Bible was completed. In 1957, the year of Ghana's independence, Methodists numbered 160,000, meeting in 1,200 places of worship. The Church became an autonomous conference in 1961, its role in education and the nation's history firmly established. It has similarly been active in inter-Church relations, forming with the Presbyterians and Anglicans the Ghana Christian Council (formerly the Christian Council of the Gold Coast, founded in 1929). The Salvation Army joined it in 1934. At the founding of the World Council of Churches at Oslo in 1948 and at the second meeting at Evanston, Illinois, in 1954, Ghanaian Methodism played an active part; a Ghanaian Methodist was elected to the Central Committee at the Evanston meeting. At the meeting of the Second Vatican Council in 1962 the President of the Ghana Methodist Church pledged earnest support for its deliberations.

Equally significantly, the Ghana Methodist Church began sending its own missionaries to other parts of Africa, a fitting tribute to the African initiative in the Christian awakening of the continent.

The African Methodist Episcopal Zion Church

The African Methodist Episcopal Zion Church (AMEZ) had its beginnings in New York in 1796 with a group of Afro-Americans who in 1821 formed themselves into a separate Church. It was introduced to West Africa by John Bryan Small, who had served in Ghana between 1863 and 1896 in the West Indian Regiment as a recruit from Jamaica. Small returned and while in America registered as a member of the AMEZ Church of which he was later consecrated bishop; he always maintained an active interest in affairs in Ghana. In 1898 branches of the Church were founded respectively at Cape Coast and at Keta, accompanied by the expression of nationalist sentiment. The first of these was organised by Thomas Freeman, the son of the great pioneer of the same name, under the authority of Bishop Small. The bishop himself visited Ghana in July 1902, in pursuit of an energetic africanisation policy, the consequence of which had led to the sending of J. E. K. Aggrey, born at Anomabu, for further education to the United States. Aggrey, later to become one of Africa's most famous sons, went to the AMEZ Church College of Livingstone in North Carolina in 1898. He returned in 1920 after a distinguished scholarly career in America. The AMEZ Church in Ghana was led by a group of distinguished Africans, some of them fired by the ideals of a new era of nationalist agitation. One of the most outstanding men of this sort was the Rev. Dr. Ata Osam Pinanko who embraced the nationalist cause with passion, seeing Christianity and politics as natural allies in the struggle to liberate the Black race.

It was thus under the stimulus of Christianity that 'Ethiopian' sentiments began to circulate freely until they crystallised into Christian Separatism or the Ethiopian Movement. Whatever else may be said about Christianity in Africa, it cannot be said to have prevented Africans from adopting the path of political activism. In this, as in the work of the Church, Ghana played a leading role, suggesting perhaps a deeper logical connection between Church and politics than is customarily realised.

6

CHRISTIAN MISSIONS AND AFRICAN EDUCATION AND SOCIAL IMPROVEMENT

The Church is charged with the commission to make the truth entrusted to it available to each generation... The spread of education is not therefore a secondary consideration of the Church, but stands at the very core and centre of the Christian message, bidding the Christian in obedience to Christ to seek truth and to see that the young are truly nurtured in His way through the family, the schools and the other institutions society has created for their nurture... [But] we must be clear that...there is a point past which education cannot go. Persons cannot be educated into conversion.

Christian Education in Africa (1963)

Introduction

No single subject has attracted as much consistent attention and resources in the history of Christian penetration of Africa as education, and no subject was as effective in the revolutionary transformation of African societies. Consequently education assumed a wide range of roles. In the hands of the missionaries it was often used as an instrument of conversion and nurture. Whether in fact it was effective as such is open to question. In the hands of conservative and some liberal philanthropists, education was conceived as a means of social control, to instill in the African a proper attitude of subservience towards the white man, usually in connection with tilling the land and producing the raw materials needed to feed western industries. Partly to answer the rising chorus of derision at the African spoilt by book-learning, some wild agricultural projects were dreamt up to set the record straight. Then again, in the eyes of the traditional Muslim leaders, modern education represented the scourge of infidel Christians, and it was approached with the greatest defiance or reluctance. Finally, for many African populations, especially those living in the coastal belt, education was welcomed as the gateway to a new and secure future. In all these instances modern education produced results and repercussions far greater than could be envisaged from any single standpoint. It shattered old ideas, created a new class of people and a new social environment, encouraged a fresh interest in African's ancient heritage and undermined the foundations of the European colonial structure, completing the paradox of ignorance as the justification for colonialism by adding to it the solvent of the existence of an educated class of Africans as the necessity for its end. Scholars will continue to argue about the actual benefits of western education to Africa; but, whether missionaries educated Africans to suppress them or to advance their welfare (there was indeed something of both), no one can now doubt the incisive nature of the instrument they were wielding. Africa would never be the same again.

Different approaches

The subject of this chapter can be studied from many points of view. One way is to look at the missionary side of the story and describe the aims, policies and personalities of the people who directed the missionary project. This approach would concentrate on the views of those who attempted to bring change in African societies, examining their motives and setting these in the context of the African experience. This has been the traditional approach and it has yielded much of value in the form of books and scholarly articles. I do not, however, intend to repeat that approach here or to compete with it.

Another approach is to investigate the subject in terms of African political response. This way of dealing with the subject seeks to tell a story about the growth of African nationalism, and it does this by looking upon the first generation of educated Africans as hidden national figures whose work was completed by a later generation of Africans. The intention of missionary educators is subordinated in this approach to the unconquerable spirit of African independence, so that missionary education achieved the unintended result of stiffening African resolve and directing it on the path of political and cultural emancipation. The missionary motive of service to Africa is thus impugned, the religious strand in their work made to fuse with the popular fashion of nationalist reaction, and the schools they founded to become the nursery beds of African resistance. This approach does not deny the revolutionary character of the change modern education has wrought in Africa. It assumes that, but seeks to make Africans, not the missionaries, the architects of that change.

This political approach has much to commend it. Its value has been to call our attention to the important theme of local response to missionary education and to caution us against proceeding only on the basis of official declarations of policy and intention. On the ground in Africa, we are being told, the story was dominated by Africans, whether in terms of educational excellence or by virtue of becoming the victims of missionary oppression. While acknowledging the importance of the shift of emphasis this approach represents, I do not wish to follow it here for reasons that I have alluded to in the Introduction and which I should now proceed to set out.

There is a third approach in which the focus is maintained on the field in Africa. Missionary education is investigated in terms of its impact on African society, but it is done in such a way as to preserve the continuity of the Christian religious theme. The African response then is seen from the point of view of Africa, not in relation to the political awakening of the continent, important as that is, but in the context of the spread of Christian influence and the pivotal religious role Africans played in it. That is our approach here.

The reasons for choosing this last approach for our purposes should be obvious. The history of the interaction of Christianity and Africa is a large and significant enough subject to be treated independently of other aspects of European contacts with Africa. Secondly, the African interest in the religious message of Christianity is similarly detachable from other factors that the presence of Christianity created. Thirdly, combining the two elements of the above points, there is enough evidence to suggest that some Africans at least perceived the opportunities that modern education opened to them in terms of an explicit responsibility to further the spread of Christian influence. Their agency in the dissemination of Christianity in different parts of West Africa and beyond is an integral part of the history of Africa, and to isolate it in order to study it better is an important step towards understanding that history. So much, then, for preliminaries.

The scope of the field

The presence of Europeans in Africa triggered a demand for western education. European traders could operate better if a certain number of Africans were literate, and so they set about encouraging this. But the western Christian lobby was anxious to protect Africa from some of the worst features of European civilisation, particularly the trade in slaves that had prospered with the trans-Atlantic stimulus and the habit of alcohol consumption which the traders encouraged. The potential of an educated Africa for the future of Christianity was immediately realised. The continent was being opened up to new influences, some of them not altogether benign. Christian circles in Europe were already beginning to feel that material restitution was due to the Black man for the wrongs of the slave trade and slavery. The opportunity to demonstrate such contrition of spirit was now being afforded by the desire of Africa to acquire useful knowledge and dedicate her sons and daughters to the service of her people. All that was needed was a scheme to cater to this need and the resources to support it. The field of opportunity was indefinite, with the restriction only of definable resources.

Early demands for education: the Sierra Leone story, 1769-1815

In the early days Africans travelled to Europe to obtain the education they desired. Often rulers sent their sons to be educated abroad, some even taking the precaution of looking to different places at home and abroad to make sure they obtained the best that was going. For example, in 1769 a king of Sierra Leone sent one son to Lancaster in England to learn Christianity and another to Futa Jallon to study Islam. Another ruler showed even more resourcefulness. This was King Naimbana of the Koya Temne of Sierra Leone. After ceding a piece of land to the French in 1785, he gave them his son Pedro (or perhaps Bartholomew) to be educated in France. He made arrangements for another son to be brought up a Muslim. A third, John Frederic (later named Henry Granville), was sent to England to be educated by two clergymen. He aroused high hopes, his benefactors wishing that he 'would be as useful in Africa, as Alfred and the first Peter were in their respective countries'.[1] His father, the king, died in February 1793, and he returned in June that year, 'dreaming of preaching the Gospel to his countrymen'.[2] However, he was carried from the ship on which he arrived disheartened and dying. His brother Bartholomew returned safely.

The example was followed by many other traditional rulers. In March 1794, Henry Kolkelly, the son of a Temne chief in Sierra Leone, was sent abroad with an official to be educated, together with another local boy, John Wilson, from the Bulom Shore. The interest of local rulers in the new religion of Christianity was obvious. If they adopted it personally they ran the risk of occupying a subordinate position *vis-à-vis* its official spokesmen; if they rejected it completely there was equally the grave risk of ignoring an influence which might gain support among their subjects and cause disaffection. Many resolved the dilemma by offering their sons as propitiatory gifts to the new forces entering the land. Committed to the logic of seeking the welfare of Africa, Christianity at this point was prepared to be guided by local considerations: the demand for education must be met as far as possible, even if the best available was of an *ad hoc*, temporary nature.

In this process Africans were among the early pioneers. Some were engaged to teach the sons of chiefs brought to Freetown. One was Mingo Jordan, a Nova Scotian, who was hired as a special teacher to introduce chiefs' sons to English. Another teacher was Boston King who went to the Bullom Shore in a missionary role. 'The few schoolmasters could not cope with the demand for schooling within the Colony, where adults as well as children sought education. Almost everyone literate enough was employed to teach. The Governor examined the schoolchildren. Teachers were enjoined to enforce personal cleanliness and morality, and take their pupils to church twice on Sunday.'[3]

1. Fyfe, *History of Sierra Leone* (1962), p.30.
2. ibid., p.54.
3. ibid., p.55.

The Colony authorities, short of personnel and funds, co-operated gladly with missions. When Macaulay, soon to be the new Governor, returned from England in March 1796, he was accompanied by two Scottish schoolmasters to take charge of the Colony school, then consisting of about 200 children and meeting together in the church. Now it was possible to reorganise the school and divide it up. An English widow from Clapham, Mrs Wilkinson, was put in charge of the girls, with a Nova Scotian schoomistress to assist her. The Sierra Leone Company (then the legal authority in the Colony), perhaps encouraged by hopes that others would be willing to pay for education, began cutting back its participation; it stopped supplying stationery to the children, although school fees were not charged except to those parents who refused to sign the declaration of not possessing looted property. Those living outside the Colony were also charged a fee. But such restrictions failed to deter the enterprising. One Cape Coast trader, for example, maintained a girl at the school for an annual fee of £14, which included board and lodging. The missionary teachers at the school worked alongside those employed by the Company. Chiefs continued to send children to the school, and no fees were collected from them. They were given lodgings in Macaulay's house, where he introduced them to Christian prayers and on Sundays gave them lessons on the catechism.

Nevertheless the tradition of looking to education for the cuts it felt necessary hardened with the Company into a popular dogma. In January 1799, it was announced that fees would be introduced for all children except for those whose parents had paid quit-rent. Now quit-rent was a deeply contentious issue, arousing in the Settlers fears of reverting to slavery. Its invocation in the context of education confirmed old suspicions about the inherent treachery of authority, suspicions compounded of the bitter experience of slave plantations in the United States and the disappointments in Nova Scotia. The children were almost at once withdrawn from the school, and a relaxation of the rule a year later failed to overcome Settler opposition completely. Some sixty parents returned their children, but most stayed away. The Company had added to the problem of shortage of funds that of a shortage of goodwill, and with that had cast a cloud over its future.

The Settlers looked elsewhere to educate their children. When Macaulay left for England in April 1799, never to return, he took with him twenty boys and four girls. Intended for a school in Edinburgh with generous provision by a local philanthropist, the children, at Macaulay's own instigation, ended up at Clapham where, ironically, they were supported by the directors of the Company. Eighteen of them were eventually baptised there. Many of those who returned to Freetown later went into official posts. One became an apothecary, another a boat-builder, another a government printer, and others clerks. Some left Freetown to settle elsewhere in Sierra Leone.

In 1807 the African Institution was founded (to be distinguished from the African Association founded in 1788 and closely associated with William Wilberforce) and included as one of its aims the object of promoting African education. It was also to keep a wary eye on the slave trade. But the African Institution became the subject of bitter controversy, involving a Freetownian of Maroon descent, Samuel Thorpe, who accused it of dereliction of responsibility in the face of abuse on a wide scale. The Institution in fact was hampered by lack of funds from carrying out its aims. It had managed to bring African boys to England for education and under its aegis a European schoolmaster went to Freetown in 1815 (to return the following year). When its effectiveness was questioned in Parliament and elsewhere, the Institution declined rapidly. It held its last meeting in 1827 and ceased to exist shortly thereafter.

A new era of educational work: the Recaptives, 1814-1907

It can safely be said that the fresh population of African recaptives which poured into Freetown as a safe haven (see chapter 4) constituted a turning-point. By a remarkable coincidence of history this period overlapped for a significant number of years with the governorship of Sir Charles MacCarthy, a man of tremendous energy and administrative foresight, though, like all mortals, a man who was not without his foibles. When he was appointed Governor in 1816 MacCarthy inherited a Colony with the most ramshackle educational system. The CMS had neglected education in Freetown and turned instead to the Rio Pongas in the hinterland. The Wesleyan Methodist Mission took over some of the school work, but was hampered by lack of personnel. In 1814 the CMS obtained a plot of land at the foot of Leicester Mountain, Freetown, which it used to found the Christian Institution, a school designed more for vocational training for recaptive children who would also be taught farming than for book-learning. In 1819 the school was closed down and a small nucleus transferred to Regent in 1820 to form a seminary of higher education, the brainchild of the enterprising Governor rather than of a reluctant CMS. Perhaps that factor alone sealed its fate, for in 1826 the two remaining pupils of the Christian Institution were dismissed and the place was shut down for lack of interest and teachers. That was more or less typical of the weakness of education in Freetown when Sir Charles MacCarthy arrived on the scene. The man matched the moment.

One writer commented on the impression the Colony made on MacCarthy when he saw it. He 'was shocked by the miserable settlements round Freetown where recaptives had been dumped, without help or instruction, to refashion their lives as best they could on alien soil, Where previous governors saw an administrative problem, how to settle them cheaply, he saw a heaven-sent way of transforming Africa by changing them into Christian communities, orderly villages, each grouped round its church tower, instructed and cared for by benevolent European guidance.'[4]

Under a scheme worked out by MacCarthy with the British Treasury, money was made available to reorganise the Colony and its satellite recaptive settlements into parishes. These parishes would be under the charge of CMS clergymen paid by the government. The government would also build churches, schools and parsonages while the CMS would provide and pay for the teachers. The scheme encouraged the CMS to turn its attention to the Colony for work among recaptives, winding down its unrewarding work in the Rio Pongas. MacCarthy surveyed the entire scene with the imaginative purpose of a pioneer. If God made the world he saw about him, then it would be his privilege to bestow upon it the adornment that high office by providence made possible. He 'spared no expense to make the villages reflect his vision. Bells, clocks and weathercocks were ordered from England for church towers, forges for village blacksmiths, scales and weights for village markets. Quill-pens and copy-books, prayer books and arithmetic books were ordered for the schools, with tin cases for the children to carry them in, lamps to read them by. Hats were ordered for the men, bonnets for the women, shoes for all; gowns and petticoats, trousers and braces — buttons, too, with needles, thread and thimbles, soap and smoothing-irons, even clothes-brushes; nothing was forgotten. As well as ready-made clothes, he ordered yards of pretty patterned cottons — for schoolgirls to make up into shirts and dresses.'[5]   In 1819 he began a grandiose school project with two wings, one for boys and the other for girls. When Major-General Turner took over as Governor in 1825, the school was still unfinished, and it was only completed in 1830.

In 1824 the CMS revised the terms of its involvement in the 'parish scheme' set up by MacCarthy. It argued that missionary recruitment would be less difficult if missionaries could be relieved of administration in the recaptive villages and if the government would pay lay superintendents. The CMS would also take over responsibility for the Colonial School in Freetown.

Was the 'parish scheme' a success? From the point of view of those who wished to transplant a slice of English culture to Africa and make it flourish, it was hardly a success story. From the point of view of orderly administration, it was undoubtedly a success, even an imaginative project. In terms of the African response the 'parish scheme' harnessed the institutional customs of Africa and forged a

4. Fyfe, *History of Sierra Leone* (1962), p.128.
5. ibid., p.131.

sense of community among the displaced and uprooted. The notion of village elders, age-set groups, initiation rites and even of tribal solidarity received a tremendous boost under the scheme. Traditional religious customs and ideas, a sense of Yoruba national feeling, of a Fulbe national identity and of a Muslim communal awareness were rejuvenated through the unwitting instrument of MacCarthy's plan and its continuation. In that ironic sense the scheme was a huge success, carrying with it far-reaching consequences for much of West Africa.

Wracked by a high mortality rate among its missionaries, the CMS turned to recaptives to revive the work. For example, between 1804 and 1824 it lost through death thirty-eight of its seventy European missionaries, a mortality rate of over 54 per cent, and seven returned ill. It was an appalling casualty rate, and in situational terms it was not necessary. Africans could be trained to take over the jobs white missionaries had done in teaching and other areas, and do them sometimes more effectively than they had been done before. That in fact was the plan the CMS embarked on. Under the direction of the German missionary the Rev. Charles Haensel, it was decided to restart the then defunct Christian Institution. It was reopened on a new site at Fourah Bay in April 1827. Samuel Ajayi Crowther was enrolled as one of its first pupils and made a monitor, and he wrote a weekly journal of events at the place which was sent to London. Crowther left in 1829 to go to Regent as teacher, and later to Wellington. Another prominent pioneer pupil of the Institution was John Langley, an Ibo recaptive. He went to teach at the village of Kent.

Demand for education continued to expand in the 1830s and beyond. The CMS and the Methodists began charging a nominal fee, a halfpenny a week. That appears to have put a price on education, with parents clamouring for places for their children. Existing schools were filled, children were turned away as a consequence and new schools were opened. By 1840 it is estimated that over 8,000 children were in school, which was nearly 20 per cent of the population. In that year some English Quakers agreed to pay for the training of two recaptives as teachers in London. One was Charles Knight, an Ibo recaptive at Gloucester, and the other was Joseph May, an Aku. Both made excellent progress and both returned as teachers: May reorganised the New Town West school into one of the best in Freetown and in 1849 went to Georgetown, in the Gambia, as a missionary teacher in the new Wesleyan Methodist mission.

In 1845 the CMS opened the Grammar School to provide secondary education for boys. The school was started by the missionary the Rev. Thomas Peyton, but it was open to all without denominational prerequisites. The subjects taught were mathematics, Greek, Biblical and English history, Geography,

History, Music and Latin. Day boys paid four guineas a year, boarders £15. Within twenty years over four-fifths of the boys had their fees paid by their parents or local benefactors. For that reason it was not a charity or a missionary college. Of the first eight boys to leave, only three went to the Christian Institution (later Fourah Bay College) to read for orders. One became a teacher, two found employment as government clerks and two went into business.

The first names on the Grammar School register included the sons of a chief from the Gallinas and a Temne from Port Loko. Within a few years boys were sent there from Badagry, Abeokuta, Liberia and Fernando Po. It had become a truly West African educational establishment.

In 1845, to show that a great future lay ahead, Dr William Fergusson, the first governor of African descent, laid the foundation stone of a new building at Fourah Bay after the CMS decided once again to take up responsibility for the Christian Institution. The four-storied stone-built house was opened in 1848, and the first principal was the Rev. Edward Jones, of African descent. Students lived in, and were fed and clothed. The curriculum included Greek, Latin and West African languages. In 1847, the Rev. Sigismund Koelle, the eminent linguist, came to teach Greek, Hebrew and Arabic, although his fame actually rests on his original work on West African languages, *Polyglotta Africana,* completed in 1854, which records the vocabularies of over 200 African languages. In the early 1850s, when the Vai script was discovered by Commander F.E. Forbes, Koelle went to study it, in Gallinas country.

The success of the Grammar School showed that local demand for 'pure' knowledge as opposed to vocational training was real and buoyant enough. The old Settlers and their new recaptive compatriots, now known as Creoles, were unmistakably clear about the importance of formal education and strove by every available means to ensure that their children received it. But the CMS was coming under increasing fire for neglecting agriculture and the mythical abundance of tropical Africa and instead concentrating scarce resources on book-learning. To its chagrin the Home Committee, under the Rev. Henry Venn, concurred with the criticism. This forced the CMS to seek to combine the sublime with the absurd: Grammar School boys were rested from their Latin classes to learn cotton growing. But even the forceful climate of prejudice against book-learning could not rejuvenate the gravelstones of the Colony, and cotton never repaid the investment of time and money put into it. But to show that myth in this case is stronger than fact, the idea of teaching Africans how to plant cotton kept being revived in spite of repeated failure. In 1850 the CMS started an Industrial School and a Normal School to train teachers. But the virtue of agriculture was to be inculcated in the students. They planted cotton. Schoolchildren at Regent and Bathurst also grew cotton and coffee. The students at the Christian Institution similarly ploughed and made a garden. Missionary honour, if gallantly defended by such examples of Africans as tillers of the soil, was not completely redeemed by the results. The CMS continued to face mounting criticism in liberal circles at home. Sir Richard Burton, the eminent patron of the Anthropological Society of London and a man of considerable influence, wrote disparagingly of missionary education, saying that it depraved Africans and made them unfit for a useful life. His caricatures and stereotypes, widely disseminated in English newspapers, were erected as sacred facts of science and stiffened with the august authority of the Anthropological Society. Then along came Winwood Reade, flashing with popular prejudice, to stock up anthropological resources with unproved opinions, some of them fleshed out with naive medical accounts. His book, *The Martyrdom of Man,* had a profound effect on, for example, H.G. Wells, although it was his *Savage Africa* which propagated his African observations. Both he and Burton did great harm by casting missionaries in the role of villains and Africans as their defenceless victims, a circuitous way of preaching the inferiority of Africans by repudiating the effective agents of African advance. Anthropology has remained a suspect science ever since.

As it happened, the Grammar School survived the diversionary excursions into cotton growing and thrived. In 1863 the Rev. James Quaker was appointed principal. Born at Kent village in 1828, he and his brother, William, a pastor at Hastings, had been among the first boys at the school, which, under his leadership, became self-sufficient and therefore less vulnerable to liberal English prejudice. The CMS provided only twenty scholarships. Quaker set up an Endowment Fund from the proceeds of the school income. When the Government introduced civil service entrance examinations in 1868, Quaker supervised them. When we come to consider the spread of educated Creoles in other parts of West Africa, we should see that many of them had Grammar School connections, and that equally significantly the idea of the Grammar School was taken to other places where similar provision was made. For example, in 1859 a Grammar School was opened by the CMS in Lagos. More will be said about Nigeria later.

Attention was also directed to girls' education. In January 1849, the CMS opened a Female Institution under Miss Julia Sass, which was to be a complement to the Grammar School. Girl boarders were admitted at £13 a year, and day-girls at £4. As usual there were more applicants than places. The CMS tried to reduce pressure on the school by exploiting moral scruple for administrative purposes: the illegitimate daughters of Europeans would be refused places at the school. Their well-off fathers, it was felt, could afford to educate them elsewhere; and the CMS would be spared the embarrassment of appearing to grant approval to an irregular moral code. But a predictable uproar among those affected followed, although a scheme to mobilise official support for an alternative school failed after a year.

Plans were made to enlarge the Female Institution. In 1858 a plot of land was acquired and drawings were made for new premises. When it was finished in 1865 it had cost £2,500, well above the original estimate. In 1877 the school was renamed the Annie Walsh Memorial School, after the daughter of the English benefactor, the Rev. James Walsh. It was rebuilt in the 1890s by an English architect who stayed on to teach building, plumbing and carpentry.

A survey was carried out in 1868 by James Laurie, an English school inspector, which officially listed seventy-eight schools with an average attendance of 7,830. But Laurie in fact visited ninety-five schools, which means that the official list had underestimated. The attendance figure of 7,830 was out of an estimated population of 50,000 i.e. about one in six, compared to England where it was one in seven. All the schools were supported from fees charged to the pupils. Teachers had low wages and had to farm or trade to supplement their income. Very few received any training. School managers had little money to spend, and consequently schools were sparsely furnished. On the basis of James Laurie's report, the government acted to improve conditions, setting up a Model School as a means of setting the standards towards which other schools ought to strive. An annual grant-in-aid scheme was established to help those schools with the right attendance and with an acceptable pass rate in the examination set up by the inspector. A Director of Public Instruction was appointed to head the Model School and inspect other schools. Teachers were examined as well. Reading matter for pupils was made to include Shakespeare and the *Arabian Nights* besides the staple diet of text-books.

The work at Fourah Bay College continued to expand, although its suitability for training village pastors was questioned by the resident bishop who had the number of students reduced. But when it was reopened in 1864 as 'Fourah Bay College', it admitted a few students (fee-paying) for secular education. Shortly after this Samuel Ajayi Crowther paid it a visit as a former pupil, but now as Bishop of West Africa outside British jurisdiction. The next move was to upgrade Fourah Bay College as an institution for higher education. The stimulus for this came from the famous Dr Edward Blyden. His idea was for a West African university to be established where African teachers would instil in their students pride in their own traditions instead of what he considered the sterile mimicking of European habits. In this Dr Blyden echoed the racial sentiments of people like Sir Richard Burton and Winwood Reade, and argued, like them, that missionary education was having deleterious effects on African authenticity for which, again like them, his cure was an unmitigated dose of Islam in a heady mixture with African traditions. Governor Hennessy, to whom Dr Blyden sent his views, was carried to lyrical heights by the idea, with Dr Blyden's fluid flattery getting to his pen. Hennessy wrote:

> The Negro plays his part
> Within Nigretia's virgin heart.[6]

William Grant, the successful trader brought up by John Langley and a devout churchman, was fired by Blyden's idea of a West African university. Deeply respected in CMS circles (Henry Venn once described him as his ideal of an African), Grant requested the CMS to make Fourah Bay College into an institution for higher learning which would be open to all. This was accepted, and in 1875 the step was taken to open the College to any student of good character who passed the matriculation examination. Students were to be charged £5 per term for instruction and £8 for board and lodging. The CMS provided two scholarships and paid for those who went on to study theology. To safeguard standards, the College was affiliated to Durham University in England, with students sitting the Durham degree examinations which were sent by post and returned for marking. When it opened in this form on 1 February 1876, the Rev. Metcalfe Sunter was appointed principal. The staff included the Rev. C.A. Reichardt, a German missionary, the Rev. J.B. Bowen, a Mende recaptive, and later a professor of languages, the Rev. Alexander Schapira, a converted rabbi and an Arabic scholar. He opened a school in Freetown for Muslim children. Of the first sixteen students (three of them came from Lagos) nine read Arts subjects, five Theology and two for a Medical Registration Examination. The College was destined to play an indispensable role in the education of several generations of leading Africans, and it was not until national universities were established in Ghana and Nigeria from 1948 onwards that its pre-eminence was seriously challenged.

In 1906 Bo School was opened, intended for the sons of chiefs. One writer commenting on the philosophy behind the creation of the school says: 'Here the doctrines of Blyden, Burton and Rousseau united uneasily to inculcate the dignity of labour while eschewing the indignity of becoming educated. The boys were to retain what was deemed their native simplicity of manners uncontaminated by pretensions to intellectual superiority. Creole schoolmasters were excluded...in a school which turned its back on a century of West African education.'[7] That same tortuous logic which despised Africans for proving themselves the intellectual equals of Europeans

6. Fyfe, *History of Sierra Leone* (1962), p.390.
7. ibid., p.616.

now demanded that they promote those traits by which Europe had first learnt to denigrate them. A leading Creole called attention to this at the time, saying that the romantic illusion of pitting unspoilt native virtues against the pretensions of educated Africans would be short-lived when Europeans found that they were raising a class of educated Africans no less objectionable than their Creole counterparts: education was no less offensive in a native mind than in a Creole one.

The United Brethren in Christ Mission ignored the prevailing prejudice against the 'europeanisation' of Africa and instead established in 1904 in Freetown a school designed for boys from the Protectorate. It was called the Albert Academy. The idea was to expose the Sierra Leone hinterland through its sons to the wind of change that was sweeping through Africa's coastline. It is an instructive historical coincidence that the first Prime Minister of an independent Sierra Leone, Sir Milton Margai (1895-1964), was a product of the school. Sir Milton came from a United Brethren school in Bonthe and later entered Fourah Bay College. Then he qualified as a medical doctor from Durham University and spent some twenty-three years practising in Bonthe and Bo. Through his agency the people of the Protectorate began to make their full contribution to the progress of the country, something which their isolation could have denied them. The advantages of modern education for individual advancement are clear enough, but its significance for national progress is equally clear. It is perhaps an adequate comment that those who extolled the virtues of native simplicity were themselves educated people. The United Brethren and their allies were vindicated by their critics, and doubly so by the products of their schools.

While the country was being opened up with the setting up of the Protectorate in 1895 and the beginning of the railway, missionary bodies continued to push inland, opening stations under the shadow of friendly chiefs. In many cases colonial boundaries were following the lines established by missionary pioneers, although it is not always possible to say that missionary activity was stimulated by the knowledge that the flag would replace the Christian ensign.

One of the most significant initiatives in the social life of the people of the Protectorate was the opening of a boarding school for girls at Moyamba, called the Harford School for Girls. The first serious attempt at female education in that part of the country, it was opened in 1907 by American Methodist missionaries. This may be the right point at which to turn to the Methodist contribution to education.

The Methodist contribution to education: Sierra Leone

The controversial Methodist missionary Benjamin Tregaskis, already discussed in chapter 4, planned to establish a Wesleyan Boys'

High School, no doubt stung into action by sectarian envy. But, afraid to let Claudius May, the Creole earmarked for the job, have the glory, he delayed its opening as long as he could, and when it was finally opened in 1874, his recall already ordered, Tregaskis contrived that there would be no opening ceremony — an appropriate gesture from a man never distinguished for magnanimity. Nevertheless the school flourished under Claudius May, its first principal, and in time was able to challenge the dominance of the rival Grammar School. Tregaskis' departure (he had to be dragged away, convinced of his indispensability and predicting the imminent collapse of the cause in Freetown) also ushered in an era of amicable relations between the Church and the school, for his post of Superintendent was taken over by the Rev. Charles Knight, the first African to hold that position. One of the distinguished people associated with the Wesleyan Boys' High School — he was a tutor there — was W.J. Davies, the first Sierra Leonean to take a degree from London University. From there he went to the United States under a changed name as Orishatukeh Faduma and took a BD at Yale University. He was principal of a school in North Carolina for seventeen years before returning home.

In January 1880, a Wesleyan Female Institution, later the Wesleyan Girls' High School, was opened. But it was not run by the Mission, one further example of African partnership in educational work. James Taylor, a local benefactor, was manager and virtual proprietor; the school ran at a loss and it was his money that kept it going. Boarding facilities were created for girls, and the curriculum included domestic as well as academic studies. Debates were held there and published in the newspapers. On the subject of girls' education, the daughter of Bishop Crowther, Mrs Juliana Thompson, ran a school at Senehun, though not exclusively for girls.

Methodist efforts in education in the Gambia, 1821-1955

The first Methodist missionaries to the Gambia, John Morgan and John Baker, perceived education as essential to their missionary duties. Soon after arriving in 1821 Morgan set about organising a school which met in his house. In 1824 Hannah Kilham came out and started her educational work, putting into practice her ideas of introducing a completely uneducated community to literacy by reading in the vernacular and leading up to English. Kilham's party in the Gambia included two Africans who had been slaves and were redeemed from slavery and educated by the Quakers in England. Kilham went to work at a girls' school on St Mary's Island (Bathurst, now Banjul). When she left, the school was handed over to Mrs Hawkins.

The educational effort was continued by William Moister and his wife Jane, who came out in March 1831 when the school had twenty-five girls and fifty boys. John Cupidon, an African, was put in charge of the school with a salary. Moister and Cupidon then went to MacCarthy's Island (hereafter Georgetown) to build a school, a preaching room and a missionary's apartment. The only textbook available at the time was Hannah Kilham's *African Lessons.* Missionary work in Georgetown was stimulated by the landing there of Liberated Africans from Freetown, following a request from the Gambia for a labour force; at the end of the 1830s, there were roughly 253 of these immigrants there. Until about 1875, the Georgetown School was to absorb many of the resources of the Mission. Its importance was acknowledged by the Methodist District Meeting which was held there in March 1842. Church membership was 266 as against 286 in Bathurst. But the school population was much lower: there were thirty-two boys and thirty girls compared to 125 boys and sixty-five girls in Bathurst schools. The Georgetown School had cost over £1,000 to build, exceeding the original estimates. An African convert, Pierre Sallah, went there to teach after Moister's departure in 1833, joining John Cupidon and Thomas Dove and his wife, the missionaries. During this time a new school too was opened in Bathurst, later to become the Wesley Day School (September 1840). As already noted, Joseph May went from Freetown to teach at Georgetown in 1849, returning home in 1854. The Georgetown School was to have a chequered history, closing and opening often, and never really able to fulfil the dream of attracting the children and the support of the adjoining Fulbe population. At one time there were in fact two schools in Georgetown and one at Nyanibantang nearby where Pierre Sallah taught until he was withdrawn to Georgetown. But the schools were patronised mainly by the Liberated African community, with neighbouring rulers occasionally sending their sons.

The Gambia Methodist Church was administered from Freetown by the Methodist Superintendant, an arrangement which greatly irked the Gambia church. Local voices were tardily heeded in 1916 when the Gambia was created a separate district from Freetown, although a joint chairmanship was instituted in 1923 with Freetown as the base. One of the effects of the relationship with Sierra Leone was to open the Gambia to Creole agents, both religious and commercial, and, equally important, to provide in Freetown training opportunities for Gambians. It was under this joint arrangement that Benjamin Tregaskis presided over the church in the Gambia between 1865 and 1874. He was a committed advocate of education, once writing: 'You may sooner think of closing your chapels than of extending religion without education.'[8] Tregaskis was an iron

8. Prickett (1971), p. 100.

disciplinarian and he drove the people under him to conform to exacting standards of organisation and accounting. But, predictably, he found the remoteness of the Gambia a factor tending to the diminution of the kind of dictatorial control he was naturally inclined to exercise, and wrote despairingly in these terms, either to be rid of the Gambia or to have unfettered control over the Church there: 'I will not have responsibility where I cannot have control.'[9] Yet he would turn up punctually at Synod meetings in Bathurst, surmounting enormous physical obstacles to preside in person and to 'mend or end' those who earned his displeasure. Schools and accounts were better organised, reports made to follow a format laid down in the rules, and church finances stabilised.

Perhaps it is not surprising that after Tregaskis left there was a period of disorganisation, for he had taken on himself the running of the Church's affairs. The greatest difficulty, however, was lack of personnel, and the church continued for a few years without any minister at all. But the educational work was revived under the Rev. James Fieldhouse who came out in April 1875 to take charge of the schools. In September the same year the High School was opened. Sixteen pupils enrolled, with two ministerial students and one pupil teacher in training. The curriculum included Religious Knowledge, English, Higher Mathematics, Greek, Latin and Music. Fieldhouse argued for a similar institution for girls, but, largely due to the absence of local demand, that idea took another forty years to be realised. Fieldhouse, emphasising the strength of local support for the High School, said that the building alterations which were necessary were 'entirely subscribed by the people'.[10] Charles Augustus McKie, a man believed to be of West Indian orgin, helped Fieldhouse with the school.

The High School, like much else concerned with education in the Gambia, suffered all the vicissitudes of sudden, unpredictable changes, the lack of personnel and resources and the absence of training facilities. However in 1882 the government passed the first Education Ordinance which made grants to schools dependent on attendance and performance, with the added requirement that schools be inspected by the government to establish their eligibility. Similarly with the inauguration of a regular steamer service up river with the *Mansa Kilah* in 1897, attempts were made to revive the dilapidated school at Georgetown.

In June 1901 the government offered £300 a year towards an Industrial School to be run by the Mission: it became better known as the Technical College. While it was making good progress, the High School went under a cloud. For example, in 1904 the Technical College had twenty-one pupils while the number at the High School

9. ibid., p.110
10. ibid., p.119

had slumped to six with no qualified teacher. Fresh life was infused into the school only after the arrival of the Rev. C. L. Leopold, a Sierra Leonean who was to serve there for the next thirteen years. Numbers increased sharply, so that by the time Leopold left there were sixty boys on the roll. Apart from pupil teachers whom he trained himself, Leopold did all the teaching in the school. He was succeeded by a lay missionary, A. Nelson Walker. In 1909 when the Rev. W.T. Balmer, an educational missionary in Sierra Leone, visited the Gambia, he found discipline in the schools high, although ironically Scripture teaching appeared to be neglected unless, of course, his own expectations in this area were unreasonably high.

Concern for girls' education led to a site being offered for that purpose in 1915. For the first two years the school met in a basement, with twenty girls, and a missionary wife (a volunteer) in charge. She left in 1917 and the school was abandoned until 1921 when it re-opened, headed by Mrs Rebecca Savage, a Gambian, with another local woman, Mrs Ruth Carrol, as her assistant. The school moved into more appropriate accommodation when it took over the premises vacated by the Technical School after it closed. It became in effect the Girls' High School and a companion to the Boys' High School. It was decided to open the two schools to government inspection to qualify for financial support. The Girls' High School flourished. In 1939 there were 100 girls on the register. At the end of the Second World War extension work was undertaken towards which £656 was raised — the government and the missionary society each giving £200 and local people the rest. In 1945 another major step was taken under the new principal, Miss Nora Senior, who reorganised the school, grouping the girls into classes nearer their age, so that the anomaly of twenty-one-year-olds sharing the Third Form with twelve-year-olds was ended. In 1954 there were 226 girls on the school books. The first two girls from the school obtained the School Certificate in 1945.

The Boys' High School continued to expand, though not at the same rate as the Girls' High School. In 1948 there were eighty-eight boys on the rolls, with the number increasing to 132 in 1954. In 1951 the West African Schools Examination Council was formed. In the same year the Baldwin Report called for one co-educational school under a Committee of Management, not under Synod. This was put into effect in 1958, resulting in the present Gambia High School.

The Georgetown School was not abandoned, although if it had, the fact could have been plausibly attributed to an act of God: so many men had died trying to serve there. It was temporarily shut down in 1932 after C.T. Taylor, the resident Creole schoolmaster, fell ill (he died in 1937). The school re-opened in 1934 for two years under J.C. Coker, another Creole schoolmaster. He returned there in 1948 and was to serve for over ten years during which the school expanded, eventually being taken over by the government as a primary school.

Armitage School, also a government school founded in 1926 as an agricultural school, grew into a secondary school with an academic curriculum. Georgetown also boasted a teacher training college which was moved to Yundum in the early 1950s after the failure there of the Colonial Development Corporation Egg Scheme.

To return to Bathurst, the Mohammedan School was opened in 1903, with pupils of both sexes, under a committee of management composed of six leading Muslims. It received a government grant of £110 per annum.

The Roman Catholics were also involved in education, although it was well into the present century before they provided secondary education. The first schools were opened in 1849 with four Sisters of Charity who started a boarding school for orphans and abandoned children. In the 1860s the Holy Ghost Fathers and Sisters of the Immaculate Conception began their work, which was mainly concentrated in Bathurst. In 1872 there were three priests, two brothers at the boys' schools and several sisters at schools for girls. A girls' school, St Joseph's Convent, and a boys' school at Hagan Street which was to become better known as St Augustine's Secondary School, were the chief educational establishments of the Catholic mission. Schools were also opened in Basse and Fulabantang up-river, both in predominantly Fula-speaking areas.

Some primary school work was also carried on by the Anglicans, although like the Catholics they entered the field much later. A boarding school was run by them at Kristikunda near Basse, but later closed down. Thus the main burden of secondary education was borne by the Methodists.

Some concluding remarks may be offered at this point. For a significant period of its educational history, the Gambia was another Creole frontier. The little education that was brought there came largely because of the Creole presence. And whatever effectiveness education had, especially in the critical early years, was due largely to Creole agents, both local and Sierra Leonean. The Rev. C.L. Leopold at the Boys' High School and Joseph May at Georgetown, to name but two outstanding men from Sierra Leone, and John Cupidon and J.C. Coker, to single out only two names from a distinguished list of local Creoles, all stood in the line of educational pioneers. It was largely their heritage and that of their English missionary colleagues which passed over to the government.

The other remark relates to the matter of admitting Muslim pupils into Christian schools. In the Gambia this happened without much difficulty. The pressure to leave Islam as a precondition to admission appears to have been minimal, if it existed at all. For example, in 1955 the Methodist Boys' High School had 140 pupils on its books. Of these twenty-nine were Methodists, twenty-four Anglicans and eighty-seven Muslims. In 1956 the Scripture Prize was won by a

Muslim boy from Bansang. A glance at the membership records of the Church will show that numbers were little more than maintained, with any upturn being the result of an influx from Sierra Leone or elsewhere, not through conversion from Islam. Whatever else Christian schools may have done, they cannot be said to have dug deep inroads into Muslim ranks. Tregaskis' singleminded confidence that education was the natural ally of missionary outreach seems to have foundered on the rock of Muslim resistance. Yet education continued to be offered to Muslims with few illusions about their final confessional status. Few missionaries bothered to learn anything about Islam or the Muslims among whom they served, as if to confirm the view that no reward would attend such labours. Yet however indifferent to Islam the missionaries might be, their commitment to education was unshakable, even to the extent of being able to override the motive of conversion. The Muslim intake at the schools continued to grow without any apparent drift towards Church membership. The agreement with the government about maintaining an open-door, non-sectarian admission policy cannot alone account for this consistent picture. Yet one modern missionary wife, anxious to exonerate those missionaries who had succeeded in using education as a tool of conversion, has written: 'It may be said that some of the missionaries wanted to indoctrinate rather than to educate, but in fact if you teach people to read, even if you only intend them to read the Bible and the catechism, you have started something which it is not in your power to stop.'[11] But there was little cause for anxiety that missionaries in the Gambia would be embarrassed with a successful haul of well indoctrinated converts. It did not happen. If conversion to Christianity as the result of missionary education is deemed a failure, then the story of missionary endeavour in the Gambia should be adjudged a complete success, one that perhaps should make the fields of failure across the fence look enviably green.

The final observation concerns the familiar official policy of encouraging education for the trades and agriculture with the idea that academic learning was harmful. It was partly this belief which kept the Georgetown School going. Land was acquired by the Mission for use as farmland on which pupils would be employed to learn the dignity of manual labour. At least three other projects were sponsored in this way, all on the strength of a forlorn hope that Africans would be appropriately fitted to lead useful lives with their roots in rural simplicity. The pattern, however, was the familiar one of schools with an academic curriculum faring better than those of the vocational type. The reasons were the obvious ones of finance and the nature of local demand, not the preferable official prejudice that Africans looked down on industriousness. Industrial schools, needing

11. Prickett (1971), p.229.

expensive equipment and trained instructors, were a drain on scanty resources. Furthermore, job opportunities for those who finished their training at these schools were disappointingly few. Whereas the demand for clerks in government offices and European firms kept the pressure on schools to produce people with book knowledge. Equally important, academic schools cost less to operate than technical and agricultural institutions. One dedicated teacher, such as the Rev. C.L. Leopold or a missionary wife ensconsed in a basement room, could make a school one of the standard-bearers of literary education and add to that the comfortable knowledge that a secure job lay outside the doors of the school. Both missions and the government, whatever their public pronouncements to the contrary, recruited Africans with the traditional academic backgrounds, of which there were never enough. Thus the contradictory picture of a government or mission official delivering an impassioned lecture on the virtues of manual labour and following this up with presiding at the opening ceremony of a grammar school was familiar up and down the entire length of West Africa. Neither in the Gambia nor anywhere else was academic learning out of step with demand. Nothing nearly as confident could be said about technical education.

Christian missions and education in Ghana, c.1850-c.1925

Up to about 1850, education in Ghana remained relatively stagnant and characterised largely by a lack of organisation or of a disciplined curriculum. What we have come to regard as the flowering of learning in terms of schools geared to an academic syllabus was largely missing, though gifted individuals might do better than keep the books of local merchants. Often an invidious comparison is intended between African education and its European counterpart. In this respect Europe itself was by no means ahead of the times. A Census report of 1851, for example, reported that in Britain education was far from being pursued for its own sake; rather, learning was motivated by a desire for material advantage, a circumstance which accounted for widespread disenchantment with schools among the working classes. Place alongside this the disarming logic of the Ashanti people that they would not consent to their children being released from productive labour only to sit down all day long idly learning 'hoy, hoy, hoy'. But the time would come when new economic opportunities created a demand for literary education by virtue of which many rose to positions of wealth, property and influence.

The period from about 1850 to the end of the century witnessed tremendous developments in education, at least in terms of social attitudes. There was of course some carry-over from the past, especially from the brief but epochal legacy of Sir Charles MacCarthy in 1822-4, but only in the 1860s did new energies stir in the field, with missions leading the way. The Wesleyan Methodist missionary, the Rev. W. West, wrote in the 1860s that the classic function of education was to provide a nursery bed for the church. Like his contemporary Tregaskis, West was convinced that schools were a Christian prophylactic against idolatry and acted to seal the first generation of converts against relapse. Wesleyan schools were erected in the colony area while the Basel ones were planted along the Ridge in the Akwapim hills. Increasingly, traditional rulers began to demand schools, with an incipient rivalry among them over whose area could attract schools. At that point a significant transition has to be made from the declared principles of missionary education to the perceived interests of the Africans who received it. It is also a transition from the eloquent slogans of mission to the quiet awakening of a sense of African identity. Education became, not the wayward mistress of *déraciné* Africans but the legitimate handmaid of those wishing to transform a state of subservience into one of freedom. The seeds of the nationalist awakening were sown in the grounds of mission schools, as colonial authorities were not slow to appreciate.

The Basel Mission followed the lead of the Wesleyan Methodists and established their first schools in 1843. By 1889 the Mission had made great advances. It had ninety-two schools catering for about 2,500 pupils. By the close of the century the number enrolled had doubled to nearly 5,000. During this period government assistance was negligible.

The main centre of attraction for educational work remained Ashanti where, after the exile of the King, Prempeh I, in 1896, new opportunities presented themselves. The Wesleyan Methodists proceeded at once to penetrate the area, although the Basel Mission continued to be cautious. Instead they prospected on the peripheries of Ashanti at Abetifi where they opened a station in the 1870s. In 1896 the Mission established a firm base in the Ashanti capital at Kumasi which F.A. Ramseyer occupied. By the close of the century, the Mission operated fifteen schools in Ashanti.

The Basel Mission established a pattern of six years in primary school followed by four at secondary level, and this became standard practice for all of Ghana. A government ordinance passed in 1887 recognised two types of schools, the extremely small government sector and what was called the 'assisted' schools into which the mission schools were grouped. The Basel Mission criticised the ordinance for the way it downgraded African languages at primary level and the inadequate attention it paid to religious subjects. The ordinance was tidied up in 1909, so that grants could be made on the basis of efficiency and not by results obtained in examinations. The Mission had also placed some stress on Middle Boarding Schools where the discipline was strict and academic standards were high. Its cause for the use of African languages was greatly helped by the provision of vernacular instruction enshrined in the 1925 Education Ordinance.

The subject of the African factor in missionary education emerges with great clarity within Methodism, and there we must pursue it. In 1868 occurred a widespread movement designed to resist the imposition of Dutch control over the forts then assigned to them by the British in an exchange arrangement. Involved also were anti-Ashanti feelings in the Accra and Fante areas. Mankessim became the headquarters of the movement with Elmina and Ashanti as their chief targets. The leaders were all Methodists, men such as R.J. Ghartey, F.C. Grant (described as 'a native gentleman'), J. deGraft Hayford, James F. Amissah and James Hutton Brew. In 1871 these men formed the Fante Confederation in a bid to roll back the frontiers of Ashanti penetration. In a letter to the governor at Cape Coast the Confederation pledged as one of its aims 'the social improvement of our subjects and peoples, the growth of education and industrial pursuits'.[12] Thus at the point of effective British colonial take-over, a sense of African nationalism had developed to make education its keen ally. Schools continued to be looked upon as fertile nurseries, never as an end in themselves, and in this sense the missionaries and the Africans were speaking a common language. But the jump from this notion to the idea that they would be the foundation for an independent nation and productive enterprise is so great that only Africans could have made it so cleanly, with missionaries still wedded to the theory of trying to produce African Christian offspring that would perpetuate their European pedigree.

In the 1870s, the demand for more and better schools increased and in this the Fante Confederation served as a catalyst. It announced its desire 'to erect school houses and establish schools for the education of all children within the Confederation, and to obtain the service of efficient schoolmasters'.[13] In 1870, after a Commission of Enquiry was set up by the governor, some recommendations were made to improve education, but it was the Methodists and not the government who acted on the report. It was partly from this that the Wesleyan High School (later Mfantsipim) was opened in 1876, as already described in the preceding chapter. This was at Cape Coast. In 1884 a High School for boys was opened at Accra, with voices being raised at the same time for a similar school to be opened for girls: in the words of a memorandum, 'the demand for a superior education for the daughters of our more respectable people, and their expressed willingness to defray the cost...have induced us to make arrangements for the opening of a female branch of the High School.

12. Bartels (1965), p.88.
13. ibid., p.89.

Circulars have been issued and satisfactory promises of support have been received.'[14]

In May 1884, Wesley Girls' High School was opened alongside Mfantsipim. The school paid its way, including the salary of the Headmistress, a local woman.

With the Church rapidly achieving self-sufficiency in support of the work, missionaries did not need second sight to realise that full autonomy was the only logical climax of the developments. In June 1880, the missionary chairman of the Church, the Rev. James Fletcher, drafted a memorandum to London in which he made a bold outline for a radical 'africanisation'of the Church. Under his scheme, the sending of missionaries would be drastically curtailed and a local man would be trained to take responsibility for educational work. In addition he provided for a time when missionary personnel would be withdrawn completely, except for occasional visits, with the entire work being handed over to Africans. The proposals, however, fell on stony ground. Fletcher stayed only a little more than a year, and his successor had other furrows to plough.

The other matter was the language issue. The Methodists were criticised by the Basel Mission for continuing to use English extensively in junior schools, and some unrestrained correspondence was exchanged in the process. It is relevant to our considerations in the next section of this chapter that the Methodist Church defended the practice from expedience and demand, not from any theoretical commitment. English, the Church said, quite apart from its being required by the Education Ordinance, was in great demand and there was great use for it. Government offices as well as mercantile houses required it. Even the administrative machine of the Basel Mission itself demanded its use. Equally important, those educated in the vernacular at Basel Mission schools had a struggle to find jobs, for no one was keen to employ them without a knowledge of English. The Church concluded by drawing attention to the fact that the commercial establishments of the Basel Mission depended on the services of people many of whom had received their English training in Methodist schools. Such disputes would hardly be relevant to us were it not for the fact that the outline of the argument summarises the case very well. It was not, of course a new position taken by the Church, for Freeman had waxed eloquent to a similar end.

The Church soon discovered that embarking on education opened it not merely to the demands of concerned parents and other individuals but to some painful scrutiny by government authorities. In 1884, the Rev. Metcalfe Sunter, Her Majesty's Inspector of Education previously based at Fourah Bay College in Freetown, submitted a report which contained a blistering attack on the system of education in use. He pointed out for special mention the

14. Bartels (1965), p.97.

inadequate provision for the training of teachers at Mfantsipim School, saying that the responsible department was no more than a theological seminary and that the people it produced were unprepared for the work of education. Sunter also reprimanded the Church for using unsuitable premises, mostly in a deplorable state of disrepair, dark, damp, unhygienic and with make-shift accommodation that could not be called a solid structure. Sometimes classes met in some rented or borrowed mud building that was lamentably unfitted for the purpose — many such places were tumbledown, full of chinks and fissures in the roofs and walls, and as such collecting points for rain water. There was no order as to where schools might be located — in a master's house, a bamboo shed or in the cellar of a chief's house. It was a damning catalogue, with the slight consolation that Methodists were an exception in the field. Yet, in spite of all the circumstances that seemed unconducive to fruitful scholarly labours, Sunter said he was astonished that pupils in Methodist schools did well at all.

Sunter also blamed the Methodist practice of making the support of schools depend entirely on local effort. He pressed the need for a trained European educationist to supervise the schools and breathe order into the system. The Church heeded this call, and asked for two local men, then being trained in England, to proceed to the educational field. They returned in 1888 and plans were immediately made to engage them at Mfantsipim. In 1892 a technical boarding school was opened at Cape Coast into which some twenty young men were enrolled, including the future Dr Aggrey (then aged seventeen) who was shunted down the path of training for the ministry. His course at the school included Greek, Latin, History, Logic, Bible and Exegesis. He was to make his mark as a senior master at Achimota School (founded in 1924 as a result of the Phelps-Stokes Commission Report).

An important social development was the founding of the so-called Reference Group, the intellectual and spiritual heir to the Fante Confederation, its membership composed mainly of the intelligentsia, including those educated in England. This was formed in reaction to the introduction of English in the morning service of the Church, replacing the usual vernacular. The Group became deeply involved in attempts to keep the language issue alive, pressing for the availability of Scripture in the indigenous languages. Shortly after a meeting at Cape Coast the Group assumed the character of a pressure group, agitating, for example, that one of the two young men trained at Richmond College, London, should succeed as Headmaster of Mfantsipim. Attoh Ahuma, one of those in question, eventually became Headmaster.

The Basel Mission had a much greater concentration of European missionaries than its Methodist counterpart. The main base of its educational work outside Ashanti was Akropong where in 1856 Zimmermann arrived as Principal in charge of seven students. Some of these students and a few others recruited later formed the basis of the United Training College, the forerunner of the Akropong Training College. Teachers trained there served throughout the educational system in the country, thus making the college a decisive influence in Ghana's educational history. Soon after its founding, in 1863, a boys' boarding school was added, following the recommendation of Johann Gottlieb Auer, the Mission's Inspector of Schools. The thickening cluster of schools run by the Mission was staffed with Africans trained at Akropong. The Mission was also prominent in women's education, extending the work to Aburi where a girls' school was established which became the Aburi Girls' Secondary School, a leading school of its type in the country.

Between them the Presbyterians (Basel Mission, and later the Bremen Mission) and the Methodists carried the largest share of the educational work in the country. To that extent Ghana's educational history can be said to be essentially that of the missions and the Churches they sired. Much of this work was achieved in the twentieth century, but since we are only concerned with the historical roots of the story it is not necessary to describe that part in any depth. It is clear that Ghanaian nationalism was born and bred under the wings of the Church and it is equally clear that education provided the women of the country with an effective instrument for social and personal advance.

We may point out here that many of the educational battles the Churches fought against the government continued after national independence in 1957. Undoubtedly, a certain jealous regard for its educational power often drove the Church into political opposition. Nevertheless, its attitude was not always determined by considerations of loyalty to the colonial regime. The part that Churches have played in Ghana's political and educational history suggests that they also had altruistic motives, although the lyrical vein in which such ideals are expressed tends to excite censure rather than respect. Yet such intellectual gadflies should not detract from the scale of the achievement. Behind the slogans and fluid dreams persists a reality that shares a deep affinity with Ghana's national spirit and its international outlook.

Christian missions and education in Nigeria, 1848–c.1960

The educational enterprise in modern Nigeria was promoted on the old idea that Africans should be educated as much as possible in industrial and agricultural schools so as to maintain a healthy respect for working with one's hands and attachment to the land. All those who preached this doctrine were convinced that an uncontrolled influx by Africans into academic schools would create grave social distortions and produce uneconomic reservoirs of talent in the midst of rampant need. Yet the alliance between such utilitarians and the great mass of Africans who were claimed to be just as concerned with the alienating influence of educational élitism failed to take the wind out of the academic sails. Schools offering the traditional grammar school curriculum continued to expand, with most of their pupils landing respectable jobs at the end of their schooling. By now, of course, it is a familiar enough story, but the irony is no less poignant that those agents and agencies who were in the forefront of the revolutionary transformation of African societies should have been so strident in their call to turn the clock back to a mythical age.

At the Methodist District Meeting at Cape Coast (which at that time included Badagry and Abeokuta) in 1848, attention was directed to the question of missionary education and the well-publicised criticisms of its adverse effects. The presiding chairman of that meeting was Thomas Birch Freeman, who was eminently suited to answer the critics. Missionary education, the meeting said, should aim at teaching children to read, write and count, and do this under the best possible conditions. How society chose to reward those with this type of education was in the end beyond the control of the teacher and the school, although of course the Mission was not indifferent to it. The best way to respond, it was argued, was to expand missionary education to try and keep in touch with the growing demand rather than hold back because of a mistaken assumption that society ought to be set on a different course altogether. Freeman had never been one to be excessively afflicted with self-doubt, and his energetic spirit appears to have stiffened the resolve of the District Meeting on this matter.

Not so the CMS. Its General Secretary, Henry Venn, declared, in imitation of the Basel Mission in the Gold Coast, that the CMS should seek not to repeat the mistakes in Freetown by creating grammar schools but instead should establish self-supporting industrial schools. In these schools the pupils would be taught agricultural and trade skills, combining fruitful labour on the field ('self-supporting') with mental discipline in the classroom. Students were to be educated in brick-making, carpentry and masonry, among other things. Other missions eagerly joined the CMS in its disdain of grammar schools, though all of them would be forced to temper the severity of principle with practice. An industrial training school was established by the CMS at Abeokuta in 1851, where the students were taught to pick and clean cotton for export, and the skills of brickmaking, carpentry and printing. Another school was established at Onitsha in 1861 and another at Bonny in the 1890s, both of the same character as the Abeokuta one. The CMS was also involved in the setting up of the Hussey Charity Training Institute in Lagos in

1890. For their part the Roman Catholics were equally convinced of the value and future of industrial schools. A training school for agriculture called the St Joseph Institution was established near Badagry in 1875; here the idea was to create a model Christian village whence the virtues of hard work and decent living would be spread to the surrounding areas by envoys of the Gospel. In 1895 the Presbyterians, with government assistance, founded the Hope Waddell Institute at Calabar. It had a grammar school section, but the main emphasis was to be on industrial training in trades such as printing, masonry, tailoring, carpentry and bakery, where most of the resources were committed. Traders on the Niger — for example, David Macintosh of the United Africa Company — urged the setting up of an industrial school, contending that it was an effective lever by which Africa would be raised. One of the richest Nigerian businessmen, R.B. Blaize, donated £1,000 to the Anglican Native Pastorate in 1895 to set up an industrial school in Lagos. When that did not materialise, he bequeathed £3,000 in his will to the Egba United Government, with which the Abeokuta Industrial Institute was opened in 1908. The Institute, unlike many others, continued to flourish, although the example was not followed with equal success elsewhere. In many of the grammar schools founded in the nineteenth century it was felt necessary to secure a plot of land where a school farm would be established. Even some of those grammar schools which were prospering under their own academic steam felt compelled to trim their sails to the prevailing wind of prejudice against book-learning. It is now time to look at the history of these grammar schools.

The impact on education in Nigeria of people educated in Freetown is one of the most significant and consistent factors in the founding of grammar schools. The story can be followed right from 1859, when the CMS Grammar School was opened in Lagos, to 1923 with the founding by the Baptists of the Boys' High School at Abeokuta, and in each case the impetus, direct or indirect, came from people familiar with the Freetown educational scene.

The first principal of the Lagos Grammar School was the Rev. T.B. Macaulay, who had been educated at the Fourah Bay College and at the CMS school at Islington in London. He returned to Lagos in 1852 and went to work at the CMS training school at Abeokuta. Associated with academic learning Macaulay fell victim to the anti-academic prejudice which had been virulently personified in the CMS missionary in charge of the field at the time, the Rev. Henry Townsend. Townsend moved him around in an attempt to disperse his academic influence, and finally, from lack of anywhere else to send him, agreed to let him start the grammar school in Lagos for which he had long pleaded. A Nigerian businessman, J.P.L. Davies, advanced £50 for the purchase of books and equipment. Of the first twenty-five boys admitted, eight were the sons or wards of merchants, fourteen those of traders, with only one the son of a clergyman, and the other two the sons of a Scripture Reader and of a carpenter. Thus was the unwilling CMS dragged into the sponsorship of grammar school education in Nigeria. The Lagos Grammar School was fee-paying, like its counterpart in Freetown, which made it self-sufficient and enabled it to withstand persistent criticism.

Then in 1872 a Female Institution, again in imitation of Freetown, was created for girls. Here the Methodists were soon to follow: the Methodist Boys' High School was founded in 1876 and the Methodist Girls' High School in 1879. The Roman Catholics, so prominent among those who derided the Lagos Grammar School for its academic curriculum, produced the academically oriented St Gregory's College in Lagos in 1881, while St Joseph's School near Badagry, the training school for agriculture, acquired the reputation of a correction centre. St Gregory's in fact became a leading grammar school.

While some others might quibble about the propriety of providing academic education, the Methodists appear to have remained faithful to the bold spirit of Freeman. The principal of the Methodist Boys' High School wrote in a prospectus for the school that it was desired to prepare young men 'for a commercial and literary life', and promptly went on to offer an exceptionally stiff load as a supplementary option to the syllabus, no doubt aware that it would appeal to rich Lagos merchants and society patrons. The school, despite its impressive-sounding prospectus, was poorly staffed, with only the principal and two assistants. Leading Methodists of Lagos had decided to invite a missionary principal to open a grammar school and provide competition to the CMS, raising some £500 for the purpose. It was that move which led in the first place to the founding of the school. That example of local enterprise lay behind the founding of most grammar schools, although many such schools in fact were little more than glorified primary schools. The Baptists also responded to popular demand and founded their Academy in Lagos in 1883.

The pace at which secondary schools were founded accelerated well into the twentieth century. In Abeokuta, for example, after the founding of the Blaize Industrial Institute, the educated Egba people clamoured for an Egba Grammar School. The Anglican Church, unable to oppose the demand, agreed to set up the Abeokuta Grammar School in December 1908. Its first principal was Rev. M.S. Cole, who had been vice-principal of the Lagos Grammar School. In January 1913, the Ijebu-Ode Grammar School was founded by two clergymen, S.J. Gonsallo and J.G. Cole. In the same year the Rev. A.B. Akinyele opened the Ibadan Grammar School in a temporary building. In 1919 the Ondo Boys' High School was founded by the Rev. M.C. Adeyemi. Apart from their academic orientation all these schools had one other thing in common: all were founded by men educated at Fourah Bay. Beset with chronic shortages of staff and books, the schools were more distinguished for their aspirations, well articulated by their founders, than for their conformity to a grammar school syllabus, but they thrived on their slim academic base mainly because the communities in which they were founded supported them.

The habit quickly spread to other areas, with or without missionary encouragement. There was the Eko Boys' High School, founded in 1913 in Lagos, which tried to remain independent of missionary control. Others included the Duke Town Secondary School founded in Calabar in 1919 and the Baptist Boys' High School founded at Abeokuta in 1923. The Methodists founded a grammar school at Uzuakoli in 1922, while the CMS established the Dennis Memorial Grammar School at Onitsha in 1925. In 1932 the Enitona High School in Port Harcourt was founded by the CMS with the Catholics founding Christ the King School in Onitsha. The Catholics also created a school in Lagos in 1933, to develop later into St Theresa's College, now at Ibadan. An independent school, the Oduduwa College, founded at Ile-Ife in 1932, worked in close collaboration with church-related schools elsewhere. Other schools founded in this period were the Ibadan Boys' High School and the Kalabari National College, both established in 1938, and the Aggrey Memorial College founded by Alvan Ikoku.

Three important developments may be signalled at this stage. Up to now we have mainly described the involvement in education of missionary or Church bodies and local individuals, some of whom were independent of missionary control. The third category of involvement was the government. Although inclined to be sceptical of the value of secondary education, particularly after the influential Phelps-Stokes Commission produced a damaging report against academic learning in schools, the government was nevertheless driven against its will to enter the field. In 1922 it started what it called a Higher College at Katsina in Northern Nigeria, later bringing it to Zaria as Government College, for a time the only secondary school in the whole of the North.

The publication in 1922 of the Phelps-Stokes Commission of Inquiry report led to the promulgation of the Education Code of 1926. The Education Code tried to regulate the private sector by making grants to them dependent on numbers and performance, with the aim also of encouraging industrial and technical education. But government intervention produced results far different from the intention behind it, tending rather to strengthen the existing academic bias in schools. A smattering of arts and crafts and some agriculture were tacked on to curricula more as an embellishment and a safeguard than from philosophical conviction. On the other hand, academic standards continued to rise. Faced with the undeniable evidence of the growing strength of secondary schools, the government accepted the inescapable logic of making a contribution itself. It created Government Colleges at Ibadan and Umuahia for boys and in Lagos Queen's College for girls in 1929. Earlier, in 1909, it had founded a school for boys in Lagos, King's College, in an attempt to fill vacancies in the clerical ranks of the Civil Service. All the signs pointed to a confident future for grammar schools, not their decline as the report of the Phelps-Stokes Commission darkly warned.

The second major development was the introduction of overseas examinations for local schools from about 1910 onwards. Two major examinations were the Cambridge and the Oxford Local Examinations. By the 1930s Cambridge had largely taken over the field and was to remain the dominant force in the West African Examinations Council. These overseas examinations set the seal of international respectability on grammar school education, providing the major impetus behind educational development in much of West Africa. The academic trophies they awarded were eagerly acquired by schools and individuals as guarantees to reward and recognition. Between 1940 and 1945 new schools were founded or old ones refurbished to take on the new look required by the overseas examining boards. In 1940 Okrika Grammar School was founded. The Catholics redoubled their efforts to make up for lost time. In 1942 they founded the Queen of the Rosary School in Enugu and the Holy Family School at Abak in the same year. Then in 1944 followed St Patrick's School at Asaba. The Baptists founded the Boys' High School at Oyo in 1945. Government itself became more active, thrusting aside the reserve of earlier years. By 1947 there were some forty government and grant-aided grammar schools in Nigeria. In the next few years the numbers had increased dramatically, so that in 1955 there were seventy-two of these schools in Western Nigeria alone. Between then and 1961 the number rose to 193. With the expansion of university education in Nigeria, beginning in 1948 with the founding of University College, Ibadan, sixth form education took root and spread, the natural bloom of the academic learning that had been diagnosed with such pessimism. An excessive emphasis on academic learning in schools under any educational system must be criticised for the obvious faults it perpetrates. It is equally easy to attack book-learning for its élitist tendencies. Developments in the curricula of grammar schools since about 1960 suggest that grammar schools could get stuck in unimaginative and inert habits, cutting themselves off from local stimuli and materials. But having said that, it remains a fact that grammar school education has acquired greater significance even if the curriculum it offers is no longer uncritically accepted. There is no reason, for example, why the Yoruba language should not improve by having the discipline and industry that used to be devoted to Latin and Greek in the old syllabi, brought to bear on it, so that academic learning can be made to flourish in the revitalising soil of Africa.

The third point is the stimulus education had on local initiative. This itself is a large theme, but it can be restricted here to one historical development which grew out of the general criticism of grammar schools and their allegedly alienating influence. A National Education Movement was started in the 1930s by Eyo Ita who was educated in the United States where he came in to contact with some of the ideas of Booker T. Washington, the famous ex-slave. Eyo Ita preached self-reliance for Africans and criticised the extent of missionary control in African education. Booker T. Washington was educated at Hampton Institute, the all-Black college in Virginia, and later founded Tuskegee Institute in Alabama as an all-Black college, with the emphasis on agriculture and the trades. He believed that only in a special educational environment can Blacks be advanced, an idea that clearly inspired Eyo Ita. In his wish to separate African schools from both government and missionary influence or control, Eyo Ita argued for authentic education for Africans, one that should 'africanise' them and not alienate them by indoctrination with strange European values. He made a clarion call for relevance in education. 'Education', he said, 'can no longer remain the opium of the people. It must now become a powerful dynamic force to liberate the people, soul and body... Education must make them creators, efficient producers and creative consumers and not mere parasitic consumers.'[15]

Eyo Ita founded the National Institute at Calabar in 1938, and, with the assistance of Professor N.D. Oyerinde, the Ogbomosho People's Institute, all in pursuit of his ideals. He also tried to bring together other independent schools into a National Education Movement, which he succeeded in doing to a certain degree. But the movement soon ran out of steam, and for obvious reasons: it was trying to reverse a process by which the grammar schools had come into prominence, and this at a time when the flow of the tide was irreversibly set towards the creation of more grammar schools. In this sense he was a century too late. He has described how at his own institute each student was allocated a plot of land on which to cultivate timber, food, fruits or raise poultry. In addition the boys would be able to choose between woodwork, pottery and making soap or paper as useful hobbies. But the academic owl of Minerva had cast the evil eye on those vocational projects, as Eyo Ita himself conceded. The interest 'in Cambridge Examinations and Civil Service jobs', he wrote, 'and the corresponding disinterestedness in these activities

15. Ajayi (1963)., p.532.

have greatly dampened our enthusiasm in both agriculture and industrial arts.'[16]

Christianity and social innovation in Nigeria, c. 1857-1930

Henry Venn of the CMS had declared in 1857 that the aim of missions in Africa should be to create a strong middle class, members of which would become leaders in society: in Church, commerce and politics. These men, he said, would form 'an intelligent and influential class of society and become the founders of a kingdom which shall render incalculable benefits to Africa and hold a position among the states of Europe'.[17] Legitimate commerce, centred around the cultivation of an export crop in which Africans would lead the way, was a central element in the scheme. It was to ensure this that Venn had envisaged an educational policy under which industrial education would be provided by the missions. A parallel innovation was to be initiated in the Church, which would be self-supporting, self-governing and self-propagating. It would depend for its future on African personnel utilising local languages and incorporating traditional religious elements in its worship and devotion. The business of mission, he said, was to build an African Church, not an Anglican Church, just as British commercial activity should be directed to the creation of national states, not the perpetuation of colonial dependencies. He deplored the fact that in many places along the coast Christianity had all the symptoms of an underdeveloped child hanging on to the apron-strings of the mission. A prominent Sierra Leonean, responding to Venn's despair, sought to dispel it by the challenge: 'Treat us like men and we shall behave as men',[18] a point which Venn immediately took to heart, thus aligning himself with African sentiments long before most missions were ready. It is a measure of the man's influence that he was able to carry the CMS along with him even though not many in it shared his bold, radical vision of an African Church. Several decades later Venn was still being acclaimed by the leaders of African Christian Independency, a tribute to his foresight as well as a sad reflection of the spirit of paternalism which returned after his death. It is of course quite clear that some of those who supported Venn's 'africanisation' policy did so from less exalted motives, for example the anthropological lobby of Burton and Reade. But Venn was able to keep close to the African reality by maintaining close contact with African correspondents whose stream of letters helped to check the racist bias in official reports. The practice of encouraging African Christians to write direct to the CMS was discontinued after Venn,

16. Ajayi (1963), p.533.
17. Webster (1963), p.420.
18. Webster (1963), p.421.

and thus an invaluable source of information was deliberately suppressed.

As a result of Venn's vision of a productive African labour force making economic use of the abundance with which nature endowed Africa, a cotton-growing project was started at Abeokuta. it inevitably failed. But in its heyday in 1859 the project had between 200 and 300 gins and five to six presses. Exports increased. Support came from England from the African Aid Society which was formed in 1860. The Society's journal, *The African Times,* harped on the theme 'the Bible and the plough'. The catchy slogan into which it was expanded — 'Civilization and Christianity must go together in Africa, if either is to go forward at all'[19] — echoed beyond Africa, encouraging in one case a scheme for the 'repatriation' of Canadian Blacks to Africa. A similar agricultural project was started in Senegambia by Bishop Kobes. In 1862 he had 240 acres under cultivation, employing 150 labourers, and two years later the acreage and labour force had doubled. An industrial school run by four priests and seven lay brothers was training 100 agricultural and twenty-five industrial apprentices. Although the two schemes operated under different managerial concepts in that the Abeokuta scheme envisaged a preponderant role for Africans, whereas the Senegalese one maintained a strong French presence, both failed. Cotton, a fragile crop, was too susceptible to the harsh climate of tropical Africa (it in fact originated in Persia), and in Senegal a blight descended on the fields in the form of locusts.

The Bible and the plough began to make a successful combination only when the mythical devotion to cotton was abandoned and palm oil and cocoa were promoted instead. Palm oil flourished at Akropong in Ghana under the Basel mission, a society long associated with the CMS in Africa. The Basel Trading Company, later the Union Trading Company (UTC), was chiefly built on the trade in palm oil though it derived additional strength from cocoa. The success of the Basel Mission in latching the mission to the plough had a direct bearing on experiments in Nigeria.

Some of the African Churches that seceded from the CMS after the reversal of Venn's policies sponsored agricultural schemes with which to try to establish self-supporting schools. One local benefactor donated a large tract of land to be held jointly by three such Churches. J.K. Coker, another enterprising local figure, sponsored a student to Tuskegee Institute in the United States to undertake agricultural and technical training, and then provided him on his return with a large tract of land at Ifako as the site of an industrial school. Coker similarly imported American Blacks to help with the

19. Webster (1963), p.423. Buxton had written: 'It is the Bible and the plough that must regenerate Africa' *(The Slave Trade and its Remedy,* London, 1840, p.483).

school. The scheme, however, declined, fatally held as it was between the twin prongs of anti-Garveyite government measures and the economic slump of 1921.

Another scheme was launched between 1895 and 1908 under Dr Mojola Agbebi, assisted by the West Indian J.E. Ricketts. Agbebi regarded himself as a follower of Venn, preaching what he called 'the gospel of coffee, cocoa, cotton and work as well as the scripture'.[20] He also came into contact with some of Dr Blyden's ideas when he supported the Lagos Training College and the Industrial Institute which Blyden had proposed. Both schemes failed. Agbebi then secured a tract of land at Agbowa near Ijebu-Ode: under Ricketts the project developed first a farm, then a school and finally a church, an order dictated by economic logic. The farm had coffee, rubber trees and sugar cane, cocoa and palm oil, with plans for cotton and kola nuts. Some 800 farmers attended an inaugural meeting of the Agbowa Farmers Association organised by Ricketts. Produce from the farm was reaching Lagos weekly. But when Ricketts died in 1908, the scheme passed quickly under a cloud, never to emerge except as a shell. Ricketts had clearly proved impossible to replace.

The Agege agricultural project, in which the enterprising hand of J.K. Coker was also much in evidence, rose to prosperity at the time of Agbowa's decline, its prosperity based mainly on cocoa. It is claimed that cocoa reached Nigeria from Akropong, where cocoa seedlings were first raised and distributed to farmers in 1865. J.P.L. Davies, who had a cocoa plantation at Ijan, near Agege, grew the first cocoa in Nigeria. He had captained a ship which sailed regularly between Freetown, Lagos and the Niger throughout the 1870s, and it is thought that the idea came to him during his travels in Ghana. J.K. Coker eventually leased the Davies farm and worked it alongside his Ifako plantation at the turn of the century. The link between the two men was strengthened by the marriage of Davies' second daughter to Coker's twin brother.

Coker's energies were not completely exhausted by his economic activities, for he was one of the founders of the secessionist African Church. In this way he gave prominence to the new link between Christianity and cocoa in Nigeria, fulfilling Venn's twofold dream of economic self-sufficiency and ecclesiastical self-rule. Between 1893 and 1930 Coker was the guiding spirit behind Agege. Initially it went through some trying times, although Coker was able to do well at his Ifako plantation where he was reported to have planted 30,000 cocoa seedlings. By 1910 most of the problems he inherited on his father's death in 1904 had been solved. By 1914 he had risen to new heights of prosperity with an annual income of £5,000 which increased to about £20,000 per annum shortly afterwards. He had about 2,000 acres under cultivation at Agege as well as owning valuable property in

20. Webster (1963), p.426.

Lagos and Ebute Metta. Agege began to attract African planters, since for once agriculture was paying handsomely. One Lagos lawyer, feeling the contraction of his practice, went to Agege to look for land where he also attracted the legal business of the planters. While Africans were being squeezed out of business by European traders in Lagos, many found shelter in and near Agege. But by far the most significant group of men was that associated with the African Church movement. With the introduction of the railway, Agege received a valuable boost, although its construction drew labour from the same pool and was a serious drain on the Agege labour supply. At the height of its growth Agege had 10,000 labourers, many of whom had families. While on the farm the labourers acquired literacy in the Yoruba language and were armed with the Yoruba Bible which many took with them throughout the length and breadth of the country. The farmers had turned missionaries under African direction. It was a tremendous encouragement for the African initiative in Christian expansion. Coker himself spent generous portions of his enormous wealth on furthering the cause, travelling extensively to preach, exhort and advise on cocoa production. As time went on it became clear that Coker had envisaged a subordinate role for his Agege plantation which he wanted to use for the greater service of the Gospel. As African churches mushroomed in the interior and the need for clergymen became correspondingly acute, Coker's interest in Agege waned. The Christian chariot, first driven by cocoa, had built up enough momentum for it to strike out on an independent course, a fact which requires, among other things, the economic historian to abdicate to the religious specialist.

However, economic considerations continued to play an active part in the development of branches of the African Church. The growth of the Church was fuelled in large measure by the earnings from cocoa. On the other hand the increase in membership of the African Church enabled it to provide much-needed labour for the Agege plantation when labour became expensive because of the demand created by the railways. The Superintendents of the Agege farm recruited members of the African Church as labourers while on preaching duties. Coker was quick to reward those churches that had sent labourers into the field. Such an interdependence between farm and church had of course long been the dream of people like Buxton; nevertheless, Agege's adaptation of this dream to the special conditions of Nigeria was an original innovation. The idea that commerce and industry would form the saddle in which Christianity and civilization would ride in triumph was repudiated in that combination, and its classical advocates were suitably unhorsed. In their place Agege hitched the much more effective yoke of agriculture and Christianity behind the integrative force of African culture. Coker and his associates rejected the notion that Africa would have to be remoulded to suit a predesigned European form of Christianity, and with it the invidious assumption that civilization could only refer to European notions of it. Their achievement confirms the view that traditional Africa constitutes a fitting prelude to the Gospel. It was on the basis of that kind of success that the new enterprise of African theological reflection began to take meaningful strides.

Education, Creoles and wider frontiers, 1857-c.1900

Education increased the social and geographical range of Africans, and in many places educated Creoles were the cutting edge of this advance. By the very fact of high professional qualifications Creoles constituted a new modern élite with an influence far out of proportion to their relatively small numbers. The irony of course is that the emergence of this élite in the second half of the nineteenth century coincided with a period of racist-inspired colonial measures, which barred educated Africans, Creoles included, from high office. To compensate for this loss of status, many Creoles entered the legal profession or went into medicine, often to set up in private practice. Others went into the Church. Unable to realise their ambitions at home, large numbers went further afield in search of new opportunities, a dispersion that both spread their influence and affirmed their identity. Without investigating fully the reaction produced by the Creole presence in other parts of Africa, it would be appropriate to expound this Creole factor in terms of the spread of Christian influence and modern education.

A Creole community had been well established in Nigeria by the middle of the nineteenth century. When the Sierra Leonean the Rev. James Beale died on a visit to Lagos in 1857 some 400 Creoles turned out for his funeral. We have already seen the prominent role Creoles played in the Niger Mission and in education in Lagos and other places. Some played an equally important role in business. One such was J.P.L. Davies, who entered the Lagos business community and was later associated with J.K. Coker, as already described. Many entered the colonial service in other territories. Christian Cole, the grandson of an Ibo recaptive and educated at the Freetown Grammar School, went to England where he obtained a B.A. degree from Oxford University in 1876. Conscious of the obstacles in his way in the colonial service, he prudently went to the bar, being called at the Inner Temple in 1883. Eventually, after qualifying, he went to practice in East Africa but died of smallpox in 1886 in Zanzibar, aged only thirty-four. Another was Joseph Renner Maxwell who at a mature age read law at Oxford, graduating in 1880. He practised in government service in the Gold Coast before going to the Gambia where he became Chief Magistrate in 1887. He retired in 1896 and died in 1901, one of the very few Creoles to have lived to the age of retirement. Another Creole with a Gambian connection was D.P.H. Taylor, the son of an Aku trader. Educated first at the Freetown Grammar School he proceeded to Wesley College at Taunton in England and thence to King's College London in 1874 to read medicine. He went to practise in the Gambia and died there in 1904. His son by an English mother, Samuel Coleridge Taylor, achieved fame as a composer. Most senior positions in the Gambia Civil Service open to Africans were filled by Creoles.

In Nigeria Creoles took the initiative in many fields. They provided the first unofficial members of the Legislative Council in Lagos — J.P.L. Davies, Rev. James Johnson and C.T. George. Other prominent Creoles included J. Otunba Payne, (from Kissy village) a Registrar in Lagos; H.A Caulerick (from Hastings), a Chief Clerk at the Treasury in Lagos; W.E. Cole (born at Charlotte), who was carried accidentally to Lagos on a steamer and rose to become Postmaster; and Charles Pike, who went to Lagos in 1870 as Chief Clerk at the Customs and subsequently became Colonial Treasurer in the Gold Coast, with a seat on the Executive Council and a CMG. C. Jenkins Lumpkin qualified in medicine from University College, London, went to Brussels for specialisation in 1884 and then to practice in Lagos. Nathaniel King after qualifying in medicine at Aberdeen University, Scotland, went to practice in Abeokuta and then at Lagos where he died young in 1884. Nathaniel Davis, the first to pass the Durham B.A. examinations, went to Lagos to teach at the Grammar School.

Creoles also feature prominently in Ghana, the former Gold Coast. We have already mentioned Charles Pike. Sylvester Cole, who studied medicine with Nathaniel King at Aberdeen, practiced in Accra before dying young in 1890. John Farrell Easmon, of Nova Scotian descent, was appointed Assistant Colonial Surgeon at Accra in 1879, after a brilliant academic career, first at University College, London, where he carried off several prizes, and at Brussels. In 1893 he was promoted Chief Medical Officer. His work on blackwater fever is the first original contribution by an African doctor to modern medicine. There were Creoles also in other branches of the Gold Coast Civil Service. Rowland Cole was Postmaster at Accra for twenty-eight years. D.B. Yorke (died 1892) was District Commissioner at Pram Pram. J. Bright Davies (died 1920) went to Accra as Chief Clerk at the Secretariat, but later turned to journalism and edited the *Gold Coast Independent* and then the *Nigerian Times.* Our final example is Peter Awoonor Renner who was called to the bar at Lincoln's Inn in 1883 and then went to practise in the Gold Coast.

Liberia also received Creoles from Freetown. One of the most famous of these was C.T.O. King who left Murray Town in the 1870s and was eventually Mayor of Monrovia. His son C.D.B. King went to Freetown Grammar School, and became President of

Liberia, an indication of the formative role played by Creoles in the modernization process in West Africa. Only a small trickle of Creoles reached East Africa, but their impact was out of proportion to their numbers. The United Free Methodists, for example, sent Creole missionaries to East Africa from Freetown: the Rev. W.H. During in 1879 and later F.A. Heroe.

Creole enterprise followed an equally vigorous course at home. They contributed significantly to African political awakening, contrary to allegations that they were docile victims of a rootless Europeanising influence. J. Bright Davies turned to journalism to help lead African political opinion. Dr Africanus Horton, the son of an Ibo carpenter at Gloucester, studied medicine at Edinburgh and, entering the Army in 1859 as Assistant Surgeon, was posted to the Gold Coast. A prolific writer, Horton replied to the unscientific claims of the Anthropological Society. He propounded views on African political advancement, argued for the extension of the colonial frontier to make Freetown more viable as an economic unit, and defended academic education for Africans against the critics, asserting that Sierra Leone ought to dispel any doubts of the value and effectiveness of modern education. In another book he wrote that sanitary conditions should be improved in Freetown, and recommended the employment of a corps of sanitary inspectors to inspect and disinfect cesspits. In 1867 a Board of Health was created and a Sanitary Inspector appointed. Horton also called for greater government expenditure on education. In 1866 money was voted for a Board of Education, which was set up the next year under an Inspector and a Secretary. But it was dissolved by the Secretary of State in London and instead an Inspector was sent out to report on schools and determine need. Small wonder that Africanus Horton has been hailed as a far-sighted patriot and a pioneer of African advancement.

In the same mould though of a different temperament was Sir Samuel Lewis, the son of an Egba recaptive who settled at Murray Town, a compact community of Yoruba-speaking Africans and a Methodist stronghold. Lewis was born in 1843 and went to school at Buxton Wesleyan School before transferring first to the Government Boys' School and then to the Grammar School where he assisted the Principal, James Quaker, in the latter's weekly naval chaplaincy work. He then went to help in his father's business which had been prospering, but was to emerge from his father's shadow destined for a legal career in which he was to achieve unprecedented distinction. The militant Tregaskis had provided suitable introductions for Samuel Lewis when he left to continue his studies in England. He entered University College, London, as a non-matriculating student in October 1866, and in January 1867 was admitted to the Middle Temple. In 1870 he won an Inns of Court exhibition worth 20 guineas a year for two years study of the law of real property, and was called to the bar in 1871. In Freetown, when he returned the following year, professional success awaited him. Merchants, property owners and the larger European firms retained him for his special skills in property and commercial law. His services were also in demand beyond Sierra Leone. In 1882 he answered the call of family by going to the Gambia to defend his brother against a charge of larceny, but returned there again in 1884 and in 1885 to take other cases. He went to Lagos on legal business in 1891. In 1888 he appeared for one Jacob Sey of Cape Coast (which Lewis visited during the conduct of the case) in a Chancery action in the English High Court. In Freetown itself, apart from his normal business, he served the colonial government and the City in a number of capacities. In fact he was unable to disentangle himself from the busy life of Freetown to take up the offer of the Chief Magistracy in Lagos. He acted often as Queen's Advocate and once as Police Magistrate. As acting Queen's Advocate Lewis sat on the Legislative Council, which he was later to join as an unofficial member in 1882. A strict constitutionalist, he used his position in the Council to advance the interests and represent the grievances of what he broadly called 'the community'. He saw the Council as more than a formal committee acting as a rubber stamp for the wishes of the Secretary of State, and in several famous conflicts with high administrative officials he displayed a resolute will and a determination to defend principle regardless of the consequences, some of which he did not always ride successfully.

Lewis became heavily involved in local government politics — in addition to his ill-rewarded efforts in colonial and imperial politics. He helped steer through measures which led to the establishment of a Freetown City Council. In the subsequent elections he was elected on a low poll. Suspicions about taxation and the unsavoury associations with past servitude still lingered, with Lewis paying the price for his undisguised enthusiasm for introducing taxation. But the elected members had no such scruples, for they elected Lewis as Mayor by 13 votes out of the 15. This was in 1895, a year that was to bring him other honours as well. (He was to be re-elected Mayor three times.) In that year Governor Cardew, still unknighted himself and far from being indulgent towards African sentiments, recommended Lewis for a knighthood, which was conferred at New Year 1896. He was the first African to be knighted, a distinction that appears not to have turned his head. For example, he pursued Governor Cardew, his chief sponsor, with dogged determination over issues in which he felt principle was at stake. Currying favour was the least of his failings. With equal persistence he urged the extension of the colonial frontier and wrote lucidly on the issue. He also invested heavily in agriculture on a farm he had bought near Waterloo. It was to lose him a large sum of money, especially with the coffee crop he so lavishly cultivated. But his efforts and lectures on crop husbandry provided the stimulus for a botanical garden in Freetown which was eventually to lead to a Department of Agriculture. Not a mean achievement for a man supposed to have been made unfit by a literary education. Lewis died in 1903, aged sixty.

We should consider something of his Christian character. He remained a pillar of Methodism to which he rendered yeoman service. Even in his busiest years, with failing health, he attended to his Christian duty with ungrudging devotion. 'No claim on his time', his biographer writes, 'had precedence over the Wesleyan church.'[21] He was Circuit Steward, Sunday school teacher and honorary legal adviser to the mission, the last of these a particularly onerous task. He remained throughout his life 'an austere and commanding figure, of unimpeachable moral character and authority'.[22] Elsewhere his biographer observes: 'His character, formed by hard work, a cultivated intelligence, strong will, and firm religious faith, would have assured him of distinction in any society offering opportunities to talent. On the relatively narrow stage of Sierra Leone, his pre-eminence was acknowledged ... by administrators ... and by Africans.'[23]

This seems the natural point at which to consider whether the dream of a substantial African middle class, taking a responsible position in religion, commerce, education and politics, had been realised in West Africa, and whether in fact any progress had been made towards the ideal of someone like Henry Venn of a 'euthanasia of mission'. Those familiar with the achievements of people like Dr Easmon, Dr Horton and Sir Samuel Lewis would be less dubious about what Dr Horton called the inherent capacity of Africans to advance themselves when given a chance. Did this new élite perform the role assigned to it by history? The answer may be less emphatic but no less confident. Tempered by the fires of enslavement and racial prejudice it was to forge the modern image of a resurgent Africa. History is conditioned to measure matters of significance in terms of their observable impact on existing patterns. Religious history, however, needs to signal decisive change without first identifying an upheaval, for it is not necessary to uproot a plant in order to know if the roots are sound. The successful transplanting of Christianity in Africa occurred behind the lines of dramatic imperial conquest, at slave auctions, in schools and farms and in the pervasive mood of expectation triggered by the encounter of Africa with Western civilisation. What is surprising is not that Christianity made

21. Hargreaves (1958), p.63.
22. ibid., pp. 63–4.
23. ibid., p.103.

use of the imperial carriage to consolidate its gains, but that those gains had in several key areas been impeded by the anti-imperial defensive reflex, and sometimes neutralised by a liberal humanistic code which mimicked Christianity in order to subvert it. Yet the success of Christianity in areas strongly attached to traditional African values suggests that there must be a deeper spiritual affinity. Perhaps the voice of the ancestors did acquire a greater range with the introduction of the Christian Scripture in local languages, with African Church leaders being the fulfilment of a redeemed heritage.

The important question of assimilating and adapting Christian teaching receives fuller treatment in the following chapter. It is sufficient here to remark that the establishment of a branch of the Gentile Church in Africa could not have been done in bleaker circumstances. On the collapsed ruins of generations of enslaved Africans a new hope was nurtured and brought to realisation. By means of literacy and the proliferating Christian schools and other social institutions, Africa would abide under the shadow of that tree that had adorned Golgotha. Whether or not education touched all who came wihin its range with the spirit of a higher purpose, its availability had often been by virtue of a sense of vocation not unworthy of Apostolic preaching and example.

7

THE RISE OF AFRICAN INDEPENDENT CHURCHES

There are times when it is more helpful that a people should be called upon to take up their responsibilities, struggle with and conquer their difficulty than that they should be in the position of vessels taken in tow, and that for West African Christianity, this is the time.
James Johnson (19 July 1892, cited in Webster, [1964], 1)

By the end of the nineteenth century it was clear that the question which most exercised the minds of people concerned with Christianity in West Africa was not the defensive one of whether the religion would survive but the more creative one of the form in which it would emerge. In the regions of the greatest population density, such as Yorubaland and the Niger, great stirrings were taking place as new economic and political forces delivered hammer-blows to traditional institutions and ideas, with the quiet impact of modern education softening up pockets of psychological resistance thrown up by ancient pride before the final retreat. The process began long before the imposition of colonial rule, and was to persist in spite of it. Into this historic ferment Christianity was introduced and adopted as a power capable of answering the new questions that a changed historical circumstance had forced upon people. To do that well, Africans had to take a leading role in the transmission and adaptation of the religion. In the days before the colonial enterprise, such a role was naturally assumed and promoted by Africans, sometimes encouraged in this by far-sighted missionary leaders like Henry Venn. But with the arrival of European colonial overlordship, white control began to be seen as indispensable to the effective management of the Church, and Africans were consequently removed from positions of influence.

It was of course a retrogressive step, a fundamental repudiation of historical experience and practice, but one which produced a surprisingly mild reaction among African Christians. Missionary confidence in the ability of Africans and of their equality in the Church had been considerably undermined by the racist doctrines of anthropology. But until the imposition of imperial rule, this confidence, though crumbling, had not been entirely overthrown. Imperial rule, however, provided the appropriate political setting for the abandonment of the African policy in mission and its replacement by a European one. In view of the crude manner in which racist considerations were allowed to overwhelm canon law and ecclesiastical convention, it is surprising that only very few Africans stepped over into doctrinal schism, and that those few did so with the greatest reluctance and after the olive branch had been offered and spurned. Many saw themselves as stalwart defenders of Biblical orthodoxy, not its challengers, and the missionaries as its flouters. Thus in assessing the historical importance of Christian Independency in Africa we have to take account of the century or so of effective African agency before the arrival of imperialism and the essentially religious motivation of the men in the Independent churches. In relative terms it is only in the recent history of Christianity in Africa that missionaries rejected Africans as partners, and in that way they were much closer to their seventeenth-century counterparts. By the time this rejection occurred, Christianity had taken on the familiar hue of the African terrain over which it was vigorously spreading, able to survive the racist-inspired obstacles placed in its path. Many Africans saw their slighted labour in the redeeming light of Apostolic example. Christainity was destined to remain on the African continent, thanks largely to their faith and perseverance.

The turning-point: the humiliation of Bishop Crowther

The adverse view the CMS came to take of the work of Bishop Crowther in the Niger Mission was a significant factor in generating an active reservoir of separatist sentiment from which Independency was to gush forth in bursts of quick succession. It is a familiar and favourite theme, with variations on it fashioned by the penitent and then eagerly set to patriotic choreography. And still it continues to cast a strong spell over the future course of the missionary enterprise and the sharp questions it forced Africans to face.

The momentous drama in which Bishop Crowther was intended as the sacrificial victim had been confidently staged on the dismantled policy of Henry Venn, with missionary lightweights propped up to challenge Crowther's episcopal authority and alienate his achievement. Through irregular procedural arrangements, the CMS allowed Crowther to be outflanked until the substantive powers he held as bishop were effectively curtailed, his priestly stature was diminished and the man himself was reduced to a sorry sight.

The stages of that drama, as already indicated, have been carefully examined by scholars and missionary writers, so that it is not necessary to repeat all the details here. But some of them, as well as the broad outlines, need to be reviewed. Crowther had been appointed bishop with the intention that he should lead the Niger expedition in 1864. He had earlier, in 1857, been on the Niger and had established new stations at Onitsha and Igbebe, the latter being removed later to Lokoja. He returned to the Niger in 1859, dragged along by Venn's irresistible persistence. In 1864 he opened a station at Bonny and another one at Brass in 1876, both in the Delta. Brass proved a particularly successful project, with a strong Church quickly coming to life.

However, Crowther, wearied by the difficulties of travel and advancing age, pleaded to be relieved of direct responsibility for the Niger. But the Lord, in the determined shape of Henry Venn, answered self-doubt with the challenge of higher office. Crowther was duly consecrated bishop, with the Lord's rod prodding him to catch a glimpse of future greatness. What Venn had in mind was that Crowther should lead a team of Africans on the Niger, establish new Churches, create a village pastorate of self-reliant and self-perpetuating congregations, and in so doing bring about the realisation of a 'euthanasia of mission'. There would then be an African Church, reared on its own indigenous roots, bearing fruit under the stimulus of its own environment and sustained by the proprietory labours of those it served. A dream would then neatly come true — 'independent of foreign aid or superintendence', as Venn said.

In an ironic way, the Niger Mission, because of the dream out of which it was born, did not have European missionaries associated with it. From their Olympian distance these missionaries used their separation as an opportunity to sit in hostile judgement over the project as a whole. Even before Crowther was enthroned, Townsend, the senior CMS missionary at Abeokuta (over which Crowther was never given charge although he was held responsible for things going wrong there) was busy sharpening his racial carving-knife.

Crowther was surrounded by enormous problems on the Niger, and it was a cruel fate that determined that he should have had his colours nailed so ostentatiously to so false a mast. Transport up the Niger was difficult; when it was available, it was in boats owned and operated by grudging European trading companies. The entry of these companies into the Niger trade, aided and abetted by Crowther himself, complicated relations along the Niger. African traders were resented, and missionaries were suspected of favouring African commercial enterprise. Their presence in the Niger area was thus warily watched and discouraged, and they were eventually denied space on the trading boats on the grounds that space was not available. Since responsibility for the area had been placed in Crowther's hands, he felt compelled to explore alternative means of access. In 1877, on a visit to England, he obtained a vessel, suitably named the *Henry Venn,* for his missionary work. European traders objected that it would be diverted from its proper purpose and used to promote African trade behind a cloak of religion. This objection was met by Crowther agreeing to have the *Henry Venn* put in the charge of a lay Englishman, J.A. Ashcroft, who was officially designated as Accountant to the Mission and was to become the centrepiece of the scheme to make an expiatory example of Crowther. Ashcroft in effect assumed the underhand role of monitor of the Niger Mission, with incitement to file adverse reports on Crowther and his team of African agents.

By 1880, after African traders had been squeezed out of the Niger, Ashcroft turned over the *Henry Venn* to trade and profit, with the CMS authorising the move in disregard of the original intention and without any reference to Crowther. The *Henry Venn* began carrying potash from Nupe down to Lagos in a joint venture with the Niger Company. Ashcroft had thus entered the scene only to ensure that Crowther had neither an independent means of travelling up the Niger nor the hope of collaboration from European traders whose enterprise he had himself personally fostered. Having thus cut off Crowther from the field, Ashcroft used his commercial ally, Captain McIntosh, as a willing mouthpiece to enunciate the need for European supervision in mission in which Africans were to revert to a subordinate position. McIntosh enticingly placed the resources of the Niger Company at the disposal of the CMS on condition that a European be appointed to head a new mission at Egga on the Niger — in other words, a European alternative to Crowther. Then the CMS organised a no-confidence move against the Niger Mission by vesting its management in a finance committee based on Lagos and controlled by a majority of Europeans. An inquisition into the affairs of the Mission was then ordered under a European.

Few men, least of all Crowther, could have missed the meaning of the straws in the wind. But he was unable to discharge the burden of episcopal honour that Providence had laid on him. He did not have the aggressive and assertive nature which the situation demanded. Others would have to choose the ground and manner of his demise.

The investigation into the Niger Mission was not really a fact-finding exercise, although some facts did come to light. It was a vendetta against Crowther and his African agents. The Rev. J.B. Wood, the secretary of the Finance Committee, was chief inquisitor. He subordinated his method — of proceeding by on-the-spot investigations — to his aim, which was to prove the Niger Mission a sensational failure. His method consequently suffered, for he culled material from anonymous and unverifiable sources and from hostile individuals, but his goal of damaging the Mission was attained. He produced a report which made scurrilous attacks on the people connected with the Mission, and sent it to the CMS in London under a self-protective cloak of confidentiality. None of the people charged had been shown the report or confronted with the evidence and given a chance to challenge it. Crowther's unquestionable right of access to the report was ignored. It was later, after it was printed and circulated by the CMS, that the conscience-stricken head of the CMS asked for Crowther to be shown a copy. By that time European traders on the Niger had seen it. And then, almost as a price for being shown it, Crowther was asked to eat humble-pie and act on the report. However, the hunter was himself being hunted: the CMS Secretary, Hutchinson, was forced to resign after an inquiry into his conduct of the Society. Ashcroft was also dismissed for insubordination to Crowther. The Finance Committee itself was dissolved and replaced by a fresh one at Bonny. During what in hindsight was a brief intermission, the CMS was trying to salvage something from the wreckage caused by Wood and his accomplices.

Smoke always rises, and the smouldering forces released by the Wood report surfaced again after a change at the head of the CMS some nine months later. Confidential reports started to reach the Parent Committee in a steady trickle, all animated by a spirit of mischief-making. Little by little, Crowther had his African agents disaffiliated, their conduct and worth impugned in reports they were never allowed to challenge. Crowther himself was never attacked, publicly or privately, but his agents were to serve as decoys for staging a show-down with the Bishop. By tearing down the African agents, European missionaries were advancing closer to their main target. A group of young missionaries, most of them young enough for Crowther to be their grandfather, assailed the work of the Niger Mission, accusing it of extravagance, materialism and lack of spiritual zeal. They wanted Crowther and his African collaborators out of the way so that they could show the world how the Kingdom of God should be established in Africa. The Finance Committee established at Bonny but meeting at Onitsha in August 1890 was to be the arena for the trial of strength with Crowther. Some missionaries later expressed acute remorse for what happened.

Crowther was spiked on the twin prongs of a sharpened European imperial drive into the African interior and the exploited mixed fortunes of the Niger Mission. Reared on the notion of partnership with Europeans of an earlier age, he was assailed by the double reflexes of monopoly enterprise and political control. Both as a success and a failure the Niger Mission became the target of an aggressive europeanisation policy. At the Onitsha meeting the Rev. F.N. Eden, the English secretary of the Financial Committee, presided and overruled Crowther as Chairman. On the basis of charges pressed against African pastors of the Mission and remitted to London without being disclosed to the Committee, Eden proceeded to cut down Crowther's assistants. They were suspended from their priestly duties. Driven into a corner by this assault on the men he ordained, Crowther sought to redeem honour by offering a defence of the Africans. He challenged the Secretary, asking whether he 'alone is empowered to dismiss and suspend and do everything else in the Mission... Will you write down, say, please, Bishop Crowther expresses surprise at the statement of the Secretary that he has power as the representative of the CMS to suspend any clergyman from his duty. . .'[1] Crowther was reprimanded for defending the censured pastors and charged with conduct unworthy of his sacred office. He was suspended from the Committee. It was the *coup de grace* of a wretched plot. He went down characteristically meek and mild. 'Few scenes', one authority is moved to write, 'could have been more painful to watch than the grey-haired ... Bishop of over 80 ..., tormented and insulted by the young Europeans, trembling with rage as he never trembled before, as he got up to announce his resignation from the committee.'[2] From first to last the initiative was not his.

The legacy of the Niger incident

Crowther's conciliatory personality acted as a brake on separatist sentiment in the Church. Broken down by the humiliation at Onitsha, he still believed that he could pursue genuine discussions with the CMS on the desirability of a Niger Delta Pastorate, to be set up independently of foreign missionary control. He died on 31 December 1891, at the height of the discussions which eventually came out against the idea, although a modified form of the scheme was put into effect in 1892. But the question of Crowther's own successor acted as a further spur on Independency. Here too the CMS were determined to hold the line against deferring to African wishes. The African clergy, imbued with indelible streaks of quiescent loyalty, fell into line behind a towering CMS, but the congregations, beckoned by the robustly independent figure of the Rev. James Johnson, chose separation in the United Native African Church, on which more presently. At just about that time moves were being made to organise African nationalist opinion, which linked up with growing religious discontent in the Church. Africans were resolved to resist CMS attempts to repudiate the Niger Mission as a failure, with the implication that Africans could not be trusted to stand on their own feet and become leaders in the church, and this coalesced with the strong feeling that, contrary to CMS intentions, Crowther's successor should be an African. The removal of twelve of the fifteen African missionary agents on the Niger between 1880 and 1890 fuelled separatist sentiment. Five of those dismissed later joined the Niger Delta Pastorate. In spite of known local feeling on the matter, to resist which had been made into a virtue, the CMS vested control in European hands, and Africans were obliged to wait till the 1950s for the substance of Venn's dream to be fulfilled.

1. Ajayi (1963), p.253n.
2. ibid., p.253.

The Native Baptist Church

The storm which threatened over the Anglican Church with the Niger Mission debacle had in fact broken across a different frontier: the trail to Independency which beckoned the disaffected African elements had been blazed by the Baptists. What in the CMS was the result of a conscious design of the statesmanship of Venn was, in the Baptist Church, the consequence of an historical accident. The experience of self-reliance in the Baptist Church in Nigeria was significantly boosted between 1863 and 1875 when funds were cut off as the result of the American civil war and American missionaries returned home. Black Baptists, African and Afro-American, struggled to keep the Baptist work going, and succeeded in establishing a measure of financial independence for the congregations. With the resumption of American missionary leadership, strains began to be felt as a result of the changes which had taken place. Africans were unwilling to turn back the clock, and missionary insistence that this be done produced all the classic signs of a separatist scenario. One African Baptist was quick to point out the double irony of the American civil war achieving the liberation of American slaves and simultaneously facilitating self-reliance among African Churches. It is an apt comment on the perception of how African Christianity (and African history) is interlocked with events in the wider world. The missionary answer was to demonstrate superior financial resources by undertaking the building of prestige projects, including the Baptist Academy in Lagos. But missionary heavy-handedness exacerbated the spirit of strife. The Africans protested that established procedures were being ignored by the missionaries in their desire to exercise absolute control over the affairs of the Church. Reacting to the attempt to cow them into submission by the display of wealth, the Africans said that if the new Church just completed was intended as a barracoon, they would leave it, a terse warning that separation was imminent.

Actual separation followed in March 1888, when a group of disaffected Baptists, including those expelled by the missionaries, began holding their own services in Lagos. They called themselves Native Baptists, taking with them all the great African pioneers of Baptist work in Nigeria. The flame of revolt spread to Ogbomosho. Then Dr Blyden swept into Lagos in December 1890, preaching Church independence and fanning the embers of secession. A little fire lit by a small coterie of African Baptists intensified until it threatened to encircle the entire range of missionary justifications for retaining power in white hands.

The appearance of Dr Blyden on the scene coincided with a period of heightened nationalist feeling. Although that subject is strictly outside the scope of this book, its relationship to Christian Independency may nevertheless be briefly indicated here. As the pace of imperial conquest quickened with the 'Scramble for Africa', many African Christians, reeling from the effects of the Niger episode, struck out on the path of Independency. In response to Dr Blyden's strident call, a West African Church was inaugurated in March 1891, conceived as a Pan-African organisation which would be capable of responding meaningfully to the international nature of the challenge posed by world-wide imperialism. However the Church was stifled at birth. Many of the leading African Christians failed to join it. It was intended not only as a political pressure group but as a schismatic movement, and that was enough to frighten away many potential supporters. Separation and Independency are one thing, but a full-blown doctrinal schism was something quite different. We shall explore a little further the connection between colonial subjugation and Independency in a moment, but first the reasons for the failure of Dr Blyden's project should be analysed. By way of contrast to the West African Church, there was the African Church Movement, and especially the United Native African Church conceived as the positive instrument for the evangelisation of Africa by Africans. If the Movement was set apart from western missions that was because it was considered more effective and in the long run more likely to endure. The African Church was thus only incidentally a racial response to missionary racial attitudes. It deliberately eschewed the philosophy of racism precisely because that philosophy undercut the confident basis for the proclamation of the Gospel. In addition, of course, racism is hard to defend on any sound theology. The malignant growth of the failure of love which the African Church Movement identified in white missionary Churches would not become less virulent if transplanted to African conditions. Dr Blyden, less gifted with a sense of Christian vocation, would merely sow for others to reap.

The era of the 'Scramble for Africa' was to create a wide circle of disaffected Africans, many of them Christians. We have already referred to the effects of the German take-over in the Cameroun on the local Baptists who rejected the Basel Missionary Society and instead founded an independent Baptist church (see Chapter 5 above). These Baptists sought contact with their fellow-Baptists elsewhere. For example, the Cameroun Baptists appealed to their brethren in Lagos for assistance in a legal dispute with the German missionaries. The Methodists in Togoland similarly opposed the German take-over, while those at Porto Novo (Republic of Benin) stood out against the coming of French rule. Many of them fled to Lagos from persecution by the French. Thus Independency was bolstered by the advent of direct colonial rule. In Nigeria itself the subjugation of Yoruba kingdoms increased the number of disaffected Christians and widened the gap between them and the missionaries. For example, the invasion that led to the overthrow of Ijebu-Ode in

1892 produced a strong reaction among African Christians, many of them critical of the support missionaries lent the British. In other cases there is more than a hint of African reaction to the consolidation of alien rule, and in the numerous movements of Christian Independency, political and economic factors played an important role in galvanising the religious resolve.

The United Native African Church

Shortly after the failure of Dr Blyden's concept of a West African Church (although James Johnson appears to have retained something of that inspiration in an endowment fund for the Niger Delta Pastorate), a movement was launched to give further strength to the African initiative in mission. It was called the United Native African Church, first set up in August 1891 in response to African discontent with the Niger Mission and to the shabby treatment accorded to Bishop Crowther. But it did not go far enough. It refused to provide sanctuary for those expelled from the mission Churches, for fear that it might be derided as second-best. On many issues it fudged and would not take a lead. But its mere existence was provocative enough, a signal to others that a vast field of religious enterprise lay unoccupied — a field which, although its potential was greater than anything about which the missions could have dreamt, was nevertheless ignored or rejected. People were not slow to move into that uncontested territory. It is a remarkable fact that in the proliferating undergrowth of secessionist sentiment, CMS intransigence on the African question was the single most critical irritant. Even in the case of Methodist separatism the atmosphere had been conditioned by postures struck elsewhere. The United Native African Church in the end allowed the torch of Independency to pass into steadier hands from which its light rapidly spread in uncontrollable flares.

The African Church Movement

In the aftermath of the dissolution of the Niger Mission as Crowther's heritage and the refusal to replace him with an African bishop, the CMS resorted to the slightly anomalous practice of creating assistant bishoprics for Africans serving under Europeans. Thus James Johnson was created assistant bishop of the Niger Delta, which came under direct CMS control. Johnson tried to keep alive the idea of a Niger Delta Native Pastorate by establishing a £10,000 endowment fund to be raised from local subscription up and down the west coast. The real likelihood that he would succeed drove the CMS into a panicked reaction. In July 1901, Johnson was sacked from his Church in Lagos and his belongings were dumped in the street. It of course had the predictable effect on his parishioners. Led by the Rev.

S.A. Coker, a group broke away as a consequence and became known subsequently as the 'Bethelites', after Bethel Church which they built in December 1901. Thus was laid the foundation of the African Church Organisation, which widened the rift with Anglicanism.

Several important issues were to dominate the early history of the African Church Movement. One was the question of African forms of music and worship. Drumming and African versions of Western hymns were introduced. The other was the related problem of dealing with foreign elements in Church life and organisation, with some people intent on keeping close to the historic mission Churches from which they had seceded, while others were determined to eradicate any vestigial remains of an earlier epoch. Another problem was what today would be known as faith and order, the question being what form of ecclesiastical order should be adopted, the choice ranging between a lay-oriented, congregational type of Church at one extreme and, at the other, an episcopacy emphasising the historical continuity with Apostolic authority. The dust of controversy which surrounded this issue was raised by the attempt to combine the experience of people from different Church backgrounds. The other contentious issue was polygamy. The African Church Movement settled on the expedient formula of allowing polygamy for the laity but insisting that the clergy adhere to the monogamous rule. It was hardly a consistent policy. The arguments which made polygamy a defective institution for the clergy would not suddenly disappear merely by drafting in the laity. And, no less important, men who relied significantly on the contribution of women in the work of the Church would be more likely to preserve that tradition through schemes of equality, not through continued male dominance.

The men who led the African Church Movement were substantial owners of property, important government officials and other prominent leaders of society. One was the wealthy entrepreneur, J. K. Coker, described in chapter 6 above. The other was J. W. Cole, another wealthy Lagos entrepreneur and a generous benefactor of the United Native African Church. He was for two years (1895–7) a member of the Legislative Council in Lagos. Two others, with civil service connections, were H. A. Caulcrick (decorated by the colonial government for distinguished service in the Treasury) and E. H. Oke, who had been in the Judiciary Department and after his retirement was a member of the Legislative Council in 1924–30. He was active in cultural circles in Ibadan where he was based and was president of the Ibadan branch of the Pan-African nationalist organisation, the National Congress of British West Africa. Finally we should mention G. A. Williams, who had been an African agent on the Niger with the CMS and left for Lagos after Crowther's demise. He became active in popular journalism, eventually owning and editing the *Lagos Standard* which he turned into a mouthpiece of the African cause. He and the others formed the highest cadre of the African Church, occupying the rank of elders. The elders performed a characteristically African function: the provision of largesse to their followers and display of wealth and influence in the community, whereby they acquired a reputation for open-handedness in contrast to foreign-inspired parsimony. Below the elders were the junior leaders who received patronage from the elders and distributed benefits among supporters. Then came the clergy, recruited from among the junior leaders and expected to occupy a relatively neutral position. The clergy were seen as brokers, not principals, in the quicksand of local politics. Theoretically untainted with partisan stigma, the clergy were in fact for the most part humble men, distinguished only by their piety and spiritual authority.

At the base of the organisational structure was the congregation which exercised its authority through the vestry meeting. But an intricate pattern of wheeling and dealing behind the scenes prevented the vestry from becoming an arena for interminable wrangling. It voted the elders into office and kept a close watch on the observance of established procedure. Scholars have of course pointed out how African Church orgánisation in this instance closely followed traditional Yoruba political ideas, and a similar phenomenon can be described in places as far apart as Ghana and Malawi, or Ivory Coast and Tanzania, to take a few examples. This kind of reciprocity, needless to say, is the key to the successful adaptation of Christianity to African conditions, and as a process it has long historical antecedents.

United African Methodist Church

A serious rift threatened in the ranks of the Methodist Church in April 1884, but it was averted through the timely intervention of the British Methodist Conference. The issue was on a point of constitutional principle, and the Lagos Synod challenged the authority of the missionary Chairman in his conduct of Church affairs. Traditionally power in the Methodist Church is devolved upon the District Synod at its statutory annual meeting, and when the missionary Chairman tried to overrule the Synod, he was acting contrary to Methodist rule and discipline. It is true that other missionaries of the same era had acted *ultra vires* with impunity, carried along as they were by the strong tide of imperial subjugation. But the Methodist Church, unlike the Anglican Church, was not an established Church and had its roots in historical circumstances strikingly similar to those of African Christian Independency. This time, at least, the Chairman was suitably reproved by a commission of enquiry set up by the British Methodist Conference, in language well suited to the mood of expectancy among Africans. 'It is a far nobler thing', the committee wrote to the Chairman, 'to guide others in their efforts to govern than to act simply as an autocrat. A fair and real self-government is one of the chief objects which your predecessors have aimed at realising, and any success of theirs is a result which we cherish with gratitude.'[3]

That crisis passed. When separation came, it was over a completely different issue and happened under a Chairman whose disciplinarian temper made him unpopular with both Europeans and Africans. Thus the racial factor was not important, with the consequence that the separatist legacy in Methodism was not unduly bedevilled with bitterness.

In 1917 the Methodist Chairman, the Rev. G.O. Griffin of Lagos, in a crackdown on what he considered reprehensible laxity in the Church, decided to expel those leaders who were guilty of polygamy. It was like opening Pandora's Box: the ten original leaders he intended to expel were joined by fifty-five others who admitted at a public meeting that they too were polygamists. They were summarily expelled, and the nucleus of a separatist Church was thus created by the action of the Chairman, for the expelled men, determined to continue worshipping as Christians, began holding their own services. There were few recriminations. The Methodist Church looked upon them as brethren fallen from grace, but still as brethren, while the separatists regarded themselves as good Methodists. They did not repudiate Methodist rule and practice, and were not anathematised by the mission.

Thus was born the United African Methodist Church. It held its first services near the Lagos fish market, eliciting by that the derogatory nickname *Eleja*, fishmongers. By the mutation of fashion the separatists proudly donned the name under Scriptural warranty as 'Fishers of Men'. But whatever its attractions the UAM (Eleja) could not make polygamy the forcing bed of anything more daring than popular virtue, and remained a relatively small separatist Church. By 1920 it had some 500 members, though with a high *per capita* income. Apart from their insistence on treating polygamy as an acceptable practice for Christians, the UAM (Eleja) were basically conservative in their churchmanship. There were no real innovations in doctrine nor any shifts in rules of Methodist discipline. Their significance lay less in what they claimed to offer than in what they symbolised, the proof that Africans, from external historical pressure and internal local stimulus, had arrived at a sense of responsibility for the future direction of the Church in their continent. The next stage of our discussion is ample testimony to the fact that that sense of responsibility had matured considerably and that whole communities were ready to come forward to help shape the Church's future. If

3. Ajayi (1965), p.259.

such a turn of events was resisted by foreign missions, it must have been because it threatened to demonstrate the greater significance of African agents as assimilators over against the subservient role of missionaries as historical transmitters. The answer to missionary prayer had come as an ironic challenge to missionary attitudes.

Charismatic Churches and Prophet movements

A special category of Churches arrived on the scene of Christian Independency by a second, internal wave of African reaction to foreign domination. The first wave had borne those Churches which broke away from mission-related Churches by repudiating European administrative control. These churches, however, had made little innovation to the content and expression of Christianity, although greater use seems to have been made of African languages. The second category by contrast adopted the twin paths of administrative independence and ritual adaptation. Charismatic Churches is one way of describing these bodies, so called because of the emphasis put on charismatic or spiritual gifts such as prophecy, healing, prayer and holiness. Interest thus shifted away from institutional structures and administrative forms and turned instead to inner renewal and personal wellbeing. A process of internal change was thus initiated in which African Christians sought a distinctive way of life through mediation of the spirit, a process that enhanced the importance of traditional religions for the deepening of Christian spirituality. The Charismatic Churches, therefore, combined the two fundamental elements of Christianity and African culture in a way that advertises their Christian intentions without undervaluing their African credentials. Biblical material was submitted to the regenerative capacity of African perception, and the result would be Africa's unique contribution to the story of Christianity.

Few areas of African Christianity have been so abundantly written about as the Independent Churches, and within that subject considerable space is devoted to Prophet movements and Charismatic Churches. It would be impossible to try here to reflect the importance of the subject in either the treatment of the theme or the range of scholarly approach. But within existing constraints an attempt ought to be made to introduce the two areas of Charismatic Churches and of Prophet movements. In the final section on the phenomenon of Christian Independency, an attempt will be made to measure the strength and extent of Christian renewal in Africa.

Prophet Garrick Braide. Garrick Braide was nurtured in the tense and fraught atmosphere of the Niger Delta Pastorate, established with some measure of independence from the CMS in 1892. By the turn of the century, the Niger Delta area was stirring with the leavening expectancy compounded of hope and frustration — hope because Christianity, having arrived on the scene, was seized upon as the instrument by which forces of change could be meaningfully harnessed, and frustration because foreign control had threatened to set back a promise that was within easy grasp. Braide would be the man to embody this historical irony. By his rise and fall he epitomised the ambiguous role of Christianity under colonial domination.

Braide was born about 1882 and grew up at Bakana, a centre of Christian missionary work. He was baptised in 1910 and confirmed by Bishop James Johnson two years later. Johnson was later to repudiate his spiritual protégé, but for a while he had the highest opinion of Braide's religious activities. Contemporary accounts speak of Braide's intense religious disposition; for example, he used to spend whole nights at prayer in the Church with the Bible at hand. He was preoccupied to an unusual degree with the state of his soul. Once he said he heard a still small voice calling him to preach the Gospel and some over-enthusiastic writers have embellished the story of his call with an account of Braide receiving a vision. Two other stories tell of his miraculous powers. Both concern rain-making. Once a rainstorm enveloped the land as a direct result of a prayer Braide directed against those who defied his ruling on keeping the Sabbath. The second story concerns another rainstorm which Braide caused in a duel with traditional rain-makers. In the atmosphere of heightened tension the boundary between ordinary coincidence and the supernatural recedes rapidly, leaving the Prophet free to inflate his powers for the benefit of the credulous. Braide's reputation spread as a result of these stories and people quickly flocked to his cause. By 1915 he had emerged as the most popular religious figure in the Niger Delta, with a formidable following. The authorities began to regard him as a danger, and a net was thrown around him within which his words and movements were monitored.

The two principal themes of Braide's preaching were complete dependence on God and the requirement that his followers abandon idols, fetishes and the use of charms. On the social side he preached an uncompromising abhorrence of alcohol — the scourge of the Niger Delta, as indeed of other coastal areas affected by European trade. For example, it is estimated that each year some 3 million gallons of gin and rum were consumed in the Delta towns of Brass, Kalabari, Bonny and Opobo. There is evidence that Braide's invective against alcohol had the desired effect, and consumption fell drastically. One of the effects was a dramatic drop in excise revenue, a point which the colonial authorities took seriously enough for them to list falling revenue as a charge against Braide.

It is difficult for the purposes of historical analysis to assess the precise effect of Braide's teaching about faith in God, that being an intangible element. But something of his success can be learnt from the statistical evidence of response to his preaching. The number of those inquiring after Christian baptism increased by 150 per cent between 1912 and 1918, the years of Braide's active career, and a still larger increase is noted in the number of baptised Christians in the areas affected by his preaching. In 1909 this number was 902, and in 1918, the year of his death, it was 11,694. Between 1918 and 1921, Braide's own followers numbered some 43,000, split though they were into three main sections.

On the matter of abandoning idols, fetishes and charms, the position is less simple. Braide repudiated these symbols of traditional religious life because he believed them to be ineffective or even harmful agents of the supernatural. But he did not deny the reality of the supernatural world; he merely offered what he considered to be more effective ways of dealing with that world. In his duel with traditional rainmakers, for example, he settled the dispute by calling on what he regarded as a higher power to achieve precisely what his opponents had previously achieved by calling on intermediary powers. It is clear that Braide had merely asserted the power of a Christian God over a territory of long familiarity, rather than shifting the religious contest to totally new ground. Furthermore, his own charismatic powers transformed him into a familiar local figure, the powerful medicine man who this time achieved miracles by the use of Christian religious symbols. Thus Christianity might come to challenge traditional religions, and sometimes even to displace them, but initially at least it did so by compensating the converts in recognised currency. To say this is not to deny the revolutionary impact of Christianity on traditional Africa but only to direct attention to the significant points of contact and the transition stages along that route. Genuine change is often the result of a prior parallel encounter.

In perpetuating old religious values Braide appeared in the deliberate guise of the Old Testament prophet, drawing a parallel between himself and Isaiah and Malachi. He called himself Elijah II and gave Bakana the title 'Israel'. He attributed his gift of efficacious prayer to the God of the Bible, and he practised healing by the use of that gift. He stressed fasting as an indispensable spiritual exercise. When called to perform healing, he would agree to go on condition that he preached his message. As his reputation for holiness grew, so too did a superstitious reverence for his person: people sought physical contact with him in order to receive healing or protection from danger. The water in which he washed was collected and dispensed as containing magical properties. His words were received as charged with spiritual force. But Braide became something more than the idol of popular devotion: the historical circumstances of his movement cast him in an inevitable political role. He did not need a profound insight into contemporary history to appreciate that

European colonialism had begun to transform political relations in Africa. In fact he preached on the subject of white alien rule, though his predictions and prescriptions showed an underestimation of the strengths of the new reality.

Both the colonial authorities and the leaders of African political opinion drew political conclusions from Braide's movement, and on that kind of subjective evidence Braide was tracked down and eventually arrested. James Johnson had decided after a meeting of the Board of the Niger Delta Pastorate in February 1916 that the movement should be proscribed; he accused Braide of heresy and excesses and was determined, he said, to root out the movement. In pursuit of this aim he wrote to the colonial authorities asking them to imitate his own policy of taking strong disciplinary action against Braide. The paradox of James Johnson, the pre-eminent patriot, appealing to the agents of foreign domination to put down a popular leader of Christian Independency can be explained only by the thoroughness of that domination. Braide was arrested in March 1916, and charged with causing civil unrest and the unauthorised raising of funds. His principal supporters were also pulled in for 'riot, assault and unlawful assembly', the familiar catch-all for culpable offence in those days. At this time Braide's support was calculated at well over 1,000,000. But that did not help him. He was as much a victim of the historical circumstances as was Johnson in a different way, the one comprehensively beaten by the forces which the other had astutely utilised to his advantage.

Braide's significance for African political opinion was demonstrated in an extended comment in the nationalist paper, the *Lagos Weekly Record,* on 18 November 1916. Yet even this unimpeachable source of nationalist pride was driven to dilute its heady political message with some vague religious predictions:

The God of the Negro it would seem has arisen as a strong man from a deep sleep and surveying the wreck and ruin — the physical and moral degradation of the dusky sons of Africa has gathered up his loins together to redress the balance of the old regime and already has begun to raise up instruments of his sweet will. Prodigies like Garrick or William Waddy Harris are neither impostors nor false prophets. They are merely temporary vehicles for some manifestations of the divine will.[4]

While Braide was in prison, his followers continued to meet, their numbers continually growing. They subsequently formed a separatist Church calling itself Christ Army Church. This was in 1916. In January 1917, with the reality of the new international political order finally dawning, the Church applied for affiliation to the World Evangelical Alliance in London; it had become conscious of the need

4. Cited in Tasie (1978), p.192.

to demonstrate outside influence and contact. Soon after its founding it was already suffering from internal dissension.

Shortly after his release from prison, Braide suffered a short illness from which he never recovered, dying in November 1918 a broken man, although popular support for him never waned. In the popular imagination he remained Elijah II, the prophet who achieved for his people a double victory over the power of local spirits and over the disintegrating civilization ushered in by the new colonial order. In the ranks of enlightened African opinion Braide was undoubtedly a hero. Both S.A. Coker and Otomba Payne, men of outstanding distinction of their age, considered him a worthy son of the soil. In terms of the prospects before the Churches in Africa, Braide's work again points firmly to the future, an early harbinger of the changes that would burst upon the scene throughout the continent. In linking him with the Prophet Harris, the *Lagos Weekly Record* had instinctively stumbled on the grand theme of African Christianity. Chapter 5 above has already described some of the effects of the Prophet's work, but the description given there does scant justice to the great man whose life and work has now been studied in great detail.[5]

If Braide was a channel which officialdom was resolved to choke with restrictive measures, the movement we are about to examine broke upon the scene with the intensity of a raging fire. The numerous bright flares of charismatic Christian bands which swept across the face of Yorubaland and beyond would merely intensify under the heat of official repression. A vertible spiritual revival was to foreshadow a political retreat.

Church of the Lord (Aladura) and other charismatic Churches

In the world-wide influenzia epidemic of 1918, an Anglican lay leader from Ijebu-Ode, Joseph B. Shadare (died January 1962), had a dream as a result of which he formed a separate prayer group within St Saviour's Church at Ijebu-Ode. He offered spiritual help against the plague. At about the same time Sophia Odunlami, a relative of Shadare and a teacher in a nearby Anglican school, claimed to have received inspiration by the Holy Spirit, and preached against the use of modern medicine. She promised healing through water and that a miraculous rain would fall. The prayer group which she and Shadare led was given the name Precious Stone or, alternatively, Diamond Society (Shadare had himself been a goldsmith). It was in effect a Pentecostal prayer and spiritual healing group. At about the same time literature from an American Pentecostal group, Faith Tabernacle, reached the Precious Stone movement. Faith Tabernacle stressed prayer, healing, personal holiness and the millennial return of Christ. It is clear that the Precious Stone band were little

5. Shank (1980).

influenced by Faith Tabernacle in these matters, but in the emphasis on the necessity of adult baptism and the rejection of infant baptism Faith Tabernacle had a direct effect. The issue was to form the basis of a serious conflict between the Anglican Church and the Precious Stone people; about 1921 it became clear that the Precious Stone movement had to withdraw from the Anglican Church, and about the same time a branch was begun in Lagos.

The movement spread to other areas. At Ilesha a prayer group was formed under the headmaster of an Anglican village school. His collaborators included the local catechist, Babatope, and a tailor, Fasah. They repudiated divinatory forms of healing and modern medicine and instead stressed the use of prayer for healing. Following contacts with Shadare and others, Babatope and his group established a separate branch of Faith Tabernacle in Ilesha, with Babatope as leader.

At Ibadan similar efforts were to lead to the establishment there of a branch of Faith Tabernacle. The movement began in Anglican circles. Isaac B. Akinleye, a member of St Peter's Anglican Church, Aremo, Ibadan, had been a recipient of Faith Tabernacle literature from America. After a healing experience in 1926, he abandoned medicines of any kind till his death in 1964. He was a prominent local leader, having been Olubadan of Ibadan and the recipient of a knighthood. (His brother became the Anglican bishop of Ibadan). In October 1924, J. Ade Aina, a young Ijebu agent for a Lagos leather merchant, was transferred to Ibadan where he obtained access to material on Faith Tabernacle, Philadelphia. On inquiring from them he was put in touch with Akinleye and two others, and together they began organising a regular service at Akinleye's house in 1925. Akinleye ceased attending Anglican synods from that time. Shortly after this the tenuous connection between Faith Tabernacle in America and its Ibadan counterpart was severed. Another Western Pentecostal group, the Faith and Truth Temple of Toronto, stepped into the breach for a while, but the association with the Ibadan Faith Tabernacle was soon terminated. Disentangled from the inhibiting influence of foreign religious organisations, Faith Tabernacle entered on its phase of expansion.

The Revival of 1930. An orchestrated movement was started in the branches of the Faith Tabernacle to pray for revival and miracles. A Lagos leader, Daniel Orekoya, went into retreat and emerged prophesying that the answer to prayer had been assured him when certain conditions were fulfilled. These were the avoidance of idolatry, the recognition of the value of prophecy, and generosity with money and possessions. This message was widely distributed.

The revival got under way in the weakest and most isolated of centres, Ilesha. It began with a young semi-skilled man, Joseph

Babalola, then aged twenty-four, who had been the driver of a road-roller. According to his own account he heard voices telling him to leave his job and to go and preach. He resisted the voices until the third day, when his engine seized up and he could not get it going. He interpreted the incident as a rebuke to his stubbornness and yielded. His resistance overcome, he returned home to pray and fast, and during that period of retreat he had visions calling him to preach repentance and judgement, the destruction of idols and the promise of healing through prayer.

A number of important introductions followed this. He was introduced to Babatope and in 1929 was invited to Ibadan and then to Lagos where he met Shadare and Odubanjo, another charismatic figure. In Lagos Babalola had phenomenal success. He prayed, prophesied and healed. When he returned to Ilesha it was the homecoming of a prodigy. His fame spread from Ilesha, igniting the highly charged atmosphere of charismatic expectancy. In another little-known town a similar revival had been getting under way quite independently of Ilesha.

Josiah Olunowo Oshitelu. The man who was to become the founder of the Church of the Lord (Aladura), Josiah Olunowo Oshitelu, had had intense visionary experiences from about 1925. In 1926 he broke with the Anglican Church and then went to a remote village to receive spiritual training. He emerged and began his public preaching in June 1929, at Ogere. He pronounced judgment on idolatry and native medicines, upheld faith healing and baptism of the Spirit, and taught about the gift of prophecy. He linked up with the Faith Tabernacle people who had been praying for revival; he also met Babalola who came from Ilesha to visit him. At this point Oshitelu's authority appears much greater than that of Babalola. Oshitelu was also received by Shadare whom he visited in Ijebu-Ode. Tension developed between Shadare and Oshitelu, especially over the latter's campaign against witchcraft, a campaign Shadare and others questioned on the grounds that weak and suggestive people were condemned for nothing more serious than a twinge of conscience at small infringements of the moral code. Shadare in fact charged that confessions were extracted under duress and that malice was the main element in most cases. He declared a more fundamental objection: 'Knowledge that somebody is a witch can bring no benefit to anybody.'[6]

The other major bone of contention with Oshitelu was his claim that he was vouchsafed certain mysterious 'Holy Names', names which he claimed were capable of bringing about miracles. One prominent follower who later broke away from Oshitelu claimed to have been told in a dream: 'These names can bring no forgiveness,

6. Turner, vol. I (1967), p.22.

salvation or benefit of any kind. . . .'[7] He testified that 'Christ came and showed us His real name and as we are promised everything in the name of Christ, all other names should be left aside.'[8] It is clear in all this ferment that Oshitelu had struck a rich vein of religious vitality, although many local groups would feed on this with the stimulus of independent figures. A living spiritual movement must be transmitted in a chain of living witnesses, each witness an independent link that contributes by its strength to the growth and development of the chain. Therefore, the absence of a central authority at this stage in the history of the charismatic revival is not a sign of weakness but of life. Oshitelu, however prominent, would be just one link in the unfolding story of the Spirit's wooing.

Oshitelu came into conflict with the colonial authorities over his inflammatory pronouncements on politics, economics and colonialism. This was between 1930 and 1931. He talked about the judgment to come and the Kingdom of Christ which would expose the fraud and falsehood that characterised the earthly kingdom. Nevertheless his reference to Europeans in Africa was in the context of Africa being able to offer Europeans a knowledge of God and secular benefits. He also predicted a catastrophic end for the older churches because of their love of money. An over-sensitive colonial government took offence at these pronouncements. The need to secure some form of Western religious contact was again felt, if only to give a semblance of respectability to what had been a local development. We shall describe this aspect of the Aladura movement (*aladura* is Yoruba for prayer) presently.

To return to Oshitelu, there is strong evidence of Islamic religious materials having been an influence on his life. It would be more consistent to discuss that in a separate chapter. What is clear is that the diction of Arabic prayers, set to the music of Yoruba tones, performed for Oshitelu a suitable revelatory function. The idea that the mysterious Divine Being could be efficaciously approached through the mystery of language and charismatic gifts had been a familiar aspect of Yoruba Islam. Whatever the distance between Oshitelu and this Yoruba Islamic heritage, the fact that he drew upon such sources cannot be doubted. In his role as a transmitter of spiritual power, he fashioned from available religious sources the instruments by which he would arrive at his own version of man's response to the transcendent. For example, to show that he was the child of a universal spirit he had the title 'Doctor of the Psychical' conferred on him in 1948 by the National Union of Spiritualists of Nigeria.

Oshitelu set about the work of organisation and expansion of his Church. His mother became the first lady president of the whole

7. Turner, vol. I (1967), p.23.
8. ibid.

movement, and when she died in 1948, was succeeded by her married daughter, Mrs Dorcas Oyetola Sodipo. But the problem of pastoral leadership was acute. For example, in 1962 the movement could claim only seventy-three ministers and ten ordinands, called 'followers'. The size of the Nigerian membership was estimated at 3,000. To turn to the expansion side of the story, here there were significant successes. Between 1938, when the movement spread west to Ife and Oshogbo, and 1956 when a branch was opened at Aba in Eastern Nigeria and by which time a foothold had been created in Northern Nigeria, large numbers of people had joined or become affiliated to the Church of the Lord (Aladura). Although its appearance in the islamised North of Nigeria was restricted mainly to the Southern immigrants there, nevertheless it was an important breakthrough. An African Church, established by Africans and drawing on religious materials which embraced an africanised form of Islam, was bound to make an impression. However, only a few Muslim converts from Kano joined the Church, although the present writer can remember on a visit to Sokoto in 1971 the near-awe with which the building of the Church of the Lord (Aladura) was pointed out by his guide, a Muslim police officer.

The pioneer Church of the Lord missionary in the north of Nigeria was S.A. Ogunnaike, who established branches in all the main northern towns. A rival Church was established in Jos by Mother D.M. Oluwole. The phenomenon of secession was widespread in the movement and most of the separatist and splinter groups were dominated by individual personalities rather than by groups. A major breakaway group was the Church of Christ (Aladura) led by a retired Creole civil servant living in Nigeria. Another secessionist Church was the Regeneration Church of Christ, founded by a defector from the United Native African Church, A.A. Banjo. He stressed the role of the Bible and the life and teaching of Jesus Christ as the ultimate standard of life and faith in contrast to the central role given by the Church of the Lord (Aladura) to visions and dreams. Banjo took a more rational view of ritual and the sacraments, with an equally tolerant attitude towards the place of women in the Church. He returned to the fold in July 1963.

It is a striking fact that the tribal factor played little or no role in the splits, striking because ethnicity appears to have fed most of the political agitation of this period. Religious dissent seems to have been the result of genuine disagreements over religious issues, which we need to bear in mind when we make religious movements the by-products of social and political forces.

To turn our attention to this social and political theme, Oshitelu appears to have had little success in winning over the social and political élites. One example makes clear his difficulties in this area. In about 1950 the new Oba of Ede was sponsored by the Church of the Lord (Aladura). After he received the political title, he remained sympathetic to the Church and gave a large tract of land as the site for a new church. By 1960, however, his support had weakened until Church officials were complaining publicly of his failure to support the cause. Another example shows Oshitelu and his Church people in a desperate light. In 1933 an approach was made to the Oba of Ijebu-Ode who was given a vision with the practical suggestion that he would be an obedient king. Five years later the Oba was not penitent enough, and Oshitelu accordingly descended on him with a barrage of rebukes and dire warnings, with the usual prescription that he would avoid a harsh fate if he gave material support to the Church. We are not told if the Oba was moved by Oshitelu's threats and demands; but it is clear here and elsewhere that traditional political hierarchies were in general ambivalent towards the overtures of the new religious men, no doubt exercised by the familiar dilemma of whether to submit and thus impair their authority or resist and thus risk ignoring a force which might alienate a more responsive section of the citizenry. On the whole it was people from the lower strata of society who were attracted to the new religious movements, with a sprinkling of professional men and senior civil servants who sought the type of charismatic ministration that the Churches were able to offer.

As remarked earlier in this chapter, Oshitelu was just one more link in the growing chain of revival groups which sprang up in various places. He had been in contact with Faith Tabernacle, but as Oshitelu's reputation grew the two movements went their separate ways. Nevertheless it was obvious that Oshitelu shared with the other religious leaders a common historical experience and a common approach to issues of the religious life. If history and the common idiom of Yoruba culture had not united them, a significant overlap of religious perception and practice would have brought them together. It was on the basis of this wide and rich common ground that there were at least three important attempts to make common cause. In 1941 a 'Prophets' Union Meeting' was proposed, to link together the various parts of the Aladura revival movement. Personal considerations prevented Oshitelu from giving continued support to the scheme, and after a couple of meetings the idea was dropped. Then again in 1952 a federal body was formed in Ibadan similar in its aim to the 1941 scheme. The Ibadan group succeeded for a short time in arousing public interest, a high point being reached in 1955 when it organised a general procession of Aladura members in a thanksgiving service on the occasion of the elevation of Akinleye as the new Olubadan (a chiefly title). A series of combined prayer meetings followed during the first week of the new year, but interest declined quickly after that and the movement lapsed.

In 1956 the third movement was launched, called the General

Council of the Christian Praying Bands, which held a joint Palm Sunday service in 1956. Aladura Churches have mostly shown a willingness to join in ecumenical efforts to mark events or occasions, such as the setting up of the Billy Graham campaign of 1960. However the creation of a permanent ecumenical structure was to elude the Churches for some time. The internal pressures of having to cope with a large influx of members, as well as the demands of administering Churches scattered over a wide area, left the new Churches with few resources to devote to ecumenical projects. Lack of education has also seriously impeded the leadership in playing a meaningful role in such ventures. However, by the time Oshitelu died in 1962, the Charismatic movement had become an established part of the African religious scene.

Other members of the Aladura revival movement

The Precious Stone Church continued to function, but more than many other similar movements it was particularly hard hit by the opposition of older Churches and by restrictive government measures. It sought association with Western religious organisations to offset these handicaps. The response from the West often proved disappointing. In matters of doctrine and practice the Precious Stone remained largely independent. It practised adult baptism by immersion, held to the monogamous rule in marriage, rejected all forms of medicine, relying instead on faith-healing, and stressed the gift of prophecy. Personal holiness was also stressed, not as the self-righteous badge of a heroic individualism so prevalent in Western religious movements, but as a mark of selfless devotion to communal life and experience. As part of the general activity of Faith Tabernacle, the Precious Stone was to be eclipsed by the emergence of new religious groups, particularly the Cherubim and Seraphim Church, to which we now turn.

Cherubim and Seraphim Church. In the 1920s a prayer group was led in Lagos by an illiterate prophet, Moses Orimolade Tunolashe, who placed great emphasis on faith-healing. In June 1925, he was called to the assistance of a fifteen-year old Anglican girl, Christiana Abiodun Akinsowon, who had gone into a prolonged trance after witnessing a procession in Lagos on the festival of Corpus Christi. Orimolade gained her confidence well enough to be able to pray successfully for her recovery. The news of this spread quickly, and before long Abiodun and he were organising a spiritual society. Abiodun began employing special prayers and holy water for healing, which she claimed had been shown her during her trance. Many enquirers called on them. Orimolade decided they must have a name for their society, and so for three days they went into retreat to fast and pray.

In September 1925, they adopted the name Seraphim after angels had appeared to them in visions. That name became their popular identity, although two years later they added Cherubim to it. In the early stages of the movement the followers were encouraged to attend their own Churches, and Seraphim prayer meetings and healing services were arranged so as not to clash with the times for church services, but this state of affairs did not last. But while it did, several leading clergymen from the historic churches maintained a close connection with the Cherubim and Seraphim. Pastors and ministers from the African Church and from the Anglican and Methodist Churches, for example, served on various committees of the movement. There was of course opposition to the new movement, although the charge that the Seraphim society was wrongfully denouncing traditional religions shows how easily the critics had been misled. In several crucial ways the Aladura churches behaved as integral parts of the Yoruba traditional world view, as an illuminating sociological study has shown. Furthermore, some of the critics themselves, such as the Anglican leader the Venerable T.A.J. Ogunbiyi, were prominent in Aladura activity. Ogunbiyi in fact wrote a best-selling Aladura pamphlet. He advised on the efficacious use of Psalm 127 against witches, in spite of having publicly denounced Aladura campaigns against witches! Although a graduate of Fourah Bay College and therefore a member of the modern African élite, he nevertheless performed as an expert handler of traditional means of spiritual mediation.

Orimolade became known as *Baba Aladura,* a title he acquired through the gift of prayer. The phrase means 'Praying Father' and was resisted by Church authorities as making Orimolade a source of rival authority. The Praying Band which he and Abiodun led was known as *Egbe Aladura.* It is clear that the focal point of the life and practice of the group was prayer. Prayer was understood in two specific ways. First, it was the means whereby the individual received certain benefits, including the fulfilment of wishes and desires, and secondly, it was the obtaining of guidance. In this way personal need and control, which used to form a prominent part of traditional religious life and practice, acquired a new lease of life in a Christian setting. The *orisha,* intermediary powers, provided answers to one's needs while Ifa divination, the science of discerning things in the spiritual world, helped to ascertain the mind and will of Olodumare, the Supreme Being in Yoruba traditional religion. The structure of this belief system was adopted almost without change in the new Christian religious movements, and Cherubim and Seraphim as members of the Aladura revival were leading users of it. Often instructions were given about how to read certain parts of the Bible, especially the Psalms, in order to achieve a desired end, and the instructions became more complex when dreams and visions were involved. The need to interpret dreams and visions and prescribe by them required expert advice for which one normally went to *Baba Aladura* or his colleagues. Such skill, established and recognised in the leaders, proved the most fruitful source of doctrinal and ritual innovation, a revolutionary instrument bringing changes which might have been difficult or impossible to introduce otherwise. Used in an effective way, it sometimes departed significantly from the pre-established course set by the *orisha:* people receiving a new experience through prayer and dreams might decide on a radical course of action, such as absolute abstension from *ogun,* traditional medicines. But such permutations in the traditional world view, however major, could not disguise the fact that Christianity was performing the function of a powerful medicine, with the additional advantage of being able to offer a rational explanation for the bewilderingly new world which Africans were entering in increasing numbers.

As the numbers increased, attempts were made to introduce some organisation into the Cherubim and Seraphim. But this excited the factional spirit. The first major split was between *Baba Aladura* himself and 'Captain' Abiodun, as she was widely known. The quarrel involved a certain girl from Ijesha who had come to Orimolade for prayer help and was feared as having an undue influence on her patron. The dispute went to the Administrator of the Colony who (in March 1929) ordered Orimolade and Captain Abiodun to go their separate ways. After a number of turbulent incidents, involving fights between the two groups, an attempt to make peace resulted in a second split, for both Abiodun and Orimolade spurned the peace-makers, accusing them of partisan manoeuvres. At the root of the splits was the educational factor: the Lagosian members of the Praying Band, all educated, were deeply mistrusted by the illiterate Orimolade and his partisans. It is the kind of tension that surfaced earlier in the Niger Delta Pastorate, with the Creole élite largely mistrusted or even resented by a local leadership lacking in self-confidence.

The splits did not hinder the growth of Cherubim and Seraphim. Captain Abiodun and her party went to Abeokuta where the Alake (chief) and other Egbas, including a group of Egba Creoles, responded warmly to them. The movement slowed down for a time in 1928 but revived in 1929. The leaders next went to Ibadan, where parades and processions were organised in the streets. Two groups were organised: one around the Seraphim and the other under the Cherubim. Ijebu-Ode was the next town Captain Abiodun visited. After this first trip the movement began to spread rapidly. A branch was established at Ilesha in September 1927, to be followed in 1928 by a visit from Abiodun who told a hard-pressed Owa (ruler) that a worrying drought would end only after intercession by the angels. She was given a house from which to evangelise. A branch was created at Ile-Ife, where the Oni once asked the society to pray for a sick son. At Ondo a highly successful campaign was launched by the daughter of Chief Awosika, Christiana Olatunrinle, a woman of great influence and popularity in the town. After one public campaign some 1,500 people enrolled, with a great ceremony where idols and jujus were burnt in the churchyard — 'a signal triumph for Christianity',[9] as one report put it. Lagos continued to be the main centre of activity, and from there evangelistic parties were sent into most of the important centres of Yorubaland and beyond. But decline soon set in. Factional disputes had whittled away much of the power and authority of *Baba Aladura*. Delegates from seven Yoruba towns met in Ile-Ife to organise themselves into a new conference which would be neutral in the quarrels of Lagos. In the meantime Orimolade's health was failing. Compared to the prominence with which he had earlier emerged into public view, he died (in October 1933, aged fifty-six) in relative obscurity, overshadowed by the momentous developments taking place in Cherubim and Seraphim circles outside Lagos. The progress towards separate churchhood was now irreversible.

With the remarkable Aladura revival of 1930 behind them, the members of the Cherubim and Seraphim were now presiding over a burgeoning movement which required an explicit identity in relation to the other Churches. The representatives of the seven Yoruba towns who met at Ife constituted themselves into the Western Conference. One of their first serious tasks was to come to terms with the Pentecostalism of the 1930 revival; the person who led this Pentecostal interest, Christiana Olatunrinle, had proceeded to stake a claim to the leadership of the group, which was largely conceded when she was accorded the charismatic title *Iya Alakoso,* 'mother superintendent'. The concession in effect turned the Cherubim and Seraphim from a religious society to a Church, with its own discipline and order.

An important aspect of life in the Cherubim and Seraphim Church was the close connection between Church and society. Many of the important Church officials were active in society, something that is also true of the other Aladura churches. Most of the early leaders of the Church at Ijesha were traders, a group of active men who were part of the mobility of the new order. At Ibadan the large Church established by them had no permanent personnel based there despite the fact that there were over 700 names on the Church records. The total membership of the Church was estimated in 1958 at about 50,000. It had some thirty primary schools under its care in 1963. In 1941 the Church lost Madam Olatunrinle through death, and another important leader, W.F. Sosan, died at Abeokuta in 1957. But Captain Abiodun continued to be active in directing the

9. Peel (1968), p.80.

Church's affairs, surviving all the main personalities of the splits of 1934. A leader of the Oke Bola branch of the Church in Ibadan, J.A. Adegbite, had worked most of his life as a clerk in the Post and Telegraph office of the colonial government, and had been moved around before coming to settle in Ibadan; he was never considered a charismatic figure in the sense in which significant figures of the Aladura revival were, but he led a small prayer circle following a vision in 1943, and his congregation grew to about 200. He worked part-time for the Seraphim until his retirement from the government service. Numerous others served in a similar capacity, with the result that while the Cherubim and Seraphim excelled in creating a spiritual élite, it suffered many splits because of inadequate administrative experience. Yet its growth in spite of internal divisions suggests that it was able to act as a point of transmission for the new forces unleashed by the impact of Christianity on traditional Africa. Although they were careful to prepare for evangelistic campaigns, the Cherubim and Seraphim had obviously learnt to march from spiritual prompting, and not from the formal precision of bureaucratic design.

Christ Apostolic Church (CAC). The Christ Apostolic Church may be considered among the élite of the charismatic Churches: it was closely identified with the legacy of spiritual gifts by which the other Churches gained prominence, but it also drew on the considerable administrative experience of its members to organise congregations.

In July 1941, Akinleye, Babalola and Odubanjo constituted themselves and their followers into the Christ Apostolic Church, a step which effectively institutionalised the mainstream of the Faith Tabernacle movement. That step also set these men apart from the Apostolic Church with which they had been associated, for the Apostolic Church, directed by English missionaries, would not forgo the use of modern medicines as the CAC insisted. After the break, the CAC went through a period of great expansion, and became so self-confident that it was making rival claims to Christian orthodoxy against the other Churches. It considered itself the foremost Christian Church in Nigeria, and in a more extended comment expounded its role in military terms: prayer, which had been such an activating force in its life, it likened to gunpowder, and the Holy Spirit, that terror of the powers of evil, it regarded as the gun, with the Bible as the ramrod. The early Christians it conceived as the first line of soldiers, and, peering down its own peculiar telescope, it saw itself as the second line of stalwarts. The first line of defence, distracted by worldly pursuits, fell back before the enemy, whereas the second line stood firm. Hardly an accurate historical analysis, but the intention of the CAC was clear. In the struggle with the world, the forces of good were pitted against those of evil. For a large part history, the record of that fundamental struggle, had been taken over by the evil forces, but this setback was only temporary. Hard on their heels was the élite corps of the Lord's army who would retrieve history and rehabilitate it for its original purpose.

The enemy, lodged in the numerous maladies that afflicted the flesh, must be driven out and muzzled. Thus spiritual healing came to acquire a prominent place in the CAC's life. It was the indisputable sign of the victory of faith, the proof that the spiritual warfare was a genuine contest. The knight of the grand commission in this contest was undoubtedly Joseph Babalola, and his role in the revival movement as a whole demonstrates the crucial place prophets occupy in the life of these Churches. The prophet channels the forces of healing into the community, presides over the awakening when it arrives, and sustains prayer as the essential supply-line of the struggle.

The CAC also stressed the importance of the Holy Spirit, who is regarded as the source of transforming power in the life of the Church. Many of the early Church members testified to being filled with the Holy Spirit, and as a consequence received spiritual gifts. Some of these early pioneers were keen to draw a parallel with the first Pentecost. One pastor spoke of the way the first followers of Faith Tabernacle huddled together in small timid groups, just as the first disciples behaved after the Crucifixion, only to experience a new power and confidence in the Apostolic Church with the repetition of the triumph of the original Pentecost. These spiritual gifts were an additional blessing to the Christian life, not a pre-requisite for salvation. Some of the leaders of the CAC wrote explicitly on this point, emphasising the confirmatory work of the Holy Spirit, and calling attention to the fact that these gifts were capable of being misused. The specific gifts of healing, prophecy, speaking in tongues, wisdom and interpretation were the concentrated sign of the Holy Spirit, who was nevertheless still active in keeping alive an awareness of moral qualities through a more diffuse indwelling of His presence.

Whereas in some of the charismatic Churches, such as the Church of the Lord (Aladura), the sense of Christ's unique life and work was only rather vaguely glimpsed behind all the colour and sound of processions and testimonies, in the CAC Christ occupied a central place. He was the rule by which all prayers were commissioned, the authority by which intercession was made, and the assurance that needs would be satisfied when His name was invoked. In fact Christ served an invaluable mediatory role, effectively outflanking the *orisha,* the lesser spirits, by merging the role of intermediary agent with that of source of the divine will. Sometimes CAC practice gave prominence to Christ as agent, with the slight hint that His function as source of the divine will had weakened in relative terms. Put in traditional religious terms, the *orisha* remained prominent in everyday experience, but this time their role was performed by Christ the mediator, while Olodumare, the Father of the *orisha* and of Jesus, continued as a remote, distant being who was seldom directly approached. However, such an interpretation of the significance of Christianity limits it to a subservient role without taking full account of the potential for far-reaching changes it brings with it. Our analysis of this theme must therefore keep together the complementary aspects of challenge and fulfilment.

Unlike the Cherubim and Seraphim, the CAC stressed the Bible as the written authority for its doctrines and of the pastor in expounding it. After the initial stress period of the epidemic during which faith-healing became an important part of charismatic life, the Cherubim and Seraphim, less equipped with knowledge of the written sources, continued to uphold the principle of spiritual healing while the CAC modified this considerably. Similarly, the CAC broke ranks with the other Churches in placing less emphasis on visions and dreams, although it did not repudiate these entirely. However it insisted that these spiritual gifts should be brought into conformity with Scriptural teaching. In advertising its services, the CAC often appealed to people in terms of spiritual help against the forces of evil and against psychological and physical disorders. In fact we have — in the detailed lists it prepared of the ailments to be cured — all the symptoms of people uprooted and bewildered by the forces of change. Among some thirty more or less specific items mentioned are indebtedness, depression, legal prosecution, insomnia, bad dreams, insecurity, indiscipline, child mortality, fear of death, loveless marriage and a general wretchedness. In this the CAC was a true outgrowth of the forces of the time, sharing with the other Independent Churches a similar response to changes that were rapidly appearing in African society. It confidently taught the reign of Jesus, and assured people that 'there is power in the blood of Jesus', as the line of one of its popular chants has it. This confident and articulate use of Christian language and symbolism in order to diagnose and prescribe for the African condition was an imaginative, almost visionary achievement. By that spiritual consolation Africans would be spared the ultimate humiliation of colonial defeat. But the chariot of ancient wisdom in which the spirits of the old dispensation once paraded would henceforth rock with the hope of the Gospel.

The importance of the CAC in Nigeria was amply clear from the early membership statistics. By 1958 its congregations had 83,000 members, and by 1965 the numbers had risen to 100,000. Not given to an old-fashioned rejection of the world, it was heavily involved in modern education. In 1963 it had 110 primary schools, twenty-two secondary modern schools, four grammar schools and a teacher training college. The Church itself was mostly concentrated in the chief Yoruba centres: at Ibadan, Efon, Ijebu, Awe, Oshogbo and so on. In addition numerous village congregations became affiliated to the CAC. Thus in numerical terms, as well as in terms of its involvement in modern education, the CAC was a major force in African Christianity.

The Church had its breakaway groups. An important secessionist movement was that connected with Prophet Peter Olatunji, a man considered second in rank only to Babalola himself, who worked actively to establish branches of Aladura Churches and was especially prominent in the Oyo area (1941-3) and in the Oke Ogun area (1945-6). In 1947, as the result of a vision, he established a permanent Church at Ibadan. Henceforth he regarded the branches of the Church he had founded as semi-autonomous. His break with the Church came over the issue of his wishing to divorce his wife and marry another, but it had been building up over other issues. For example, he claimed spiritual authority to ordain people by virtue of visions, in opposition to the Church's position of proceeding by practices and rules supportable from the Bible. Olatunji was also opposed to the rule by committee in the CAC, a committee on which he was not allowed to sit even though he was designated Assistant General Evangelist. He complained of the power which pastors wielded over prophets, lamenting that the spiritual fervour of the early generation had weakened and been replaced by lower ideals. He produced a manifesto to this effect. The Church replied by emphasising that to cut visions loose from the control of Scripture was to open the way for error. The rift was unbridgeable. Olatunji and seventeen of his branches seceded in 1948, adopting the name Christ Gospel Apostolic Church (CGAC). In the mid-1960s the number of its branches reached fifty-three, and by that time too the CGAC had started applying a pattern of authority similar to that of the CAC. Obviously personalities played an important role in religious developments.

The question of secessions within African Christian Independency cannot be adequately explained without reference to the general level of religious expectation and activity. Otherwise a scholarly interest in the matter would act as an excuse for adopting a negative stance based on a superficial understanding. Many of the secessions occurred in defence of what was perceived as orthodoxy, and often in response to developments in other parts of the religious scene. The example of individuals locked in a quarrel and then thrashing about for partisan support which had not existed was rare. Thus numerous secessions shared with the entire phenomenon of Christian Independency a similar character: that of seeking to express a sense of Christian commitment in a dynamic religious style. We should now explore this theme in the wider context of West Africa.

The expansion of the Church of the Lord (Aladura) beyond Nigeria

The extension of the work of the Church of the Lord (Aladura) beyond Nigeria is, with a few possible exceptions, largely the story of one remarkable man, E.A. Adejobi, who so confidently interpreted the first vision of Oshitelu of April 1927 and was instrumental in setting up what was to become the largest church building of the movement in Lagos in about 1943. In 1944 he helped set up the Elegbata branch on Lagos island. To his considerable administrative and spiritual gifts he added the qualities of a frontiersman. He was the sharp edge of the pioneering spirit of the movement.

Sierra Leone. Shortly after establishing the Elegbata branch of the Church, Adejobi had a vision calling him to do similar work in Freetown. At about this time, in late 1946, Oshitelu, seeking to encourage him, sent him off with S.O. Oduwole for missionary work in Liberia, where the Church had been invited by a Liberian lawyer. It was one step nearer to the realisation of the Sierra Leonean dream. Some preparatory work was going ahead in that direction through the agency of a Creole couple who had attended Adejobi's services in Lagos, and in March 1947 Adejobi and Oduwole with six others landed at Freetown on what was expected to be a short visit. In the event it was a full year before Adejobi could return to Nigeria. At first he had the use of a small room, but through the interest and help of a Creole, Mrs Laura Dove Savage, he and his nucleus of followers moved to more spacious accommodation a month later. Thus began the Freetown work.

Freetown did not receive Adejobi with open arms. On the contrary, he and his followers were beset with obstacles, not least of which were the hostility and ridicule of the Creole community. He was pilloried in the popular press as a muddleheaded religious adventurer with a beguiling effect on the simple and ignorant. But Adejobi was more than equipped to take these aspersions in his stride, and his persistence won him the admiration of important friends, not least in the press. A local Creole medical doctor offered generous support for the new Church; in June 1947 Adejobi was able to move to premises offered by the doctor, and Church meetings were transferred to another place on the old site of the boarding department of Albert Academy. In December that year, a harvest thanksgiving service, of long duration, was held, which over 1,000 people were reported to have attended; a lot of money was collected, with a single cash gift of £100 from the medical benefactor. Thus when Adejobi left in March 1948 for a brief return to Nigeria, he had guided the fledgling Church through some rough seas and secured for it a recognised base in Creole society. The Sierra Leonean membership was estimated at 600.

Adejobi returned to Freetown with a Yoruba wife who shared his work, being recognised as 'Spiritual Mother' in the Church. Two issues dominated the first phase of the history of the Church in

Freetown: one was the need for ministerial training, with the challenge to establish a Creole ministry, and the other, not unrelated, was the need to adapt Church discipline and practice to Freetonian conditions. An auspicious start had been made in tackling the first problem, with a Creole pastor remaining in active service at Bo, but if more men and women were to be attracted to the service of the Church some means of support had to be found. In 1952 the Church opened the Oke Murray Temple, which cost £7,000 to build, and Oshitelu, the Primate, came from Nigeria to preside at the opening ceremonies, which an estimated 2,000 people attended. By involving more people in its life, especially those who might be able and willing to contribute to its work, the Church was laying the foundations for its expansion.

The second probem was never satisfactorily resolved, namely, how to adapt to the special conditions of the Creole experience. Adejobi tended to view dissent as evidence of disloyalty, and to regard concessions as surrender. This problem has little in common with the history of Christian missions from the west: Adejobi would see Church of the Lord (Aladura) practice as deeply African and regard its critics as being unduly influenced by western conventions. However, the question of responding positively to Creole demands lay at the heart of the issue of acceptance of the Church. Its hesitations suggest that it would remain slightly suspect in traditional Creole circles, a fate which was to follow it to other parts of West Africa.

Adejobi then made ambitious plans to strike further inland: Bonthe, Yoni and as far afield as Segbwema. Prospects in these distant vineyards were not encouraging; traditional rulers, responding more from curiosity than genuine interest, declined to commit themselves. Local populations refused to rush in where chiefs would not lead. Thus the work did no more than scratch the surface. Adejobi was moved to write a gloomy assessment: 'Apart from Freetown', he said, 'all other fields or towns in Sierra Leone appear very hard soil for the propagation of the Church of the Lord's Dogma, Doctrine, and Teachings.'[10] But whereas disappointments might cast down a man of less determination, Adejobi seemed to see them as an invitation to further attempts elsewhere.

Ghana, Liberia and elsewhere. The extension of the work to Ghana was at the instigation of a woman from Kumasi who first approached Oshitelu. He in turn asked Adejobi. It was to prove the most promising development of the work outside Nigeria. Even in the new issues it raised for the Church as a whole, it was to mark a watershed in the definition and practical application of the concept of central

10. Turner, vol. I (1967), p.125.

authority in the Church of the Lord (Aladura). Only the briefest of summaries can be attempted here.

Adejobi made frequent visits to Ghana, the first being in March, 1953, to be followed by another the following year. Ghana was prosperous, a leader among African countries. Its promise was obvious, and to none more so than to Adejobi. One of the most important people to have been touched by his message was Princess Victoria Prempeh, the daughter of the King of Ashanti who had been exiled in the Seychelles. She had returned with her father from exile in 1924 and subsequently trained as a nurse. She had already been receiving visions and had been looking for spiritual assurance when in 1953 she heard Adejobi preach in Kumasi. She immediately backed him and made her house available as a meeting place. In 1957 she herself entered the ministry of the Church and went to Freetown to be trained. By 1962 she had served in several churches and was still keen on learning more about spiritual healing by going to Britain.

Adejobi went on to Sekondi where, through the assistance of the chief, the first services were held in the native court hall. Then other places followed: Swedru, Winneba, Koforidua and others, in all of which what he called 'divine messages' were carried to the chiefs. At Swedru, for example, he said special prayers for chiefs and public men, and made 'predictions that were sharp, stirring and remarkable'. He made a similar impression on the chief of Koforidua. Traditional rulers on the whole exhibited caution towards the new religion that was appearing among them; most offered hospitality and encouragement but stopped short of enrolling. The reasons should be clear by now, and in Ghana especially those reasons have long and venerable roots.

Adejobi then decided to appeal to other public men and women, and here his rewards were less in dispute. For example Kojo Botsio, the prominent Ghanaian politician, and his wife patronised the Church of the Lord (Aladura), although they did not enrol as members. Mrs Botsio continued to support the Church enthusiastically, beginning with a healing experience in 1955. Another local politician who backed the new Church was Mrs Grace Ayensu from Sekondi, who at critical points offered mediation in the tangles of Ghanaian politics into which the Church got itself. Her mediation almost certainly saved the Church from political retribution from Nkrumah's Marxist militancy.

An important year for the Church in Ghana was 1959. Its claim to the first ranks of the Church's international branches was established beyond question. Clearly some of the prestige then enjoyed by Ghana had affected and enhanced its stature. One instance of this national prestige may be given. An elder of the Church's branch in Freetown visited Ghana in 1959 and reported back on his impressions. He remarked on the wealth of the country, its healthy and active people, with big houses, impressive cars, large and orderly markets, well-seated lorries in which people could travel in decent clothes, and good trains. He described in glowing language the life of the Church in Ghana: the generous offerings, seating arrangements and the quality of the religious life. He proudly confessed: 'Ours is but a toy! So to Ghana, not to the U.K. when on leave, to see how things should be done.' The confidence of the visitor from Freetown was justified when, after only a few years of endeavour, the Church of the Lord (Aladura) membership was around 2,800. Ghana also became one of the most generous of the Church's branches, sending an annual contribution to Nigeria.

The remarkable work of Adejobi in Ghana, particularly in Kumasi, bore fruit in the tangible shape of a permanent church building which Oshitelu came to consecrate in November 1959. £900 was raised as a personal gift to the Primate, out of which a car was bought as a present for him, the balance being taken as a cash gift.

At this point the work of the Church in Liberia ought to be recounted in so far as it had a bearing on the Ghanaian situation. Adejobi's successes in Ghana revived the whole question of the proper jurisdiction of his work in Sierra Leone (the base for his operations in Ghana) and that of Prophet Oduwole who was based in Liberia and in whose jurisdiction, at least in theory, Ghana was. When Adejobi entered Ghana, Oduwole, in a move charged with great meaning, decided to challenge him by entering the country as well, not paying much regard to the fact that Adejobi was acting on higher orders. Thus in June 1953 Oduwole came to Accra from Monrovia, establishing congregations in Accra and at other points along the coast at Cape Coast. The two arms of the Church, the one based at Kumasi (the more prosperous of the two) and the other centred on Accra, became involved in a dispute about the proper limits of responsibility between the Sierra Leonean branch of the Church and the Liberian counterpart. Oduwole, reacting from a much weaker position than Adejobi, adopted the path of direct confrontation with the Primate at Ogere by repudiating his authority and declaring himself under no obligation to him. Oshitelu acted swiftly by dismissing Oduwole and summoning him to Ogere. Oduwole came to Ogere — not, surprisingly, in answer to the letter of recall, but to recant and do severe penance for his insubordination. That appears to have mended him and he was subsequently reinstated at Monrovia.

But the dispute within Ghana itself was far from settled, with many people there unhappy at the confused state of affairs that had been such an important factor in the rift between Oduwole and Adejobi. The conflict has many complex features but for our purposes we may point out five possible elements. The first is the lack of central planning in the expansion of the work into Ghana. Although the

Primate had asked Adejobi to do the work, he had done so by overturning a principle of responsibility which he himself had laid down. Secondly, Adejobi and Oduwole were active in the two areas of Ghana with a history of political rivalry, and in their case this rivalry happened to have economic roots as well. Thirdly, the political climate in Ghana at that time, with President Nkrumah's brand of strong nationalist sentiment, exposed the Nigerian connection of the Church to inevitable challenge and criticism. Fourthly, the hegemony of the Convention People's Party, the party of Nkrumah, largely acknowledged in the Accra region, was at times contested in the Ashanti area. A religious initiative taken in Accra would therefore be viewed rather differently in Kumasi. The final factor needs stressing. The apparent aloofness of the Primate from the situation encouraged many in Ghana to believe that separation from Nigeria was only a matter of time, with the first prize going to those prepared to seize the opportunity. The proof that separation did not have an independent appeal may be found in the fact that when Oshitelu took decisive action and installed a Nigerian as the head of the Ghana Church, with a frank statement about the necessity for this in view of Ghana's inexperience, there was general acquiescence. Had he shown a similar decisiveness earlier he might have prevented much blood-letting.

Prophet Oduwole and the Liberian mission

It should be clear that the role of Oduwole in the conflict in Ghana was, if anything, that of a catalyst. The elements of the conflict were constituted mainly from local factors, and Oduwole's removal from the scene affected neither the scale nor the direction of the dispute. However his place in the history of the Church in Liberia is much firmer.

Oduwole came to Liberia in April 1947. After a few months he met President Tubman and by that connection secured important political recognition for his Church. In this sense Oduwole was of course fitting into an established pattern of Church life in Liberia, where political patronage had always been a necessary concomitant of religious activity. Oduwole had come to Liberia as a result of enquiries by a Liberian public figure, Justice Anthony Barclay, brother of a former President of the Republic, and his wife. Both had been to Nigeria where they came into contact with the Church of the Lord (Aladura), having visited Ogere and met Oshitelu. They were interested in the doctrines and practice of the Church, particularly in spiritual healing. However when Oduwole finally arrived on their doorstep in Monrovia, the Barclays were less than enchanted at the prospect of hosting what would in effect be a popular religious movement. However, Oduwole would not be put off and resorted to extreme spiritual pressure to overcome this unexpected resistance, finally making do with a room downstairs in the house of the Barclays. But the contact was clearly without promise, and a little later, after much unpleasantness, Oduwole and his party moved to different premises.

The Americo-Liberians responded to Oduwole in the manner of their Freetown counterparts. They were unhappy with the practices of the new religion and demanded changes more in conformity with existing Church practice in Monrovia. Oduwole, like Adejobi, substituted obstinacy for flexibility, making a virtue of persistence where the greater virtue lay in patience; for him the need to demonstrate the prominence of the new religion on the Liberian stage was paramount. In January 1949 the Church was incorporated in Liberia; then a grandiose scheme was launched for a $70,000 cathedral project. The foundation stone was laid in 1959, with President Tubman himself laying the corner-stone in February 1961. The President also donated $500 towards the cost, with a promise of a further $6,000. The popular imagination may be impressed by such prestige projects, but the danger is always present that when pursued too singlemindedly they may consume much of the vital energy needed to preserve the momentum of a fledgling movement and thus tend to diminish its original vision. There is evidence that the Church became a confined phenomenon of the Monrovia scene, unable to break out in any significant way into the larger hinterland beyond.

The failure to establish a significant presence outside Monrovia was not for lack of trying. Oduwole and his assistants prospected seriously along the coast between Monrovia and Harper to the east and inland as far as Gbarnga. A congregation was established at Bomi Hills to the north of Monrovia. By 1962 twelve centres had been established in Liberia, but apart from Monrovia most of these centres were weak, and their contribution to general Church funds was small. The total Liberian membership was approximately 600.

Nevertheless Oduwole was instrumental in helping to bring the Church of the Lord (Aladura) to the notice of people in the United States. One of his spiritual disciples, Mrs Angeline Toles, introduced it to friends in Atlanta, Georgia, where she was a student. She organised a group of interested people into the Samuel Oduwole Spiritual Club which eventually spread among Baptist and Methodist circles in Atlanta, New York and Philadelphia. The groups held weekly meetings and an annual convention. Oduwole himself kept a regular correspondence with inquirers in the United States. He had intended to travel to America, no doubt to a hero's welcome, but had wanted to wait until the cathedral was completed and dedicated. His dream remained unfulfilled. He was stabbed to death on 7 April 1965 in Monrovia by a mental patient for whom he was praying. Adejobi preached at his funeral, which was marked by a state-declared day of mourning and attended by President Tubman and several members of his Cabinet.

Adejobi: prophet, pioneer and crown prince

In September 1961, Adejobi travelled to Britain to enrol as a student at the Glasgow Bible Training Institute on a two-year course. He had done so at his own expense and against the advice of his Church. People naturally feared that study might prove detrimental to his faith or — equally bad — make him critical of Church practices. Neither seems to have happened. His studies helped to develop his grasp of Biblical material, which he applied in a positive way to the teachings of the Church, and his new wider contacts in Pentecostal circles strengthened his faith in the efficacy of spiritual means.

But the prophet marched in step with the pioneer. After leaving Glasgow he came to London where he began a series of evangelistic meetings. He set up house in a South London suburb and on 12 April 1964 inaugurated there what he called the First West African Christian Church in Europe. The people it served included Sierra Leoneans, Ghanaians and Nigerians, and a small number of white Britons. Adejobi returned to Nigeria in May 1964, and this event brought him into serious contention as the crown prince of the movement. He arrived in June, to be met with a number of special services and functions in tribute to a successful son of the movement. All eyes now were on him, to see whether he would conform to Church practice in worship and doctrine. But Adejobi had not deviated on any point, and himself led a personal thanksgiving in which he made public testimony of faith and undertook the spiritual exercises of rolling on the floor, jumping, bowing, clapping and prostration, with the characteristic shouts. He did each of these things seven times in front of the altar.

Having passed that test he had to face the Primate, who questioned him closely on several points of Church doctrine. The Primate also observed Adejobi's manner in case the prestige of having been a student in Britain had created in him illusions of personal grandeur. Again Adejobi emerged from the scrutiny unblemished. Oshitelu was obviously dealing with a genuine reward of answered prayers, and he proceeded accordingly to invest Adejobi with a commission second in importance only to his own.

One more act of moral duty needed to be discharged before Adejobi could settle down to his appointed work. This was the duty he felt of visiting the first Church he established outside Nigeria and which had maintained close contact with him during his years of absence, namely that in Freetown. He made a trip there in August 1964, coinciding with the season of spiritual renewal in the Church. He also went up-country, visiting and strengthening the branches there. In Freetown he met the Prime Minister and organised a national day of prayer for the country involving Pentecostal groups in Freetown. Late in 1964 he returned to Freetown for a brief visit, but henceforth his main preoccupation was with establishing a Spiritual and Bible Training Institute in Nigeria where he could put the training and experience he had received in Glasgow to further use. If the Church of the Lord (Aladura) has acquired a deeper knowledge of the Bible and a greater sense of its place in the life and teaching of the Church, then no small part of that is due to Adejobi's ability and vision. He succeeded to the Primacy on the death of Oshitelu in 1966.

It is perhaps appropriate to conclude this rapid review of West African Christian Independency by considering for a moment St Augustine's encounter with the Donatists of North Africa, described in some detail in Chapter 1. In his *Letters,* Augustine appealed to the Donatists not to allow their concern with the establishment of an African Church to blind them to the universal mission of the Catholic Church. He begged them not to step over into open and permanent schism, holding before them the timeless merits of Christ's sacrifice. The sincerity of Augustine's concern with the reconciliation of the Donatists is obvious, but he was equally concerned with upholding the true teaching of the Catholic Church and afraid that by their actions the Donatists might turn against this in an erroneous bid for a national Church. The encounter of the Church of the Lord (Aladura) and the Catholic Church has of course never been on as sustained a level as that between the Donatists and Augustine. Indeed, where we have evidence of contact with the Catholic Church, as in Sierra Leone, the Church of the Lord (Aladura) ministers appear not to have got beyond anything deeper than first impressions, and those were often influenced by sectarian fervour. Nevertheless, that aspect of Augustine's concern that an African Church should seek, and remain in, communion with the wider Church has not been entirely absent from the calculations of the Church of the Lord (Aladura) in these early decades of its existence, or indeed from those of other Independent Churches. A true ecumenical spirit seems to have penetrated the thinking of the leaders of African Christian Independency, although writers do them an injustice by attributing this ecumenical spirit to nothing more than a desire for Western recognition. Indeed three of the most significant factors that have motivated the men of Christian Independency may be listed as the spirit of ecumenism, the search for ecclesiastical rectitude and a striving after Biblical orthodoxy — not an inconsiderable advantage at the start of the pilgrimage of faith which many have joined so earnestly.

The scope and character of Christian renewal in Africa: A postscript

Nearly 5,000 independent Church movements have been identified throughout Africa since about 1862. In 1967 the estimated membership of these movements was some 7 million adherents drawn largely from just under 300 different peoples. Of these by far the largest numbers came from Southern Africa, with just over 3,700,000. The Republic of South Africa had slightly above 3 million adherents. By contrast Islamised North Africa was virtually untouched by the phenomenon of Christian Independency, with the small exception of Egypt. There a small separatist movement began in 1869 which called itself Plymouthism and grew into a 9,000 strong Brethren denomination. A movement was also started in 1925 by dissidents within the Coptic Church, calling itself the Society for the Salvation of Souls. However, on the whole, Islam appears to have interposed an impenetrable barrier to the spread of Independency. We shall return to this subject later.

One of the most important movements of Christian Independency in the whole of Africa was that founded by Simon Kimbangu in Zaire, when it was the Belgian Congo. Kimbangu himself, born in September 1889 at Nkamba, embarked on an independent religious career in March 1921, after a number of years in association with Baptist missionaries. He named his religious centre the New Jerusalem and performed several miracles there. His followers gave him the title *Ngunza*, 'Prophet/Messiah'. A few months after he began public preaching, Kimbangu came to the attention of Belgian officials, who immediately arranged to have him arrested. This was done in September 1921. There was a clamour in colonial circles to make a final example of the man and have him executed, and indeed the death sentence was passed on him. However, the Public Prosecutor, overcome by the extremity of the sentence for a crime involving no loss of life, violence or damage to property, made an emotional and unprecedented plea for the prisoner's life. The sentence was finally commuted to life imprisonment, and Kimbangu died in prison in 1951. While he was serving the sentence, his wife took over his movement.

Kimbangu was by all accounts an extraordinary man. During his brief public appearance he created a powerful following and taught the main tenets of his movement. Although the colonial authorities made much of the claim that he preached race hatred and encouraged the crowds to despise the white man, the fact remains that the Prophet was engaged in a struggle to tame the beast of the tribe: he attacked fetishism, lewd dancing and similar feats of exhibitionism, and condemned polygamy, that pride and virtue of the patriot. On his followers he riveted the chains of discipline by banning theft, fraud and unlawful profiteering, and capped it with a prohibition of the sale and consumption of alcohol. 'To make palm-wine', he declared, 'is to create sin — to sell it or offer it is to spread sin'.[11] It is cause enough

11. Lisembé (1979), p.155.

to stop and consider why people should respond in such numbers to a religious movement imposing severe tests on physical and spiritual endurance against the widely available and officially backed alternative of gradual assimilation in the historic Churches.

Kimbangu's movement took on the official name, the Church of Jesus Christ of the Prophet Simon Kimbangu, with the French initials EJCSK. It is more commonly known as the Kimbanguist Church. By 1966 his followers were estimated to number some 500,000, the largest single group in the entire history of African Christian Independency. As a tribute to its ecumenical outlook, it became one of the affiliated members of the World Council of Churches in 1969. At Kinshasa the Kimbanguist Church has founded a theological college.

To gain an insight into the character of Christian renewal within Independency, we can do worse than look briefly at some of the teachings and prayers of the Kimbanguist Church. We have already seen some of Kimbangu's social teachings. We should now turn to his religious teachings. Kimbangu summed up in his own person the destiny of his people and their age. In his prayers he pleaded for their weakness, their hardship, their poverty and suffering, their powerlessness and apathy, and above all their capacity for evil and their need of deliverance. In the attempt to minister to a condition he had himself diagnosed with such authoritative comprehensiveness, Kimbangu called on the ancestors to share in the work of awakening and renewal. Having first proceeded to dismantle the cults which had offered themselves as effective vehicles of spiritual contact, he reintroduced the ancestors by the new route of the Christian faith and discipline. As we have observed many times before, meaningful change often rides on the back of what preceded it. A contemporary witness has this to say: 'Neither Kimbangu nor his apostles have ever appealed for ancestor worship to be abandoned; their tombs were kept clean, paths leading to them were laid out and their return to life was going to initiate the Golden Age.'[12] Confronted with the overwhelming sight of a disillusioned people, Kimbangu sought to infuse in them a dynamic sense of purpose, a notion that they were appointed for greater ends than humiliation under foreign conquest. One prayer speaks well of this:

O Jesus, Saviour of the world, we come to rest ourselves in You. We trust in You; we shall not be lost for eternity... Oh soldiers of Jesus do not lose heart! Be brave... The Kingdom is ours. We have it! They, the whites, no longer have it... None of us shall be discouraged. Let us praise God, our Father, who will come on the clouds.[13]

12. Lisembé (1979).
13. ibid. p.154.

Yet, contrary to what the scholars of reductionism would have us believe, the horizon of Kimbanguism was not confined by the powerful economic and political forces that had convulsed Congolese society and thrown up a mass of dispirited people. If Kimbanguism responded to history, it also charted its course. Kimbangu's vision, so thoroughly religious, was extended by the broadening stimulus of Christian commitment, with local circumstance acting only as a necessary context. Another of his prayers makes this clear:

I thank Thee, Almighty God, Maker of heaven and earth...heaven is Thy throne and earth...Thy footstool. Thy will be done on earth as it is in heaven. Bless all peoples of the earth, great and small, men and women, whites and blacks. May the blessing of heaven fall on the whole world so that we all may enter heaven. We pray to Thee trusting that Thou dost receive us, in the name of Jesus Christ our Saviour. Amen.[14]

To conclude our study of the subject, we should mention a few points about the life and worship of the Kimbanguist Church. The church calendar is dominated by three principal events: 6 April, to commemorate the beginning of Kimbangu's ministry of healing and evangelism; 12 October, to mark his death in prison, and of course Christmas Day with its usual associations plus notions of divine fecundity and the blessing of children. The Eucharist is celebrated on these occasions only. In general the Christian 'mysteries' are not stressed in the worship life of the church, although in December 1966, the sacrament of communion was introduced on a regular basis. In doctrine the Kimbanguist Church is extremely orthodox. 'No one', Kimbangu once wrote, 'could buy his salvation. That is the gift by faith.' The sense of a missionary calling is strong. Kimbangu urged upon his followers 'to bear the message of our Lord Jesus Christ to all countries of the world, as enjoined by Holy Scripture'.[15]

In a special study prepared by the World Council of Churches and devoted to the Kimbanguist Church,[16] the following observations are made. Worship in the Kimbanguist Church is a joyful, fraternal festival lasting several hours. The lay nature of the worship is underlined by the role of the leader who acts in effect as master of ceremonies. He announces in turn each item in the service. There are congregational hymns and singing by special choirs; prayers are also offered from the congregation, sometimes by women. A compulsory reading of one of the Psalms of David is prescribed, as well as other Scripture readings. In the sermon, which follows, the preacher is not afraid to address questions to the congregation who reply unanimously and joyously. When money collections are taken, the

14. Martin (1975), p.49.
15. Handspicker and Vischer (1967).
16. ibid.

congregation responds generously, fervently and cheerfully. The atmosphere of the service may be enhanced by the display of palm leaves, which people wave above their heads while singing hymns in a syncopated rhythm. Surprisingly, there is no dancing in the church. People arrive for the service in the dignity of a palm-waving procession, and, if particularly touched, some may sway and rock before the spirit makes a sedate, unannounced exit. On special occasions, such as when visitors are present, a little procession may gather and approach the visitors and offer gifts. Then it moves forward in a controlled, graceful rhythm full of gentleness and reverence. On such occasions, rare as they are, the spiritually-minded may indulge a certain restrained liberty and acknowledge the presence of the spirit. However, the Church discourages such spiritual adventures, in interesting contrast to the majority of Christian Independent movements. The transition from the service proper to the social part of the meeting is often imperceptible.

Most movements of Independency combine a respectful regard for custom and tradition with a bold, radical application of Christian discipline and teaching. For this reason, if for no other, African Christian Independency is more than simply a decorative vehicle for old religious traditions. It makes bold demands on religious loyalty and challenges inherited attitudes with a fundamental assertion about the nature and purpose of the Creator. There is little doubt that for those who want to continue their pursuit of the religious vocation, Independency has offered as bracing an opportunity as many are likely to find in some of the historic Churches. Furthermore, in the adaptation of Christianity to African conditions, Independency can consider itself in the first ranks of the pioneers.

8

CHRISTIANITY, ISLAM AND AFRICAN TRADITIONAL RELIGIONS

In the flash left by the passing colonial comet it has been difficult to see the transformation which the old Africa has wrought within Christianity, or the subtle changes it has made to the Islamic religious law, with the result that a legacy of rivalry and antagonism has eclipsed real gains which are only now beginning to come into full view.

Journal of Religion in Africa, XI, 1 (1980)

Introduction

From the first century of its encounter with West Africa, missionary Christianity has encouraged the view that the overtaking of Islam is an overriding consideration. Thus whatever the real history of relations with Muslims, and however genuine the attempts to arrive at a sympathetic understanding of Islam, the myth has been perpetuated that Christianity is locked in a bitter rivalry with it, with Africa serving as the arena and the prize. Western colonialism merely bolstered this competitive myth and invested it with greater potency.

It is a view that has produced some of the most regrettable consequences on a number of fronts. First, it subordinates the actual events of the history of missionary penetration in Africa to the myth of carrying on a contest with Islam. Secondly, it imposes on the frontiers of missionary activity an imaginary Islamic menace, even if Islam has made little or no appearance on the scene. Thirdly, it induces in missionaries a sense of false alarm and, withal, a certain lack of confidence, believing themselves to be helpless against Islam. Fourthly, it creates a false picture of the nature and size of Islamic gains in Africa, a picture which deepens the mood of pessimism among disheartened elements of the Christian faithful. Fifthly, it lends attraction to the proposition that the two world religions are moving, along with other religions, towards an inevitable predestined convergence, a proposition which provides the illusion of escaping from the competitive myth without actually abandoning it at all. Then there is the fact that this competitive perspective makes us prone to ignore or belittle the significance of African religions and their effect on the two world religions. Finally, in the prime setting of African nationalism and the sentiments of reaction that preceded it, this imported view has ignited into a full-blown ideological device which brings Christianity within the same firing range as the colonialism it seeks to demolish, with Islam now serving the role of favoured bystander. Thus the mental outlook inherited from the Crusades is allowed to impose itself in a situation where every reasonable circumstance militates against it. But if historical reality diverges so clearly from cherished myth, then to dispel myth we need to allow the details of historical contact to shape our formulations and determine our view.

The historical evidence, once stripped of the trappings of myth, reveals a rather surprising picture of the encounter of Christianity and Islam in Africa. Further, we discover that African religions played an important role in moulding the two missionary religions. One effect of this has been the transformation of the ancient rivalry between Christianity and Islam by confronting them with the decisive issue of indigenization. Across the path of a self-confident missionary faith Africa has erected the solid barrier of traditional religions, which neither Christianity nor Islam was able to ignore. In the response to this barrier, Christianity and Islam were immersed in a process of which the direction and momentum no longer reflected the prejudged priorities of the two religions. For this reason we can talk of the African response to Christianity and Islam as constituting an independent religious phenomenon, so that what emerges from the process of africanisation reveals as much about Africa's ancient religious heritage as about the separate opportunities of the two missionary faiths. The stage is thus set to concede to African religions the pride of place they had lost through the persistence of rival caricatures.

First, we must define the nature of our approach in this chapter. Our interest in African religions is limited to those features which were brought into sharp relief from the impact of Christianity and Islam: these would be the features which attracted both the approval and the censure of the two religions. We also need to examine areas of fruitful contact and assess the nature of the resulting changes, and, in view of the myth that one religion, usually Islam, is more adaptable than the other, to assess the responsiveness of African religions to outside religious influences. Finally, it is necessary to try to relate Christianity and Islam in a way that brings out the significance of the African medium through which they have been submitted, thus effectively taking apart the edifice of competition by which myth was made to lose connection with reality. This is bound to enlarge our view not only of the importance of African religions but of the enriched world of the two missionary traditions.

Having thus defined the nature and scope of the subject, we must point to an obvious limitation in our approach. Our concern is not with the central teachings of African religions, or even with an exposition of their distinctive claims, which can be more suitably studied elsewhere. We cannot in this book attempt anything like a comprehensive picture of the many religious traditions in Africa. What we present of these religions will be short snatches glimpsed through situations of encounter. Even if such encounters are staged on frontiers of suspicion and antagonism, the view that traditional religions may form of the challenge of Christianity and Islam constitutes a relevant factor in the new religious climate. Without therefore plunging into the heart of African religions as such, we can nevertheless appreciate something of their inner vitality in their interaction with an aggressive Christian or Muslim tradition.

As to the procedure we shall follow in this chapter, it would be appropriate to set the scene with the Christian interaction with Islam before considering the challenge of traditional religions. In the later parts of the chapter, we shall re-evaluate the significance of the indigenous religions and ask whether or not they represent a positive factor in religious assimilation. Our primary concern remains Christianity, but we should keep before us the valuable dimension of the comparative Islamic tradition.

The encounter of Christianity and Islam

The story we are about to investigate persists through missionary Christianity into African Christian Independency. The sub-theme of the account of European travellers, sometimes marred by speculative assertions, affects the picture very little. Some of this material will be presented here.

Islam filtered from North Africa across the Sahara into West Africa along the well-plied trade and caravan routes. At first it was the religion of small foreign communities who resided near political capitals to conduct trade and other business; but in time political rulers in the medieval West African states came into contact with the religion which they tolerated within their kingdoms. It accorded well with their role as transmitters of new influences. However, rulers mostly tried to maintain their position as mediators between the old and the new and as upholders of the balance between competing interests in their states. The exclusive sponsorship of Islam which might be required of them was often incompatible with the prerequisites of political office. For this reason Islam long remained a stranger-religion, and from this position it entered palace circles as an isolated religion. As such it performed a ceremonial function on royal occasions and provided diplomatic facilities with outside officials. The advisers and functionaries of the palace might be recruited from Muslim ranks or might be Muslim converts. Their position of influence would further extend the power of Islam. Consequently the ruler might feel it advisable to take on a Muslim identity, bringing with him his retinue of officials and subordinates. But because of his political role, the ruler often found it more in keeping with his position to maintain contact with traditional religions, the rites of which would continue to influence ceremonial functions at court.

Political rulers in the medieval African kingdoms consequently served two complementary roles. One was to facilitate the introduction of Islam into their states, and the other was to help expose it to local religions. When Islam finally took root in African societies, particularly in those places where the ruling class were the first to be islamised, it assumed a flexibility imposed on it by the host environment. This is one of the reasons why, in the attempts to purify Islam, Muslim reformers have sought to drive a wedge between the orthodox cause and traditional political hierarchies. For several centuries after its introduction into West Africa — say, between about 1100 and 1600 — Islam relied for its survival on the patronage of the older African traditions. From this two extreme consequences followed. One was that many Muslim centres, cut off from outside influences, regressed and became subsumed under the preponderant traditional religious wave; and the other was that the educated Muslim élite, suffering from all the disadvantages of a minority, began to agitate and to long for a more favourable political climate. In both cases, however, we are dealing with people whose religious loyalties, whether traditional–religious or Islamic, exterted a powerful influence on their attitudes. Indeed, it can be argued that the members of the Muslim élite often envied traditional religious devotees their zeal and vitality which, they had ruefully to admit, was missing from local Islam.

Whatever the gains of the puritanical Islamic reform movements which swept across the face of West Africa between about 1700 and 1900, the legacy of tolerance and flexibility bequeathed by the host African environment has largely survived. So too has the phenomenon of Muslim dependence on indigenous religious structures and stimuli. In some ways, of course, Islamic reform was the last gasp of the 'Arabising' elements in the Muslim ranks, the desperate action of those who realised that the Arabic heritage of Islam had been effectively suppressed in the assimilating current of strong local religious activity. The centuries of Islamic reform coincided, towards the end, with the coming of Christianity and of Western colonialism. However, because of the pervasiveness of African elements in Islam, Christianity encountered an acclimatized Islam, or one that had decidedly relinquished the irritant ambition of an Arabised faith. In many places, in fact, Muslims openly acknowledged an African destiny for the faith even if that exposed them to the charge of hypocrisy from the militant spokesmen of the unreconciled Islamic élite. Thus there can be little question of the strength of the African undergirding of much of Islam.

Early travellers recount how local populations tried to combine elements of Christianity with their profession of Islam. The English traveller Richard Jobson wrote in the 1620s how local Muslims in Senegambia used the Cross to decorate their dresses and houses. He also says that the name of Jesus was used by them as a charm. The Portuguese Jesuit priest Balthasar Barreira, one of the first Christian missionaries to Sierra Leone, where he arrived in 1605 and stayed till 1610, appears to have had some successes among traditional rulers, baptising several. He encountered Islam at the court of a Susu king who had invited him but who eventually opted for Islam. Traditional political rulers continued to play a role in the encounter of the two religions. We have already seen how in 1769 a king of Sierra Leone sent one son to learn Islam in Futa Jallon and another to study Christianity in England. Often trading opportunities with Freetown encouraged Muslims to enter into relations with Christian missions. In 1794 two agents of the Sierra Leone Company penetrated as far inland as Timbo, where the Fulbe arranged a deputation to travel to Freetown to arrange regular trade.

When missionaries arrived to do work among Muslims, they were preceded by extremely favourable reports of the beneficial effects of Islam. For example, when in 1796 some Methodists arrived for missionary work among the Fulbe, the Sierra Leone Company had started to develop good relations with Muslims; Macaulay, the Company representative, was impressed by Islam's affinity with Christianity and by the unwillingness of Muslims to sell fellow Muslims. Afzelius, a Swedenborgian Christian, felt that African Islam had come nearest to his idea of a native utopia. Muslim abhorrence of alcohol similarly won many admirers among European residents in Freetown and elsewhere.

In 1797 what was to become the London Missionary Society, a non-sectarian Protestant body, enabled two Scottish missionaries to travel to Sierra Leone to revive the work among the Fulbe; they were joined by six others later the same year, and a Susu mission developed from this initiative, but it did not last long. The missionaries almost immediately set to work on local languages: Susu and Temne principally. These missionaries were in daily contact with Islam.

Some of the early CMS bishops and other missionaries showed sympathy towards Islam. Bishop John Bowen, who succeeded John Weeks at Freetown in 1858, was a linguist with knowledge of Islam. When he visited Magbele he surprised the local people with a quotation from the Qur'an in Arabic. In the 1800s, under Henry Venn's leadership the CMS adopted a major initiative towards Islam by appointing Dr Edward Blyden, whose sympathy with Islam was well-known, as an agent in Sierra Leone. He set about developing the work of Bishop Owen Emeric Vidal, who died on a return journey to

Freetown from the Niger Mission in 1854, and Bishop John Bowen; he was intent to make something positive out of the common ground he believed existed between Christianity and Islam. His knowledge of Arabic won him the confidence and admiration of Muslim leaders; however, his radical ideas on Islam made him many enemies in CMS missionary circles, who eventually succeeded in getting the CMS to dismiss him. Blyden then turned to secular patronage in the form of Governor Kennedy to promote his ideas of using an africanized Islam as a vehicle for bringing about beneficial changes in African societies. Kennedy responded positively and Blyden was fitted out to visit Muslim centres in Falaba and adjacent areas in 1872. The trip confirmed his views on Islam, and after he returned in March of that year he began editing a newspaper, *The Negro,* to foster African opinion.

Meantime Kennedy had been temporarily succeeded by John Pope Hennessy in whom Blyden found another enthusiastic supporter for his cause. Through *The Negro* Blyden propounded his views on the need for a West African university in which Muslims would play an important role, and which could also publish his controversial views on what he considered the negative effects of Christian education, with the solution lying in the use of Islamic educational methods. As we saw in Chapter 6, the proposals for a West African university prepared the ground for the creation of Fourah Bay College. Together Blyden and Pope Hennessy pursued the myth of the native utopia 'within Nigretia's virgin heart', as Pope Hennessy put it (see Chapter 6, p.138). Both were completely unperturbed by the fact that this unspoilt native genius was supposed to find fulfilment in the most contaminated of settings, namely an institution of higher learning. Schemes of perfection must always tend toward the ultimate compromise.

Both men ventured into the interior of the country. Blyden went as far as Timbo, and they both visited Gbile on the opposite bank of the Scarcies where they saw a Qur'an school by which they were greatly impressed. The existence of a centre of learning in otherwise undistinguished country appears to have strengthened the prejudice against missionary education and the attendant European influence. Blyden's patronage of Islam bore tangible fruit in the appointment of a local Muslim, Muhammad Sanusi, as government Arabic Writer. Blyden was instrumental later in the setting up of a government-backed Muslim Board of Education, which he headed. He helped in getting a local Muslim, Harun al-Rashid, employed for a year as a teacher of Arabic at Fourah Bay College. Blyden's vision of an organised system of Muslim education, with official support, was realised when a government inspectorate was established to oversee the running of Muslim schools. The Colonial Office gave its blessing to the scheme under which Metcalfe Sunter, then principal of Fourah

Bay College, was employed as Inspector, with responsibility for the four West African colonies. This was in 1882. In 1890 Sunter got the Muslims to apply for a government grant to open a school in Freetown. Gheirawani, a local Muslim, was put in charge. Blyden offered instruction to the senior pupils of the school during his frequent visits in the period when he was based elsewhere in West Africa.

This Muslim school was later to decline, the victim of factionalism in the local Muslim community. But it was a time which coincided with considerable official support for Muslim education in general. For example, the acting governor, Sir Matthew Nathan, was sympathetic to Islam and wanted government help for Muslim schools, pledging government support once the schools proved efficient. Blyden himself was busy organising Muslim opinion around the idea of an institute of higher Islamic learning. Only limited resources stood in the way of government support. In 1901 Blyden was appointed Director of Muhammadan Education with responsibility for supervising local schools.

The picture that begins to emerge here is that Islam received considerable encouragement from the colonial authorities. One of the most enthusiastic was the governor, Sir Samuel Rowe, who became well-known for his patronage of local and visiting Muslims. One *sharif* from Morocco, a descendant of the Prophet Muhammad, travelled through West Africa spreading stories of the generosity of Governor Rowe who had treated him kindly in Freetown. Another *sharif* from Fez turned up in Freetown, but he, in contrast, fared ill. One of his legs had to be amputated and, feeling forlorn in a strange country, he threw himself on the Samaritanly mercy of Governor Rowe who fitted him with a wooden leg. At the feast of ᶜid al-fitr at the end of Ramadan in 1879, Rowe entertained over 700 Muslim guests at Government House and, in deference to Islamic teaching, served non-alcoholic beverages. He also took an active interest in the factional troubles of the Freetown Fulah Town Muslim community, offering his personal mediation. Trade caravans from Muslim areas flowed into Freetown. In early 1879 a party of over 1,000 arrived from Segou on the Niger. Thus we find that, at least for most of the period before the Scramble, a wide chasm separated the men of practical policy from the eloquent myth-makers.

The other aspect of the picture is the unquestionable influence of Dr Blyden, whatever the inconsistencies of his pronouncements. On the Sierra Leone scene, as much as elsewhere, his impact was enormous. He pushed along two frontiers simultaneously. On the Christian side he tried to build on the shared ground between the two monotheist faiths. A public debate was held on the subject in 1888 and subsequently reported in the popular press, with much being made of Dr Blyden's claim that Christianity and Islam are kindred faiths. On the secular front Blyden secured the support of colonial governors on behalf of his scheme to promote and co-operate with a strengthened Islam.

Some of his ideas continued to influence the academic direction of Fourah Bay College (see Chapter 6 above). When, mainly for financial reasons, government failed to implement Blyden's programme for a West African university, the CMS were approached by a protégé of his to make Fourah Bay College an institution of higher learning open to all without denominational barriers. When the college opened in its new form, a converted rabbi, the Rev. Alexander Schapira, was the professor of languages. Schapira was an Arabic scholar with an interest in local Muslims, and he opened a school in Freetown for Muslim children. Schapira was of course carrying on from where Sigismund Koelle left off. Koelle had arrived in 1847 to teach Arabic, along with Hebrew and Greek, at what was then a theological college. Dr Blyden himself, in his antediluvian period with the CMS, had begun translating the Bible into Fula, using the Arabic script. Whether in the relations between Christianity and Islam or in the fermentation of African nationalist sentiment, the overspill of Blyden's ideas must be measured in broad international terms.

This may be the convenient point at which to pursue the theme of Christian-Muslim encounter to Nigeria, where Dr Blyden's ideas also found a good response. The subject has been studied in considerable detail in Nigeria, and it is therefore straightforward enough to deal with it in our survey. On the whole the situation in Yorubaland conformed to pattern. European missionaries, impelled by the ambition to vindicate myth, stumbled after an imaginary Islamic menace, ignoring the reality of an hospitable traditional religious environment which had clearly influenced Islam. African Christians, on the other hand, while often reminded by their missionary mentors of the menace lurking in expected places, nevertheless acted from living experience and not from reconstructed theory. Indeed, as adapters of Christianity to African conditions, that was the natural role for them to assume. There were of course exceptions on both sides, with people sometimes ignoring the battlelines. The fact remains, however, that those battlelines were drawn, and drawn by divesting actuality of contextual meaning.

With the negative reaction provoked by the imposition of British rule, many Muslim centres at first resisted Christianity, and with it the modern schools that accompanied it. Faced in the long run by the inevitablity of foreign rule and the great social changes that followed, Muslim resistance weakened, a process encouraged by colonial measures designed to reward Muslim collaboration. Two phases may thus be identified in Muslim attitudes. In the first, Muslims warily watched the advent of Christianity and mounted a sort of passive resistance. In the second, they became increasingly responsive to Christian presence and began to view Christian schools, both mission and independent, with less suspicion.

Bishop James Johnson typified the first phase when he wrote in 1878: 'The Mohammedans show no desire for the education that may be had at our schools.'[1] Elsewhere Johnson observed the strong negative reaction of Muslims to Christianity. He said: 'Young Mohammedans were scolded, flogged and prevented by their elders and priests from attending Christian schools and Churches and even conversing with their Christian friends on religion.'[2] The Muslim resistance to Christian schools was helped by the great number of Qur'an schools which proliferated, especially in country areas as well as Lagos and the other main centres of colonial influence. Boosted by a significant group of Sierra Leonean Muslim immigrants (locally called Saro), Lagos Muslims were to the fore in the encounter with Christianity, which they had known about in Freetown. In the Lagos schools the number of Muslim children was extremely small, although even that small number suggested that the resistance was beginning to give way. In 1893, for example, there were 412 Muslim pupils in the thirty-three mission schools. By contrast, in the same year there were some sixty Qur'an schools in Lagos with a Muslim enrolment of about 1,400 pupils. These schools taught little more than rote learning of the elementary portions of the Arabic Qur'an, but they provided a psychological barrier against the impact of modern schools under Christian sponsorship. Given this psychological inhibition, even those Muslim pupils attending Christian schools resisted Christian conversion. One unmollified missionary, reflecting on this, wrote faintheartedly: 'The effect of our school gospel teaching on some of our Mohammedan friends continues to be nullified at home.'[3]

Sometimes opposition to Christian influence went beyond the negative fear of the unknown. Some Muslims felt that Islam was theologically a superior religion to Christianity, a comforting thought for those who felt Christianity was the religion of the imperialism that had forced their subjugation. In Abeokuta, for example, one missionary testified that the Muslim 'claims to be in possession of the last, best and truest revelation of God's will given to man'.[4] Consequently, the missionary went on, Muslims held themselves 'as much superior to the Christian'.[5] Perhaps as a tribute to his own ability to listen, the missionary was right to make the distinction between God revealing His will — an important point of Islamic

1. Gbadamosi (1978), p. 134.
2. ibid., p.139.
3. ibid., p.137.
4. ibid., p.142.
5. ibid.

theology — and God revealing Himself as Christian theology affirms. However these distinctions were often lost in the heat of controversy. One Yoruba clergyman was engaged by a group of local Muslims on points of disagreement between the two sides. Such public disputations were generally good-natured, and protagonists in a religious debate would be disappointed if one side declined to take part. In this particular instance (in December 1887) the result was a stalemate and a certain mutual satisfaction, with the clergyman as contented to leave the Muslims as he found them as they were to part with him. The interest of African Muslims in matters of deep theology would surprise and even confound the average Christian, African or Western. The unpreparedness of many Christians when faced with such unremitting Muslim pressure led them to resort to handy caricatures of recrimination. Only by keeping in mind the extent to which the competitive myth became a triumphant substitute for reality can we explain the remarkable slowness of Christian leaders to proceed by positive signals on the ground, and their corresponding haste to use aggressive language in support of their cause. James Johnson, with more than his fair share of responsibility on the ground, reacted to the missed opportunities by commenting wistfully: 'Our activity has provoked their own. They were never warmer in the defence of their religion.'[6]

The shift in Muslim attitudes which marked the second phase occurred in different places at different times, but a significant turning point was undoubtedly the defeat of Ijebu-Ode by the British in 1892. Johnson commented: 'This event in a great measure helped us to get access to the country in a larger way than had been previously the case.'[7] Between 1899 and 1900, Christianity made significant inroads into Ijebu-Ode, leading the missionary the Rev. N.T. Hamlyn to remark on the extraordinary progress of the faith in the area. Parallel with these developments on the political front were efforts to involve Muslims in modern schools, and since the predominance of Christians in that field was self-evident, approaches were made to missions to encourage them to include the teaching of Arabic to attract Muslims.

In July 1889, a Committee of the Board of Education was set up to investigate the general matter of poor attendance in Lagos schools, in which the issue of Muslim attendance was taken up as a special problem. The Governor was to meet leaders of Muslim opinion to raise the matter with them. Christian schools should be offered financial inducement to introduce the teaching of Arabic in the syllabus; and finally, Qur'anic schools should be encouraged to incorporate elements of the modern syllabus into their teaching. Two successive governors took up the cudgels on behalf of the Muslims but

6. Gbadamosi (1978), p.134.
7. ibid., pp.139–40.

came up against the difficult barrier of Arabic. Qualified teachers in the language were rare enough, and Christian schools could not be expected to make it a priority within existing constraints. Just when it seemed that Muslim education was predestined for its own separate course, a glimmer of hope appeared from Sierra Leone.

Two men were to help keep alive the prospect of greater Muslim involvement in modern education, and by that a corresponding increase in the level of Christian-Muslim encounter. One was Dr Blyden whom the Governor, Sir Gilbert Carter, appointed Agent of Native Affairs in 1895. A major assignment in the appointment was for Blyden to try to prevail on Muslim parents and guardians to send their children to modern schools, and encourage Muslims to take advantage of government provision for financial help. Blyden succeeded in placing one Muslim school, better organised than most, under government assistance. It was opened in June 1896 as the Government Muslim School with an initial enrolment of eighty-six. Support for the school in the Lagos Muslim community was widespread, with the desire on the part of many to imitate the Christian example. Armed with proof of Muslim interest, the Governor called for greater support for the school, whose success began to inspire Muslims in other parts of Yorubaland. It also emboldened Dr Blyden to resuscitate his dream of an institute of higher Islamic learning.

The other man from Sierra Leone to have made an impact on the Muslim educational scene in Lagos was Harun al-Rashid, Blyden's protégé. The fact that al-Rashid had taught Arabic at Fourah Bay College made him a popular hero in Lagos. He addressed several meetings, calling upon his fellow-Muslims to avail themselves of the new opportunities offered by modern education. His own continuing Muslim vocation demonstrated to his admirers that fear of Christian indoctrination was largely unfounded. It was a witness which indirectly advanced the Christian cause. Improvements in the atmosphere of Muslim relations with modern schools were evidence that the negative reaction to colonial conquest had been replaced by a spirit of co-operation and active dealings with the colonial authorities. Islam stood to gain from the conditions of imperial rule, and Christianity was no longer the feared foe it once was.

Unburdened of the wearisome myth of confrontation with Islam, Christians assessed Islam in the more favourable light of its local manifestation, the natural milieu towards which the religion tended. Many missionaries expressed admiration for a religion which taught sobriety, personal discipline and lay participation, and which inspired self-giving and enforced a moral code. Many had their eyes opened to the phenomenon of African Muslims acting as effective missionary agents for their faith without the support of a powerful and wealthy foreign missionary structure. Johnson isolated this last point for special comment, saying that the progress of Islam was in spite of the handicap of Arabic. It is a point well made, for at the heart of the question of indigenization is the matter of local languages, which Christianity developed but which Islam sought to bypass by the insistence on Arabic as the exclusive vehicle of revelation. Islam might spread by African agents, but not seemingly through the devoted cultivation of the languages of those agents. It is clear, however, that once a sense of realism prevailed about local Islam, a more positive perspective was restored to the Christian encounter with it. We should nevertheless be wary of the excessively rosy picture painted of the exploits of Islam, for behind this flattering portrayal lurks the competitive dragon. One missionary, William Allen, put his finger on it when he observed in 1887 that at Abeokuta and Lagos the Muslims 'appear to be friendly disposed and devoid of that fanatical spirit which characterise them in the Turkish dominions'.[8] African religious and cultural values had persisted into newly-acquired religious loyalties. In Nigeria, as elsewhere in Black Africa, the family was the upholder of this heritage. Within the family a variety of religious confessions existed in an amicable way. Religious differences were overtaken by the stronger bonds of mutual tolerance and personal interdependence. It is a precious heritage in a divisive world.

We should now begin to lay the Christian missionary theme to rest and proceed to the situation which existed under Christian Independency. One missionary with long experience in the field wrote a report on a Christian assessment of Islam in West Africa. It is a description which draws together several threads of the fluctuating relationship between Christianity and Islam and provides a good example of the progress of one missionary out of provocative stereotypes through competitive skirmishes into the reassurance of the African armistice, with the old habits still not completely dormant. The missionary in question, William Maude, had served for several years in Sierra Leone, the Gambia and Ghana in the period beginning in December 1867 to about 1916. Otherwise he is an undistinguished figure, the apt representative of a whole species of missionary men and women who tried to serve without the guarantee of reward. In a valedictory note to the Missionary Committee, Maude wrote:

The evangelism of West Africa does not depend on what Mohammedanism may be doing, although if Mohammedanism can provoke and shame the Christian Church into doing its duty, that is something to the good. Whether in any other way Islam prepares the way for Christianity may be doubted but I think it should be recognised that it is at least an advance on paganism, and in one particular at least it is an advantage to the country, in that it teaches

8. Gbadamosi (1978), p.146.

and to a large extent enforces, abstinence from all intoxicants, and so promises to save the peoples of interior Africa...from the curse at their door... When we have a policy...it will take time and money to work it out... Force and cruelty are no longer being used to spread Islam...the Mohammedan teacher is everywhere. He needs no society behind him, no funds to sustain him. He goes forth as the first Christians went with his staff and his wallet, and wherever he goes he is at home! He is everywhere welcomed — though perhaps not more freely than the Christian teacher would be. Both have the prestige of being Bookmen and God men. The Christian teacher goes as a stranger among foreigners and must be supported from without. The Mohammedan teacher gets paid in kind for blessing crops, sells charms etc. and he doesn't do anything for nothing. The Christian teacher is debarred from these methods of livelihood, and consequently must be kept or starve... The wonder to my mind is, not that Mohammedanism has spread among the pagan tribes, but that it does not spread more rapidly, and that it should make no impression on the multitudes of professed Christians whose Christianity is so immature and all whose instincts and tradition are in this direction... People who have tried to convert Moslems (who are always willing to listen and usually to pray with Christian teachers) have begun by disputing instead of trying to conciliate and understand. Even the native ministers and European missionaries show not only lack of special training but want of sympathy and local knowledge...a certain aloofness and assumption of superiority... 'I belong to a superior race. I condescend to come among you but should never think of living with you or even eating with you.' The Arabic teacher will squat round some calabash and dip his hand in the same dish.... We must make ourselves neighbourly. . .[9]

With that eirenic appeal Maude showed that his African experience was real enough to alter the image that was the standard equipment of official teaching. His plea for Christian sympathy, local knowledge and a neighbourly attitude could not be more relevant. It is a fitting tribute to those who took part in the adaptation of Christianity to Africa, of whom a surprising number were missionaries. Maude of course was not entirely free of the tendency to represent Islam as larger-than-life, and therefore was not free of the competitive attitude. Nevertheless he was prepared to allow local contact to guide his thinking and attitude, thus becoming perhaps a better missionary, if a little ahead of his time.

African Christian Independency and Islam

The striking parallels between Christian Independency and African Islam have been noted by a good number of writers. However, a certain caution is again necessary in approaching this material. In describing such parallels many writers have proceeded on the unstated assumption that Christianity has remained an alien religion, with the future lying along the path of closer imitation of Islam. The

9. Cited from Prickett (1971), pp.164–4.

decisive African context is thus ignored, and on the basis of the adversary view of Christian-Muslim rivalry the significant achievement of African Christians is undervalued. Even African Christian renewal, which is such a critical element in the history of Christianity on the continent, is seized on as proof of the foreignness of the religion rather than what it demonstrably is, namely, the sign that the African religious heritage is being engaged by a profound attention to Biblical material. Unless this is recognised, our perspective on the entire phenomenon of the history of religion in Africa will be gravely distorted.

Right from the beginning, the leaders of Christian Independency were closely involved with Muslim religious figures. The practice of prayer and divinatory activity provided two of the most fertile settings for mutual influence. However, contrary to the popular view, Muslim prayer activity as such had little influence on religious attitudes in Independency. Except in the historical sense that local Muslims preceded their Christian counterparts in drawing on African religious materials, Independency outpaced Islam in the bold use of religious symbols. As one writer puts it, the 'Yoruba have little confidence in Muslim methods and refer contemptuously to Hausa diviners playing with the sand (geomancy, *khatt*). They consult Muslim diviners only in connection with specifically Islamic ceremonies such as the time for the payment of *iso-yigi* (bride-price). African Islam does not have a special class, for divination is a clerical function, but diviners like Hausa *mai-duba* exist in all Islamic communities. A Hausa cleric is not called *mai-duba,* though the practice is called *duba.* The old terminology is not normally transferred but a new one invented, and a Yoruba cleric when divining is called *alafoshe.*'[10] Given this decisive African factor in religious practice, there should be little surprise at the separate initiative of Independency *vis-à-vis* Islam.

Moses Orimolade Tunolashe, of the Cherubim and Seraphim, was lodging with a Muslim in a run-down part of Lagos when his fame as a prayer leader began to spread. Relations between Cherubim and Seraphim and Islam continued to be extremely cordial, as evidenced in a number of visions in the latter commending Islam. At Abeokuta a member of the Church was told in a vision in 1932 that people were to keep the Ten Commandments and to observe the Sunday Sabbath of 'the followers of Ise', Ise being the Arabic name for Jesus. Members were also enjoined to keep 'the day called Jimo [Friday] for which Mohammed petitioned the Lord and was allowed; for upon this day his predecessor was crucified and on this day he ascended into Heaven.'[11] It then referred to churches and mosques and all other places where the name of the great God was being called upon.

10. Trimingham (1959), p.120; see also pp.110–17.
11. Peel (1968), p.233.

Another vision commended Muslims for their 'clean' worship. Muslims were equally prominent in Seraphim circles: an important Muslim official in the court of the Olubadan patronised Seraphim services. On one occasion he came to make personal thanksgiving and offer testimony: there was no pressure on him to abjure Islam, though several of his children were Christian. At the colourful celebrations in 1965 for Captain Abiodun on the fortieth anniversary of her vision, one of the two chairladies, a kinswoman of Abiodun's and a wealthy trader, was a Muslim.

A similar fraternal spirit existed among the other Churches of the Aladura movement. In Ibadan a wealthy Muslim produce buyer, Salami Agbaje, had strong Aladura connections. In spite of its dogmatic abrasiveness on the matter, the CAC had extensive Muslim contact. The CAC church building in Ondo is constructed in the style of the prominent hexagonal central mosque of the town. Conversions from Islam took place and were encouraged: Muslim rosaries, abandoned by new converts, were put on display as signs of genuine repentance. Nevertheless, as Akinyele advised, conversion of Muslims should be by precept only and not by aggressive attacks on their religion. When we look closely, we find that informal contacts between Muslims and members of the Aladura movement were extensive. More on this presently.

The tradition for contacts with Islam is a venerable one in the Aladura movement and goes back to Oshitelu himself. In his journal he recorded how in April 1926, he had a vision in which he saw a 'book open, written in strange Arabic language'.[12] On the basis of these visions which occurred through the year, he produced the 'holy script' in which he clearly tried to emulate the Arabic script, writing from right to left in a style reminiscent of the square Kufic writing, with elements of Greek style. His use of the 'sacred script' as seals of power is also reminiscent of Muslim amulets. Similarly the use of water in healing and sacramental life must have been stimulated by the Yoruba Muslim environment, although this phenomenon occurs in non-Muslim traditions, with Braide, for example, as one of the most conspicuous to have popularised it among his followers in the Niger Delta (see Chapter 7). In the use of the peculiar Holy Names, the resemblance with Islam is at times remarkable. 'Allah', the Islamic name for God, occurs in the complex form used by Oshitelu, 'Jehovah Joffellah'. The Yoruba word *aladura* itself, meaning prayer, is not native to the language but is derived from the Arabic *al-duᶜa*, meaning supererogatory prayer. Arabic words like *allahumma*, 'O my God'; *al-rabb*, 'Lord' and *majubah*, 'answer, response', find more than echoes in the Holy Names of the Church of the Lord (Aladura).

The special case of prayer needs discussing in a little more detail. In the prayer the prophet and his acolytes prostrate themselves in the

12. Turner, vol. I (1967), p.41.

manner of the Yoruba custom and of the Muslim *sujud,* and repeat the seal word *ajubah.* The five daily prayers of the Islamic religious canon find a parallel in Church of the Lord (Aladura) practice where services are held five times a day: at 5 and 9 in the morning and at 3, 6 and 9 p.m. Enclosures called 'mercy grounds' are marked out adjoining the chapel in a fashion similar to Muslim prayer grounds. At the benediction the worshippers raise their arms with their hands open to catch the blessing from heaven just as Muslims do at the end of the first chapter (*surat*) of the Qur'an. The shedding of shoes at the entrance to the church duplicates Muslim practice at the mosque. When the name of Jesus is called upon it is followed by the praise words, 'Adore His Holy Name', in a way evocative of the Muslim practice, 'Muhammad, on whom be peace [*calayhi salam*]'. Many other parallels can be drawn.

In the social teachings of the Church, similarities with Islam occur also. In the marriage law Islam permits up to four wives. The Church of the Lord (Aladura) allows three 'in order that [the man] may at all times be able to satisfy his natural desires'.[13] The dietary rules of the Church prohibit the consumption of alcohol and the eating of blood and the flesh of dogs, rodents, snakes and pigs. Although clearly this is in consonance with Old Testament teaching (see Leviticus 11), the stimulus of Maliki Islamic rulings cannot be altogether denied. Other regulations concerning women covering their heads and not entering the church during menstrual periods, and of the ministers not being allowed to cut their hair, as well as of prohibiting corpses from being brought into the church at funerals are also drawn from Leviticus and other parts of the Old Testament. Nevertheless a certain affinity is shared with Islam in the detailed attention to rules of the written code.

Muslims have felt at home in the surroundings of the church. At a special service and rally held in a church in Freetown, a Muslim presided as Chairman and gave a short address. He acknowledged that his faith was different, but emphasised to his Christian audience that all of them worshipped one God and that there was no cause for antagonism between them: a gracious speech, to which his audience heartily responded. The Muslim visitor had clearly been anticipated. Even the long white robes of members of the Church of the Lord (Aladura) catch the reflection of Muslim ceremonial attire.

Appearances, however, can be deceptive. In spite of such strong parallels, resemblances, similarities and echoes, there is no doubt that Independency must in the final analysis be explained by its own terms. Take, for example, the prominent use of *Jah* as a Holy Name in the Church of the Lord (Aladura). The word occurs in Islamic tradition with reference to the spiritual stature and high rank of notable religious figures. Yet in the practice of the Church the

13. Banton (1956–7), p.62.

sanction for its use is found in Psalm 68.4 ('extol him that rideth upon the heavens by his name JAH, and rejoice before him'). Also the use of consecrated water may resemble a similar procedure in local Muslim practice: the Holy Script, written on the Qur'an school wooden slate, is washed off and the water thus used is collected in a bottle to be dispensed for medicinal purposes. Yet Independency has firmer Biblical roots in the matter: the teaching of Jesus about the necessity for a person to be born of water and of the Spirit in order to enter the new life (John 3.5), and the use of water in Christian baptism generally. Such ritual significance of water probably gave the impetus to the development of a sophisticated theology of water. But there is little doubt that the pervasive importance of the element in traditional religions provided the underpinning for what was to become a full-scale ritual practice in many Independent Churches. For example, in Yoruba religion Oba is a river goddess and is regarded as the third wife of Shango, the god of lightning and thunder. In addition, Olokun is a deity of the sea and is worshipped by those who dwell by the sea and by those who have much to do with it, such as fishermen and canoemen. When the worshippers gather at the sea front, the men are clad in dark dresses while the women wear white. A series of prostrations and genuflections follow, with a simple meal at the end. Then comes bathing and then an elaborate meal. The remains of the food are tossed into the sea as a sacrifice to Olokun. It is by this kind of ritual culture, therefore, that we have to interpret much of the practices of the Church of the Lord (Aladura), especially the services held on the sea front.

Biblical material merely complements and confirms what is familiar and deeply valued in the traditional religious heritage. The therapeutic value of water would be enhanced, for example, by the detailed prescription for its use as such in the Old Testament. In one place a guilty woman makes amends and undergoes an elaborate ritual of purification involving the use of holy water. The curse is removed by the priest writing the words of a verse in a book and then blotting them out with bitter water which he causes the woman to drink. She then makes a jealousy offering, part of which is burnt and given to her in a mixture to drink. Involved in the procedure is a trial by ordeal, for guilt that is denied may be detected through the adverse consequences that the holy water will produce. Innocence may be established by child-bearing, that is the annulment of barrenness (Leviticus 5.11-29). To those members of traditional religions whose ears are instinctively tuned to the rush of rivers and streams and the sound of waves, the Biblical theme, however discreetly introduced in Christian teaching, would act as an amplifier. In this sense, of course, the teaching of the Apostles that the light of truth which in the end was focused in Christ had been widely diffused in God's universal Providence can be testified to by Christian Independents and others (e.g. Hebrews 1.1-2, Ephesians 1.4 and Acts 10.34-35).

A final theme to be considered before we proceed to the next stage is why people like Oshitelu should set so much store by the use of mysterious language and signs, especially if, as some scholars believe, religious faith is merely a shorthand for assimilating pressures from the social and material environment. It is much more straightforward to take some of this religious evidence at face value. In that case we may discern the following process at work. The use of mysterious language is an appeal to a vehicle of communication which is unstained by the stigma of original sin and therefore is immune from the contaminating consequences of the curse. Such a language would act as a lever to raise humanity to the divine level and to recover the heritage lost through the curse. The only thing which both necessitates and justifies such a religious language is faith in the supernatural, the belief that God not only exists but that He is also efficaciously accessible. Unlike traditional religious clerics or the Yoruba Muslim *alafoshe*, Christian Independents make unusual assertions about the centrality of God in the context of dealings with Him on a regular basis, thus making Him part of the living experience of ordinary people. Whether or not traditional religious people, set loose in the flux and mobility of modern Africa, would have arrived inevitably at a monotheist faith, as has been ably argued, the step that is taken from a passive acknowledgement of the existence of God to an active engagement with Him is a revolutionary one, and challenges traditional attitudes. This is one of the reasons why Christianity needs to be viewed both as a fulfilment and as a radical force, enabling people to look back in confidence and to march forward in hope at the same time.

Encounter with African religions and customs: Islam and traditional religions

A fact worth noting in the encounter of Christianity and Islam with Africa is their sharply contrasting attitudes to African religions and customs. Representative Muslim figures adopted an attitude of deep hostility, with the world neatly divided in their minds between those who call others to honour (*amal ma^cruf*) and those who incite others to what is forbidden (*munkar*). Indigenous innovations are stigmatised as satanic (*bida^c shaytaniyah*) and seen as *casus belli*. This attitude provided the ideological motivation for the nineteenth-century Islamic reform movements. Christian spokesmen, by contrast, whatever their antipathy to indigenous custom and practice, lacked any comparable Biblical authority and certainly did not have the assurance in the Bible of a religious state that would enforce the religious code. Where such an assurance exists, as in Islam, it has the effect of anathematizing the existing social and political order. We have seen enough of the colonial attitude to Islam to know that even the colonial rulers could not be relied on to support the Christian cause. Without this political power Christian missionaries might preach against traditional religions, but they would be unable to back it up with a precise programme of legislation. The Muslim reformers, for their part, waged war and legislated in response to the prescriptive requirements of the faith. Those Muslims who continued to dabble in traditional religions did so either in gross ignorance or in wilful disregard of the law, and, in theory at least, they deserved to be classed as reprobates (*murtadin*). If, therefore, in the African situation we find Muslims adopting elements from the local religions and blending these with their practice of Islam — as in fact happened — then it is clear that the Islamic code as it exists in the law books has been displaced as a determinant of religious perception. Similarly, we should expect to find in the written sources a self-conscious attack or disapproval of traditional religions, which again contrasts sharply with some vivid parallels Christians drew from those sources. The contrast we have in method of presentation of material, therefore, is a reflection of the nature of the material itself, and not due to any prior sense of commitment.

It would be appropriate to begin with the Islamic picture. In the first detailed account of significant Islamic conversion in West Africa, an eleventh-century Arab writer describes how Islam gained a foothold in the kingdom of Mali. Although it had been present in the kingdom for some time, Islam had to wait until the traditional religious clerics were discredited by their inability to bring an end to a disastrous drought before it earned the attention of the hard-pressed king. A visiting Muslim cleric responded to the king's request for prayer to end the drought by first requiring him to embrace the faith and to accompany the cleric on prayer devotions lasting the whole night. At the end of that period, if we may believe the account, the land became shrouded in rain clouds, and there followed a downpour which effectively completed the demise of the local clerics. That round of the contest went to Islam; yet we know enough of the ambivalence of political rulers and aristocrats towards new religious influences to predict that if Islam was to survive at court at all it would have to be a very mixed form of the religion — in spite of its prescriptive standards. Politics and religion are strange bedfellows.

Of such mixing in royal courts we have abundant evidence, with Mali again providing a good example. Ibn Battuta, the celebrated fourteenth-century Arab traveller, describes a visit to the court of Mali in 1352 during the feasts of ^c*id al-kabir,* which is normally timed to coincide with the pilgrimage sacrifice at Mecca, and of ^c*id al-fitr* after Ramadan. The king was seated on the royal platform, called *pempi,* surrounded by men in ceremonial attire. There were armour-bearers with quivers of gold and silver, gold-ornamented swords with golden scabbards, gold and silver lances and crystal maces. Then there were army commanders, Islamic officials and subordinate provincial rulers. With the formal political and Islamic sphere thus clearly defined, the traditional sphere came into its own with the local musician Dugha, with his roots deep in ancient usage and custom, and people Ibn Battuta calls poets, who followed Dugha, all of them rather ornately dressed. In fact the poets appeared in masquerades, one of them 'a figure resembling a thrush, made of feathers, and provided with a wooden head with a red beak, to look like a thrush's head'.[14] They addressed the king, reminding him of his obligation to preserve custom, uphold the deeds of his predecessors and advance their good name. Ibn Battuta, somewhat offended by these old customs, commented: 'I was told that this practice is a very old custom amongst them, prior to the introduction of Islam, and that they have kept it up.'[15] Thus Ibn Battuta depicts the pluralist world of the Muslim king of Mali, surprised that what elsewhere he called their assiduous practice of the faith did not seem to prevent the people from participating equally sincerely in African practices. He would have been just as surprised at the suggestion that Islam might be enriched by those practices.

The two spheres of institutional Islam and indigenous custom and religion, which often co-existed in royal courts, sometimes collided on a course set by Islam's universal ambition. The state of Songhay in the fifteenth century was the stage for a conflict that was to set an example to many other places. What happened there should shed light on the nature of the encounter between Islam and traditional religions. The *de facto* creator of the Songhay state was Sonni Ali who, in about 1465, succeeded in repudiating the Mandinka overlordship of Mali. Sonni Ali epitomised the religious ambivalence of society in Songhay, and he was at the centre of a bitter controversy concerning the role of traditional religion in the life of the state. He acted severely against Muslim scholars, especially those he suspected of harbouring sympathy for the Tuareg, the nomadic people of Timbuktu and beyond, and launched a wave of persecution against the scholars of the great Sankore mosque, the seat of learning in Songhay. He so decimated known Muslim figures that those who remained could, in the laconic words of the chronicler, 'be gathered under the shade of one tree'. He forbade the observance of Islamic law among members of his court, placing an interdict, for example, on the keeping of Ramadan. Yet Sonni Ali did not repudiate Islam completely; on the contrary, he made a show of keeping it. He pronounced the Muslim creed, rewarded those scholars who had not earned his wrath with concubines taken from military raids, and performed the Muslim prayer (*salat*). The seventeenth-century chronicler, after having

14. Ibn Battuta (1929), p.329.
15. ibid.

catalogued Sonni Ali's outrages against Muslims, added: 'Notwithstanding all the wrong and pains Sonni Ali inflicted upon the scholars, he acknowledged their eminence and used to say: ''Without the scholars the world would be no good.'' He did favours for other scholars and respected them.'[16]

Why this painful ambivalence towards Islam? Sonni Ali regarded himself as the chief patron of the traditional religion which was under increasing pressure from Muslims. He felt that the survival of his power depended on a successful defence of the older religious heritage. Islam had threatened to become a state within a state by challenging the traditional religion, thus rejecting the pluralist tradition that had sustained the old order. Yet, on the other hand, tolerance of Islam would be in conformity with that older tradition and might even bolster the king's political authority. His function as chief patron of the old and the new would reinforce his power. Keeping the two forces in balance, however, proved problematic and caused the violent swings in his policy towards Islam. Sonni Ali had fears for his sovereignty as he witnessed the rising power of Islam in rivalry to his own. What happened subsequently justified his fears.

The *askiya* Muhammad Ture, the new king of Songhay who toppled Sonni Ali in a *coup d'état,* had few illusions of the importance of traditional religions, justifying his rebellion against Sonni Ali in terms of a struggle against the powers of darkness and error. As the champion of the Arabised militants in the Muslim party, the new *askiya* helped to crystallise the Islamic objections to traditional religions and their African Muslim patrons. Sonni Ali became the embodiment of traditional religious attitudes. The *askiya* wrote of him:

His mother was from the country of Far, and they are unbelievers [*qawm kuffar*] who worship idols of trees and rocks, and making offerings to them, and asking their needs of them. And they do not raid until they ask their advice, and if they return from a journey they repair to them and dismount there. And these idols have custodians who serve them, and among them are soothsayers and magicians to whom they repair in the same way. Now Sonni Ali, from his infancy to his maturity used to spend much time with them, until he grew hoary among them, becoming impressed with the imprint of their polytheism [*shirk*] and customs. Then after the death of his father he sought power... It was characteristic of him that he pronounced the two Muslim professions of faith, and similar Muslim utterances, and fasted in Ramadan and gave much alms by immolations and by other means at the mosques and similar places, but despite that he venerated certain trees and stones by making sacrifices at them and by making offerings and [kindling] fires for them and seeking fulfilment of his needs from them, and asking their help, and the help of the magicians and soothsayers in all matters. . .[17]

16. Al-Sa^{c}di, *Tarikh al-Sudan* (French transl. by O. Houdas, Paris, 1911), text 67, tr. 109.
17. Hiskett (1962), pp.579–80.

Although the Islamic sources are nearly all hostile and therefore tendentious, we can nevertheless discern in the accounts a certain envy of the power of traditional religions, their organised strength and their success in integrating society and state. This is clear from the following passage, referring to Songhay: 'They have temples which are venerated by them. They do not appoint a ruler, nor do they honour anything, whether great or small, except on the authority of the custodians of their great temples.'[18] Precisely the role that Muslims would have liked for themselves, and the fact that it existed under the old dispensation made it a practicable goal for Islam.

It is also not surprising that the cutting edge of the Muslim opposition consisted of the Arabised militants. They campaigned for the reassertion of the Arabic heritage of Islam and the setting up of political structures according to the written sources of the 'pious' cAbbasid caliphate of Baghdad. A keen recruit to this élite group was cAbd al-Karim al-Maghili (died 1505), a Muslim scholar from Tilimsan in North Africa where he was known for his stern anti-Jewish views. He visited both Songhay and Hausaland, disseminating radical Islamic ideas. In Songhay he commented with acrid humour on the traditional Muslim teachers who would pass themselves off as authorities. He said: 'One of their characteristics is that they are not Arabic-speaking; they understand no Arabic except a little of the speech of the Arabs of their towns, in an incorrect and corrupted fashion, and a great deal of non-Arabic, so that they do not understand the intentions of the orthodox scholars.'[19]

A straight comparison between al-Maghili and his missionary Christian counterpart would be misleading. However, it is instructive to see how an expatriate religious specialist like al-Maghili could call for a return to the Arabic heritage of Islam while the Christian missionary, however unsympathetic, would in similar circumstances be seeking to make greater use of local languages. At this stage in the encounter of Islam and African religions, two general lines appear to be emerging. One is the deep impact of the African religious environment on Islam, and the other is the objection of Muslim spokesmen to the identification between the two. There is no doubt that the issue for the great majority of African Muslims was the importance of maintaining solidarity with traditional institutions and ideas. Equally, more disquiet was expressed at the level of the élite, than in the corresponding Christian case. To what extent Muslims were hindered by the inadmissibility of translating the Qur'an into local languages and to what extent they allowed the traditional world-view to determine their perception is a matter for detailed investigation. But on the divergence between experience and

18. Hiskett (1962), p.579.
19. ibid., p.580.

teaching there can be little doubt.

In some places these two converge in a frank acceptance of the power of local religion and custom. The Kano Chronicle, a nineteenth-century document drawing on much older traditions, is one of the few detailed sources we possess on religion in Hausaland before the triumph of Islam. In it the interplay between Islam and the local religions is closely described, as is the way traditional religion became integrated with state and society. The central religious shrine was at Gagua where the god Tchunburburai dwelt. It was a sacred grove which was visited for worship and for obtaining oracles on important events. The Kano Chronicle described one such pilgrimage there.

The pagans [i.e. traditional religious worshippers] stood in awe of the terrors of their god and this grove... The branches and limbs of its trees were still — save, if trouble were coming to this land, it would shriek thrice, and smoke would issue forth in Tchunburburai, which was in the midst of the water. Then they would bring a black dog and sacrifice it at the foot of Tchunburburai. They sacrificed a black he-goat in the grove. If the shrieks and smoke continued, the trouble would indeed reach them, but if they ceased, then the trouble was stayed. The name of the grove was Matsama and the name of Tchunburburai was Randaya.[20]

The first Muslim rulers of Kano came into active contact with the cult. For example, we find an early ruler, Warisi (1063-95), son of Bagoda, being counselled by a palace official about extending his conquests towards those lands where traditional religions were not strong enough to oppose him. Another *Sarki* or ruler, Gugua, (1247-90), son of Gijimasu, set himself the difficult task of penetrating the mysteries of the local religion in order specifically to control it. The chief shrine attendants responded:

The chief pagans assembled at dead of night, forty in number, at the foot of the sacred tree. Allah alone knows what took place there. They came forth when the sun rose and went to the Sarki. They said, 'O Sarki, when the night of Idi comes we will tell you the mysteries of our god.' He agreed, for he was glad at heart, and gave them gifts abundantly. That night an apparition appeared to the Sarki in his sleep — a man with a red snake in his hand. He struck the Sarki with the snake and said to him. 'Of two things choose one. Either thou mayest know the mysteries, in which case thou wilt die, or thou mayest not know the mysteries, in which case thou wilt not die.' The Sarki said, 'No! No! No!' Now when the Sarki rose from his sleep he told his men what he had seen in the vision. They said to him, 'What do you see in it?' He said, 'What do *you* see?' They said, 'We see war?' The Sarki said nothing, he spoke not a word, but suddenly he was struck blind. He remained blind for many years.[21]

20. Palmer (1908), p.65.
21. ibid., pp.67-8.

The contest continued under the next Sarki, though with less dramatic personal consequences. In fact a more conciliatory attitude prevailed this time, with the traditional religious worshippers acknowledging the Sarki's authority in return for freedom of worship. The chronicler comments: 'The Sarki...left them their customs and power. They said, "Were it not for fear of what may result we would have told the Sarki the secrets of our god." The chief of them, Samagi, said, "If we show him the secrets of our god we shall lose all our power, and we and our generation will be forgotten."'[22]

About a century later, in the reign of Kanajeji (1390-1410), son of Yaji, we find this sentiment of perpetuating the historical memory of tradition making a bold entry. Kanajeji had won great military victories, and in an ebullient mood began an armed campaign against the traditional stronghold of Zukzuk. He was repulsed with heavy losses, and sued for peace. The words of the chronicle capture well enough the drama of the defeat:

The Sarkin Kano went back to Kano in a rage and said, 'What shall I do to conquer these men of Zukzuk?' The Sarkin Tchibiri said: 'Re-establish the god that your father and grandfather destroyed.' The Sarki said, 'True, but tell me what I am to do with it.' The Sarki Tchibiri said: 'Cut a branch from this tree.' The Sarki cut off a branch. When it was cut the Sarki found a red snake in the branch. He killed the snake, and made two *huffi* [= a kind of slipper, usually yellow, with no leather behind the wearer's heel] with its skin. He then made four *dundufa* and eight *kuntakuru* [*dundufa* = tall, narrow drum which stands on the ground when being played; *kuntakuru* = small, round drum of wood hollowed-out, covered with skin] from the branch. These objects he took to Dankwoi and threw them into the water and went home. After waiting forty days he came back to the water, and removed the objects to the house of Sarkin Tchibiri. Sarkin Tchibiri sewed the rest of the snake's skin round the drums and said to Kanajeji, 'Whatever you wish for in this world, do as our forefathers did of old.' Kanajeji said, 'Show me and I will do even as they did.' The Sarkin Tchibiri took off his robe and put on the *huffi* of snake's skin and walked round the tree forty times, singing the song of Barbushe. Kanajeji did as Sarkin Tchibiri did, and walked round the tree forty times. The next year he set out to war with Zukzuk.[23]

That time Kanajeji achieved victory. Even allowing for the Islamic filter of the Arabic language through which the chronicle was processed, the impression created is of a vigorous culture of traditional religious worship. It provides details on how Islam was supplanted and how a ruler, extremely active and mobile, abjured Islam on the grounds of political utility and of greater authenticity. Local experience often acted in this way to rescind the exclusive teachings of Islam, not of course always with the same striking result.

22. Palmer (1908), pp.67-8.
23. ibid., pp.73-4.

The puritan Islamic revolutionaries of the nineteenth century, only too aware of the power of the African religious traditions, denounced those Muslims who lent a veneer of respectability to these traditions by participating in cult practices. In most places local Muslims took part in these cults as a matter of course. But where an awareness of Islam's Arabic heritage was strong, it produced a sentiment of intolerance and a self-righteous desire to abolish the old religions. In the first line of fire were the so-called Muslim compromisers, whom the reformers castigated as venal teachers who did the round of simple villages clutching a bundle of Arabic manuscripts which they did not understand, and making a show of carrying pious satchels which contained only cockroaches! War against them and eventually against traditional religious worshippers was, they counselled, an obligation imposed by the Holy Book. In other words, the process of religious adaptation was to be violently arrested and a specific programme of Islam's universal code introduced and maintained. It was attempted, at great cost, with results that bore little relationship to the original ideals.

The failure of the reform movements to sweep away completely and finally the ancient religious heritage of Africa can only be partly explained by the unorthodox motivation of the *mujahidin* (militant reformers). A greater part of the reason must lie ultimately in the absorptive power of the host-environment, for which the evidence is quite strong and unambiguous. Several stories make this clear. One account says that when Islam was first introduced to Yorubaland (perhaps in the eleventh or twelfth century) by a Hausa Muslim from the north, the traditional people of Ife at first resisted the new faith, but afterward retrieved the missionary's sack containing a copy of the Qur'an which they covered with a pot and began to worship as Odudua, the ancestor/ancestress of the race. Thus began the cult of Odudua among the Yorubas. Whatever its historical foundations, the story suggests how an in-coming Islamic influence stimulated existing religious tendencies into more explicit local formulation. The 'children of Odudua' (*Omo Odudua*), as the Yoruba call themselves, continued through history to resist total assimilation by foreign influences, whatever the motivation of their would-be captors.

A recent study of Islam in Yorubaland has tried, somewhat unsuccessfully, to describe Islam both as favourable to African religions and as posing a serious threat to them. If the author had identified Islam on one level as a client religion that was subservient to the host environment and on another as an instrument for the imposition of the Arabic heritage of the faith, he might have escaped the contradictions of his method. It is a fault he shares with better-known scholars. From Ilorin, that lone outpost in Yorubaland of the Fulani Islamic revolution in Hausaland, came religious envoys determined to spread the faith in the major Yoruba centres. They came up against stiff opposition from the traditional leaders. In the hands of modern Muslim commentators the struggle between Islam and the traditional heritage, both religious and secular, has assumed all the familiar but misleading appearance of the light in Islam overcoming the darkness in traditional areas. The Muslims launched an attack on Ogboni, an important earth cult, on the Orisha cults and their worshippers and on the whole integrated structure of traditional belief, because, as the author of the recent study puts it, these constituted 'obstacles to the progress of Islam [read, an Arabised Islam]'.[24] Traditional religious people are described in the same source as 'pagans and vermin'.[25] In places up and down Yorubaland, an over-credulous hand records the signal triumphs of Islam over the traditional culture, the scale of 'pagan' conversions emphasising the inevitable rout of enemy ranks. Yet a century or so later the traditional heritage has survived and an Arabic-controlled Islam remains a remote dream of the zealots. Meanwhile, as another detailed study has amply demonstrated,[26] the culture of Ifa and the Orisha teems with unabated vigour, and the pluralist heritage of Africa is preserved intact. The hope for Islam clearly lies through that pluralist heritage.

In other places we can observe a similar process of Islam being assimilated into an existing religious world. Poro is a secret society similar in many ways to Ogboni and the Egungun secret society. In Sierra Leone Islam came upon a highly organised Poro society, and in the ensuing encounter it was definitely Islam that played second fiddle. The Muslim cleric was adopted into the Poro hierarchy and given a role which suited his familiarity with the sacred Arabic script. He used his knowledge of the science of magic squares (^{c}*ilm awfaq*), the basis of Islamic talismans, to provide the Poro with powerful medicine for use against their enemies. The Poro society would ban the sale of oil palms to people who had contravened their rules or displeased them. To signify such a boycott, two wooden slates are filled with these magic squares and placed on oil palms in a campaign of economic boycott. The Muslim cleric himself is normally surrounded by an interlocking chain of obligations and prohibitions under the ever-vigilant authority of Poro. His identity is not denied — on the contrary, his special skills are valued — but the plough to which he puts his hand receives its power from Poro. A similar phenomenon has been observed in Liberia where Poro remained a major force, with Islam again having to seek shelter under it. The widespread use of Islamic amulets is perhaps better seen as evidence of a foreign religion having to perform 'submissive' gestures in order to be recognised by the host religious community

24. Gbadamosi (1978), p.4.
25. ibid., p.198.
26. Ryan (1979).

than as proof of its virility.

A study of Islam in the Middle Volta Basin in the pre-colonial Gold Coast[27] gives many examples of the interaction between Islam and the traditional religions and customs. Islamic ritual was absorbed into the important Dangba festival where subordinate chiefs reaffirmed their tutelage under the Paramount Chief. Muslim clerics, confronted with local cults which were better patronised, more ably organised and often longer established, gave up Islam and sought a career in the cults. Some performed as diviners in such local cults. Others passed on their skills and became silent partners with the shrine attendants. One example is given of how the priest of a medicine shrine gave umbrage to Islam by himself praying twice a day, fasting three days during Ramadan, and carrying a rosary, a Qur'an and a bundle of Arabic manuscripts although he knew no Arabic. The predilection for religious symbolism and for experimenting with spiritual power acts as a vortex into which Islam is sucked; the tolerance and adaptability which have trailed it through African communities emanated from this active centre. Muslim efforts to resist the pressure exerted by the surrounding environment would tend to suggest that the availability of religious choice is recognised as a principle of the host-environment which Islam would ideally like to replace. How traditional Africa has reacted upon the exclusive Arabic heritage of Islam remains one of the most important aspects of its inner vitality. When Christianity or Islam has been willing to enter into genuine dialogue with traditional religions, some of this vitality is immediately apparent. In turning, therefore, to the Christian side of the story we are faced with a remarkable example of authentic encounter in the history of religion.

Christianity and traditional religions

In the encounter with traditional religions, African Muslims have delineated the situation in terms of what Islam permits (*halal*) and what it forbids (*haram*). In this way judgment is made on the methods and forms of traditional religious worship and divination, not on the content and ideas. Ifa divination, for example, is assessed on the basis of whether it contravenes the religious code, not on whether it introduces people to ideas of the supernatural. African Christians, on the other hand, would seem to be attracted to those features of Ifa which prepared people for faith in the Creator and His Providence, considering as of less consequence the forms and methods of Ifa practice. It is this religious culture of African religions which acquired a new importance in the Christian setting. As a framework of the religious life it anticipated Christianity at several crucial points.

27. Levtzion (1968).

The encounter of Christianity with African religions in Freetown has been described in Chapter 4 above. We need only recall some of the details here. Both Crowther and Johnson were involved in discussions with the leaders of these religions. Crowther, for example, found that worship of Shango, the god of thunder and lightning, was particularly strong. He also found Ifa to be widely followed. One Ifa diviner answered persistent missionary criticism by saying that he normally asked his clients to call on the name of Jesus Christ before making any sacrifice to the gods. Ifa diviners made the general point that since their gods existed for the good of mankind, devotion to them must necessarily be in conformity with worship of the God of Christianity. We also saw in that section of Chapter 4 how the Egungun secret society tried to resist the encroachments of Christianity. We should now proceed to add to that material from Nigeria and elsewhere.

James Johnson was later convinced that Christianity had much of value to learn from traditional religions. His attitude here was in some contrast to Crowther's, who had much more representative views on the matter. Johnson felt that the names of Ifa could properly apply to the attributes of God: 'great, Almighty one', 'the child of God', the 'one who is mightiest among the gods and prevailed to do on a certain occasion what they could not'. The transition from this kind of language to that of Isaiah 53 is not difficult: the Suffering Servant of Scripture is a familiar figure in this setting. Johnson's confidence in the revelatory capacity of African religions is strengthened by a comparable Christian attitude to the Scriptures of the Old Testament. For many people like him, the old finds fulfilment in the new: 'Behold, the former things have been brought to pass, and the new things I bear tidings of. Before they spring forth I tell you of them' (Isaiah 42.9).

A ritual of death and resurrection, probably connected with Orisha-Beku, the deity of the mountain, in the Yoruba town of Otta was fascinatingly described by William Allen, the nineteenth-century missionary. A corpse — that is, a simulation of one — is placed on the altar. Relatives and friends come to the shrine to pray for a dead child to be raised to life. The corpse in the shrine starts to decompose. After several months a ceremonial ritual act takes place in which the resurrection rite in enacted. The decomposing corpse actually consists of bones of animals laid out in the shrine. After some elaborate rituals, during which a shrine devotee slips into place alongside the symbolic corpse, life begins to stir. The body finally rises and is found to be able to speak — but in an incomprehensible language. The cult initiate, having vividly acted out death and resurrection, is then taught the secret language of the shrine. He thus becomes the striking representation of victim, priest and intercessor. A more powerful example of the story of Christianity in traditional religions is hard to imagine.

Elements of this story occur in another account,[28] also involving the dead coming to life. However, this account is more akin to the Cain and Abel story in Genesis 4. Two brothers attended a festival in a neighbouring village from which they returned with handsome rewards for their part in entertaining the people. Each was given a thousand cowries. The older brother, jealous of the younger, murdered him and stole his cowries. He then reported the murdered brother missing to his parents. They enquired in vain all along the road, but from the decaying bones of the victim sprang an edible fungus, *olu,* which the mother tried to pluck. At that point the *olu* sang a lament of four verses, with the final verse revealing the truth about the murder. The elder brother, confronted with the evidence, admitted his guilt and was executed, whereupon the innocent brother was restored to life. The notion of sin and death, linked to that of innocence and life, belongs with an explicit moral order which overlaps significantly with Christian teaching. Those who have been nurtured in this moral order (the story was told to children in Yorubaland) cannot be total strangers in the world of Christian teaching. For many of them Christian baptism acknowledged not just their own status, for they were not alone, but the message of life and hope bequeathed by the ancestors. The powerful presence of the 'living dead', as the ancestors may be conveniently called, foreshadowed, and sometimes forestalled, the Christian 'communion of saints'.

With the rise of Christian Independency has gone renewed interest in African religions. Some of the extreme forms of Independency have preached a message of denunciation of the old religions, but, as we have seen in Chapter 7, this dogmatic stance conceals a real affinity between the two. Furthermore some spokesmen of Independency have called for a more respectful attitude towards the old religions. One leader in Ogbomosho declared: 'He who tries to proselytize without tact and patience among the people of other cults is playing with a match in a room full of powder',[29] although the message of tolerance there is strained by a certain sense of danger. Another local Christian at Ado Ekiti won approval for the way 'he urged the material advantages of Christianity and the demoralising effects of paganism...but was not bitter... He attacked Christians living a pagan life, but was not cynical... He awakened the whole Ado town to active life.'[30] Elsewhere in Abeokuta Christians were exhorted to 'preach coolly' because 'the religion of Christ does not teach you to spoil other men's religion.'[31] A chief declared: 'We all

28. Lucas (1948), p.255.
29. Peel (1968), p.53. The Ogbomosho leader in question was Dr Oyerinde.
30. ibid.
31. ibid., p.233.

worship God in our different ways,'[32] obviously concerned to forestall the political consequences of religious sectarianism.

The resemblance between the Aladura Churches and the traditional religious cults has been pointed out by many writers. It is an enormous theme in itself, but its bearing on our subject should at least be indicated. The prominent role assumed by the prophet in the Aladura Churches has been noted. His functions include the receiving of dreams and visions, and, through them, the offering of healing to members. His counterpart in traditional religion is the *babalawo,* a religious specialist with knowledge of Ifa divination and of *ogun. Ogun* is concerned both with herbal medicine for organic illnesses and magical charms for the prevention of ill-luck, bringing riches and happiness, protection against enemies and in battle, and, a modern permutation, help in passing examinations and obtaining promotion at work. While the Aladura Churches have often preached against herbal medicine along with its Western substitutes, they have mainly retained elements of *ogun* in the use of Christian materials as sources of spiritual efficacy. The prophet has assumed the functions of the *babalawo.* Through dreams and visions he discerns the will and mind of God, just as the *babalawo* did through Ifa. The invocation of angels and other spiritual beings parallels the use made of the *orisha.* Even the material means of healing, such as candles, oil and water, are shared with the Ifa cult; indeed, in one Aladura Church, a breakaway group from the CAC, two *babalawo* were associated with the healing work of the prophet in charge. This convergence between Aladura Christianity and traditional religions is strongest in rural areas. However, even in large urban centres the path opened by Ifa mediation has been eagerly followed by the Aladura Churches.

The theme of healing, when joined to prayer, represents an important point of convergence with traditional religions. The Aladura Churches were actively concerned with witches and various maladies, so much so that some scholars have characterised their Christianity as essentially this-worldly. That of course is an over-simplification, for both the Bible, on which they relied, and traditional religions do conceive of a life after death, even if traditional religions incline towards an atavistic world-view. Nevertheless it is true that dealing with intermediary spiritual forces for the wellbeing of people is an important part of the work of these Churches. Such spiritual mediation was of course the essential focus of the Ifa diviner, the *babalawo.* Prayer, understood as the attempt to discover God's mind and the utilitarian use to which that knowledge can be put, is the benchmark of Christian Independency. First and foremost, prayer is power, and to possess it is to control an invaluable resource. Thus the prescriptive use of prayer has come to dominate the affirmative, expressive nature of prayer. (Expressive prayer is

32. Peel (1968), p.233.

concerned with private and individual gratification; prescriptive prayer attempts to direct a community of worshippers towards the transcendent. Expressive prayer is justified by the action; prescriptive prayer by metaphysical norms.) It is essentially a contrast between the world-view of traditional religions and that of a Western theological outlook. To that extent African Christianity reflects the spiritual and religious values of African societies.

Many Independent Churches perceive themselves as recipients of prayer-power, the Yoruba *alagbara* (*agbara*). Even Divine Grace is interpreted by the notion of power, with God seen as Olorun. Of course 'power' in this sense is nearly universal in all primal religions, what is often called the *force vital*. This *force vital* has been portrayed as the great principle which infuses a unitary purpose into all aspects of life, so that the different areas of life are comprehended into an integrated, meaningful whole. It acquires its greatest expression in religious symbolism and language, scholars say, thus giving religion both a practical orientation and a theoretical significance in its interpretive and explanatory function. Both these aspects of religion hold true for Christian Independency. The phrase 'God is' (*Olorun mbe*) affirms this dual concept of religion: God exists as an invisible force; but He also exists as efficacious power, the one who makes promises and keeps them, and may indeed be approached to fulfil human needs. The prophet is the person who embodies this power, *agbara*. He is the person who may actualize the gifts of the Spirit, especially the gift of healing. The demonstration of these gifts used to be an inseparable part of the ministry of Christian Independency. It is almost as if Independency had to pass muster in the crucible of traditional religious culture before it could properly turn its attention to the other aspects of New Testament teaching, especially the centrality of the Person of Christ. In the end the prophet made way for the pastor. Spiritual knowledge of the unseen world was replaced as a religious category by the preacher's knowledge of the Bible as the written text. And with the advent of the preacher we arrive at the stage of the fulfilling role of Christianity.

The other point to be made before we conclude this part of the discussion is that the religious character of traditional cultures imbued them with a profound level of tolerance for the Christian message. Hence the apparent ease with which African Christians saw themselves as 'Jews', not in the specific sense of suffering through faith, but in the more general notion of a people chosen by Providence for special blessing. It gave a sharp edge to religious inquiry and invested the whole field of religion with a certain purposefulness. It is by this religious character of African societies that the momentous changes represented by Western contact and colonialism — the coming of modern education and improved means of communication, and the great social mobility occasioned by bureaucratic institutions, urbanisation and industrialization — were absorbed and expressed in emotionally and intellectually satisfying ways.

9

SOME CONCLUDING OBSERVATIONS

Several lines converge on the subject of the character of Christianity in Africa. The most significant of these is undoubtedly the contribution of traditional religions to a deepened sense of the religious potential of the message of the Bible. It is by that factor that we have to judge the African reponse to the Church. It is a recurring theme in this book, and deserves far greater attention than has been devoted to it. Merely to defend traditional religions against European missionary attack or criticism is not enough, and may, by diverting attention from the independent milieu of these religions, and making them anti-cyclones whirling in a foreign element, be counter-productive. Such a defence, however well-intentioned, is nevertheless a by-product of the strength of the missionary challenge and may not in fact be the form or substance of the response of traditional religions. Its value as a tool of conceptual analysis is thus restricted to the currency of the anti-foreign cause it espouses.

The real questions we should ask relate to the phenomenon of the rich and diverse religious life that has flourished in African societies. For example, why did people draw a careful line between the world of the divinities and that of ordinary life? By what rule did a common object, such as water or a piece of stone or wood, make the transition into a ritual symbol? Did the perception of common object and its transformation into ritual subject become a factor in the use of mediation and intercession in African Christianity? Did the recognition of the plural world of the divinities contribute to the understanding of the universal doctrines of the Bible? Did the tradition of Christian renewal and reform, so prominent in African Christianity, occur in traditional religions under the category of dreams and visions? If so, did their widespread use in the Churches owe more to such indigenous roots than to the Bible? Did the notion of religious hierarchy in traditional religions determine the way the Church was assimilated in African societies? And so on. An underlying assumption in all these questions is the continuing vitality of African religions both as influences in the ordinary perception of Christians and as a force in the organizational aspects of Christianity. The issue is more than just of academic interest. It has implications for pastoral care and counselling, and for developing a meaningful theology for the Church.

Another line concerns the *status* of Christianity in Africa. The phrase 'African Christianity' or 'African Churches' has often acted as a cloak for the perpetuation of the idea of the inadmissibility of Africans as a legitimate part of the wider humanity, so that the history of Africa and its religious heritage is consigned into an area-study category, outside the mainstream of academic teaching and research. Regrettably, many educated Africans have capitulated to this piece of intellectual apartheid by the seductive device of fashionable arguments for African authenticity and uniqueness. Not only has this conceded the inferior position of Africa in the broader field of world Christianity, but it has allowed the history of the Church in North Africa to be excluded from our concern, which is then promptly annexed as an exclusive province of the European Church. Sometimes this intellectual apartheid has been extended to the Ethiopian Orthodox Church, which is wrenched from the rest of Black Africa and made into a satellite of the Judaeo-Christian centre of gravity. Such academic categories are deeply divisive and distort profoundly the historical process of the unfolding story of Christianity from the time of the Apostles. The espousal, in strident neo-nationalist terms, of the cause of a separate, ethnic African Christianity is one of the most damaging things to have occurred since the end of the European missionary era. The vital debate now is on how to rescue the subject of African Christianity from its exotic ghetto and at the same time compel the other parts of the Christian world to lower the barrier behind which they have cultivated a political and cultural ascendancy over the entire Christian heritage. This would rectify the over-concentration of intellectual resources in Western hands, and African Christianity would cease to be the preserve of so-called European experts. Such a reversal of the existing state of affairs would help to release the energies of the Church for the service and witness of the one Lord it knows and claims.

A third factor is best described in terms of an irony. The usual conception of Christianity was to see it as bringing to Africa certain universal teachings about God which were lacking in traditional religions. In rallying to the defence of those religions, some African writers hastened to reply by latching on to the fact that since, for example, ideas of the Supreme Being were present before the arrival of the missionaries, African religions could be accorded the status of a *præludia fidei* in the Christian dispensation. In other words, the criticism of the missionaries was valid in itself, except that they had been forestalled in the case of African religions. And with that concession went the opportunity to understand those religions by the standard of their own true measure. And here is the irony, namely that missionary Christianity as the propounder of a universal God turned out to be an exclusive religion tied to an ethnocentric Western world view, whereas traditional religions, criticised as restrictive tribal affairs, offered hope and reconciliation by their tolerance of religious diversity and by their inclusive view of human community. That makes them more in tune with Biblical teaching than the politically divisive form of European Christianity. By recognising this tolerant aspect of traditional religions we may be able to discover sources of strength which a missionary Christianity forfeited through its compromising subservience to colonial politics.

This would have far-reaching implications for an understanding of the mission of the Church in Africa. The rather tarnished image of the Church as a quisling of the imperial order, particularly in the formative years of colonialism between about 1890 and 1930, undoubtedly compromised its missionary task. African Christians, labouring under such inherited difficulties, often found themselves on the defensive, becoming easy prey to the popular criticism of Christianity as an alien religion. To break out from behind that psychological barrier has taken a long time. Without our realising it, perhaps, the defensiveness has produced social barriers, with Christians inclined to enclose themselves for fear of exposure. Once a proper understanding of the religious basis of African Christian life has been acquired, it would be easier to separate it from the political role foisted on it by missionaries, and thus easier to remove defensive barriers. There is evidence that in many places Christianity has in fact moved into a more open phase.

To encourage this movement it is sufficient only to demonstrate the role of Africans as pioneers in the adaptation and assimilation of Christianity in their societies, with a corresponding scaling down of the role of Western missionaries in that process. The evidence for this is secure and needs no elaborate exegesis to establish it. The initiative passed out of the hands of the missionaries as historical transmitters and went instead to the countless Africans who presided over the reception and growth of the Church. For example, in the early period in Freetown, it was clear from the start that the Nova Scotians were the key to the successful implantation of the Church, with the Colonial Chaplaincy left floundering. With the emergence of recaptive Africans came the high-water-mark of Christian activity, with a significant outburst of missionary initiative in Nigeria and elsewhere. In Ghana similarly, the African contribution was decisive. This aspect of the spread of Christianity in Africa has been suitably dramatised in the phenomenon of Christian Independency, but that it has existed as an important historical fact right from the beginning is without question. We may characterise it as the African factor in mission and make it a fitting successor to the previous classic definition of 'the missionary factor' in African Christianity.

The question of African agency ties in with that of the status of African religions in Christianity. Those who adapted and promoted the faith in African communities remained themselves very close to sources of traditional religious vitality even if they had occasionally to make approving noises of condemnation to please the missionary who was often far removed from the scene of action. In African hands, then, Christianity spread along familiar religious channels, acquiring in the feedback a strong dose of local religious materials which the quarantined culture of the Western missionary had tried to filter out. It is not only inevitable that such an encounter should take place, but it is also immensely critical for the successful establishment of the faith. Seen in this light, the charge of 'syncretism'so often invoked against the increasing importance of African leadership in the Church loses its force. In a different sense, Christianity itself is one of the most syncretistic of religions, if by that we mean the amalgamation of ideals and realities, of principles and mundane practice, for it is a pre-eminent theological teaching that through the Incarnation the transcendent and the terrestrial merged in human focus. The Christian poet describes it well:

> He laid his glory by,
> He wrapped him in our clay;
> Unmarked by human eye,
> The latent Godhead lay.

It is a logical consequence of this insight that in Africa such teachings should take local form, and that those who resisted them were out of contact with the overwhelming sense of the message they proclaimed. Thus religious compromise, if such indeed must be the price Africans must pay for embodying the faith, has a deeper affinity with the music of the Benedictus.

To reinterpret the decisive role of Africans as adaptors of the faith requires a corresponding adjustment to the position occupied by missionaries. Under the old categories, the missionary was his own worst enemy, for by calling attention to his historical pre-eminence he minimised the roots of local assimilation whose irrepressible significance made him an easy target for attack. It is ironic that even in our own day when the African Christian idiom is an accepted part of the wider ecumenical discourse, some Western writers should still wish to insist on elevating the historical transmission of Christianity to a major status, completely overshadowing the African factor. Consequently the missionary contribution has suffered and continues to suffer: the missionary is cast in one of two roles, either as the whipping-boy of the nationalist or as the disembodied idol of the West. In both cases we are left with a caricature.

It is not before time that we should once and for all move into a constructive stage and find a reappraisal that conforms to the complex historical situation, and one too that does not detract from the African factor. A way forward is to acknowledge that the missionary signified the stage of the historical transmission of Christianity, a stage which stimulated the more powerful wave of local response. Once whipped into action, this local wave acquired a force that rose from sources of traditional religious enterprise, sustaining the Church in its intimate involvement in the life of the people. The discussion in the past has failed to recognise this. Instead the focus remained on what may be termed the missionary 'hardware' of finance, bureaucratic machinery, political alliances, and the propaganda engine of Home Committees. When we tried to consider the missionary 'software' through the men and women who passed through the Home Committees to arrive in Africa, we were hindered by the strong shadows cast over the field by the 'hardware', with the consequence that a 'tunnel' effect was superimposed on their role. Thus many writers, without even looking in detail at what happened on the ground, proceed to discuss missionaries in the light of what may be deduced from the 'hardware'. Thus is set up the abstract outline that reduces the missionary to a caricature. One line in an occasional despatch about obtaining government support for a school project, for example, is enough to set the air waves tingling with news of missionary collaboration with colonialism. A life-time of dull, grinding service, by contrast, is ignored, either because it is a statistical 'failure' in the view of the Home Committee or because its recognition by the nationalist would dilute popular rhetoric.

While it is true that the missionary occupied a marginal position at the stage of the adaptation of Christianity, his contribution may often have been crucial. This would appear to have been true over the documentation of local languages, translations of the Scriptures, in the use of the vernacular in schools and as a vehicle of preaching and other forms of local religious activity. While Africans may have the advantage over the missionary in the appreciation of the deeper nuances of their own languages, the raw material and data upon which this advantage rests were provided by the missionary. From that relative advantage Africans have gone on to establish their unrivalled command of local resources, using as their model indigenous forms of religious life. The demand by the missionaries that Africans repudiate local religions and customary practices has to be understood against this background of the increasing marginalisation of the missionary once the stage of adaptation has been reached. It should not be used in the manner of a 'proof text', for the simple reason that its *prima facie* value is nil.

On another level too, the role of the missionary needs to be investigated for the light it may throw on the whole issue of indigenisation. We would need to know more than pronouncements made from different ideological positions. It may often be the case that the missionary has stood in the way of indigenisation, either deliberately or unwittingly. But it may happen that the missionary facilitates indigenisation, not only by his linguistic labours but by the attention he allows local Christians to pay to certain cultural themes, such as hymns and sacred songs in the local language, music, the decorative arts, and the writing down of local stories, myths and folklore. Even the notion of looking to the past age of the Church is capable of stimulating an enhanced apprehension of the African sacred past. Sometimes, indeed, it is this prior sense of the sacred past which attunes the African to the message of Christianity. But, for our purposes now, the order is not decisive. The fact that religious parallelism invests the two traditions with mutual significance suggests that the African religious model is not subservient to the external one of Christianity.

There is a theological way of representing all that we have been saying so far, and, without trying to be technical, we may thus present it briefly. A distinction is made between the *missio Dei* on the one hand and on the other, the mission of the Church. By *missio Dei* is meant the unceasing work of God in the great task of reconciliation and forgiveness and a maturing sense of His love and fellowship. The mission of the Church, by contrast, is the historical response to God's initiative, and finds its most poignant expression in service, *diakonia.* But historical *diakonia* often falls far short of the *missio Dei,* and, what is equally important, other agents may be just as active in this *missio Dei* as are Christians. By implication, God's initiative has anticipated and preceded the specific version of Christian mission, so that in Africa, the 'good news' of Divine love and reconciliation, for example, was long diffused in the local religious traditions before the missionary came on the scene.[1] It is this Divine precedent which on the one hand authenticates the African religious experience and, on the other, validates the missionary vocation. Without it the African would rise to a materialist cosmology but no higher, while the missionary would represent his own cause. Furthermore, the historical fact that missionaries may have been allies of structures of privilege and power remains highly marginal from the point of view of the *missio Dei,* for it is evident that Africans proved more than adequate instruments in the extension of the Church despite the obvious handicaps of powerlessness and material deprivation. From the perspective, then, of the *missio Dei,* the Western missionary is merely heeding a call whose echo has long reverberated throughout the edifice of African religiosity. In the historic missionary vocation he attempts to connect up with the ongoing task of the *missio Dei.* Theologically the historic mission is a venture of partnership with the *missio Dei,* even if in practice it may have been prosecuted by uncouth means. As a partnership it required the divine precedent to justify it

1. See, for example, G. W. H. Lampe, *God as Spirit* (the Bampton Lectures, 1976), Oxford, 1977, pp.180-1.

and the African factor to make it efficacious.

The matter of indigenisation becomes on this basis a logical extension of the reality of the *missio Dei*. Its logical opposite is the mission station tucked away on the hill-top above the village, resolutely setting its face against contagious contact with the people it aims to serve. It is easy enough to castigate this self-defeating practice of mission. But provided we keep our eyes on the *missio Dei* we should see that the divine initiative is actively and liberatingly at work among the outcasts in the villages below, that the Good Samaritan is encamped on the Jericho road of the villagers where His purpose animates their spirit and fires their righteous indignation.

An important condition for recovering a true sense of the mission of the church is to recognise the African factor. Once this step is taken we shall see that mission is no longer a specialised department of the Church into which so-called experts are drafted, but that it forms part and parcel of the Church's life and witness. As such it elaborates the theme of discipleship and *diakonia* which constitutes the heart of the Christian life. It is therefore appropriate that the laity should play a significant part in mission, as they have done in Africa. It is a weakness of the Church that it should excel in the professional training of priests and other members of the clergy on the one hand and, on the other, lag behind in a corresponding involvement of the laity in its normal life. The African experience of responsible flexibility in Church life, so close in fact to the New Testament itself, should be set forward as a positive contribution to a Western Church that is straitjacketed in lifeless forms and conventions. Only in movement may we keep pace with the living presence of the Lord who has called us.

One other matter that relates to indigenisation is polygamy. Because it is an emotional issue, invested with high stakes by the patriot, it has been used as the touchstone of genuine indigenisation. The discussion has been so over-concentrated that it has lost sight of the important contribution Christianity has made to the emancipation of women and their equal treatment before the law. The discussion has also played into the hands of those reared on the distorted myths of popular anthropology which asserts the superhuman sexual drive of the African, who is thus laid open to the puritanical disdain of the West. To attack the puritanical roots of this distortion does not advance the African cause one iota, for it leaves unchallenged the grounds on which polygamy is defended. There is nothing inherently African about the institution of plural marriages, nor can it be said to be a universal rule applied in all societies. We need also to avoid the danger of describing it in such a way that it is made to embody all the ideals of the African past. There was much abuse in the system, and its benefits were not always the unmitigated boon claimed. Its modern proponents, who are mostly men, risk alienating a whole community of women from the social and educational pressures which may tend towards a more just world. In any case it seems inconceivable that in such a vital area as marriage and family life the Church should stand aside or else come into the picture only to make an opportunistic endorsement of an arrangement that panders to the male ego. To say that the rule of monogamy is unacceptable to the Church in Africa on the grounds mainly that it is a Western-imported institution is to misunderstand both monogamy and the West's painful inconsistency on the subject. There is a valid Christian understanding of the question, and to that discussion the church in Africa ought to contribute.

The whole area of inter-religious encounter has been investigated in the relevant chapters above. Although the value of African religions in this connection cannot be over-emphasised, we may leave them at this stage and consider only how Christianity and Islam have been affected by the African medium. It is part of received academic orthodoxy that when discussing these two missionary religions in Africa, we should proceed to apply to them standards derived from their Western and Middle Eastern incarnations. But orthodoxy in this instance is in manifest error. Christianity in its European transformation is a reconceptualisation of the heritage of the Apostles, and Islam has been no less immune to the dynamic process of historical and cultural experience. Yet in their African versions we have behaved as if these religions have existed in sterilised form from their origin, still responding to the stimulus of their immediate environment, and to that extent able to renounce the African setting as contaminating. The theoretical invalidity of such assumptions is easy to demonstrate, but it would distract us from the main issue at stake. The fact of the matter is that Africa has imposed its own character on the two religions, subjecting them to its own historical experience and immersing them in its cultural and religious traditions. Far from allowing Christianity or Islam to siphon off those elements which constituted its own spiritual integrity, Africa has dissolved much of what came to it and reconstituted the resultant phenomenon as a reinforcement to pre-existing principles of the religious life. Therefore, the most fundamental question that has faced the two missionary religions in Africa is whether and how they can reciprocate with African religions in a mutually recognisable idiom. They are not free to decide whether or not they wish to be involved, nor indeed whether the contest is being staged on propitious grounds, for the initiative lies with their African hosts. The Arabic proverb which advises the guest to visit less frequently if he wishes to be loved more greatly has an acute point to it. As permanent sojourners in the African household Christianity and Islam cannot any longer aspire to the courtesies of the occasional visitor while wishing to retain the privileges of a legal heir.

The effective transformation of these religions in Africa means that we should apply African standards to their behaviour, rather than continue to foster them on transplanted soil. This historical and cultural transposition constitutes a valid turning-point in the career of these religions. We ought to see them as religious movements which spread over different terrains and which in the African stage of their progress took on the strong hues of that tropical interlude.

Such a step is being urged because it has numerous implications for Africa, and for religion in general. The divisive measures we have adopted in summing up Africa's potential continue to affect our methodology when we apply divisive criteria to Africa's religious traditions as under-dogs at the mercy of outsiders. Often the motive is an apparently enlightened one, namely, that since Christianity and Islam have a strong Scriptural and intellectual tradition, we show a progressive spirit if we concede their ascendancy over African religions. Both the motive and the procedure share the grave flaw of received academic orthodoxy. And with that recognition we have come much nearer to understanding the local and historical roots of religious adaptation. Such an African perspective is an invaluable asset to discussions of religious encounter and dialogue. It is also relevant to questions of identity and what constitutes the normative religious model. What is clear is that there exists a plurality of normative models and that we can restore them to their rightful place by viewing them in historical and comparative perspective. There is truly no one inherently superior model of representing the human enterprise. If Africa contributes nothing else to the large stock of religious ideas now within our grasp, this comparative dimension alone should secure it an honourable place in religious and academic counsels.

Of course, there is more to it than that. Our final point concerns the destiny of African Christianity. No one can miss the vitality of the religion in much of the continent. In spite of the strident forms of political nationalism that have followed the end of colonialism, the Church in Africa has continued to play an active role in national affairs, sometimes paying a heavy price for refusing to bow to political pressure. If it were nothing more than the carbon-copy of the Western Church, the African Church would have merged with the political state and become a defender of the *status quo*. For in many parts of the West the Church has been thoroughly neutralised, its prophetic sting drawn by the effective encirclement of institutional political privilege, with a fate no better than the Church enjoys under Communist domination in the East. This fate has not for the most part overtaken the Churches in Africa, with the notable exception of South Africa. As long as support for the national cause is not exclusively identified with the cause of God, then the Church is proportionately free to be the people of God. The alternative would be to make the national anthem the hymn of orthodox faith. Given this prophetic role of the Church, it is indisputable that for much of Africa Christianity is embarked on the inexorable march of the people of God. It is salutary to recall that it was after St Paul had established the Church as the Church of the *ethnoi,* the Greek word for Gentiles, that Christianity entered upon its universal course. Who can deny that a similar phenomenon may be about to unfold before our eyes as Christianity makes unprecedented progress in an ill-rated Africa?

SELECT BIBLIOGRAPHY

Chapter 1. African Christian Antecedents in Antiquity

Alvarez, Francisco, *Narrative of the Portuguese Embassy to Abyssinia during the Years 1520-1527,* London, 1881.

St Augustine, *Retractions,* Washington DC, 1968.

—, *City of God,* London, (Penguin), 1972.

—, *Confessions,* London, (Penguin), 1980.

—, *Letters,* 4 vols, Washington, DC, 1965-77.

Bainton, Ronald, *The Penguin History of Christianity,* vol. 1, London, 1967.

Barton, I. M., *Africa in the Roman Empire,* Accra,1972.

Bede, *A History of the English Church and People,* London, (Penguin), 1981.

Boardman, John, *The Greeks Overseas,* London, (Penguin), 1964.

Budge, E.A. Wallis, *A History of Ethiopia: Nubia and Abyssinia,* 2 vols, London, 1928.

The Cambridge History of Africa, vol. 2, 1978.

Charles-Picard, Gilbert, *Carthage,* London, 1964.

Cohn, N., *The Pursuit of the Millennium,* London, 1957.

Coulton, G.C., *Five Centuries of Religion,* 4 vols, Cambridge, 1923-50.

Cross, F.L., *The Early Christian Fathers,* London, 1960.

Davis, A.J., 'The Orthodoxy of the Ethiopian Church', *Tarikh,* 2, 1, 1967, pp. 62-9.

—, 'Coptic Christianity', *Tarikh,* vol. 2, no. 1, 1967.

Ellis, I. P., 'Professor Groves and the North African Church', *The Sierra Leone Bulletin of Religion,* V, 2, Dec. 1963, pp. 66–71.

Eusebius, *The History of the Church,* London, Penguin Books, 1980.

Farquhuar, J.N., 'The Apostle Thomas in North India', *Bulletin of the John Rylands Library,* X, 1926, pp. 89.

Ferguson, John, 'Aspects of Early Christianity in North Africa', *Tarikh,* Historical Society of Nigeria, 2, 1, 1967, pp. 16–27.

—, *The Heritage of Hellenism,* New York, 1973.

Frend, W.H.C., *The Donatist Church: A Movement of Protest in Roman North Africa,* London, 1952.

Harden, Donald, *The Phoenicians,* London, 1962.

Ilevbare, J.A., 'Christianity in Nubia', *Tarikh,* 2, 1, 1967, pp. 53-61.

Jaeger, Werner, *Early Christianity and Greek Paideia,* Cambridge, Mass., 1961; London, 1977.

Jones, A.H.M., *Constantine and the Conversion of Europe,* London, 1948.

—, 'Were Ancient Heresies National or Social Movements in Disguise?' *Jnl. Th. S.N.S.,* X, 1959, pp.280-98.

Kidd, B.J., *History of the Church to A.D. 461,* London, 1922.

Lewis, Bernard, 'The Fatimids and the route to India', *Revue de la Faculté des sciences économiques,* University of Istanbul, XI, 1949-50, pp.50-4.

Ludolf, H., *A New History of Ethiopia,* London, 1684.

Marrou, H., *St Augustine and His Influence,* London, 1959.

Morris, W.D., *The Christian Origins of Social Revolt*, London, 1949.

Nock, Arthur Darby, *Conversion: the Old and New in Religion from Alexander the Great to Augustine of Hippo*, Oxford, 1933.

The North African Provinces from Diocletian to the Vandal Conquest, Cambridge, 1954.

Simpson, Sparrow, *St Augustine and the African Church Divisions*, London, 1910.

Smalley, B., *The Study of the Bible in the Middle Ages*, Oxford, 1952.

Stevenson, J., *A New Eusebius*, London, 1957.

Tafla, Bairu, 'The Establishment of the Ethiopian Church', *Tarikh*, 2, 1, 1967, pp. 28-42.

Tamrat, Taddesse, *Church and State in Ethiopia 1270-1527*, London, 1972.

Thompson, L.A., and John Ferguson (eds), *Africa in Classical Antiquity*, Ibadan, 1969.

von Campenhausen, H., *The Fathers of the Greek Church*, New York, 1959.

Wand, J.W.C., *History of the Early Church*, London 1945.

—, *Doctors and Councils*, London, 1962.

Warrington, B.M., *Carthage*, New York, 1960.

Chapter 2. The Early Pioneers

Artz, F.B., *The Mind of the Middle Ages*, New York, 1954, reprinted Chicago, 1980.

Azurara, G. de, *The Chronicle of the Discovery and Conquest of Guinea (1453)*, London, 1899.

Bane, Martin J., *Catholic Pioneers in West Africa*, Dublin, 1956.

Blake, John W., *West Africa: Quest for God and Gold, 1454-1578*, London, 1977.

Bovill, E.W., *Caravans of the Old Sahara*, London, 1933.

Boxer, C.R., *The Portuguese Seaborne Empire: 1415-1825*, New York and London, 1969, 1977.

The Cambridge Mediaeval History, vols. 5-8, 1926-36.

Chadwick, Owen, *The Reformation*, Pelican Books, London, 1966.

Claridge, W.W., *A History of the Gold Coast and Ashanti*, London, 1915 (2 vols).

Dawson, Christopher, *Religion and the Rise of Western Culture*, London, 1950.

Deanesly, Margaret, *A History of the Mediaeval Church*, 1925, reprinted London, 1979.

Debrunner, Hans W., *A History of Christianity in Ghana*, Accra, 1967.

Dickens, A.G., *Reformation and Society in Sixteenth Century Europe*, London, 1975.

—, *The Counter Reformation*, London, 1975.

Duncan, T. Bentley, *Atlantic Islands: Madeira, the Azores and the Cape Verde Islands in Seventeenth-Century Commerce and Navigation*, Chicago, 1972.

Elton, G.R., *Reformation Europe: 1517-1559*, New York, 1964.

Groves, C.P., *The Planting of Christianity in Africa*, I, London, 1948.

Hamelberg, Edward, 'The Jesuits in Sierra Leone: 1605–1617: A Whirlwind of Grace', *Sierra Leone Bulletin of Religion*, 6, 1, June 1964, pp. 1–8.

Harnack, Adolf von, *The Mission and Expansion of Christianity*, 2 vols, 2nd edn. (ed. J. Moffatt), London, 1908.

Hay, D., *Europe: The Emergence of an Idea*, Edinburgh, 1957.

Hayford, M.C., *West Africa and Christianity,* London, 1903.
Heer, Friedrich, *The Mediaeval World: Europe from 1100 to 1350,* London, 1974.
Holmes, U. Tigner, *Daily Living in the Twelfth Century,* Madison, Wisconsin, 1952.
Huizinga, J., *The Waning of the Middle Ages,* New York, 1954.
Johnston, H.H., *The Colonization of Africa,* London, 1913.
Kup, A. P., 'Jesuit and Capuchin Missions of the Seventeenth Century' *Sierra Leone Bulletin of Religion,* 5, 1, June 1963, pp. 27–34.
Lawrence, A. W., *Trade Castles and Forts of West Africa,* London, 1963.
Lodge, Sir Richard, *The Close of the Middle Ages 1273-1494,* New York, 1901, London 1906.
Major, R. H., *The Discoveries of Prince Henry the Navigator and their Results,* 1877.
Newitt, Malyn, *Portugal in Africa: the Last Hundred Years,* London, 1981.
Palmer, J.J.N., *England, France and Christendom, 1377-1399.* London, 1972.
Parry, J.H., *The Age of Reconnaisance,* New York, 1964.
Pigafetta, F., *History of the Kingdom of Congo,* Rome, 1951 (tr. Hutchinson, 1881).
Rand, E.K., *The Founders of the Middle Ages,* Cambridge, Mass., 2nd edition, 1929.
Reardon, Bernard M.G., *Religious Thought in the Reformation,* London, 1981.
Searle, G.W., *The Counter-Reformation,* London, 1973.
Scott-Moncrieff, P.D., *Paganism and Christianity in Egypt,* London, 1913.
Streeter, B.H., *The Primitive Church,* London, 1929.
Tellenbach, G., *Church, State and Christian Society at the time of the Investiture Contest,* Oxford, 1940.
Tracy, Joseph, *A Historical Examination of the State of Society in Western Africa etc.,* 3rd edn, Boston, Mass., 1845.
Tritton, A.S., *The Caliphs and their Non-Muslim Subjects,* London, 1930.
Tout, Thomas F., *The Empire and the Papacy 918-1273,* London, 1903, reprinted Westport, Conn., 1980.
von Grunebaum, G., *Medieval Islam,* 2nd edn, Chicago, 1962.
Wiltgen, Ralph M., *A Gold Coast Mission History: 1471-1880,* Techny, Ill., 1956.

Chapter 3. Missionary Activity in Benin, Warri and São Tomé, 1480-1807

Adams, John, *Sketches taken during ten years voyages to Africa between the years 1786 and 1800,* London, 1822.
Ayandele, E.A., 'Traditional Rulers and Missionaries in Pre-Colonial West Africa', *Tarikh,* Historical Society of Nigeria, 3, 1, 1969, pp. 23-37.
Bane, Martin J., *Catholic Pioneers in West Africa,* Dublin, 1956.
Blake, John W., *West Africa: Quest for God and Gold: 1454-1578,* London, 1977.
Boxer, C.R., *The Portuguese Seaborne Empire: 1415-1825,* London, 1977.
Henige, David, 'The Problem of Feedback in Oral Tradition: Four Examples from the Fante Coastlands', *Journal of African History,* XIV, 2, 1973.

Lloyd, Peter C., *The Itsekiri,* London, 1957.
—, 'The Portuguese in Warri', *Odu,* 4, 1955, Ibadan.
Moore, William A., *History of Itsekiri,* London, 1936.
Newitt, Malyn, *Portugal in Africa,* London, 1981.
Otite, Onigu, *Autonomy and Dependence: the Urhobo Kingdom of Okpe in Modern Nigeria,* London, 1974.
Ryder, Alan C., 'The Story of Dom Domingos', *Odu,* 4, Ibadan, 1955, pp. 33-9.
—, 'The Re-establishment of Portuguese Factories on the Costa da Mina to the Mid-eighteenth century', *Journal of the Historical Society of Nigeria,* 1, 3, Dec. 1958.
—, 'Missionary Activity in the Kingdom of Warri to the Early Nineteenth century', *Journal of the Historical Society of Nigeria,* 2, 1, 1960, pp. 1-24.
—, *Benin and the Europeans, 1485-1897,* London, 1969.

Chapter 4. Establishment of Christian Colonies in West Africa: Sierra Leone and Liberia

Alexander, William, *Memoir of Capt. Paul Cuffee: A Man of Colour: To Which is subjoined the Epistle of the Society of Sierra Leone, In Africa, etc.,* York, England, 1812.
Anderson, Benjamin, *Journey to Musardu,* New York, 1870, reprinted, London, 1969.
[Anon., *A Life of William*] *Allen, with Selections from His Correspondence,* 2 vols, London, 1846-7.
Aptheker, H., *The Negro in the American Revolution,* New York, 1940.
Atkins, J., *A Voyage to Guinea,* London, 1735.
Bane, Martin J., *Catholic Pioneers in West Africa,* Dublin, 1956.
Beltran, G. Aguirre, 'The Tribal Origins of Slaves in Mexico', *Journal of Negro History, XLII,* 1957.
Biobaku, S.O., *The Egba and their Neighbours,* London, 1957.
Blyden, Edward W., *African Life and Customs,* London, 1908.
—, *Liberia's Offering, being addresses, Sermons, etc.* New York, 1862.
—, *Report on the Falaba Expedition, 1872,* Freetown, 1872.
Buxton, Sir Thomas F.V., 'Creole in West Africa', *African Society, XII,* 1913, pp.384-94.
Campbell, Robert, *A Pilgrimage to My Motherland: An Account of a Journey among the Egbas and Yorubas of Central Africa in 1859 and 1860,* New York, 1861.
Carnes, J.A., *Journal of a Voyage from Boston to the West Coast of Africa,* Boston, Mass., 1852.
Cassell, C. Abayomi, *Liberia: History of the First African Republic,* New York, 1970.
Cole, Abayomi, *The Revelation of the Secret Orders of Western Africa,* Dayton, Ohio, 1886.
Coupland, Reginald, *The British Anti-Slavery Movement,* London, 1933.
Cox George, N.A., 'Direct Taxation in the Early History of Sierra Leone', *Sierra Leone Studies,* new series, Dec. 1955, 5, pp. 20-35.
Crowther, Samuel Ajayi, *Vocabulary of the Yoruba Language,* London, 1843.
Crummell, Alexander, *The Relations and Duties of Free colored men in America to Africa,* Hartford, Conn., 1861.

Cuffee, Paul, *A Brief Account of the Settlement and Present Situation of the Colony of Sierra Leone in Africa as Communicated by Paul Cuffee (A Man of Colour) to his Friend in New York*, New York, 1812.

Cugoano, O., *Thoughts and Sentiments on the Evils of Slavery*, London, 1787.

Cullen, J.B., *Life of the Venerable Mother Javouhey*, Dublin, 1912.

Curtin, P.D., *Two Jamaicas*, Cambridge University Press, 1955.

Dallas, R.C., *The History of the Maroons*, 2 vols, London, 1803.

Dickson, Mora, *The Powerful Bond: Hannah Kilham: 1774-1832*, London, 1980.

Donnan, E., *Documents illustrative of the History of the Slave Trade to America*, Washington DC, 1930-5.

Elliott, J.B., *The Lady Huntingdon's Connexion in Sierra Leone*, London, 1851.

Falconbridge, Anna Marie, *Two Voyages to Sierra Leone during the years 1791-2-3*, London, 1794.

Fiddles, Edward, 'Lord Mansfield and the Sommersett Case', *The Law Quarterly Review*, CC, Oct. 1934, pp. 499-511.

Fuller, Thomas, Jr., *Journal of a Voyage to Liberia and a visit to several of its settlements*, Baltimore, 1851.

Fyfe, Christopher, *A History of Sierra Leone*, London, 1962.

—, 'The Baptist Churches in Sierra Leone', *Sierra Leone Bulletin of Religion*, V, 2, Dec. 1963, pp. 55-60.

—, 'The Countess of Huntingdon's Connexion in Nineteenth Century Sierra Leone', *Sierra Leone Bulletin of Religion*, 4, 2, July 1962, pp. 53-61.

—, 'European and Creole Influences in the Hinterland. of Sierra Leone before 1896', *Sierra Leone Studies* (new series), 6, June 1956, pp.113-23.

—, 'Four Sierra Leone Recaptives', *Journal of African History*, II, 1, 1961, pp.77-85.

—, 'The Life and Times of John Ezzidio', *Sierra Leone Studies* (new series), 4, 1955.

—, 'The term "Creole",' *Africa*, 50, 4, 1980, p.422.

—, 'Thomas Peters: History and Legend', *Sierra Leone Studies* (new series), Dec. 1953, 1, pp.4-13.

—, 'The West African Methodists in the Nineteenth Century', *Sierra Leone Bulletin of Religion*, III, 1, June 1961, pp.22-8.

Greene, Lorenzo Johnston, *The Negro in Colonial New England*, New York, 1942.

Greenwood, O., 'Hannah Kilham's Plan' in two parts, *Sierra Leone Bulletin of Religion*, 4, 1, June 1962, pp.9-22; 4, 2, Dec. 1962, pp.61-71.

Groves, C.P., *The Planting of Christianity in Africa*, 1, London, 1948.

Hair, Paul, 'An Analysis of the Register of Fourah Bay College, 1827-1950', *Sierra Leone Studies* (new series), 7, Dec. 1956, pp.155-60.

—, 'E. W. Blyden and the CMS', *Sierra Leone Bulletin of Religion*, 4, 1, June 1962, pp.22-8.

—, 'CMS "Native Clergy" in West Africa to 1900', *Sierra Leone Bulletin of Religion*, 4, 2, Dec. 1962, pp.71-2.

—, 'Creole Endeavour and Self-criticism in Sierra Leone Church Missions', *Sierra Leone Bulletin of Religion*, 8, 1, 1966.

—, 'How Yoruba was reduced to writing', *Odu*, no.9, Sept. 1963, pp.42-3.

Hamilton, William, 'Sierra Leone and the Liberated Africans', *The Colonial Magazine and Commercial—Maritime Journal*, VI-VIII, Sept. 1841-June 1842, pp.327-34, 463-9, 29-43, 214-25, 286-96, 404-12, 37-44, 220-3.

Harris, Sheldon, H., *Paul Cuffee: Black America and the African Return*, New York, 1972.

Hecht, J.J., *Continental and Colonial Servants in Eighteenth Century England*, Northampton, Mass., 1954.

Hogan, E.M., *Catholic Missions and Liberia*, Cork University Press, Ireland, 1981.

Holman, J., *Travels in Madeira, Sierra Leone, Teneriffe, St. Jago, Cape Coast, Fernando Po, Princes Island*, London, 1840.

Howard, Horatio P., *A Self-Made Man: Cpt. Paul Cuffee*, New Bedford, Mass., 1913.

Innes, William, *Liberia or the Early History and Signal Preservation of the American Colony of Free Negroes on the Coast of Africa*, Edinburgh 1831.

Johnston, Sir Harry Hamilton, *Liberia*, 2 vols, London, 1906.

Karnga, Abayomi Wilfrid, *The Negro Republic of West Africa*, Monrovia, 1909.

—, *History of Liberia*, Liverpool, 1926.

Kilham, H., *The Claims of West Africa to Christian Instruction through the Native Languages*, London, 1830.

—, *Memoir of the Late Hannah Kilham* (ed. Biller), London, 1837.

—, *Present State of the Colony of Sierra Leone*, Lindfield, 1832.

—, *Specimens of African Languages Spoken in the Colony of Sierra Leone*, London, 1828, 3 parts.

Kingsley, Mary, *West African Studies*, London, 1901.

Knight, W., *Memoir of Henry Venn*, London, 1882.

Kuczynski, R.R., *Demographic Survey of the British Colonial Empire*, London, 1948.

Kupp, A.P., *A History of Sierra Leone: 1400-1787*, London, 1961.

Landeck, Beatrice, *Echoes of Africa in Folk Songs of America*, New York, 1960.

Lascelles, E.C.P., *Granville Sharp and the Freedom of Slaves in England*, London, 1928.

Lloyd, Christopher, *The Navy and the Slave Trade*, London, 1949.

Lynch, Hollis R., 'The Native Pastorate Controversy and Cultural Ethnocentrism', *Journal of African History*, V, 3, 1964, pp. 395-413.

—, *Edward Wilmot Blyden: Pan-African Patriot*, London, 1967.

McCarthy, J.A., *The Prospects of Christianity in West Africa*, London, (?1887).

McPherson, J.H.T., *History of Liberia*, New York, 1891.

Marke, C., *The Origin of Wesleyan Methodism in Sierra Leone*, London, 1913.

[Marrant] *A Narrative of the Lord's Wonderful Dealings with John Marrant, a Black*, London, 1788.

Matthews, J., *A Voyage to the River Sierra Leone*, London, 1788.

Maxwell, J., *The Negro Question*, London, 1892.

May, J.C., *Brief Sketch of the Life of Rev. Joseph May*, Freetown, n.d.

Mehlinger, Louis R., 'The Attitude of the Free Negro Toward African Colonization', *Journal of Negro History*, July 1916.

Melville, Elizabeth, *A Residence at Sierra Leone*, London, 1849.

Migeod, F.W.H., *The Languages of West Africa*, London, 1911.

Miller, Floyd J., *The Search for a Black Nationality: Black Emigration and Colonization, 1787-1863*, Urbana, Ill., 1975.

Moister, William, *Missionary Worthies*, London, 1885.

Newton, John, *Thoughts Upon the African Slave Trade*, London, 1788.

Norton, Mary Beth, *The Black Americans: The Loyalist Exiles in England, 1774-1789*, Boston, Mass., 1972.

—, 'The Fate of Some Black Loyalists of the American Revolution', *Journal of Negro History*, LVIII, 4, 1973, pp.402-26.

Owen, N., *Journal of a Slave-Dealer* (ed. Martin), London, 1930.

Peterson, John, *Province of Freedom*, Evanston, Ill., 1969.

Phillips, Earl, 'The Egba of Abeokuta: Acculturation and Political Change, 1830-70', *Journal of African History*, vol. X, no. 1, 1969.

Porter, Arthur T., *Creoldom*, London, 1963.

—, 'Religious Affiliations in Freetown, Sierra Leone', *Africa*, XXIII, 1953, pp. 3-14.

Quarles, Benjamin, *The Negro in the American Revolution*, Chapel Hill, NC, 1961.

Rankin, F.H., *White Man's Grave: A Visit to Sierra Leone in 1834*, 2 vols, London, 1836.

Rodney, Walter, 'The Upper Guinea and the Significance of the Origins of Africans Enslaved in the New World', *Journal of Negro History*, LIV, 4, Oct. 1969, pp.327-45.

Salvador, George, *Paul Cuffee: The Black Yankee 1759-1817*, New Bedford, Mass., 1969.

Sawyerr, Harry, 'Sacrificial Rituals in Sierra Leone', *Sierra Leone Bulletin of Religion*, 1, June 1959, pp. 1-9.

Schick, Tom W., *Emigrants to Liberia: 1820-1843, an alphabetical listing*, Newark, Delaware, 1971.

Schultz, Stanley K., 'The Making of a Reformer: The Reverend Samuel Hopkins as an Eighteenth Century Abolitionist', *Proceedings of the American Philosophical Society*, CXV, Oct. 1971.

Sherwood, Henry Noble, 'Early Negro Deportation Projects', *Mississippi Valley Historical Review*, II, March 1916.

—, 'The Formation of the American Colonization Society', *Journal of Negro History*, II, July 1917.

—, 'Paul Cuffe', *Journal of Negro History*, VIII, April 1923.

Sherwood, Mrs, *The Re-Captured Negro*, Wellington, 1821.

Sibthorpe, A.B.C., *The History of Sierra Leone*, London, 1881.

Smeathman, H., *Plan of a Settlement to be made near Sierra Leone on the Grain Coast of Africa*, London, 1786.

—, *Some remarkable Particulars concerning the rapid Civilization of the Negroes in the Colony of Sierra Leone*, Retford, 1821.

Stewart, T. McCant, *Liberia: The Americo-African Republic*, New York, 1886.

Stock, Eugene, *History of the Church Missionary Society: Its Environment, Its Men, and Its Works*, 3 vols, London, 1899.

Stockwell, G.S., *Republic of Liberia: History of Early Settlement*, New York, 1868.

Tracy, Joseph, *A Historical Examination of the State of Society in Western Africa...*, Boston, Mass., 1845.

Tregaskis, Benjamin, *An Address delivered in Buxton Chapel*, London, 1872.

Vassa, G., *The interesting Narrative of the Life of Olaudah Equiano, or Gustavus Vassa, the African*, London, 1789.

Wadstrom, C.B., *Plan for a Free Community at Sierra Leone*, London, 1792.

—, *An Essay on Colonization*, London, 1794.

Walker, Samuel A., *The Church of England Mission in Sierra Leone*, London, 1847.

Walker, Thomas H.B., *History of Liberia*, Boston, Mass., 1921

Walls, A.F., 'A Christian Experiment: The Early Sierra Leone Colony', in *Studies in Church History,* vol. 6: *The Mission of the Church and the Propagation of the Faith,* (ed. Canon Cuming), Cambridge University Press, 1970, pp. 107-29.

—, 'The Nova Scotian Settlers and their Religion', *Sierra Leone Bulletin of Religion,* 1, June, 1959, pp. 19-31.

West, Richard, *Back to Africa: A History of Sierra Leone and Liberia,* London, 1970.

Wilkeson, Samuel, *A Concise History of the Commencement, Progress and Present Condition of the American Colonies in Liberia,* Washington DC, 1839.

Williams, Geoffrey J., *A Bibliography of Sierra Leone: 1925-1967,* New York, and London.

Williams, J.J., *The Maroons of Jamaica,* Boston, Mass., 1938.

Wilson, H.S., 'E.W. Blyden on Religion in Africa', *Sierra Leone Bulletin of Religion,* 2, 2, Dec. 1960, pp.58–66.

Wilson, J.L., *The British Squadron on the Coast of Africa,* London, 1851.

Winterbottom, T., *An Account of the Native Africans in the Neighbourhood of Sierra Leone,* London, 1803.

Select Newspapers published in Freetown in the Nineteenth Century:
African Times.
The Artisan.
Methodist Herald.
Sierra Leone Times.
Sierra Leone Weekly News.
West African Herald.
West African Record.
Tables showing the number of emigrants and recaptured Africans sent to the Colony of Liberia by the Government of the United States...together with a census of the Colony etc., Official Government Publication, Washington DC, 1845.

Chapter 5. The Baptist, Presbyterian and Methodist Missions: Cameroun and Ghana

Apter, D.E., *The Gold Coast in Transition,* Princeton, NJ, 1955.

Armstrong, C.W., *The Winning of West Africa,* London, 1920.

Baeta, Christian, *Prophetism in Ghana: a Study of Some 'Spiritual' Churches,* London, 1962.

Bartels, Frederic Lodowic, *The Roots of Ghana Methodism,* London, 1965.

Birtwhistle, Allen, *Thomas Birch Freeman,* London, 1950.

Bowdich, T.E., *Mission to Ashantee,* London, 1873.

Busia, Kofi A., *The Position of the Chief in Ashanti,* London, 1951.

Christaller, J.G., *Dictionary of the Asante and Fante Language,* Basel, 1933.

—, *Twi Proverbs,* Basel, 1879.

Claridge, W.W., *History of the Gold Coast,* 2 vols, London, 1915.

Crooks, J.J., *Records Relating to the Gold Coast Settlements 1750-1874,* Dublin, 1923.

Debrunner, Hans W., *A History of Christianity in Ghana,* Accra, 1967.

—, 'Notable Danish Chaplains on the Gold Coast', I, 2, 1956, *Transactions of the Historical Society of Ghana.*

Fage, John D., 'The Administration of George Maclean on the Gold Coast, 1830-44', IV, 1, 1955, *Transactions of the Historical Society of Ghana.*

Findlay, G.G. and W.W. Holdsworth, *History of the Wesleyan Methodist Missionary Society*, London, 1921-4.

Forster, P., *Education and Social Change in Ghana*, London, 1965.

Freeman, Thomas Birch, *Journal of Two Visits to the Kingdom of Ashanti in Western Africa*, London, 1843.

Goodall, N, *A History of the London Missionary Society 1895-1945*, London, 1954.

Gray, Richard, 'The Origins of the 19th Century Missionary Movement', *Tarikh*, 3, 1, 1969, pp.14-22.

Groves, C.P., *The Planting of Christianity in Africa*, vols 2-4, London, 1954–8.

Hargreaves, John D. (ed.), *France and West Africa*, London, 1969.

Hayford, J.E. Casely, *Ethiopia Unbound*, London, 1911.

—, *William Waddy Harris, the West African Reformer*, London, 1915.

Hayford, M.C., *West Africa and Christianity*, London, 1903.

Hewat, E.G.K., *Vision and Achievement 1796-1956: a History of the Foreign Missions of the Churches United in the Church of Scotland*, London, 1960.

Jenkins, Paul, 'The Anglican Church in Ghana, 1905–24', *Transactions of the Historical Society of Ghana*, XV, 1, June 1974 (printed 1976), pp.23–39.

Keller, Werner, *The History of the Presbyterian Church in West Cameroun*, Victoria, Cameroun, 1969.

Latourette, K.S., *A History of the Expansion of Christianity*, 7 vols, London, 1937-45.

Lovett, R., *The History of the London Missionary Society 1795-1895*, 2 vols, London. 1899.

Neill, Stephen, *A History of Christian Missions*, Pelican History of the Church no.6, London, 1964.

Oliver, Roland, *The Missionary Factor in East Africa*, London, 1952.

Pascoe, C.F., *Two Hundred Years of the Society of the Propagation of the Gospel, 1701-1900*, London, 1901.

Platt, W.S., *An African Prophet*, London, 1934.

Reindorf, Christian Carl, *The History of the Gold Coast and Asante*, Basel, 1889, Accra 1966.

Robinson, C.H., *A History of Christian Missions*, London, 1915.

Smith, Noel, *The Presbyterian Church of Ghana: 1835-1960*, Accra, 1966.

Southon, A.E., *Gold Coast Methodism*, Cape Coast and London, 1935.

Stock, E., *History of the Church Missionary Society*, 3 vols, London, 1899; vol.4, London, 1916.

Thompson, H.P., *Into All Lands: The History of the Society for the Propagation of the Gospel in Foreign Parts 1701-1900*, London, 1951.

Ward, W.E.F., *A History of Ghana*, 3rd edn, London, 1967.

West, T., *The Life and Journal of the Reverend Daniel West*, London, 1857.

Chapter 6. Christian Missions and African Education and Social Improvement

Afigbo, A.E., 'Background to the Southern Nigerian Code of 1903', *Journal of the Historical Society of Nigeria*, 4, 2, 1968, pp. 197-225.

Ajayi, J.F.A., 'Henry Venn and the Policy of Development', *Journal of the Historical Society of Nigeria*, 1, 4, Dec. 1959.

—, 'The Development of Secondary Grammar Education in Nigeria', *Journal of the Historical Society of Nigeria*, 2, 4, 1963, pp. 517-35.

Azikiwe, Nnamdi, *My Odyssey: an Autobiography,* London, 1970.

Buxton, C., *The Memoirs of Sir Thomas F. Buxton,* London, 1851.

Carr, Henry, *Special Report on Schools in Southern Nigeria,* Old Calabar, 1900.

Cooke, Colman M., 'Church, State and Education: the Eastern Nigerian Experience: 1950-1967', in E. Fashole-Luke, Richard Gray, A. Hastings and G. Tasie (eds.), *Christianity in Independent Africa,* London, 1978.

Forster, P., *Education and Social Change in Ghana,* London, 1965.

Fyfe, Christopher, *A History of Sierra Leone,* London, 1962.

Graham, C.K., *The History of Education in Ghana,* London, 1971.

Graham, Sonia F., *Government and Mission Education in Northern Nigeria 1900-1919,* Ibadan, 1966.

Hargreaves, John D., *A Life of Sir Samuel Lewis,* London, 1958.

Hayford, M.C., *West Africa and Christianity,* London, 1903.

Humphreys, John, 'The Image of the educated African: British Attitudes towards the Gold Coast educated community, 1843-1914', unpublished Ph.D. thesis, Harvard University, 1976.

Ita, Eyo, *A Decade of National Education Movement,* Calabar, 1949.

McFarlan, Donald M., *Calabar: The Church of Scotland Mission, Founded 1846,* London, 1946.

Parsons, R.T., *The Churches and Ghana Society,* Leiden, 1963.

Prickett, Barbara, *Island Base,* Bo, Sierra Leone, n.d. (1971?).

Smith, Noel, *The Presbyterian Church of Ghana: 1835-1860,* Accra, 1966.

Sumner, Dwight L., *Education in Sierra Leone,* Freetown, 1963.

Thomas, Roger G., 'Education in Northern Ghana: 1906-1940: A Study in Colonial Paradox', *The International Journal of African Historical Studies,* 7, 3, 1975, pp. 427-67.

Webster, J. B., 'The Bible and the Plough', *Journal of the Historical Society of Nigeria,* 2, 4, Dec. 1963, pp. 418–34.

Chapter 7.   The Rise of African Independent Churches

Abiodun, Emanuel, *Celestial Vision of Her Most Rev. Mother Captain Mrs C. Abiodun Emanuel, which originated Cherubim and Seraphim in 1925,* Charity Press, Yaba, 4th edn. 1962.

Ajayi, J.F.A., *Christian Missions in Nigeria: 1841-1891: The Making of a Modern Elite,* London, 1965.

Ajisafe, A.K., *A History of Abeokuta,* Bungay (Suffolk, England), 1924.

Akinleye, I.B., *The Place of Divine Healing in the Church,* Ibadan, 1962.

Anderson, E., *Messianic Popular Movements in the Lower Congo,* Uppsala, 1958.

Anyanwu, K.C. and E.A. Ruch, *African Philosophy: an introduction to the Main Philosophical Trends in Contemporary Africa,* Rome, 1981.

Ayandele, E.A., *The Impact of Christian Missions on Modern Nigeria,* London, 1966.

—, *Holy Johnson,* London, 1970.

Balandier, G., 'Messianism and Nationalism in Black Africa', in van den Berghe (ed.), *Africa,* New York, 1965.

Barrett, David B., *Schism and Renewal: an Analysis of Six Thousand Contemporary Religious Movements,* London, 1968.

—, 'AD 2000 - 350 Million Christians in Africa', *International Review of Mission,* 59, 233, Jan. 1970, pp.39-54.

Bascom, W.R., 'The Sanctions of Ifa Divination', *Journal of the Royal Anthropological Institute*, LXXXI, 1943.

Biobaku, Saburi O., *The Egba and their Neighbours 1842-72*, London, 1957.

Bond, George, Walton Johnson and Sheila Walker (eds.), *African Christianity*, New York, 1979.

Charsley, S.R., 'Dreams in an Independent African Church', *Africa*, XLIII, 3, July 1973, pp. 244-57.

Dike, Kenneth Onwuka, *The Origins of the Niger Mission: 1841-1891*, Ibadan, 1957.

Eternal Sacred Order of Cherubim and Seraphim, *Moses Orimolade at Ojokoro*, Ebute Metta, (Nigeria), 1962.

Fisher, Humphrey, J., 'Conversion Reconsidered: Some Historical Aspects of Religious Conversion in Black Africa', *Africa*, XLIII, 1, 1973, pp. 27-40.

Hair, Paul, 'Archdeacon Crowther and the Delta Pastorate 1892-9', *Sierra Leone Bulletin of Religion*, 5, 1, June 1963, pp.18-27.

Haliburton, G.M., *The Prophet Harris*, London, 1971.

Handspicker, M.B. and L. Vischer (eds.), *An Ecumenical Exercise*, 'The Kimbanguist Church in the Congo', Geneva, 1967, Faith and Order Paper no.49, pp 29-36.

Hayward, Victor E.W. (ed.) *African Independent Church Movements*, London, 1963.

Horton, Robin, 'African Conversion', *Africa*, XLI, 2, April 1971, pp. 85-108.

Ifeka-Moller, Caroline, 'White Power: Social Structural Factors in Conversion to Christianity, Eastern Nigeria 1921-1966', *Canadian Journal of African Studies*, VIII, 1, 1974, pp. 55-72.

James, William, *The Varieties of Religious Experience*, New York, 1902, Lectures IX and X on 'Conversion'.

Jules-Rosette, Bennetta, *African Apostles: Ritual and Conversion in the Church of John Maranke*, Ithaca, New York, 1975.

Lienhardt, G., *Divinity and Experience: the Religion of the Dinka*, London, 1961.

Lisembé, Elebé, 'The Role of Kimbanguism in the Development of Self-Awareness of the Zaire Nation', in *Christian and Islamic Contributions towards establishing Independent States in Africa south of the Sahara*, Stuttgart, 1979.

Macgaffey, Wyatt, 'The Beloved City: Commentary on a Kimbanguist Text', *Journal of Religion in Africa*, II, 2, 1969, pp. 129-47.

—, *Custom and Government in the Lower Congo*, Berkeley and Los Angeles, 1970.

—, 'Kimbanguism: an African Christianity', *Africa Report*, Washington DC, XXI, 1, 1976, pp. 40-3.

Martin, Marie-Louise, *Kimbangu: An African Prophet and His Church*, Oxford, 1975.

Mullings, Leith, 'Religious Change and Social Stratification in Labadi, Ghana: The Church of the Messiah', in George Bond *et al.* (eds) *African Christianity*, New York, 1979.

Ndiokwere, Nathaniel I., *Prophecy and Revolution: the Role of Prophets in the Independent Churches and in Biblical Tradition*, London, 1981.

Now, magazine published by the Methodist Church Overseas Division, London: issue of May 1977 devoted to 'African Independent Churches'.

Omoyajowo, J.A. *Cherubim and Seraphim; The History of an African Independent Church*, NOK Publishers, New York and Lagos (in press).

Peel, John D.Y., *Aladura: a religious Movement among the Yoruba,* London, 1968.

—, 'The Aladura Movement in Western Nigeria', *Tarikh,* 3, 1, 1969, pp. 48-55.

Schaff, Philip, (ed.), A Select Library of the Nicene and Post-Nicene Fathers of the Christian Church, vol. IV: *St. Augustine: The Writings Against the Manichaeans and Against the Donatists,* Grand Rapids, reprinted, 1979 from the 1887 edition.

Shank, David, A., 'A Prophet of Modern Times: the Thought of William Wadé Harris', unpublished Ph.D. thesis (3 vols.), University of Aberdeen, 1980.

Starbuck, E.D., *The Psychology of Religion,* New York, 1899.

Sundkler, Bengt, *Bantu Prophets in South Africa,* London, 1948, 2nd edn 1961.

—, *Zulu Zion and some Swazi Zionists,* London, 1976.

Tasie, Godwin, *Christian Missionary Enterprise in the Niger Delta,* Leiden, 1978.

Taylor, John V., *The Primal Vision,* London, 1963.

Turner, Harold W., *History of an Independent African Church: Church of the Lord (Aladura),* 2 vols, London, 1967.

—, *Religious Innovation in Africa,* Boston, Mass., 1979.

Wainright, Geoffrey, 'Theological Reflection on "The Catechism Concerning the Prophet Simon Kimbangu" of 1970', *Orita,* Ibadan, V, 1, 1971, pp. 18-35.

Walker, Sheila S., 'Christianity African Style: the Harrist Church of the Ivory Coast', unpublished Ph.D. thesis, University of Chicago, 1976.

Webster, James B., *African Churches among the Yoruba 1888-1922,* London, 1964.

—, 'Independent Christians in Africa', *Tarikh,* 3, 1, 1969, pp. 56-81.

Wilson, Bryan: *Magic and the Millennium,* London and New York, 1973.

Zettenberg, H. L., 'Religious Conversion as a Change of Social Roles', *Sociology and Social Research (Unesco),* 36, 3, 1952, pp. 159-86.

Chapter 8. Christianity, Islam and African Traditional Religions

Ajayi, J.F.A., and Michael Crowder (ed.), *History of West Africa,* 2 vols, London, 1971.

Ajayi, J.F.A., *Christian Missions in Nigeria, 1841-1891: the Making of a Modern Elite,* London, 1965.

Al-Hajj, Muhammad, 'The Fulani Concept of Jihad: Shehu Uthman dan Fodio', *Odu,* I, 1, July 1964, pp. 45-58.

Anderson, Ch., 'Early Muslim Schools and British Policy in Sierra Leone', *West African Journal of Education,* 14, Oct. 1970, pp.177-9.

Aspects of African Religion, Open University Course Units 24 and 25, Milton Keynes, England.

Awolalu, J. Omosade and P. Adelumo Dopamu, *West African Traditional Religion,* Ibadan, 1979.

Avery, W.L., 'Christianity in Sierra Leone', *African Research Bulletin,* II, 2, 1972, pp.3-28.

Banton, Michael, 'An Independent African Church in Sierra Leone', *Hibbert Journal,* LV, 1956-7, pp.57-63.

Blyden, Edward W., *Christianity, Islam and the Negro Race,* London, 1967.

Bond, George, Walton Johnson and Sheila S. Walker, (eds.), *African Christianity: Patterns of Religious Continuity,* New York, 1979.

Conn, Walter E. (ed.), *Conversion: Perspectives on Personal and Social Transformation,* New York, 1978.

Crampton, E.P.T., *Christianity in Northern Nigeria,* London, 1979.

Dennett, R.E., *Nigerian Studies,* London, 1910.

Fisher, Humphrey J., 'Independency and Islam: the Nigerian Aladuras and some Muslim Comparisons', *Journal of African History,* XI, 1970, pp.269-77.

—, 'Conversion Reconsidered: Some Historical Aspects of Religious Conversion in Black Africa', *Africa,* XLIII, 1, 1973.

—, 'The Modernisation of Islamic Education in Sierra Leone, Gambia and Liberia: Religion and Language', in Godfrey N. Brown and Mervyn Hiskett (eds), *Conflict and Harmony in Education in Tropical Africa,* London, 1975.

Gbadamosi, T.G.O., *The Growth of Islam Among the Yoruba: 1841-1908,* London, 1978 (1979).

Groves, C.P., *The Planting of Christianity in Africa,* I, London, 1948.

Fyfe, Christopher, *A History of Sierra Leone,* London, 1962.

Harley, George W., *Notes on the Poro in Liberia,* Cambridge, Mass., 1941.

—, *Masks as Agents of Social Control in North East Liberia,* Cambridge, Mass., 1950.

Hiskett, Mervyn, 'An Islamic Tradition of Reform in the Western Sudan from the 16th to the 18th century', *Bulletin of the School of Oriental and African Studies,* XXV, 3, 1962.

—, 'The Song of the Shehu's Miracles: a Hausa Hagiography from Sokoto', *African Language Studies,* 12, 1971.

—, *The Sword of Truth: the life and times of Shehu Usuman dan Fodio,* New York, 1973.

Horton, Robin, 'African Conversion', *Africa,* XLI, 2, April 1971, pp. 85-108.

Hodgkin, Thomas, 'The Islamic Literary Tradition in Ghana', in I.M. Lewis (ed.), *Islam in Tropical Africa,* London, 1966.

Hubbard, J.P., 'Government and Islamic Education in Northern Nigeria: 1900-1940', in Brown and Hiskett, (eds.), 1975.

Hunwick, John O., 'Religion and State in the Songhay Empire, 1464-1591', in I.M. Lewis (ed.), 1966.

Ibn Battuta, *Travels in Asia and Africa: 1352-1354,* tr. and ed. H.A.R. Gibb, London, 1929 and 1963.

Idowu, E. Bolaji, *Olodumare: God in Yoruba Belief,* London, 1962.

Jobson, Richard, *The Golden Trade or a Discovery of the River Gambia: 1620-1622,* London, 1968.

Kane, Cheikh Hamidou, *Ambiguous Adventure,* London, 1972.

Last, Murray, *The Sokoto Caliphate,* London, 1967.

—, 'A Note on the Attitudes to the Supernatural in the Sokoto Jihad', *Journal of the Historical Society of Nigeria,* 4, (1967), pp. 3-13.

—, and Muhammad al-Hajj, 'Attempts at Defining a Muslim...', *JHSN,* no. 3 (1965), pp. 231-40.

Levtzion, Nehemia, *Muslims and Chiefs in West Africa: A Study of Islam in the Middle Volta in the Pre-colonial Period,* London, 1968.

—, *Ancient Ghana and Mali,* London, 1973.

— (ed.), *Conversion to Islam,* New York, 1979.

— and J.F.P. Hopkins, *Corpus of Early Arabic Sources for West African History,* Cambridge University Press, 1981.

Lewis, I.M., (ed.), *Islam in Tropical Africa,* London, 1966.

Lucas, J. Olumide, *The Religion of the Yorubas,* Lagos, 1948.

Mbiti, John S., *Concepts of God in Africa,* London, 1970.

—, *The Prayers of African Religion,* London, 1975; New York 1976.

McKenzie, Peter R., 'Samuel Crowther's Attitudes to Other Faiths — the Early Period', *Bulletin of the Society for African Church History,* III, 1-2, 1969-70, pp. 28-43.

Morton-Williams, Peter, 'The Yoruba Ogboni Cult in Oyo', *Africa,* 30 (1960), 34-40.

Muller, Jean-Claude, 'Old Wine in New Wine-skins: Traditionalists and Christians among the Rukuba (Benue-Plateau State, Nigeria)', *Archives de sciences sociales des Religions,* 38, 19 (2), July-Dec. 1974, pp. 49-62.

O'Brien, Donal Cruise, 'Towards an Islamic Policy in French West Africa', *Journal of African History,* VIII, 2, 1967.

—, *The Mourides of Senegal,* London, 1971.

Oduyoye, Modupe, *The Vocabulary of the Yoruba Religious Discourse,* Ibadan, 1971.

Olatunde, A.S., 'Islam Forbids Prostrating as a Mark of Respect [weekly sermon]', *Daily Sketch,* Ibadan, 1 June 1973.

—, 'Muslims Must Avoid Fetish Feasts', *Daily Sketch,* 15 June 1973.

Oosthuizen, G.C., *Afro-Christian Religions,* Leiden, 1979 (see Richard Gray's review, *Bulletin of S.O.A.S.,* XLIII, 2, 1980, p.415).

Palmer, H.R., (tr. and ed.), 'The Kano Chronicle', *Journal of the Royal Anthropological Institute,* XXXVIII, 1908.

Parrinder, E.G., *African Traditional Religion,* London, 1968.

—, *African Religion,* London, (Penguin), 1969.

Peel, John D.Y., *Aladura: A Religious Movement among the Yoruba,* London, 1968.

Prickett, Barbara, *Island Base* (History of the Methodist Mission in the Gambia), Bo, Sierra Leone (1971).

Ramsey, Ian T., *Religious Language: an empirical placing of theological phrases,* London, 1957.

Ryan, Patrick J., *Imale: Yoruba Participation in the Muslim Process,* Montana Harvard Dissertations, 1979.

Sanneh, Lamin, 'Amulets and Muslim Orthodoxy', *International Review of Mission,* October 1974.

—, 'Christian Experience of Islamic Da'wah, with particular reference to Africa', *International Review of Mission,* LXV, 260, October 1976.

—, 'The Origins of Clericalism in West African Islam', *Journal of African History,* XVI, 1, 1976.

—, 'Christian-Muslim Encounter in Freetown in the 19th century. . .', *Bulletin of the Secretariat for non-Christian Religions,* Rome, XII/1-2, 34-35, 1977, pp. 13-31.

—, 'Modern Education among Freetown Muslims and the Christian Stimulus', in Richard Gray *et al.* (eds.), *Christianity in Independent Africa,* London, 1978.

—, 'Muslims in Non-Muslim Societies of Africa', in *Christian and Islamic Contributions towards Establishing Independent States in Africa south of the Sahara*, Stuttgart, 1979.

—, 'The Domestication of Christianity and Islam in African Societies', *Journal of Religion in Africa*, XI, 1, 1980, pp. 1-12.

Shorter, Aylward, *Prayer in the Religious Traditions of Africa*, Nairobi, 1975.

Trimingham, J. Spencer, *A History of Islam in West Africa*, London, 1962.

—, *Islam in West Africa*, London, 1958.

Turner, Harold W., *History of an African Independent Church: the Church of the Lord (Aladura)*, 2 vols, London, 1967.

—, *Religious Innovation in Africa*, Boston, Mass., 1979.

The West African Roll-Call, Methodist Missionary Society, London, 1907.

Zahan, Dominique, *The Religion, Spirituality and Thought of Traditional Africa*, Chicago, 1979.

INDEX